LIBRARY OF HEBREW BIBLE/
OLD TESTAMENT STUDIES

736

Formerly Journal for the Study of the Old Testament Supplement Series

Editors
Laura Quick, Oxford University, UK
Jacqueline Vayntrub, Yale University, USA

Founding Editors
David J. A. Clines, Philip R. Davies and David M. Gunn

Editorial Board
Sonja Ammann, Alan Cooper, Steed Davidson, Susan Gillingham, Rachelle Gilmour, John Goldingay, Rhiannon Graybill, Norman K. Gottwald, Anne Katrine Gudme, James E. Harding, John Jarick, Tracy Lemos, Carol Meyers, Eva Mroczek, Daniel L. Smith-Christopher, Francesca Stavrakopoulou, James W. Watts

SENNACHERIB AND THE WAR OF 1812

Disputed Victory in the Assyrian Campaign of 701 BCE in Light of Military History

Paul S. Evans

LONDON • NEW YORK • OXFORD • NEW DELHI • SYDNEY

T&T CLARK
Bloomsbury Publishing Plc
50 Bedford Square, London, WC1B 3DP, UK
1385 Broadway, New York, NY 10018, USA
29 Earlsfort Terrace, Dublin 2, Ireland

BLOOMSBURY, T&T CLARK and the T&T Clark logo are trademarks of
Bloomsbury Publishing Plc

First published in Great Britain 2023
Paperback edition published 2024

Copyright © Paul S. Evans, 2023

Paul S. Evans has asserted his right under the Copyright, Designs and Patents Act, 1988, to be identified as Author of this work.

For legal purposes the Acknowledgments on pp. ix–x constitute an extension of this copyright page.

All rights reserved. No part of this publication may be reproduced or transmitted in any form or by any means, electronic or mechanical, including photocopying, recording, or any information storage or retrieval system, without prior permission in writing from the publishers.

Bloomsbury Publishing Plc does not have any control over, or responsibility for, any third-party websites referred to or in this book. All internet addresses given in this book were correct at the time of going to press. The author and publisher regret any inconvenience caused if addresses have changed or sites have ceased to exist, but can accept no responsibility for any such changes.

A catalogue record for this book is available from the British Library.

Library of Congress Control Number: 2022948376

ISBN: HB: 978-0-5677-0896-0
PB: 978-0-5677-0900-4
ePDF: 978-0-5677-0897-7

Series: Library of Hebrew Bible/Old Testament Studies, volume 736
ISSN 2513-8758

Typeset by Newgen KnowledgeWorks Pvt. Ltd., Chennai, India

To find out more about our authors and books visit www.bloomsbury.com and sign up for our newsletters.

To My Family
יְהוָה זְכָרָנוּ יְבָרֵךְ
Ps 115:12a

CONTENTS

Acknowledgments	ix
Abbreviations	xi

Chapter 1
INTRODUCTION 1
   1.1 Past Research 2
   1.2 Methodology 19
   1.3 Overview 27

Chapter 2
ARCHAEOLOGICAL EVIDENCE 29
   2.1 Areas Showing Destruction in 701 BCE 29
   2.2 Areas Showing No Destruction in 701 BCE 41
   2.3 The Recovery of Judah 49

Chapter 3
ASSYRIAN TEXTS 63
   3.1 Chronological Matters 64
   3.2 The Offensive against Phoenicia 65
   3.3 Eight Kings Submit 69
   3.4 The Offensive against Philistia 71
   3.5 The Battle of Eltekeh 74
   3.6 The Offensive against Judah 79

Chapter 4
BIBLICAL NARRATIVE ACCOUNTS 89
   4.1 2 Kings 18–19 (Isaiah 36–37) 90
   4.2 Summary 103

Chapter 5
TEXTS FROM THE BOOK OF ISAIAH 105
   5.1 Texts Critical of Hezekiah 106
   5.2 Texts Viewing Hezekiah Positively 122
   5.3 Summary 126

Chapter 6
DISPUTED VICTORY IN THE WAR OF 1812 127
   6.1 Origins of the War of 1812 128

6.2 US War Aims	133
6.3 US Opinion on the Outcome of the War	135
6.4 Canadian Opinion on the Outcome of the War	142

Chapter 7
DISPUTED VICTORY IN THE WAR OF 701 BCE 153
7.1 Origins of the War of 701 BCE	153
7.2 Diverse Opinion of the War and the War Leader	154
7.3 Judahite Opinion: Judah Won the War	156
7.4 Assyrian Opinion: Assyria Won the War	166
7.5 An Empire Perspective	171
7.6 The End of the War	172
7.7 Summary	173

Chapter 8
SCHOLARLY ASSESSMENTS OF HEZEKIAH AND HIS REBELLION 175
8.1 Modern Attitudes toward War	177
8.2 Older Attitudes toward War	184
8.3 Modern Scholarly Assessments of Hezekiah in Light of Their Social Location	185
8.4 Summary	190

Chapter 9
CONCLUSION 191

Bibliography	199
Author Index	229
Index of References	238
Index of Subjects	241

ACKNOWLEDGMENTS

The completion of this volume requires my expression of thanks to those in my life who have contributed in many ways. The nucleus of some of the following chapters were presented at several conferences such as the Annual Congress of the Canadian Society of Biblical Studies in Toronto (Ryerson University, 2017) and Vancouver (University of British Columbia, 2019) and the Annual Meeting of the Society of Biblical Literature in Denver (2018), and I would like to thank friends and colleagues in the sessions for listening to these papers and providing gracious criticism and helpful comments. I am indebted to Dr. Shawn Zelig Aster for his feedback on my chapter on archaeological evidence. I would also like to thank Dr. Gordon Heath, historian at McMaster Divinity College, for taking the time to read the chapter on the War of 1812 and providing me with an expert assessment. I also benefited greatly from interactions with the outstanding doctoral students at McMaster Divinity College who participated in my History of Ancient Israel seminars and helped me clarify my ideas and arguments during our time together in class. I am grateful to the faculty and administration at McMaster Divinity College for both their collegial support and the culture of research to which they all contribute at the institutional level. Thanks must be expressed to my graduate assistants at McMaster Divinity College, Dustin Burlet, Kevin Foth, Matthew Bovard, Tamara Mitton, and Phil Haskell, who procured books, articles, and otherwise assisted with my research during the many stages of writing this volume. I would especially thank Phil Haskell for his careful editorial work in the preparation of this manuscript, which he read in its entirety multiple times. Of course, I alone am responsible for deficiencies that remain.

The writing of this volume took place during the COVID-19 worldwide pandemic. My pandemic experience was that of extended lockdowns, excessive time spent at home, lack of social engagements, along with anxieties, frustrations, and many inconveniences that characterized this seemingly unending time of strangeness. However, during this time I have become keenly aware of how very blessed I am as the pandemic experience for many was one of widespread suffering not only of isolation but also of financial strain, job loss, sickness, and death. The writing of this book reflects my significant privilege that allowed the lockdowns and extended time at home to be a fruitful time of research, reflection, and writing. My greatest blessing is my amazing family. This book could not have been written without the encouragement of my wife, Caitlin, and my children, Chaim and Talyah, and the vital joy they bring to my life and the love we share.

While pandemic restrictions resulted in extended separation from family in British Columbia, this has led to an even deeper realization of the debt I owe to my parents, Randy and Sandy Evans, both for who they are and all they have done for me. As well I must express warmest gratitude to my brothers, Bob and Tim, for their friendship, love, and support. It is to my family that I dedicate this work.

ABBREVIATIONS

AASF	Annales Academiae Scientiarum Fennica
AASOR	Annual of the American Schools of Oriental Research
ÄAT	Ägypten und Altes Testament
AB	Anchor Bible
ABD	*Anchor Bible Dictionary*. Edited by D. N. Freedman. 6 vols. New York: Doubleday, 1992
ABRL	Anchor Bible Reference Library
ABS	Archaeology and Biblical Studies
ACEBT	*Amsterdamse Cahiers voor Exegese en Bijbelse Theologie*
ACJS	Annual of the College of Jewish Studies
AfOB	Archiv für Orientforschung: Beiheft
AHw	*Akkadisches Handerwörterbuch*. Wolfram von Soden. 3 vols. Wiesbaden, 1965–1981
ALASPM	Abhandlungen zur Literatur Alt-Syrien-Palästinas und Mesopotamiens
ANET	*Ancient Near Eastern Texts Relating to the Old Testament*. Edited by J. B. Pritchard. 3rd ed. Princeton: Princeton University Press, 1969
Ant.	Josephus, *Antiquities of the Jews*
AOAT	Alter Orient und Altes Testament
AQDJ	*Army Quarterly and Defence Journal*
Arch	Archaeology
Armed Forces Soc.	Armed Forces and Society
AS	Assyriological Studies
ATANT	Abhandlungen zur Theologie des Alten und Neuen Testaments
ATD	Das Alte Testament Deutsch
AUSS	*Andrews University Seminary Studies*
BA	*The Biblical Archaeologist*
BAR	*Biblical Archaeology Review*
BASOR	*Bulletin of the American Schools of Oriental Research*
BASORSup	Bulletin of the American Schools of Oriental Research Supplements
BEvT	*Beiträge zur evangelischen Theologie*
Bib	*Biblica*
BibIntS	Biblical Interpretation Series
BibS(N)	Biblische Studien (Neukirchen, 1951–)
BThS	Biblische-Theologische Studien
BibOr	Biblica et Orientalia
BIFAO	*Bulletin de l'Institut français d'archéologie orientale*
BJRL	*Bulletin of the John Rylands University Library of Manchester*

BKAT	Biblischer Kommentar, Altes Testament. Edited by M. Noth and H. W. Wolff
BLS	Bible and Literature Series
BN	*Biblische Notizen*
BO	Berit Olam Commentary
Br. J. Polit. Sci.	*British Journal of Political Science*
BS	The Biblical Seminar
BWAT	Beiträge zur Wissenschaft vom Alten Testament
BZAW	Beihefte zur Zeitschrift für die alttestamentliche Wissenschaft
CAD	*The Assyrian Dictionary of the Oriental Institute of the University of Chicago.* Chicago, 1956–
CBC	Cambridge Bible Commentary
CBET	Contributions to Biblical Exegesis and Theology
CBQ	*Catholic Biblical Quarterly*
CC	Continental Commentaries
CEH	*Central European History*
Child Dev.	*Child Development*
ChrEg	*Chronique d'Egypte*
COHP	Contributions to Oriental History and Philology
ConBOT	Coniectanea biblica: Old Testament Series
COS	*The Context of Scripture.* Edited by W. W. Hallo and K. Lawson Younger. 3 vols. Leiden: Brill, 1997–2002
CTN	Cuneiform Texts from Nimrud
Dalhous. Rev.	*Dalhousie Review*
Def. Stud.	*Defence Studies*
Ebib	Etudes bibliques
EgT	*Èglise et thèologie*
EHAT	Exegetisches Handbuch zum Alten Testament
EI	Eretz-Israel
ESHM	European Seminar on Historical Methodology
FCI	Foundations of Contemporary Interpretation
Foreign Aff.	*Foreign Affairs*
FOTL	Forms of the Old Testament Literature
FRLANT	Forschungen zur Religion und Literatur des Alten und Neuen Testaments
GKC	*Gesenius' Hebrew Grammar.* Edited by E. Kautzsch. Translated by A. E. Cowley. 2nd ed. Oxford: Clarendon, 1910
GM	*Göttinger Miszellen:Beiträge zur ägyptologischen Diskussion*
GtS	Grazer theologische Studien
HANES	History of the Ancient Near East Studies
HALOT	*The Hebrew and Aramaic Lexicon of the Old Testament.* Ludwig Koehler, Walter Baumgartner, and Johann J. Stamm. Translated and edited under the supervision of M. E. J. Richardson. 4 vols. Leiden: Brill, 1994–1999
HAT	Handbuch zum Alten Testament
HBM	Hebrew Bible Monographs
HCOT	Historical Commentary on the Old Testament

HdAr	Handbuch der Archäologie
HDWRCU	Historical Dictionaries of War, Revolution, and Civil Unrest
Hist.	Herodotus, *Histories*
HO	Handbuch der Orientalistik
HS	*Hebrew Studies*
HSM	Harvard Semitic Monographs
HSS	Harvard Semitic Studies
HTR	*Harvard Theological Review*
IBHS	*An Introduction to Biblical Hebrew Syntax*. Bruce K. Waltke and Michael O'Connor. Winona Lake, IN: Eisenbrauns, 1990
ICC	International Critical Commentary
IEJ	*Israel Exploration Journal*
Int. J. Psychol.	*International Journal of Psychology*
Int. Secur.	*International Security*
IOS	*Israel Oriental Studies*
Iran. Stud.	*Iranian Studies*
JAEI	*Journal of Ancient Egyptian Interconnections*
JAOS	*Journal of the American Oriental Society*
JBL	*Journal of Biblical Literature*
J. Contemp. Hist.	*Journal of Contemporary History*
JEH	*Journal of Egyptian History*
JHS	*Journal of Hebrew Scriptures*
J. Mil. Hist.	*Journal of Military History*
JNES	*Journal of Near Eastern Studies*
JNSL	*Journal of Northwest Semitic Languages*
JSOT	*Journal for the Study of the Old Testament*
JSOTSup	Journal for the Study of the Old Testament Supplement Series
JSSEA	*Journal of the Society for the Study of Egyptian Antiquities*
KASKAL	*Rivista di storia, ambienti e culture del Vicino Oriente Antico*
KHC	Kurzer Hand-Commentar zum Alten Testament
LD	Lectio Divina
LHBOTS	Library of Hebrew Bible/Old Testament Studies
LQ	*Lutheran Quarterly*
Mar.'s Mirror	*Mariner's Mirror*
MBC	Major Battles and Campaigns
MDAIK	*Mitteilungen des Deutschen Archäologischen Instituts, Abteilung Kairo*
Mil. Aff.	*Military Affairs*
MTA	Münsteraner Theologische Abhandlunger
MS	Mesopotamian Civilizations
NCBC	New Century Bible Commentary
NEA	*Near Eastern Archaeology*
NEAEHL	*New Encyclopedia of Archaeological Excavations in the Holy Land*. Edited by Ephraim Stern. 5 vols. Jerusalem: Israel Exploration Society & Carta; New York: Simon & Schuster, 1993
NEASB	*Near East Archaeological Society Bulletin*
NeHeT	*NeHet*: Revue numérique d'Égyptologie
NYRB	*The New York Review of Books*

OBO	Orbis biblicus et orientalis
OEANE	*The Oxford Encyclopedia of Archaeology in the Near East*. Edited by E. M. Meyers. 5 vols. New York: Oxford University Press, 1997
OIP	Oriental Institute Publications
OLZ	*Orientalistische Literaturzeitung*
Ont. Hist.	Ontario History
Or.N.S.	Orientalia, Nova Series
OTA	Old Testament Abstracts
OTL	Old Testament Library
OTS	*Old Testament Studies*
OtSt	Oudtestamentische Studiën
PAe	Probleme der Ägyptologie
Parameters	*Parameters: U.S. Army War College*
PBM	Paternoster Biblical Monographs
PEQ	*Palestine Exploration Quarterly*
PERA	Publications of the Egyptian Research Account
PHSC	Perspectives on Hebrew Scriptures and Its Contexts
PIA	Publications of the Institute of Archaeology
PM	Philological Monographs
PSQ	*Political Science Quarterly*
Psychol. Rep.	Psychological Reports
PTMS	Pittsburgh Theological Monograph Series
Qad	Qadmoniot
RB	*Revue biblique*
RelSRev	Religious Studies Review
RlA	*Reallexikon der Assyriologie*. Edited by Erich Ebeling et al. Berlin: de Gruyter, 1928–
SA	Serie archeologica
SAAB	*State Archives of Assyria Bulletin*
SAAS	State Archives of Assyria Studies
SAHL	Studies in the Archaeology and History of the Levant
SANER	Studies in Ancient Near Eastern Records
SB	Subsidia Biblica
SBLDS	Society of Biblical Literature Dissertation Series
SBLMS	Society of Biblical Literature Monograph Series
SBLSP	*Society of Biblical Literature Seminar Papers*
SBLSymS	Society of Biblical Literature Symposium Series
SBT	Studies in Biblical Theology
SBTS	Sources for Biblical and Theological Study
ScrHier	Scripta hierosolymitana
SHANE	Studies in the History of the Ancient Near East
SHCANE	Studies in the History and Culture of the Ancient Near East
SFSMD	Studia Francisci Scholten memoriae dicata
SJOT	*Scandinavian Journal of the Old Testament*
SMNIA	Sonia and Marco Nadler Institute of Archaeology Monograph Series
ST	*Studia theologica*
StudOr	Studia Orientalia

SzB	Schriften zur Bibel	
TA	*Tel Aviv*	
TCL	Textes cunéiformes. Musée du Louvre	
TCS	Texts from Cuneiform Sources	
TRu	*Theologische Rundschau*	
TSHB	Textpragmatische Studien zur Hebräischen Bibel	
TynBul	*Tyndale Bulletin*	
UCOP	University of Cambridge Oriental Publications	
UF	*Ugarit-Forschungen*	
USIJ	*USI Journal*	
VAB	Vorderasiatische Bibliothek	
VT	*Vetus Testamentum*	
VTSup	Supplements to Vetus Testamentum	
War	Josephus, *Wars of the Jews*	
WBC	Word Biblical Commentary	
WDOG	Wissenschaftliche Veröffentlichungen der Deutschen Orient-Gesellschaft	
WMANT	Wissenschaftliche Monographien zum Alten und Neuen Testament	
WO	*Die Welt des Orients*	
ZAW	*Zeitschrift für die alttestamentliche Wissenschaft*	
ZBK	*Zürcher Bibelkommentare*	
ZDPV	*Zeitschrift des deutschen Palästina-Vereins*	
ZTK	*Zeitschrift für Theologie und Kirche*	

Chapter 1

INTRODUCTION

War is the province of uncertainty: three-fourths of the things upon which action in War must be calculated, are hidden more or less in the clouds of great uncertainty. Here, then, above all a fine and penetrating mind is called for, to search out the truth by the tact of its judgment.

—*Carl von Clausewitz*[1]

Sennacherib's third campaign is one of the more thoroughly investigated events that intersect with so-called biblical[2] history, and the Assyrian invasion of Judah is doubtless the most documented historical event in Israel's history before the Neo-Babylonian period.[3] The Old Testament/Hebrew Bible (hereafter, OT/HB) contains multiple accounts of Sennacherib's invasion of Judah. 2 Kings 18–19, Isaiah 36–37, and 2 Chronicles 32 all provide narrative accounts. Oracles from the book of Isaiah (e.g., Isa 1:4-9; 18:1-2; 10:5-19; 14:4-21; 21:1-10; 22:9-11; the woe oracles of 28–31) also pertain to the 701 BCE Assyrian crisis and evince somewhat diverse perspectives on the Assyrian invasion.

In addition to biblical texts, Assyrian sources contain still another perspective on Sennacherib's campaign. Of most importance are the so-called annals of Sennacherib, which were written shortly after the campaign to the West.[4]

---

1. Clausewitz, *On War*. https://www.gutenberg.org/files/1946/1946-h/1946-h.htm.

2. A better term would be ancient Israelite history or the history of ancient Palestine, as historians "are historians of a place and/or period of time, not of a book." Cf. Lester L. Grabbe, "Reflections on the Discussion," in *"Like a Bird in a Cage": The Invasion of Sennacherib in 701 BCE* (ed. Grabbe; JSOTSup, 363; ESHM, 4; London: Sheffield Academic Press, 2003), 320.

3. Isaac Kalimi, "Sennacherib's Campaign to Judah: The Chronicler's View Compared with His 'Biblical Sources,'" in *Sennacherib at the Gates of Jerusalem: Story, History and Historiography* (eds. Kalimi and Richardson; Culture and History of the Ancient Near East, 71; Leiden: Brill, 2014), 11.

4. Especially the Rassam Cylinder/Cylinder B (700 BCE), Cylinder C (697 BCE), the Oriental Institute/Chicago Prism (689 BCE), the Taylor Prism (691 BCE), and the Jerusalem/Sennacherib Prism (691 BCE).

In addition, the Bull inscriptions refer to the event as do the later summary inscriptions of Sennacherib.[5] Furthermore, the campaign is reflected in some Hellenistic sources as well (Herodotus *Historia* 2.141 and Josephus, *Antiquitates judaicae* 10:1-23), which contain their own perspective on the events of 701 BCE.[6]

Besides textual evidence, there is an abundance of archaeological evidence that is thought to be relevant to the historical reconstruction of Sennacherib's invasion. While there is some debate over what data are actually to be associated with these events, the main sites of Lachish and Jerusalem are undeniably relevant. A destruction layer found at Lachish has led to a broad consensus that it should be associated with Sennacherib's invasion of 701 BCE. In addition, the massive relief from Nineveh depicting Sennacherib's siege and conquest of Lachish provides yet another type of evidence for the events of the Assyrian invasion, which is easily correlated with the excavation of Lachish and statements from the biblical text. What is more, ubiquitous destruction layers in Judahite sites from 701 BCE have been discovered in excavations, supporting the consensus that the Assyrian invasion devastated Judah.[7] While Jerusalem clearly survived relatively unscathed—with no destruction layer found from that period—the consensus is that the Assyrian invasion of 701 BCE was very debilitating to Judah, with the suffering and death of many, the loss of their fortified cities, and even the annexation of much of their territory (distributed to the Philistines).[8] However, despite the plethora of available evidence and the vigorous scholarly industry, there continue to be major debates concerning the historical reconstruction of the events of 701 BCE. How is it that both Assyrian and Judahite sources remember the war as their respective victories?

1.1 Past Research

In 1851, Henry Rawlinson reported that he had read Hezekiah's name on a bull colossi at Nineveh, which was discovered by Austin Layard.[9] In 1852, Henry

---

5. Albert Kirk Grayson and Jamie R. Novotny, *The Royal Inscriptions of Sennacherib, King of Assyria (704-681 BC)* (Rinap, 3/2; Winona Lake, IN: Eisenbrauns, 2012). The Azekah inscription may also be relevant, though this is contested. See William R. Gallagher, *Sennacherib's Campaign to Judah: New Studies* (Shcane, 18; Leiden: Brill, 1999), 3.

6. Josephus cites Herodotus and Berossus's *History of Chaldaea*. Cf. Kalimi, "Sennacherib's Campaign," 12.

7. Ephraim Stern, *Archaeology of the Land of the Bible. Volume II: The Assyrian, Babylonian, and Persian Periods, 732-332 BCE* (ABRL, 11; New York: Doubleday, 2001), 10.

8. Hayim Tadmor, "Sennacherib's Campaign to Judah: Historiographical and Historical Considerations," *Zion* 50 (1984): 65-80.

9. Henry Rawlinson, "Assyrian Antiquities," *The Athenaeum* 1243 (August 23, 1851): 902-3. Referenced in Mordechai Cogan, "Cross-Examining the Assyrian Witnesses to Sennacherib's Third Campaign: Assessing the Limits of Historical Reconstruction," in

Rawlinson published Sennacherib's account (from the Taylor Prism).[10] Various other cuneiform texts referencing the events of 701 BCE were also discovered and appeared in D. D. Luckenbill's edition and English translation in 1924.[11] The publication of other translations (without accompanying editions of the text) provided easy access to scholars and students without Akkadian.[12]

The Rassam cylinder is the oldest of the inscriptions likely dating only a year after the invasion (700 BCE). Subsequent editions of Assyrian annals appear to have copied the Rassam text. The long list of booty in the Rassam text is abbreviated in the successive editions such as the Chicago and Taylor Prisms (which are the texts usually translated in collections of ancient Near Eastern sources such as *ANET* and *COS*), which date to 689 and 691 BCE, respectively.[13] The Assyrian annals record the destruction of forty-six Judahite fortified cities, and the exile of 200,150 Judahites.

Another Assyrian text that has sometimes been associated with the third campaign of Sennacherib is the Azekah inscription. The text comprises two fragments that were originally separate (K 6205 and BM 82-3-23, 131) and thought to have come from different time periods[14] though Na'aman later convincingly argued for their unity.[15] Previously, based mainly on one of these tablets, it was

Sennacherib at the Gates of Jerusalem: Story, History and Historiography (eds. Kalimi and Richardson; Culture and History of the Ancient Near East, 71; Leiden: Brill, 2014), 51.

10. Henry Rawlinson, "Outlines of Assyrian History, Collected from the Cuneiform Inscriptions," *XXIVTH Annual Report of the Royal Asiatic Society (1852)*: XV–XLVI. For a detailed account of the history of the work on Sennacherib's inscriptions, see Louis D. Levine, "Preliminary Remarks on the Historical Inscriptions of Sennacherib," in *History, Historiography and Interpretation* (eds. Hayim Tadmor and Moshe Weinfeld; Jerusalem: Magnes, 1983), 58–75.

11. Daniel David Luckenbill, *The Annals of Sennacherib*, OIP 2 (Chicago: University of Chicago Press, 1924).

12. E.g., *ANET* and *COS*. More textual work was done by Rykele Borger, *Babylonisch-Assyrische Lesestücke* (Rome: Pontifium Institutum Biblicum, 1979).

13. Cf. A. R. Millard, *The Eponyms of the Assyrian Empire 910-612 BC* (SAAS 2; Helsinki: Neo-Assyrian Text Corpus Project, 1994), 50, 88, and 94. For the text itself, Luckenbill (*The Annals of Sennacherib*) was the standard for some time. More recent editions and translations include E. Frahm, *Einleitung in die Sanherib-Inschriften* (AfOB, 26; Horn: Selbstverlag des Instituts für Orientalistik der Universität Wein, Druck F. Berger & Söhne, 1997). Walter Mayer, "Sennacherib's Campaign of 701 BCE: The Assyrian View," in *"Like a Bird in a Cage": The Invasion of Sennacherib in 701 BCE* (ed. Grabbe; JSOTSup, 363; ESHM, 4; London: Sheffield Academic Press, 2003), 168–200. Grayson and Novotny, *The Royal Inscriptions of Sennacherib, King of Assyria (704-681 BC)*.

14. K 6205 was thought to come from the reign of Tiglath-Pileser III (cf. Paul Rost, *Die Keilschrifttexte Tiglat-Pilesers III nach den Papierabklatschen und Originalen des Britischen Museums; neu hrsg* [Leipzig: Pfeiffer, 1893], 1.18–21, ll. 103–19) and BM 82-3-32 from the regency of Sargon II.

15. Nadav Na'aman, "Sennacherib's 'Letter to God' on His Campaign to Judah," *BASOR* 214 (1974): 25–39.

thought that the name "Azriau," reconstructed in the Azekah inscription using an extant theophoric element, referred to the biblical king Azariah (Uzziah). The name "Azriau" also appeared in an inscription by Tiglath-Pileser, and the text suggests that he led an anti-Assyrian league in Syria in 738 BCE.[16] Na'aman argued that "Azriau" in the Tiglath-Pileser text is *not* the same as the biblical king but was an otherwise unknown individual (possibly not a Judahite since the name of his land is not mentioned in the text).[17] Na'aman further argued that the Azekah inscription should be associated with Sennacherib and his 701 BCE invasion of the West, and many have followed his lead.[18] In the end, identifying the Azekah

16. Rost, Die Keilschrifttexte Tiglat-Pilesers III, 1.18–21, 2. 103–19.

17. He concludes that "the name Azriau of the Annals of Tiglath-Pileser III and Azariah of the Bible—the king of Judah—should be regarded as two separate individuals, and that the identity of names is incidental, a pitfall for the modern historian." Cf. Na'aman, "Letter to God," 38–39; Nadav Na'aman, "Sennacherib's Campaign to Judah and the Date of the Lmlk Stamps," *VT* 29 (1979): 61–86.

18. There is no real consensus in regard to dating this text. Many have dated it to the reign of Sargon II. E.g., Hayim Tadmor, "The Campaigns of Sargon II of Assur: A Chronological-Historical Study," *Journal of Cuneiform Studies* 12 (1958): 80–4; James Maxwell Miller and John Haralson Hayes, *A History of Ancient Israel and Judah* (Philadelphia, PA: Westminster, 1986), 407; Mordechai Cogan and Hayim Tadmor, *II Kings* (Garden City: Doubleday, 1988), 262 n. 6; Stefan Timm, *Moab zwischen den Mächten: Studien zu Historischen Denkmälern und Texten* (ÄAT 17; Wiesbaden: O. Harrassowitz, 1989), 337 n. 319; 356 n. 50; Bob Becking, *The Fall of Samaria: An Historical and Archaeological Study* (SHANE, 2; Leiden: Brill, 1992), 3; Andreas Fuchs, *Die Inschriften Sargons II. aus Khorsabad* (Göttingen: Cuvillier, 1994), 314–15; Gershon Galil, "A New Look at the 'Azekah Inscription," *RB* 102 (1995): 321–9; Frahm, *Einleitung*, 229–32; Jeremy Goldberg, "Two Assyrian Campaigns against Hezekiah and Later Eighth Century Biblical Chronology," *Bib* 80 (1999): 360–90; Bob Becking, "Chronology: A Skeleton without Flesh? Sennacherib's Campaign as a Case-Study," in *"Like a Bird in a Cage": The Invasion of Sennacherib in 701 BCE* (ed. Grabbe; JSOTSup, 363; ESHM, 4; London: Sheffield Academic Press, 2003), 56; Robb Andrew Young, *Hezekiah in History and Tradition* 155 (Leiden: Brill, 2012), 39. Others have associated it with Sennacherib's third campaign. E.g., Na'aman, "Letter to God," 25–39; Carl D. Evans, "Judah's Foreign Policy from Hezekiah to Josiah," in *Scripture in Context: Essays on the Comparative Method* (eds. Evans et al.; Pittsburgh: Pickwick, 1980), 160–1; Nadav Na'aman, "Hezekiah and the Kings of Assyria," *TA* 21 (1994): 235–54; Walter Mayer, *Politik und Kriegskunst der Assyrer* (ALASPM 9; Münster: Ugarit, 1995), 350–1; Antti Laato, "Assyrian Propaganda and the Falsification of History in the Royal Inscriptions of Sennacherib," *VT* 45 (1995): 214; Gallagher, *Sennacherib's Campaign*, 110–12; K. Lawson Younger Jr., "Assyrian Involvement in the Southern Levant at the End of the Eighth Century B.C.E.," in *Jerusalem in Bible and Archaeology: The First Temple Period* (eds. Vaughn and Killebrew; SBLSymS; Leiden: Brill, 2003), 238–40, 243, 245; Alexander Zukerman, "'The Royal City of the Philistines' in the 'Azekah Inscription' and the History of Gath in the Eighth Century BCE," *UF* 38 (2006): 729–78. Still others have argued it is evidence of a subsequent campaign by Sennacherib to the West a decade later. E.g., William

inscription as referencing Sennacherib's third campaign is not essential to historical reconstruction of the events (but is actually more material to the reconstruction of Judahite dispositions to Assyria during Sargon's reign if dated to Sennacherib's father's regency instead).[19]

The Assyrian account of Sennacherib's third campaign can be summarized as follows: Without a battle, the Phoenician coastal cities largely surrender to the Assyrians. Instead of military conflict, Sennacherib claims "The awesome splendor of my lordship" or the "weapon of Assur my lord" simply overwhelmed these cities. Afterward, those who failed to submit (e.g., Ashkelon) are attacked. After subduing the rebels, Sennacherib replaced their rebellious king with an obedient, pro-Assyrian leader (son of their former king) who would pay the requisite tribute. As the annals turn to chronicle their conflict with Ekron, who had deposed their king Padî and sent him prisoner to Hezekiah in Jerusalem, they then describe the battle of Eltekeh with Egyptian and Cushite forces, who had come to aid those in Ekron, the outcome of which is clearly recorded as an Assyrian victory. Furthermore, Ekron is besieged and captured, and its treasonous officials killed, and guilty citizens taken as "spoil." The innocent (those "who had not sinned") of Ekron are then freed and Padî, the king imprisoned in Jerusalem, is reinstalled as king. Sennacherib then chronicles his maneuvers against Hezekiah's Judah, noting that he besieged and conquered forty-six fortified cities as well as innumerable other towns (describing the military tactics employed), claiming 200,150 exiles as spoil (along with many animals).

Regarding direct military action against Hezekiah, Sennacherib famously boasts of enclosing Hezekiah in Jerusalem "like a bird in a cage."[20] While in the past it was common to view this as an actual "siege" of Jerusalem, more recent scholarship has concluded there was no actual siege of Jerusalem, but that the

---

H. Shea, "Sennacherib's Second Palestinian Campaign," *JBL* 104 (1985): 404–7; William H. Shea, "Jerusalem under Siege: Did Sennacherib Attack Twice?," *BAR* 25 (1999): 36–44, 64. Though see the convincing critique by Frank J. Yurco, "The Shabaka-Shebitku Coregency and the Supposed Second Campaign of Sennacherib against Judah: A Critical Assessment," *JBL* 110 (1991): 35–45.

19. Most important, we have no record of an invasion of Judah by Sargon, unless the Azekah inscription is just that. Therefore, dating the inscription to Sargon's days would be more vital for a reconstruction of Judah–Assyria relations at that time, than understanding it to be from Sennacherib's invasion of 701 BCE, which makes it simply one more witness to the third campaign. Dating it to Sennacherib's regency suggests Hezekiah did not oppose Assyria early in his reign. There has also been debate over whether the royal city mentioned in the text should be understood to be Gath or Ekron. Na'aman initially argued for the former (Na'aman, "Letter to God") but later became convinced of the latter (Na'aman, "Hezekiah") due to the arguments of Mittman (Siegfried Mittmann, "Hiskia und die Philister," *JNSL* 16 (1990): 91–106). Others have since argued again for Gath. E.g., Zukerman, "The Royal City of the Philistines," 729–78.

20. Mayer's translation. Cf. Mayer, "Sennacherib's Campaign," 189.

city may have been subject to a blockade at most, or military threats at least.[21] Furthermore, the phrase "like a bird in a cage" should be understood as hyperbolic language that is used in Assyrian texts elsewhere in situations where there was no actual military success against a city.[22]

Another claim of Sennacherib in his annals is that he annexed much of Hezekiah's territory and gave it to the Philistines. On this basis, many historical reconstructions posit the severe shrinking of Judahite territory at this time and the diminishing of Hezekiah's power and influence subsequent to this Assyrian annexation.[23] Using the same language used to describe the initial success against the Sidonians, Sennacherib claims that Hezekiah was also "overwhelmed by the splendor of [Sennacherib's] lordship," which resulted in Hezekiah sending him tribute (which is described at length to conclude the account) after he returned to Nineveh.

Problems in correlating the Assyrian annals and the biblical texts concerning the Assyrian invasion of 701 BCE were seen from the beginning. Layard observed discrepancies between the biblical and Assyrian sources but nevertheless believed their reports could be correlated.[24] While both sources appeared in agreement regarding the Assyrian invasion of Judah and the tribute paid by Hezekiah—including the identical amount of gold listed in both Assyrian and biblical sources—there was clear incongruity regarding the outcome of the war. According to Assyrian texts, it was an unequivocal victory for Sennacherib, while the biblical sources record an Assyrian defeat that resulted in Sennacherib's return to Nineveh (2 Kgs 19:35).

At first, these discrepancies were seen to be due to the tendency of Assyrian kings to omit any defeat from their records. For example, when Henry Rawlinson explained the discrepancies to his brother George Rawlinson, who was writing his book on ancient Mesopotamian history,[25] he simply said it was owed to the Assyrian refusal to admit defeat. According to Walter Mayer, "This cut-and-dry explanation became the guiding force for all subsequent interpretation of Neo-Assyrian

---

21. Paul S. Evans, *The Invasion of Sennacherib in the Book of Kings: A Source-Critical and Rhetorical Study of 2 Kings 18–19* (VTSup, 125; Leiden: Brill, 2009).

22. Hayim Tadmor, *The Inscriptions of Tiglath-Pileser III, King of Assyria: Critical Edition, with Introductions, Translations and Commentary* (Jerusalem: Israel Academy of Sciences and Humanities, 1994), 79; Eckart Frahm, "The Neo-Assyrian Period (ca. 1000–609 BCE)," in *A Companion to Assyria* (ed. Frahm; Hoboken, NJ: John Wiley, 2017), 163.

23. E.g., Ernst Axel Knauf, "Sennacherib at the Berezina," in *"Like a Bird in a Cage": The Invasion of Sennacherib in 701 BCE* (ed. Grabbe; JSOTSup, 363; ESHM, 4; London: Sheffield Academic Press, 2003), 142.

24. Austen Henry Layard, *Discoveries in the Ruins of Nineveh and Babylon* (London: J. Murray, 1853), 142–5.

25. George Rawlinson, *The Five Great Monarchies of the Ancient Eastern World: The Second Monarchy: Assyria* (4 vols.; London: John Murray, 1864), 2.430–46.

historical writings."[26] Mayer's assessment is a bit hyperbolic, however, as scholars wrestled with explaining Hezekiah's payment of tribute (acknowledged in both the biblical and Assyrian sources) as congruent with an Assyrian defeat, despite the thinking that Assyrian sources were unwilling to concede loss. Therefore, various theories were employed to fit the biblical and extrabiblical evidence into a plausible historical reconstruction.

This problem led to speculations that the biblical text bears witness to two discrete campaigns of Sennacherib into the West. The first to suggest a two-campaign reconstruction was G. Rawlinson.[27] Though he admitted the Assyrian evidence did not suggest a second campaign,[28] he posited an invasion by Sennacherib in 700 BCE, during which Hezekiah surrendered, followed by another invasion, two years later in 698 BCE to which 2 Kgs 18:17–19:37 refers. Most subsequent two-campaign theorists have argued the second invasion was over a decade later. For example, Grayson writes,

> It seems obvious that the two sources [Sennacherib's annals and the biblical account] are describing essentially different events, and that we must reckon with at least one further Palestinian campaign after 701. This second campaign probably took place late in the reign (688–681), a period for which no Assyrian annalistic narratives are preserved ... Whatever happened, Sennacherib withdrew in confusion and disgrace.[29]

26. Mayer, "Sennacherib's Campaign," 169. In recent years, most have rejected the two-campaign theory as unlikely, as it is based on speculative source-critical delineations and devoid of any Assyrian evidence for a second campaign by Sennacherib into the West. Cogan argues forcefully against the notion based on the conclusion that if Sennacherib were not wholly successful in a second campaign, he could not have left Esarhaddon set up for success in the way that he did (Cogan, "Cross-Examining," 74). Contra. this supposition that there could not have been an imperfect success is Knauf's conclusion that "the Assyrian-Egyptian conflict ended in stalemate, not to be settled until 671. As for Sennacherib, after his narrow escape at/from Eltekeh he had no intention of returning to southern Canaan either" ("Sennacherib at the Berezina," 149).

27. Rawlinson, *The Five Great Monarchies of the Ancient Eastern World*, 2.430–46.

28. Ibid., 2.439 n. 4.

29. Albert Kirk Grayson, "Assyria: Sennacherib and Esarhaddon," in *Cambridge Ancient History: The Assyrian and Babylonian Empires and Other States of the Near East, from the Eighth to the Sixth Centuries* B.C. (eds. Boardman et al.; Cambridge: Cambridge University Press, 1991), vol. III, Part 2, 111. Other adherents to the two-campaign hypothesis include E. A. Wallis Budge, *A History of Egypt: From the End of the Neolithic Period to the Death of Cleopatra VII, B.C. 30, Vol. 6: Egypt under the Priest-Kings and Tanites and Nubians* (Books on Egypt and Chaldea, 14; London: Kegan Paul, Trench, Trübner, 1902), 6.133–42; Kemper Fullerton, "The Invasion of Sennacherib," *BibSac* 63 (1906): 577–634; George Adam Smith, *Jerusalem: The Topography, Economics and History from the Earliest Times to A.D. 70* (2 vols.; London: Hodder and Stoughton, 1907), 2.148–80; Alfred Jeremias, C. H. W. Johns, and C. L. Beaumont, *The Old Testament in the Light of the Ancient East* (London: Williams

The mention of Tirhakah (Taharqa/Taharqo) "King of Cush" in the biblical text (2 Kgs 19:9) in the context of Sennacherib's 701 BCE invasion was also thought to suggest a second campaign. Egyptian records show that Taharqo did not become Pharaoh until a decade later (c. 690 BCE), leading many to argue that the biblical text refers to a later, second Assyrian invasion of the Levant under Sennacherib, when Taharqo was king. Moreover, it is not only the date of Taharqo's regency but also his age in 701 BCE that is part of this debate. Initially scholars understood Taharqo to be a child in 701 BCE, meaning he would be unable to lead an army at that young age.[30] More recently, however, it has been argued that he was actually a man of at least twenty years of age and by that time he could have easily led an army.[31] A pair of stelae from Cush are central to this

& Norgate, 1911), 222–8; Robert William Rogers, *Cuneiform Parallels to the Old Testament* (New York: Eaton & Mains, 1912), 337–9; George A. Barton, *Archæology and the Bible* (Philadelphia, PA: American Sunday-School Union, 1916), 471–6; Raymond P. Dougherty, "Sennacherib and the Walled Cities of Judah," *JBL* 49 (1930): 160–71; William F. Albright, "Review of A. T. E. Olmstead, *History of Palestine and Syria to the Macedonian Conquest*," *JQR* 24/4 (1934): 370–1; William F. Albright, "New Light from Egypt on the Chronology and the History of Israel and Judah," *BASOR* 130 (1953): 8–11; J. Le Moyne, "Les deux ambassades de Sennachérib à Jérusalem; Recherches sur l'évolution d'une tradition," in *Melanges bibliques rédigés en l'honneur de André Robert* (Paris: Bloud & Gay, 1957), 149–53; John Bright, *A History of Israel* (Louisville, KY: Westminster/John Knox, 2000), 267–9, 282–7; Cornelis van Leeuwen, "Sanchérib devant Jérusalem," *OTS* 14 (1965): 245–72. More recently, the theory was defended by Shea, "Sennacherib's Second Palestinian Campaign," 401–18; William H. Shea, "The New Tirhakah Text and Sennacherib's Second Palestinian Campaign," *AUSS* 35 (1997): 181–7; Shea, "Jerusalem under Siege," 36; William H. Shea, "Hezekiah, Sennacherib and Tirhakah: A Brief Rejoinder," *NEASB* 45 (2000): 37–8. Cf. Christopher T. Begg, "Sennacherib's Second Palestinian Campaign: An Additional Indication," *JBL* 106 (1987): 685–6.

30. Miles F. L. Macadam argues that Taharqo was born in 710 BCE, making him too young to lead a military role in 701 BCE. Macadam posits a six-year co-regency between Shabatko and Taharqo. Cf. Miles Frederick Laming Macadam, *The Temples of Kawa. Vol. 1* (London: Oxford University Press, 1949), 1.18–20. Cf. Jürgen von Beckerath, "Ägypten und Der Feldzug Sanheribs Im Jahre 701 V Chr," *UF* 24 (1993): 3–8. Albright ("New Light from Egypt," 9) therefore thought it impossible for Taharqo "to take part in any military activity" in 701 BCE. Similarly, Donald B. Redford understands the Kawa inscription to mean that Taharqo was twenty years old in 690 BCE (making him only around ten years in 701 BCE). Cf. Donald B. Redford, *Egypt, Canaan, and Israel in Ancient Times* (Princeton: Princeton University Press, 1992), 351–3. Similarly, Richard A. Parker, "The Length of the Reign of Amasis and the Beginning of the Twenty-Sixth Dynasty," *MDAIK* 15 (1957): 208–12. Arie van der Kooij finds the biblical mention of Tirhakah to be pure anachronism, and he doubts his presence in the Levant at that time. Cf. Arie van der Kooij, "Das assyrische Heer vor den Mauern Jerusalems im Jahr 701 v. Chr," *ZDPV* 102 (1986): 114.

31. Kenneth A. Kitchen reexamined the Nubian dynasty's chronology, concluding that he was old enough to lead the army in 701 BCE, though he was crowned sole king in

issue.³² One mentions that Taharqo was initially summoned to Egypt by Shabatko, and the other that Taharqo was twenty years old at this time. Many understood the summons to be a call for Taharqo to fight Sennacherib in the Levant in 701 BCE.³³ However, in recent research several scholars have argued for a revision in our understanding of the conventional chronology of the Twenty-Fifth Dynasty reversing the order of succession between Cushite kings Shabako and Shabatako.³⁴

690 BCE. Cf. Kenneth A. Kitchen, *The Third Intermediate Period in Egypt (1100–650 B.C.)* (Warminster: Aris & Phillips, 1986), 161–72. Kitchen also convincingly refuted the theory of a six-year co-regency (164–172). Cf. Jean Leclant and Jean Yoyotte, "Notes d'histoire et de civilisation éthiopiennes: À propos d'un ouvrage récent," *BIFAO* 51 (1952): 17–29; Leeuwen, "Sanchérib," 260. Anson F. Rainey, "Taharqa and Syntax," *TA* 3 (1976): 38–41; Frank J. Yurco, "Sennacherib's Third Campaign and the Coregency of Shabaka and Shebitku," *Serapis* 6 (1980): 222–3; James K. Hoffmeier, "Egypt's Role in the Events of 701 B.C. in Jerusalem," in *Jerusalem in Bible and Archaeology: The First Temple Period* (eds. Vaughn and Killebrew; SBLSymS 18; Leiden: Brill, 2003), 230–2. Regarding the necessary age for a military role, Kitchen points out that Rameses II held the office of commander of the army at the age of ten years and participated in foreign military campaigns at the age of fourteen or fifteen years. Cf. Kenneth. A. Kitchen, *Pharaoh Triumphant: The Life and Times of Ramesses II, King of Egypt* (Warminster, England: Aris & Phillips, 1982), 24; See Young, *Hezekiah in History and Tradition*, 73–6; Dan'el Kahn, "The Inscription of Sargon II at Tang-i Var and the Chronology of Dynasty 25," *Or.N.S.* 70 (2001): 2, n. 10–11.

32. "Kawa IV (Khartoum Snm 2678 = Merowe Museum 52), *ll.* 7–9," in *The Temples of Kawa, Vol. 1* (ed. Macadam; Oxford University Excavations in Nubia; London: Oxford University Press, 1949), pls. 7–9; "Kawa V (Ny Carlsberg Glyptotek Æ.I.N. 1712), *ll.* 22–27," in *The Temples of Kawa* (ed. Macadam; Oxford University Excavations in Nubia; London: Oxford University Press, 1949), pls. 9–10.

33. D. Kahn explicitly states that "Shabatka [=Shabatko] summons Taharqa to fight against Sennacherib." Kahn, "The Inscription of Sargon II," 18. Cf. Kitchen, *The Third Intermediate Period*, 157–8 §127, 557 §469; László Török, *The Kingdom of Kush: Handbook of the Napatan-Meroitic Civilization* (HO, 31; Leiden: Brill, 1997), 169–70; T. Eide, ed., *Fontes Historiae Nubiorum* (Bergen: Klassisk Institutt, Universitetet i Bergen, 1994), 1.144.

34. Michael Bányai, "Ein Vorschlag zur Chronologie der 25. Dynastie in Ägypten," *JEH* 6 (2013): 46–129; Frédéric Payraudeau, "Retour Sur La Succession Shabaqo-Shabataqo," *NeHeT* 1 (2014): 115–27; G. P. F. Broekman, "The Order of Succession between Shabaka and Shabataka: A Different View on the Chronology of the Twenty-Fifth Dynasty," *GM* 245 (2015): 17–31; Michael Bányai, "Die Reihenfolge der kuschitischen Könige," *JEH* 8 (2015): 115–80; Claus Jurman, "The Order of the Kushite Kings According to Sources from the Eastern Desert and Thebes. Or: Shabataka Was Here First!" *JEH* 10 (2017): 124–51; Jeremy Pope, "Sennacherib's Departure and the Principle of Laplace," in *Jerusalem's Survival, Sennacherib's Departure, and the Kushite Role in 701 BCE: An Examination of Henry Aubin's Rescue of Jerusalem* (ed. Bellis; PHSC, 32; Piscataway, NJ: Gorgias Press, 2020), 147–51; Aidan Dodson, "The Rescue of Jerusalem: A View from the Nile Valley," in *Jerusalem's Survival, Sennacherib's Departure, and the Kushite Role in 701 BCE: An Examination of Henry Aubin's Rescue of Jerusalem* (ed. Bellis; PHSC, 32; Piscataway, NJ: Gorgias Press,

This new understanding concludes that Shabatako occupied the Cushite throne *before* Shabako. With this new understanding of the succession, Taharqo would have been summoned by Shabatako *not* in 701 but in 712 BCE, meaning Taharqo was around thirty years old in 701 BCE—plenty old to have a leading military role. On the other hand, the reversal of the succession of Shabako and Shabatako means that the calling of Taharqo from Cush to Egypt cannot have been in order to participate in the campaign of 701 BCE, since it occurred in 712 BCE. However, Taharqo's age being thirty years in 701 BCE means that the mention of Tirhakah in the biblical account does not necessitate a two-campaign hypothesis. The reference to him as "king of Cush" (2 Kgs 19:9) could be an understandable anachronism due to his later fame as the Pharaoh who resisted Assyria.[35]

However, the title "king of Cush" need not be understood as anachronistic. The term 'Pharaoh" was not used exclusively in Egypt at the time, as there were multiple rulers in the region. Besides which the title "king of Cush" (2 Kgs 19:9) is not the same as "king of Egypt" (Cush designates Nubia–modern Sudan). There were multiple dynasties in power in this time period, with Egyptologists actually differentiating them by regions.[36] The multiplicity of regencies is even evident in the Assyrian annals, which mention the "kings of Egypt"[37] and "the king of the land of Meluḫḫa [Ethiopia]"[38] as Sennacherib's opponents in the battle at Eltekeh. Although not yet the Pharaoh of Egypt, Taharqo could rightly have been referred to as the king of Cush at the time of Sennacherib's 701 BCE campaign.[39] Besides which, the Ethiopian king's list actually names Taharqo as ruler during 701 BCE.[40]

2020), 167–88; Aidan Dodson, *The Royal Tombs of Ancient Egypt* (Barnsley: Pen & Sword Archaeology, 2016), 115–49.

35. K. A. Kitchen, *Ancient Orient and Old Testament* (Chicago, IL: InterVarsity Press, 1966), 82–4; K. A. Kitchen, *Third Intermediate Period*, xxxix–xlii, 158–61, 383–6, 552–9, 584–5; K. A. Kitchen, "Egyptian Interventions in the Levant in Iron Age II," in *Symbiosis, Symbolism, and the Power of the Past: Canaan, Ancient Israel, and Their Neighbors from the Late Bronze Age through Roman Palaestina* (eds. Dever and Gitin; Winona Lake, IN: Eisenbrauns, 2003), 127–8.

36. Kitchen, *Third Intermediate Period*, 366. As Young writes, "There was in this period a confederation of kings and high chieftains who ruled smaller, local centers of power throughout Libya and Nubia, thus permitting Taharqo to be a king ruling from Napata while his brother Shebitku was recognized as a Pharaoh over Egypt" (*Hezekiah in History and Tradition*, 75).

37. RINAP 3.1:176, 22.ii.79.

38. RINAP 3.1:176, 22.ii.80. Also mentioned in RINAP 3.1:176, 22.iii.3. Cf. Luckenbill, *The Annals of Sennacherib*, 31–2.

39. Contra. Kahn who concludes Tirhakah "was not yet the King of Kush in 701." Dan'el Kahn, "Tirhakah, King of Kush and Sennacherib," *JAEI* 6 (2014): 36.

40. Alan Gardiner, *Egypt of the Pharaohs: An Introduction* (Oxford: Clarendon Press, 1961), 342. Some have argued that another inscription belongs to Taharqo's reign. Cf. Donald B. Redford, "Taharqa in Western Asia and Libya," *EI* 24 (1993): 188–91. On this basis, Shea again has argued to the two-campaign hypothesis. Cf. Shea, "New Tirhakah

Also against the two-campaign theory is the reconstruction of this period of Assyrian history. If the first campaign (recorded in Sennacherib's annals and the putative Account A) was utterly successful, as is reconstructed by proponents, why did Sennacherib campaign again so soon thereafter? Would Hezekiah rebel so soon after he was thoroughly punished? What is more, this second campaign is thought to be dated later than 690 BCE (when Taharqo was crowned sole king), which makes it occur in the years following the destruction of Babylon by Sennacherib in 689 BCE. Given the fate of powerful Babylon, it seems unlikely that this would be a time when vassal states would feel confident to rebel.[41] Further, if Sennacherib did invade again, but this time suffered a defeat, that would have meant that his son Esarhaddon would have needed to make the West submit once again, but extant Assyrian inscriptions list Hezekiah's son, Manasseh, as a vassal king.[42] Given the obvious problems with the historical reconstructions involved in the two-campaign hypothesis, and the fact that there is no hint of a second Palestinian campaign in Assyrian records, and that the OT/HB itself does not present its account as a separate invasion, the present study rejects this hypothesis.[43]

Text," 181-7; Shea, "Jerusalem under Siege," 36-44, 64. However, Cogan has convincingly refuted the hypothesis, arguing against the identification of Egyptian deportees as the Assyrian army and that a late defeat of the Assyrians does not fit into the picture of Assyrian rule as we know it. Cf. Cogan, "Cross-Examining," 74.

41. As Cogan and Tadmor (*II Kings*, 249) write, "Babylon's fate surely served as a warning of what awaited the unsubmissive." Similarly, Jossette Elayi writes, "it is inconceivable that, after the terrible ravage of Babylon by Sennacherib in 689, a western king had dared to revolt against Assyria." See Jossette Elayi, *Sennacherib, King of Assyria* (ABS 24. Atlanta, GA: SBL Press, 2018), 87.

42. Ibid., 249. Cogan reiterates this opinion later, asserting that if Sennacherib suffered a defeat so late in his reign, his son, Esarhaddon "would have had to reassert Assyria's hegemony over the West early on," but he did not. Cf. Cogan, "Cross-Examining," 74.

43. As Young writes, "To expect the deliverance of Jerusalem to have occurred twice under the same Judean king against his unchanged Assyrian overlord, with both parties acting from their selfsame physical locations, strains credulity." Cf. Young, *Hezekiah in History and Tradition*, 66-73(71). For critical responses against the theory, see Elayi, *Sennacherib*, 85-7; Cogan, "Cross-Examining," 51-74; Kahn, "Tirhakah," 29-41; Siegfried H. Horn, "Did Sennacherib Campaign Once or Twice against Hezekiah," *AUS* 4 (1966): 1-28; Yurco, "The Shabaka-Shebitku Coregency," 35-45. Yurco, "Sennacherib's Third Campaign," 221-40. Robert D. Bates, "Could Taharqa Have Been Called to the Battle of Eltekeh? A Response to William H. Shea," *NEASB* 46 (2001): 43-6; Robert D. Bates, "Assyria and Rebellion in the Annals of Sennacherib: An Analysis of Sennacherib's Treatment of Hezekiah," *NEASB* 44 (1999): 39-61. See, especially, the criticisms by Mordechai Cogan, "Sennacherib's Siege of Jerusalem: Once or Twice?" *BAR* 27 (2001): 40-5, 69; A. K. Jenkins, "Hezekiah's Fourteenth Year: A New Interpretation of 2 Kings 18:13-19:37," *VT* 26 (1976): 284-98; Evans, "Judah's Foreign Policy," 157-78; Kitchen, *Third Intermediate Period*, 550; Christof Hardmeier, *Prophetie im Streit vor dem Untergang Judas: erzählkommunikative Studien zur Entstehungssituation der Jesaja- und Jeremiaerzählungen in II Reg 18-20 und Jer 37-40*

The difficulty of correlating the payment of tribute with an Assyrian defeat also led to a source-critical approach to the problem put forward by Bernhard Stade, who separated the 2 Kings account into discrete sources, which were further refined by Brevard S. Childs.[44] The earliest source (Account A: 2 Kgs 18:13-16) made reference to the tribute Hezekiah paid to Sennacherib, while the later sources (Account B1: 2 Kgs 18:17–19:9a, 36-37; and Account B2: 2 Kgs 19:9b-35) did not, but instead narrated an Assyrian defeat and retreat from Judah. In my earlier monograph,[45] I have argued at length against the source-critical delineations of Stade and Childs, and I will not go over that ground again here other than to state that in my opinion the arguments for this hypothesis do not stand up to scrutiny. However, despite the problems of determining the exact sources behind the present biblical text in Kings, many still hold that the early A source was accurate (as it correlates with Assyrian sources), but the B sources were not (since they narrate an Assyrian retreat).

The reliability of the B source is widely maligned by scholars, as A. R. Millard described: "What we read in 2 Kings 18.17–19.37 is, in effect, no more than a theologian's fairy-tale, an interweaving of an old story with theological theory to produce a narrative which is unhistorical."[46] The poor view of the reliability of the B source appears tied to the tendency to date it quite late. Seitz concludes, "It is not a work authored in a single setting, or by an eyewitness concerned with reporting 'what really happened' in some objective sense."[47] R. E. Clements argued that the earliest date that B1 could be written is Josiah's time because it is only then that Assyrian control weakened.[48] In fact, Clements concludes B2 likely dates from the

---

(Berlin: de Gruyter, 1990), 164; Redford, *Egypt, Canaan, and Israel*, 354 n. 165; Frahm, *Einleitung* 10. Becking proposed a divergent two-invasion hypothesis, based on the reference to Hezekiah's fourteenth year, suggesting this reflects an invasion by Sargon II in 715 BCE. He suggests that the B narrative reflects this invasion but that the rest of Account A, 2 Kgs 18:14-16, reflects Sennacherib's invasion in 701 BCE. Cf. Becking, "Chronology: A Skeleton without Flesh?" 40–72. Becking's hypothesis is very close to that proposed by Jenkins years ago. Cf. Jenkins, "Hezekiah's Fourteenth Year," 284–98. Goldberg argued that 2 Kgs 18:13-16 originally referred to a "limited invasion" by Sargon in 712 BCE, which was later conflated with that of the 701 BCE invasion. Cf. Goldberg, "Two Assyrian Campaigns," 360–90.

44. Bernhard Stade, "Miscellen: Anmerkungen zu 2 Kö. 15–21," *ZAW* 6 (1886): 156–89; Brevard S. Childs, *Isaiah and the Assyrian Crisis* (SBT, 3; London: SCM, 1967).

45. Evans, *Invasion of Sennacherib*, 39–81.

46. A. R. Millard, "Sennacherib's Attack on Hezekiah," *TynBul* 36 (1985): 73.

47. Christopher R. Seitz, *Zion's Final Destiny: The Development of the Book of Isaiah: A Reassessment of Isaiah 36–39* (Minneapolis, MN: Fortress, 1991), 94.

48. Roland Ernest Clements, *Jerusalem and the Nations: Studies in the Book of Isaiah* 16 (Sheffield: Sheffield Phoenix Press, 2011), 80-1. He writes, "The earliest that such an interpretation of an event could reasonably be thought to have arisen is during Josiah's reign, when the weakness and crumbling authority of Assyrian control had become evident in Jerusalem." In fact, he concludes it must be in "no earlier than the latter period of Josiah's reign and continuing through into the reigns of Jehoiakim and Zedekiah" (81).

Persian period "when hopes for the revival of the Davidic family's fortunes revived in the late sixth century BCE."[49] Na'aman disagrees and sees it possible B1 was written shortly after Sennacherib's death, though he dates B2, with its miraculous ending, to the Babylonian exile or early Persian period.[50] It would appear that the scholarly consensus regarding the reliability and late date of B2 is intertwined with its miraculous divine intervention described at its climax, which is thought to evince later theological development. It was written, as Clements writes, "after a considerable interval of time had elapsed, and is intended to draw the maximum in the way of theological significance out of the fact that Jerusalem was not subjected to any military attack."[51] While Account A, which agrees in large part with the Assyrian annals, is thought to be written close to the event, Account B, with its view of divine deliverance of Jerusalem, must have been written much later.[52]

Childs, on the other hand, viewed B2 as reflecting historical reality due to similarities between the Assyrian messenger's speech in the biblical account and Assyrian documents, wherein an Assyrian official attempts to persuade his audience to not join in with rebels.[53] Of course, scholars have come to different conclusions regarding the Rabshakeh's speech(es) and its dating and historicity.[54]

---

49. Ibid., 131.

50. Nadav Na'aman, "Updating the Messages: Hezekiah's Second Prophetic Story (2 Kings 19.9b-35) and the Community of Babylonian Deportees," in *"Like a Bird in a Cage": The Invasion of Sennacherib in 701 BCE* (ed. Grabbe; JSOTSup, 363; ESHM, 4; London: Sheffield Academic Press, 2003), 218–19.

51. Ronald Ernest Clements, *Isaiah and the Deliverance of Jerusalem: A Study of the Interpretation of Prophecy in the Old Testament* (JSOTSup, 13; Sheffield: University of Sheffield, 1980), 59. He later writes similarly, "The story of a fortunate escape amid a ruthless campaign of destruction and barbarism has been elevated into one of miraculous divine intervention." Cf. Clements, *Jerusalem and the Nations*, 151.

52. As Clements opines, the account of Jerusalem's deliverance is "a retrospective interpretation of the reason why Jerusalem was spared the fate of Lachish and belong to the wider context of interpretation that belongs to the Deliverance Narrative of Isa 36:1–39:8. They focus on the power of Yahweh as God, the divine justice in punishing the arrogance of Sennacherib, and they look ahead to the future of Jerusalem and Judah." Cf. Clements, *Jerusalem and the Nations*, 94.

53. Childs, *Assyrian Crisis*, 78–93, drawing on H. W. F. Saggs, "The Nimrud Letters, 1952–Part I," *Iraq* 17 (1955): 21–56; H. W. F. Saggs, "The Nimrud Letters, 1952–Part II," *Iraq* 17 (1955): 126–60; H. W. F. Saggs, "The Nimrud Letters, 1952–Part III," *Iraq* 18 (1956): 40–56 + plates 9–12. Cf. H. W. F. Saggs, *The Nimrud Letters, 1952* (CTN, 5; London: British School of Archaeology in Iraq, 2001).

54. Gallagher (*Sennacherib's Campaign*) also argued for the general historicity of the Rabshakeh's speeches in 2 Kings. Gallagher holds that Isa 10:5-19 is basically a summary of the Rabshakeh's speech and contemporary to the events of 701 BCE. Contrary to Gallagher's conclusions regarding the historicity of the Rabshakeh's speeches, E. Ben Zvi and D. Rudman separately have pointed out that these speeches comprise common biblical language and even resemble prophetic language, rather than reflect actual Assyrian speech

Most hold that the miraculous conclusion of the putative B2 source must have been written later as a theological reflection on the historical event of Jerusalem's survival.[55] At the end of his study, Childs concluded that the biblical and Assyrian sources could not be reconciled unless new historical information came to light.[56]

This common view disparaging the historicity of the so-called B2 source evinces significant changes in scholarly opinion since the early position that biblical sources were preferable to Assyrian sources due to the untrustworthiness of the latter. In more recent scholarship, some even go as far as to say that "Assyrian royal inscriptions (nearly) never lie."[57] Along these lines, Baruch Halpern has put forward what he calls the "Tiglath-Pileser principle,"[58] which

---

and propaganda. Cf. Ehud Ben Zvi, "Who Wrote the Speech of Rabshakeh and When?" *JBL* 109 (1990): 79–92. Dominic Rudman, "Is the Rabshakeh Also among the Prophets? A Rhetorical Study of 2 Kings XVIII 17–35," *VT* 50 (2000): 100–10. Contra, Chaim Cohen, "Neo-Assyrian Elements in the First Speech of the Biblical Rab-Saqê," *IOS* 9 (1979): 32–48. Cf. Peter Machinist, "The Rab Saqeh at the Wall of Jerusalem: Israelite Identity in the Face of the Assyrian 'Other,'" *HS* 41 (2000): 151–68; Moshe Weinfeld, "Cult Centralization in Israel in the Light of a Neo-Babylonian Analogy," *JNES* 23 (1964): 202–12. Ben Zvi suggests Rabshakeh's speech is largely a free composition of the biblical writer (similarly Klaas A. D. Smelik, "King Hezekiah Advocates True Prophecy: Remarks on Isaiah XXXVI and XXXVII//II Kings XVIII and XIX," in *Converting the Past: Studies in Ancient Israelite and Moabite Historiography* [OTS, 28; Leiden: Brill, 1992], 98–128). According to Ben Zvi, however, the speech writer was restricted by some "collective memory" of the actual historical event that prevented the writer to put the speech into Sennacherib's mouth (or a more important official than the Rabshakeh). He concludes the speech was "not contemporary with the events" and speculates dating its composition to "post-monarchic Judah." Cf. Ben Zvi, "Who Wrote the Speech," 92. Rudman ("Is the Rabshakeh Also among the Prophets," 101) also examined the speech and drew attention to parallels and shared language with other biblical literature. Some have doubted the historicity of the Assyrian delegation of the Tartan, Rabsaris, and Rabshakeh, given that the Isaiah account has only the Rabshakeh sent to Jerusalem. But it makes sense that Sennacherib would travel with such an entourage. While some think it strange that the lowest ranking official does the speaking (the Rabshakeh), it seems likely this is due to his fluency in the local language. Cf. Cogan and Tadmor, *II Kings*, 230.

55. E.g., Clements (*Deliverance of Jerusalem*, 60–1) asserts that the attribution of Jerusalem's deliverance to the angel of Yahweh had "only been introduced into the narrative of the events of that year at a comparatively late stage. It marks a high point in the growth of the tradition ... but, consequentially changes substantially the perspective."

56. He writes, "In terms of the specific historical problem of 701, it seems unlikely that a satisfactory historical solution will be forthcoming without fresh extra-biblical evidence" (Childs, *Assyrian Crisis*, 120). Although he also considers the possibility that "a very new handling of the known material" may help. Ibid., 118.

57. Knauf, "Sennacherib at the Berezina," 141.

58. Baruch Halpern, *David's Secret Demons: Messiah, Murderer, Traitor, King* (Grand Rapids, MI: Eerdmans, 2001), 124–32.

holds that Assyrian documents never outright lie, though they "put extreme spin on real events."⁵⁹ Thus this "principle" implies that when biblical sources diverge from Assyrian claims the latter's opinion should be trusted at the expense of the former. For example, E. A. Knauf views the Assyrian and biblical sources as irreconcilable, and sides with the Assyrian version of events, asserting that 2 Kings 18–19 (and Isaiah 36–37) "is not a source at all for the events of 701, but a piece of propaganda from the second siege of Jerusalem by Nebuchadnezzar."⁶⁰ N. P. Lemche opines that "the biblical narrative that follows the payment of the tribute [i.e., 2 Kgs 18:17–19:37] is invented history or simply fiction."⁶¹ Mayer similarly holds that the biblical narration that concludes with Sennacherib's retreat "belongs to the body of postexilic legends that arose during the time of rivalry between Jerusalem and Samaria."⁶² Frahm similarly holds that due to the "theological concerns" driving the authors, the biblical texts "paint a rather distorted picture of the outcome of the campaign."⁶³ Thus, instead of Assyrian sources being unreliable, with their unwillingness to admit defeat, for some it is biblical claims that are suspect, and even deemed "invented," "fiction," "distorted," or simply "legend."⁶⁴

Of course, some scholars (often labelled maximalists) may privilege the biblical text above all other sources and take the data from the OT/HB as historically reliable unless they have been otherwise disproved. While not always stated, this approach may be based partly on a view of the biblical text as inspired and therefore accurate.⁶⁵ Such scholars may still hold to a version of the early position that Assyrian sources do in fact purposefully deceive and not just put "spin" on events.

59. Ibid., 126.
60. Knauf, "Sennacherib at the Berezina," 146.
61. Niels Peter Lemche, "On the Problems of Reconstructing Pre-Hellenistic Israelite (Palestinian) History," in *"Like a Bird in a Cage": The Invasion of Sennacherib in 701 BCE* (ed. Grabbe; JSOTSup, 363; ESHM, 4; London: Sheffield Academic Press, 2003), 153.
62. Mayer, "Sennacherib's Campaign," 171.
63. Frahm, "Neo-Assyrian Period," 184.
64. As Clements says of the biblical account, "The record has been adjusted and elaborated." Cf. Clements, *Jerusalem and the Nations*, 97.
65. Regardless of its motives, the position that the biblical text should be accepted unless falsified by extrabiblical sources contemporary to the events is problematic given the paucity of available sources and the randomness of their discovery. Cf. William W. Hallo, "Jerusalem under Hezekiah: An Assyriological Perspective," in *Jerusalem: Its Sanctity and Centrality to Judaism, Christianity, and Islam* (ed. Levine; New York: Continuum, 1999), 44. For the same reason, the so-called minimalist approach of demanding clear verification of all biblical claims by contemporary extrabiblical evidence is equally problematic. The problematic nature of both falsification and verification principles is brought into view in an instance like the Assyrian invasion of Judah in 701 BCE, where a wealth of sources exists but firm conclusions have not been drawn.

Determining the extent to which both Assyrian sources and biblical sources are deceptive depends upon the accepted historical reconstruction of the events of 701 BCE. Key to assessing the claims of these texts is the issue of measuring military success. Was Hezekiah's rebellion disastrous or successful? Was Sennacherib's campaign completely successful or somewhat of a mixed bag in that regard? Some unequivocally state that the Assyrians were completely successful[66] and that Sennacherib fully achieved his war aims.[67] Others view the supposed complete-and-utter-success of Assyria more critically. For example, even though he completely rejects the biblical accounts as relevant for historical reconstruction of the events of 701 BCE, Knauf suggests that Sennacherib's clash with the Egyptian forces on this campaign "ended in stalemate, not to be settled until 671" and that the Assyrian king only narrowly escaped from the battle of Eltekeh and "had no intention of returning to southern Canaan."[68]

Others judge Sennacherib's aims by the speeches of the Rabshakeh in 2 Kgs 18:19-35 and conclude that Assyrian goals were *not* completely met.[69] The Rabshakeh speaks of Assyrian plans for a long siege of Jerusalem (18:27) and the deportation of its inhabitants (18:32), neither of which were accomplished. In light of the Assyrian policy to depose rebel rulers and to place a new pro-Assyrian king on the throne,[70] other scholars find it problematic that Hezekiah remained

---

66. Nadav Na'aman, *Ancient Israel and Its Neighbors: Interactions and Counteractions* (Winona Lake, IN: Eisenbrauns, 2005), 112. Frederick Mario Fales, "The Road to Judah: 701 B.C.E. In the Context of Sennacherib's Political-Military Strategy," in *Sennacherib at the Gates of Jerusalem: Story, History and Historiography* (eds. Kalimi and Richardson; Culture and History of the Ancient Near East, 71; Leiden: Brill, 2014), 248.

67. E.g., Elayi (*Sennacherib*, 83) argues that Sennacherib "achieved his aims"; Similarly, Cf. Finkelstein and Silberman suggest, "Sennacherib fully achieved his goals." Israel Finkelstein and Neil Asher Silberman, *The Bible Unearthed: Archaeology's New Vision of Ancient Israel and the Origin of Its Sacred Texts* (New York: Touchstone, 2001), 264. As Bagg writes, "Even if the Judah episode did not end with the conquest of Jerusalem, it was successful." Cf. Ariel M. Bagg, "Assyria and the West: Syria and the Levant," in *Sennacherib at the Gates of Jerusalem: Story, History and Historiography* (eds. Kalimi and Richardson; Culture and History of the Ancient Near East, 71; Leiden: Brill, 2014), 272.

68. Knauf, "Sennacherib at the Berezina," 149. Nadav Na'aman, "Forced Participation in Alliances in the Course of the Assyrian Campaigns to the West," in *Ah, Assyria ... Studies in Assyrian History and Ancient Near Eastern Historiography Presented to Hayim Tadmor* (eds. Cogan and Eph'al; Jerusalem: Magnes Press, 1991) argued that Sennacherib intended to weaken Judah, which was the strongest nation in Egypt's vicinity, thus preventing further rebellions. More recently, Cf. N. K. Matty argued similarly that the Assyrian objective was not destruction of their enemies in the campaign but eliminating opposition to Assyria, which Sennacherib effectively accomplished without removing Hezekiah or taking Jerusalem. Nazek Khalid Matty, *Sennacherib's Campaign against Judah and Jerusalem in 701 B.C.: A Historical Reconstruction* (BZAW, 487; Berlin: de Gruyter, 2016), 46.

69. E.g., Gallagher, *Sennacherib's Campaign*, 158.

70. E.g., COS 2.119B:302–303, COS 2.119A:300–02.

king in Judah if there was a complete Assyrian victory.⁷¹ In sum, strong arguments have been made on both sides of the debate over how to understand the extent

71. E.g., Grabbe, "Reflections on the Discussion," 313. Stephanie Dalley put forth the thesis that Sennacherib did not aim to conquer Jerusalem due to his being married to a Judahite princess, Atalia, whose remains have been found in a Nimrud tomb and whom she thought had the Yahwistic theophoric element in her name. Cf. Stephanie Dalley, "The Identity of the Princesses in Tomb II and a New Analysis of Events in 701 BC," in *New Light on Nimrud: Proceedings of the Nimrud Conference, 11th–13th March 2002* (ed. Curtis; London: British Institute for the Study of Iraq; The British Museum, 2008). Earlier Dalley suggested that Atalia was Sennacherib's mother; Stephanie Dalley, "Yabâ, Atalyā and the Foreign Policy of Late Assyrian Kings," *SAAB* 12 (1998): 97. While provocative, her thesis has not been widely accepted and remains speculative at best. It is not clear that Atalia was from Judah nor that Sennacherib purposefully treated Jerusalem with any leniency. Dalley's argument has been assessed at length by Reinhard Achenbach and K. Lawson Younger, both of whom do not think the names of the Assyrian queens Dalley examines are Judahite. Cf. Reinhard Achenbach, "Jabâ und Atalja–zwei jüdische Königstöchter am assyrischen Königshof? zu einer These von Stephanie Dalley," *BN* 113 (2002): 29–38; K. Lawson Younger Jr., "Yahweh at Ashkelon and Calah? Yahwistic Names in Neo-Assyrian," *VT* 52 (2002): 207–18; K. Lawson Younger Jr., "Aubin's the Rescue of Jerusalem: An Assyriological Assessment," in *Jerusalem's Survival, Sennacherib's Departure, and the Kushite Role in 701 BCE* (ed. Bellis; PHSC, 32; Piscataway, NJ: Gorgias Press, 2019), 221–46. Younger ("Yahweh at Ashkelon and Calah?" 207–18) convincingly demonstrated that the Assyrian Atalia does not have the Yahwistic theophoric element represented in her name. Zadok also demonstrated that the Hebrew name Atalia could not be connected to this Assyrian Atalia because the first component of the name clearly does not correspond properly. Cf. R. Zadok, "Neo-Assyrian Notes," in *Treasures on Camels' Humps: Historical and Literary Studies from the Ancient Near East Presented to Israel Ephʿal* (eds. Cogan and Kahn; Jerusalem: Magnes, 2008), 327–9. Cf. Frahm, "Neo-Assyrian Period," 185; Eckart Frahm, "Family Matters: Psychohistorical Reflections on Sennacherib and His Times," in *Sennacherib at the Gates of Jerusalem: Story, History and Historiography* (eds. Kalimi and Richardson; Culture and History of the Ancient Near East, 71; Leiden: Brill, 2014), 206–8. As Fales ("The Road to Judah," 226) concludes, there is "nothing to be deduced from the available evidence as to whether Atalia's presence and role at the Assyrian court had any bearing on Sennacherib's approach to the Judahite question in 701 or not." Achenbach ("Jabâ und Atalja," 29–38) further argues against Dalley's reconstruction and concludes that the biblical texts do *not* give an account of Tiglath-Pileser III or Sargon II marrying a daughter of a Judahite king and that Judah did not get special treatment by the Assyrians. Elsewhere Dalley speculates that the reason Sennacherib could let Hezekiah remain on the throne, despite his breaking of his oaths to Assyria, was due to "ritual purification" procedures performed by the king. Thus, "based upon such procedures Assyrian rulers could keep Hezekiah and then his son as client kings, even though an oath had been violated." Cf. Stephanie Dalley, *Esther's Revenge at Susa from Sennacherib to Ahasuerus* (Oxford: Oxford University Press, 2007), 29.

to which Sennacherib's campaign and Hezekiah's rebellion were successes or failures.⁷²

Regardless of which position or variation on a position is held, scholarship evidently finds great difficulty in reconciling all the available sources for a historical reconstruction.⁷³ M. Cogan probably represents the general consensus when he asserts that after the Assyrian and biblical accounts are "pitted against one other," then "the unavoidable judgment [must be] made that some are more trustworthy than others."⁷⁴ It is with this point that the present work contends. While the political and theological spin put on real events in both texts is indisputable, do the different perspectives of Judahite and Assyrian texts make it necessary to conclude one is true while the other is not? To be sure, a modern reconstruction searches for truth, but our assessments of ancient accounts must be cautious not to critique them for not agreeing with our modern conclusions.

As George Iggers has argued,

> This distinction between truth and falsehood remains fundamental to the work of the historian. The concept of truth has become immeasurably more complex in the course of recent critical thought. To be sure the postulate of "an absolute objectivity and scientificity of historical knowledge is no longer accepted without reservation." Nevertheless the concept of truth and with it the duty of the historian to avoid and to uncover falsification has by no means been abandoned. As a trained professional he [sic] continues to work critically with the sources that make access to the past reality possible.⁷⁵

At issue in an attempt to properly assess the trustworthiness of the available sources for use in historical reconstructions is how success in war is determined and perceived in the ancient world. In this instance, judging by the sources available, both Assyrian and Judahite sources perceived a victory in the same campaign.⁷⁶

---

72. As Cf. Na'aman writes, "The rebellion was a complete failure and left its mark on the kingdom for many years to come." Nadav Na'aman, "Let Other Kingdoms Struggle with the Great Powers—You, Judah, Pay the Tribute and Hope for the Best: The Foreign Policy of the Kings of Judah in the Ninth-Eighth Centuries BCE," in *Isaiah's Vision of Peace in Biblical and Modern International Relations: Swords into Plowshares* (New York: Palgrave Macmillan, 2008), 70.

73. A. Anthony Spalinger, "The Foreign Policy of Egypt Preceding the Assyrian Conquest," *ChrEg* 53 (1978): 38.

74. Cogan, "Cross-Examining," 73. Similarly in his commentary co-written with Tadmor, he asserts that the "disagreements" between the biblical and Assyrian records are "blatant and seemingly irreconcilable." Cf. Cogan and Tadmor, *II Kings*, 248.

75. Georg G. Iggers, *Historiography in the Twentieth Century: From Scientific Objectivity to the Postmodern Challenge* (Hanover, NH: Wesleyan University Press, 1997), 12.

76. Contra. Dan'el Kahn who asserts, "The Assyrian inscriptions and visual art, as well as Biblical passages, claimed victory for the Assyrian king." Cf. Dan'el Kahn, *Sennacherib's*

Na'aman writes, "Historically, the rebellion was an utter failure, bringing about large-scale destruction, mass deportation, desolation of large districts, loss of extensive territories, and worse subjection than ever before."[77] Yet he concludes that Hezekiah's "rebellion, which brought about such catastrophic results for the kingdom of Judah, is treated favourably by the [Deuteronomistic] historian."[78] How is it that the rebellion was utterly catastrophic but remembered fondly and positively?

Gallagher has offered different explanations for tensions between biblical and Assyrian sources. He writes,

> One source may have false information; perhaps we do not fully understand what a source is saying; perhaps we have misunderstood the background of one of the sources; perhaps the chronological order in a source has been disrupted; a source may lack a few important details which could clarify the obscurities.[79]

Of course, determining which the case in each source is may be difficult to discern. Therefore, Gallagher suggests considering "relevant information of all sorts" that could help one to decide upon such matters.[80]

1.2 Methodology

The present study would like to set aside far-reaching claims or "principles" concerning the trustworthiness of sources and instead reexamine the historical claims of both the Assyrian and biblical texts anew, drawing insights from what could be called indirect evidence from the study of military history.[81] Throughout history, how is victory in war assessed? How is victory perceived by the participants in a conflict? What type of expectations did peoples have regarding their participation in a conflict? To what extent did victory have to be clear-cut to be perceived successful? While caution must be used in drawing conclusions from such evidences, when combined with other evidences, a new hypothesis for understanding the character of both the Assyrian and biblical accounts of the 701

Campaign against Judah: A Source Analysis of Isaiah 36–37 (SOTS; Cambridge: Cambridge University Press, 2020), 124.

77. Nadav Na'aman, "The Deuteronomist and Voluntary Servitude to Foreign Powers," *JSOT* 65 (1995): 51.

78. Ibid., 52.

79. Gallagher, *Sennacherib's Campaign*, 5.

80. Ibid., 5.

81. Military historian Michael Howard defined military history as "the history of armed forces and the conduct of war." Cf. Michael Howard et al., "What Is Military History?" *History Today* 34 (1984): 5.

BCE war can be formulated. In historical study, such revisions in opinions are often necessary as later perspectives provide different vantage points with which to view events and historical persons. Historians must reexamine older views and revise them accordingly to provide realistic assessments based on the best information available. In the opinion of this writer, knowledge of military history will assist in this reevaluation.[82]

1.2.1 Assessing War in Military History

The study of military history will provide a necessary perspective on assessing the success of Sennacherib's third campaign from the perspectives of all those involved. Not that military history will provide a cookie-cutter comparison between the war of 701 BCE and other conflicts, but it will provide wide parameters that will be instructive in assessing the evidences and ancient perspectives regarding the outcome of the third campaign. There will be no attempt to formulate a system or model that would explain definitively what victory meant to different peoples in different contexts.[83] As Lanskoy notes, "Since contingency plagues history, no system can take account of the myriad details of a given situation—the quirky personalities, the unintended consequences, the missed opportunities,"[84] and so on. However, despite changes in the logistics, military technology, and historical circumstances, military history provides helpful parallels that will prove methodologically advantageous in our assessment.[85] In other wars throughout history, how was success determined?

1.2.1.1 The Capture of a Symbolic Item or City There are a variety of ways in which victory in war is claimed in military history. Sometimes a claim to victory involved taking something symbolically significant of the enemy: something that is "the

---

82. In study of the war of 701 BCE, some scholars have drawn on military history to some extent to better explain and understand the events. E.g., Knauf made brief reference to the Napoleanic wars in a short article, "Sennacherib at the Berezina," 142, n. 4; 147, n. 16, n. 17; Gallagher compared propaganda from the Second World War to the Rabshakeh's speech in 2 Kings 18–19 (*Sennacherib's Campaign*, 174–86).

83. As John David Lewis observes, the study of military history reveals "no single strategic pattern, no universal 'theory of war,' and no moral 'rules' divorced from context or purpose." Cf. John David Lewis, *Nothing Less Than Victory: Decisive Wars and the Lessons of History* (Princeton: Princeton University Press, 2012), 10.

84. Miriam Lanskoy, "When Personalities Clash: Assessing the 1994–1996 Russian-Chechen War," *Nationalities Papers* 28 (2000): 586.

85. As Victor Davis Hanson opines, "The wisdom of the past concerning how conflict begins, is deterred, and ends is more critical now than ever, however unwelcome such lessons may be." Cf. Victor Davis Hanson, *The Father of Us All: War and History, Ancient and Modern* (New York: Bloomsbury Press, 2010), 68.

essential source of ideological and moral strength, which, if broken, makes it impossible to continue the war."[86] Often taking the enemy's flag and/or replacing it with one's own standard was a way of declaring victory. In the ancient Near East, victors would often take their enemy's gods/idols and parade them or relocate them to their own temples to show their conquest.[87] Another claim of victory in a war is the taking of prisoners by the victor. Claims of massive amounts of prisoners were often primarily rhetorical claims to superiority, but the actual taking of many prisoners was meant to indicate victory.[88]

Often the capture of a capital city would be viewed as victory. If the enemy cannot protect their capital, they cannot be said to be victorious. Alternatively, the failure to capture the enemy's capital mitigates against understanding the war to be an unqualified victory. Of course, the significance of the capture of a capital is not always viewed the same in each conflict or for each belligerent. For some, the capital is most significant, for others the army is most significant: it all depends upon what the "center of gravity" (as Clausewitz called it) is for each side.[89] For example, Clausewitz suggests that at the beginning of the French Revolution "if Paris had been taken in 1792," the revolution would have ended; whereas "in 1814, on the other hand, even the capture of Paris would not have ended matters" due to the size of Napoleon's army.[90] Clausewitz explains further, "For Alexander, Gustavus Adolphus, Charles XII, and Frederick the Great, the center of gravity was their army. If the army had been destroyed, they would all have gone down in history as failures. In countries subject to domestic strife, the center of gravity is generally the capital."[91] Thus, the consequence of the capture of a capital city has different significance for different peoples and circumstances, but can often indicate victory or defeat.

1.2.1.2 Forced Act of Humiliation Often victors in war took measures to humiliate the vanquished. Sometimes people were made to serve as a human footstool to shame the enemy. This can be seen in the iconography of ancient Near East (and Mediterranean) as well as in biblical texts (e.g., Ps 110:1).[92] Modern warfare often

---

86. Lewis, *Nothing Less Than Victory*, 6.

87. Morton Cogan, *Imperialism and Religion: Assyria, Judah, and Israel in the Eighth and Seventh Centuries* B.C.E. (SBLMS, 19; Missoula, Mont.: SBL and Scholars Press, 1974), 40.

88. Descriptions of massive numbers of prisoners are commonplace in both ancient and modern warfare. Of course, Sennacherib claims the taking of 200,150 people (though the number may include animals taken as well). As Knauf writes, "This is nearly twice as many as the whole kingdom of Judah had inhabitants; the Shephelah had had some 60,000–65,000." Cf. Knauf, "Sennacherib at the Berezina," 146.

89. Lewis, *Nothing Less Than Victory*, 5.

90. Carl von Clausewitz, *On War*; trans. E. Howard and P. Paret (New York: Routledge, 2004), VIII.4, 595.

91. Ibid., VIII.4, 596.

92. As Brad E. Kelle observes, biblical images of victory (e.g., Ps 47:3; 68:21) find parallels in ancient Near Eastern literature and iconography with Assyrian or Egyptian "kings

ends with the victor making their victory explicit with the signing of a treaty. For example, following the Great War, the treaty of Versailles explicitly made Germany take the blame for starting the war and admit defeat at the hands of the allies.[93] In the ancient world, treaties were also common, with many ancient Near Eastern treaties found that adjudicate the relations between polities. In the case of Judah and Assyria in 701 BCE, no treaties have been found, so we cannot see conditions that were placed on either side after the conflict.

1.2.1.3 War Aims Another way victory in conflict is determined is by the war aims. If an army set out to conquer another country and did not in fact conquer the country, it is perceived that they lost the war. For example, in Napoleon's offensive against Russia in June 1812, the French had set out to conquer Russia. A key battle was the battle of Borodino, which involved a quarter of a million troops, of which 70,000 died in the battle—the bloodiest day in the Napoleonic wars.[94] In the battle, the French drove back the Russians, who abandoned their positions and lost their final chance to prevent the conquest of their capital. While the French took Moscow a week later, the French actually lost more soldiers in the battle than the Russians. Despite taking the capital, the French invasion failed as they retreated in October that year with no way to force the Russian Czar to surrender since the Russian army was not defeated decisively enough. Historical accounts of the fighting vary considerably depending on whether their provenance was French or Russian. In the battle of Borodino, the French consider it a victory because they continued to advance (and they occupied Moscow),[95] while the Russians considered themselves successful since the French sustained more casualties, had to retreat, and French war aims (the conquest of Russia) were not achieved.[96]

---

striking down enemies and placing them under their feet." Cf. Brad E. Kelle, "Warfare Imagery," in *Dictionary of the Old Testament: Wisdom, Poetry & Writings* (eds. Longman and Enns; Downers Grove, IL: IVP Academic, 2008), 829.

93. Versailles Treaty, June 28, 1919. http://www.firstw orld war.com/sou rce/ver sail les.htm. Though this treaty was not written and adopted until 1919 at the Paris Peace Conference. Cf. William R. Keylor, *The Legacy of the Great War: Peacemaking, 1919*; Boston, MA: Houghton Mifflin, 1998). The "War Guilt" clause (Article 231) states, "The Allied and Associated Governments affirm, and Germany accepts, the responsibility of Germany and her allies for causing all the loss and damage to which the Allied and Associated Governments and their nationals have been subjected as a consequence of the war imposed upon them by aggression of Germany and her allies."

94. Keegan, *History of Warfare*, 360.

95. Dyer, *War: The New Edition*, 234.

96. Cf. Ziony Zevit's understanding of Sennacherib's war aims: "A close reading of Sennacherib's remarks about the Judah part of his campaign indicates that it was *a qualified success* but only if it is assumed that its strategic objective was Judah's complete and total devastation and subjugation. *I do not assume this.* His sweep through the Levant threatened destruction by selectively demonstrating the thoroughness with which he could execute it,

1.2.1.4 Taking of Territory Another clear indication of victory can be seen in the expansion of the victor's land holdings and the reduction of the enemy's lands. A classic example of a disputed victory that is seemingly indicated by geographical boundaries is the famous battle of Qadesh between Hittite forces under king Mawattalli and Egyptian forces under Rameses II in the thirteenth-century BCE. Though Rameses claims victory in multiple accounts and in artwork, the Hittites also claim victory in the battle.[97] Most of the evidence comes from the Egyptian side, which claims an unequivocal victory. Of course, the victory is described fantastically with Rameses setting out to battle by himself, with no one to aid him, calling on his god, and then killing the enemy soldiers.[98] Needless to say, this Egyptian description of Rameses's heroics is viewed as fanciful by historians. However, even the fact of an Egyptian victory is questioned by historians as many view the battle as a "draw at best."[99] Reasons for this skepticism are the fact that subsequent campaigns by Rameses were stopped much further south and that "Egyptian influence over Amurru and Qadesh seemed to have been lost forever."[100] Despite the fact that the Hittite king Mawattalli died shortly afterward and his sons fought for succession, Rameses did not take advantage of this weakness and made no incursions into their territory and subsequently sued for peace and made a defensive alliance.[101] Claims of victory ring hollow when territory is not taken by the victor.

1.2.1.5 Winning the Last Battle In military conflict, it is often viewed as essential to be victorious in the final battle of the war. Despite early success, if an army fails in the final battle, early successes are irrelevant. It is the army that is successful in the end that will be crowned victor. In fact, early losses during a war can be ultimately discounted in the end if the final battle is won. This despite the fact that

---

but destruction was not his objective. Sennacherib used war to achieve political objectives. He intended to leave loyal allies behind him, not to create certain enemies [emphasis mine]." Cf. Zevit, "Implicit Population Figures and Historical Sense: What Happened to 200,150 Judahites in 701 BCE?" in *Confronting the Past: Archaeological and Historical Essays on Ancient Israel in Honor of William G. Devers* (eds. Gitin et al.; Winona Lake, IN: Eisenbrauns, 2006), 361–2. While Zevit has his own ideas of what Assyrian war aims were, it is likely that Judahites had their own thoughts about this. In fact, Judahite perspectives of Assyrian war aims may have been different than Assyrian ones.

97. Nicolas-Christophe Grimal, *A History of Ancient Egypt* (Oxford: Blackwell, 1992), 256.

98. Miriam Lichtheim, *Ancient Egyptian Literature II: The New Kingdom* (Berkeley: University of California Press, 1976), 65.

99. Marc Van de Mieroop, *A History of Ancient Egypt* (Chichester: Wiley-Blackwell, 2011), 400. Similarly, Michael G. Hasel, *Domination and Resistance: Egyptian Military Activity in the Southern Levant, ca. 1300–1185 B.C* (PAe, 10; Leiden: Brill, 1998), 155.

100. Van de Mieroop, *A History of Ancient Egypt*, 400.

101. Ibid., 404.

earlier battles could have been disastrous. An example can be seen in the Battle of Moscow in the Second World War between Stalin's Red Army and Hitler's Axis forces.[102] The former sustained three times more casualties than the latter, but ultimately the Russian counterattack resulted in the German withdrawal.[103]

1.2.1.6 Historical Perspective Sometimes victory is decided not by initial success but by the long-term outcome. For example, when Hitler attacked Russia, he initially experienced widespread success. This success led to his decision to take Kiev before going on to take the capital of Moscow.[104] Hitler's success continued with the successful capture of Kiev, wherein he captured greater than 600,000 Russians in the process.[105] However, his success actually mitigated his ultimate victory since the victory in Kiev delayed the Germans too long, making the taking of Moscow impossible due to the arrival of the Russian winter.[106] Here war aims come into play again. While Hitler had widespread success early in his war against Russia, in the end his war aims of Russian conquest were *not* successful.[107]

Sometimes the success of a war is determined even later, with historical perspective. A modern instance could be the Iraq War of 2003, wherein the United States and some of its allies invaded Iraq, which was initially deemed a great success. The primary objective of removing Saddam Hussein and his regime from power was achieved quickly and efficiently. Shortly after the "victory," George W. Bush famously declared "mission accomplished" to his military.[108] The larger purpose of removing Hussein was to prevent Iraq from having nuclear weapons or other weapons of mass destruction (WMDs) and to cut off its support

---

102. Michael K. Jones, *The Retreat: Hitler's First Defeat* (New York: Thomas Dunne Books, 2010).

103. David M. Glantz and Jonathan M. House, *When Titans Clashed: How the Red Army Stopped Hitler* (Lawrence, KS: University Press of Kansas, 1995), 293.

104. John Keegan, *The Mask of Command* (London: Jonathan Cape, 1987), 262–6; Glantz and House, *When Titans Clashed*, 293; Stephen G. Fritz, *Ostkrieg: Hitler's War of Extermination in the East* (Lexington: University Press of Kentucky, 2011).

105. Keegan, *The Mask of Command*, 263; John Keegan, *A History of Warfare* (New York: Vintage Books, 1993), 373; Glantz and House, *When Titans Clashed*, 94. Cf. David M. Glantz, "The Soviet–German War 1941–1945: Myths and Realities" (paper presented as 20th Anniversary Distinguished Lecture at the Strom Thurmond Institute of Government and Public Affairs. Clemson University, 2001).

106. Keegan, *The Mask of Command*, 264.

107. Knauf points to the battle of Berezina wherein Napoleon and his army lost at *c.* 20,000 troops during the battle (possibly nearly 30,000), which would normally count as a crushing defeat, but it is remembered as a French victory only due to Napoleon's escape, which turned it into a victory of sorts. Cf. Knauf, "Sennacherib at the Berezina," 148, n. 16.

108. May 1, 2003, in a televised address on the USS Abraham Lincoln aircraft carrier.

of Al-Qaeda, the terrorist group held to be responsible for the attacks on the twin towers in New York City on September 11, 2001. Of course, as is well known, investigation after the "victory" revealed that Iraq did not have any WMDs, and no ties to Al-Qaeda were uncovered. While the initial war was brief, the occupation that followed was long-lasting, with the United States only withdrawing its troops about nine years later. In historical perspective, many now view the war in less victorious terms. First, the monetary cost of the war to the United States has been estimated to be trillions of dollars.[109] What is more, the war aims, despite the initial success, were not met. The war did not "promote democratic governance on the western model, economic prosperity, peaceful change or regional order" as it had aimed.[110] Thus, the Iraq War has been widely criticized for its failure to achieve the outcomes desired.[111]

Louise Fawcett has examined the "longer-term implications" and legacy of the Iraq War, ten years after its conclusion and has found reasons to assess its legacy differently. First, she suggests that the fall of Saddam Hussein may be linked to the Arab Spring and the downfall of other dictators in the Middle East.[112] She concludes,

> The Iraq War may therefore be seen as a critical juncture in a continuing and protracted process of transformation in which popular mobilization, demands for greater liberalization of politics, a new regional balance of power and shifting international alignments all feature.[113]

After the war, regional alliances in the Middle East emerged, with Saudi Arabia and Qatar being front-runners due to their connections to the West, strong economies, and religious status.[114] The effects of the war were widespread, and some are still developing today. The matter of assessment is complex. In the end, the Iraq War, while initially lauded in the West as an amazing success, in due course was assessed in a diametrically opposite fashion, so much so that some have concluded that "the US lost" the war.[115]

---

109. Joseph Stiglitz and Linda Bilmes, "The True Cost of the Iraq War: $3 Trillion and Beyond," *Washington Post*, September 5, 2010.

110. Louise Fawcett, "The Iraq War Ten Years On: Assessing the Fallout," *International Affairs* 89 (2013): 327.

111. Ibid.

112. She writes, It is hard to imagine that there was no link between the downfall of the Iraqi dictator in 2003—and the subsequent dissent it unleashed." Ibid., 325–43.

113. Ibid., 342.

114. Ibid., 327. She writes, "A clearer pattern of regional alliances and rivalries started to emerge, with the GCC monarchies, headed by Saudi Arabia and Qatar, as front runners on the regional stage, drawing on economic stability and western connections as well as claims to religious legitimacy."

115. Stephen Walt, "Top 10 Lessons of the Iraq War," *Foreign Policy* (2012).

The Iraq War offers some points regarding the assessment of victory that are instructive. First, initial dispositions regarding the success of a war are often reassessed. This can occur very shortly after a conflict, or later in historical perspective. Second, the assessment of a war is complex, with multiple factors involved. Despite the fact that Iraq's military could not stop the onslaught of the US invasion, the result of the conflict was not a clear victory for the United States. The long-term result was not the rise of pro-American democracy in Iraq, resulting in greater security of American interests in the area.

Later historical perspective is important when assessing the war of 701 BCE. As scholarly consensus holds, the biblical accounts of the Assyrian invasion were written well after the fact.[116] On the other hand, Assyrian annals were written shortly after the events of 701 BCE. They clearly portray the war as an Assyrian victory. Did this initial position get reassessed thereafter? Or perhaps many years later? After Sennacherib's assassination by his son, to what extent was his third campaign thought to be a success? Why did Esarhaddon again campaign West, but not touch Judah or the rebel states? Was this due to their compliance or wanting to avoid the mistakes of his father? Historians have noted that Esarhaddon thought the untimely death of his father (and grandfather) was due to "divine punishment" and he was "eager to avoid the sins of his fathers."[117]

The biblical texts, being written well after the historical events, may be understood as having a longer historical perspective. Perhaps, if the Assyrians had been more successful, the author(s) of Kings may have judged it differently. As we will see in our survey of material archaeological evidence, Assyrian short-term achievements gave way to a burgeoning Judahite success story in the early seventh century, which may have led to speculation of the possible demise of Assyrian power in the region.[118] Despite Assyrian aggression and destruction, Judah proved resistant to external pressures for change. So, in the end, the long-term legacy of the war of 701 BCE may have been that Judah felt greater regional autonomy and self-reliance rather than subservience to Assyria.[119] Given the later

---

116. Of course, there is not a complete consensus on the dating of the biblical texts, but all would agree that significant time passed between the historical event and the writing of the texts.

117. Frahm, "Neo-Assyrian Period," 186–7.

118. An interesting parallel might be the Iraq War. As Fawcett ("The Iraq War," 336) comments, "Had the war been more successful, history might have judged it differently. As its short-term military achievements gave way to widely advertised long-term failures, this led to intense speculation about the possible demise of US power and reputation in an emerging multipolar system." Fawcett further writes, "There was undoubtedly reputational and soft power damage" (337).

119. Fawcett (ibid., 341) writes similarly of the aftereffects of the Iraq War. "When the dust finally settles on the Arab Spring, it may be the fact of greater regional autonomy and self-reliance, rather than dependence on the West, that becomes the long-term legacy of Iraq."

historical perspective, it is open to question whether the biblical narratives' view of the outcome of the war of 701 BCE was more genuine rather than deceptive historiography.

1.3 Overview

The following investigation will begin with a survey of archaeological evidence relevant to historical reconstructions of the war of 701 BCE. Our study will then examine the Assyrian annalistic accounts of Sennacherib's third campaign, followed by a survey of biblical texts often considered relevant in reconstructing both the events and Judahite opinions regarding the rebellion against Assyria. To better assess the evidence thus surveyed, the present work will then examine an extended example from military history wherein both sides of a conflict deem themselves the victor in the end (the War of 1812). Incorporating insights drawn from military history, we will then reassess the archaeological and textual evidences surveyed and come to a new perspective on Judahite historical accounts. In the end, the consideration of military history will support the thesis of this book that both Assyrian and biblical texts were not principally deceptive in their presentation of the war as their own victory, but that both had reasons to see themselves as the victor in the conflict. Finally, to better understand modern assessments of Hezekiah and the war of 701 BCE, we will take into account the social location of modern scholars, which will shed light on such assessments in the academy.

Chapter 2

ARCHAEOLOGICAL EVIDENCE

A key type of evidence for historical reconstruction of the war of 701 BCE is material archaeological remains. There is plenty of well-known evidence for widespread destruction by the Assyrian forces in their assault on the Levant, the chief piece of evidence being the destruction layer in Lachish Stratum III. Lachish has been extensively excavated, and therefore identifying pottery found in destruction levels at other sites as similar to that of Lachish III is one of the main grounds for dating that destruction level to 701 BCE.[1] Much of the devastation about which Sennacherib boasts in his annals and is acknowledged in the account in the book of Kings can be verified through archaeological excavations.[2] However, the extent of the damage was not universal across Judah as there is also plenty of evidence that the entire country was not devastated in the same way.[3] In this chapter, we will survey the archaeological evidence as relevant to the question of measuring victory in the war of 701 BCE. As we survey the extent of the Assyrian devastation, we should keep in mind the important question: Were the devastation and economic hardship detrimental to the perception of ancient Judahites that the war had been worthwhile?

2.1 Areas Showing Destruction in 701 BCE

There exists a fairly broad consensus concerning which archaeological sites showing a destruction layer should be associated with Sennacherib's third

---

1. Olga Tufnell, "Excavations at Tell Ed-Duweir, Palestine, Directed by the Late J. L. Starkey, 1932–1938," *PEQ* 82 (1950): 76–9; Miriam Aharoni and Yohanan Aharoni, "Stratification of Judahite Sites in the 8th and 7th Centuries BCE," *BASOR* 224 (1976).

2. Stern, *Archaeology of the Land of the Bible*, 405, 438.

3. As Zevit ("Implicit Population Figures," 363) points out, "The Assyrian records suggest that, although many cities were captured, destruction was only partial." Zevit suggests Sennacherib redistributed territory to ensure a loyal vassal (Philistine) would bring the tribute to Assyria, rather than Hezekiah. He writes, "In effect, he redrew political borders by transferring Judahite cities to the control of vassals loyal to Assyria. This insured that Judah's future taxes would be delivered by loyal Philistines and not by Hezekiah" (Ibid., 364).

campaign. Criteria for dating such archaeological evidence to the war of 701 BCE is largely dependent upon whether destruction layers in archaeological sites are congruent with the material culture from Stratum III of Lachish. In addition, the presence of *lmlk* seals found on storage jar handles (*c.* 1,700 have been found) assists in dating material remains to this time period.[4] After much scholarly debate about the dating of *lmlk* seals, it seems fairly clear they were used for a limited time largely during Hezekiah's tenure and were part of Judah's preparations for an Assyrian assault.[5] Of course, this preparation should not be viewed as some last-minute stockpiling of provisions. As Vaughn writes, "Hezekiah's siege preparation probably began several years before Sennacherib's invasion, and that preparation included economic buildup and a strong infrastructure."[6] Consensus would also hold the construction of the Siloam tunnel as part of Hezekiah's preparations for the inevitable Assyrian attack foreseen by the king at least when he ceased paying tribute—if not shortly after the fall of Samaria in 722 BCE.[7]

---

4. Such jar handles were found in more than seventy sites in the vicinities of ancient Judah. Cf. William G. Dever, *Beyond the Texts: An Archaeological Portrait of Ancient Israel and Judah* (Atlanta, GA: SBL Press, 2017), 551. For the most thorough treatment of the subject of the *lmlk* seals, see Andrew G. Vaughn, *Theology, History, and Archaeology in the Chronicler's Account of Hezekiah* (ABS, 4; Atlanta, GA: Scholars Press, 1999), 81–167. Cf. Oded Lipschits, "The Long Seventh Century BCE: Archaeological and Historical Perspectives," in *The Last Century in the History of Judah: The Seventh Century BCE in Archaeological, Historical, and Biblical Perspectives* (eds. Filip Capek and Oded Lipschits; SBLAIL 37; Atlanta, GA: SBL Press, 2019), 15.

5. Dever, *Beyond the Texts*, 551. The jars appear to have been only in use for a relatively short period of time as evinced by the names of officials (which would only have been useful for a limited time) and the location of some *lmlk* stamps in territory that was not controlled by Judah before Hezekiah's regency.

6. Vaughn, *Theology, History*, 167. Cf. Seymour Gitin, "Tel Miqne-Ekron in the Seventh Century B.C.; City Plan Development and the Oil Industry," in *Olive Oil in Antiquity: Israel and Neighbouring Countries from the Neolithic to the Early Arad Period* (eds. Eitam and Heltzer; HANES 7; Padova: Sargon, 1996), 219–42. Of course, Oded Lipschits has challenged this view, claiming many of the handles are later. Cf. Oded Lipschits, Omer Sergi, and Ido Koch, "Royal Judahite Jar Handles: Reconsidering the Chronology of the Lmlk Stamp Impressions," *TA* 37 (2010): 3–32; Oded Lipschits, "Judah under Assyrian Rule and the Early Phase of Stamping Jar Handles," in *Archaeology and History of Eighth-Century Judah* (eds. Farber and Wright; ANEM 23; Atlanta, GA: SBL Press, 2018), 337–55. However, others have convincingly countered his assertions and defended the consensus. See David Ussishkin, "The Dating of the Lmlk Storage Jars and Its Implications: Rejoinder to Lipschits, Sergi, and Koch," *TA* 38 (2011): 220–40; more recently, see Andrew G. Vaughn, "Should All of the LMLK Jars Still Be Attributed to Hezekiah? Yes!" in *Archaeology and History of Eighth-Century Judah* (eds. Farber and Wright; ANEM 23; Atlanta, GA: SBL Press, 2018), 357–62.

7. Shawn Zelig Aster, *Reflections of Empire in Isaiah 1–39: Responses to Assyrian Ideology* (ANEM 19; Atlanta, GA: SBL Press, 2017), 180–1.

2.1.1 Destruction in the Shephelah

The Shephelah was the most heavily inhabited region in Judah in the eighth century.[8] As is well known, the Assyrian invasion destroyed most of the sites in the area.[9] What is more, from the textual evidence, it would seem that during their assault the Assyrians stayed, for the most part, in the Shephelah. Besides Jerusalem, both biblical and Assyrian texts emphasize towns in the Shephelah exclusively.[10] The towns mentioned in 2 Kings 18–19 (Lachish, Libnah) and Micah 1:8-16 (Gath, Beth Le-Ophra, Shaphir, Zaanan, Beth-ezel, Maroth, Moresheth-gath, Mareshah) are all in the Shephelah, suggesting this focus was an Assyrian strategy.[11] It is possible that Sennacherib's aim was to encircle Judah but not attack the highlands. After all the Shephelah was somewhat of a border area between Philistia and Judah, who were both the focus of the third campaign.[12] As the survey below will show, it appears that only the Shephelah suffered destructions

---

8. Magen Broshi and Israel Finkelstein, "The Population of Palestine in Iron Age II," *BASOR* 287 (1992): 52, 54.

9. Israel Finkelstein estimates 85 percent of the settlements were destroyed in 701 BCE. See Finkelstein, "The Archaeology of the Days of Manasseh," in *Scripture and Other Artifacts: Essays on the Bible and Archaeology in Honor of Philip J. King* (eds. Coogan et al.; Louisville, KY: Westminster John Knox, 1994), 173.

10. Avraham Faust, "Settlement and Demography in Seventh-Century Judah and the Extent and Intensity of Sennacherib's Campaign," *PEQ* 140 (2008): 182. Knauf, "Sennacherib at the Berezina," 143. Mayer, "Sennacherib's Campaign," 184.

11. Yohanan Aharoni, *The Land of the Bible: A Historical Geography* (Philadelphia, PA: Westminster Press, 1979), 392; Anson F. Rainey and R. Steven Notley, *The Sacred Bridge: Carta's Atlas of the Biblical World* (Jerusalem: Carta, 2006), 243. As Bloch-Smith writes, "In spite of Assyrian assertions, archaeology reveals selective targeting of prominent sites and no wide-spread destruction of small towns or villages. Assyrians attacked strategically located, fortified sites along the major highways and at critical road junctions." Cf. Elizabeth Bloch-Smith, "Assyrians Abet Israelite Cultic Reforms: Sennacherib and the Centralization of the Israelite Cult," in *Exploring the Longue Durée: Essays in Honor of Lawrence E. Stager* (Winona Lake, IN: Eisenbrauns, 2009), 36. Similarly, Zevit ("Implicit Population Figures," 362) suggests Assyrian strategy was not to destroy Judahite cities and reduce their population as much as it was to secure important trade routes and stop the Egyptian-backed revolt. Cf. Dever, *Beyond the Texts*, 578. For an alternative location of Le-Ophra, see Matthew Suriano, "A Place in the Dust: Text, Topography and a Toponymic Note on Micah 1:10-12a," *VT* 60 (2010): 433–46.

12. As Dagan writes, "Following Sennacherib's campaign the settlement in the Shephelah went through an acute change—the number of sites decreased significantly, many settlements were destroyed and abandoned, and the settlement did not regain its former size." Cf. Yehudah Dagan, "The Settlement in the Judean Shephela in the Second and First Millennium BC: A Test-Case of Settlement Processes in a Geographic Region" (PhD Dissertation, Tel Aviv University, 2000), 208. Cf. Avi Ofer, "The Monarchic Period in the Judaean Highland: A Spatial Overview," in *Studies in the Archaeology of the Iron Age in*

from which sites did not recover.[13] While there were cities destroyed elsewhere in Judah, most recovered afterward, and many new sites were founded as well.

2.1.1.1 Lachish (Stratum III) The Judahite fortress of Lachish (Tell ed-Duweir) provides the clearest archaeological evidence of Assyrian siege and destruction available to date.[14] Of course, as is well known, the destruction of Lachish is corroborated by Sennacherib's detailed relief depicting the siege and capture of Lachish, which he had created for his throne room in Nineveh. Excavators found more than 400 *lmlk* jar handles in the ruins.[15] The biblical text also underscores the importance of Lachish (2 Kgs 18:14, 17; 2 Chr 32:9), though the Assyrian annals are silent regarding the city.[16] Both the exterior Assyrian siege ramp and the interior counter ramp were found at the southeast corner of the city, matching Sennacherib's throne room artwork.[17] As Grabbe has observed, the city's extensive defenses suggest that the city was prepared for the Assyrian invasion.[18] The city was razed, and the casualties were many, as evinced by the mass grave containing 1,500 cadavers found on-site. The awful destruction had lasting consequences with only a very limited recovery in the seventh century suggested by the archaeological evidence.[19] The recovery in late seventh century was of a diminished size without reaching its pre-701 capacity.[20]

Israel and Jordan (ed. Mazar; JSOTSup 331; Sheffield: Sheffield Academic Press), 27; Faust, "Settlement and Demography," 169.

13. Faust, "Settlement and Demography," 11; Avraham Faust, "The Shephelah in the Iron Age: A New Look on the Settlement of Judah," *PEQ* 145 (2013): 214–15.

14. David Ussishkin, *The Conquest of Lachish by Sennacherib* (PIA 6; Tel Aviv: Tel Aviv University, Institute of Archaeology, 1982).

15. Dever, *Beyond the Texts*, 560.

16. Contra. Dever (*Beyond the Texts*, 559) who repeatedly claims the Assyrian annals mention Lachish and criticizes the biblical account saying, "Ironically, the Hebrew Bible dismisses the whole incident in one verse, noting simply that Sennacherib had been at Lachish"; William G. Dever, "Archaeology, Material Culture and the Early Monarchical Period in Israel," in *The Fabric of History: Text, Artifact and Israel's Past* (eds. Clines and Davies; JSOTSup, 127; Sheffield: JSOT Press, 1991), 107–8.

17. Ussishkin, *Conquest of Lachish*; DavidUssishkin, "The Assyrian Attack on Lachish: The Archaeological Evidence from the Southwest Corner of the Site," *TA* 17 (1990): 53–86; David Ussishkin, "A Synopsis of the Stratigraphical, Chronological and Historical Issues," in *The Renewed Archaeological Excavations at Lachish (1973–1994)* (ed. Ussishkin; Tel Aviv: Institute of Archaeology of Tel Aviv University, 2004), 90–2. Cf. Olga Tufnell, Margaret A. Murray, and David Diringer, eds., *Lachish III (Tell Ed-Duweir): The Iron Age* (Oxford: Oxford University Press, 1953), 45, 48, 55–6.

18. Grabbe, "Introduction," 8.

19. Faust, "Settlement and Demography," 172.

20. Ussishkin, *Conquest of Lachish*; Ussishkin, "A Synopsis of the Stratigraphical, Chronological and Historical Issues," 90–2; Faust, "Settlement and Demography," 169.

2.1.1.2 Tel Ḥalif (Stratum VIB) This Judahite site shows evidence of destruction that has been dated to 701 BCE (the dating is based upon the four *lmlk* handles[21] and Lachish-like pottery found) after which it was only partially rebuilt (Stratum VIA).[22] While the pre-701 town was flourishing, showing evidence of both weaving and pottery industry (with a cemetery and inner space with many "four room" houses), the subsequent stratum (VIA) was on a smaller scale.[23] However, the return to the site is evidenced shortly after Sennacherib's invasion.[24] It appears the town only existed during the period of Pax Assyriaca, as it appears to have been abandoned later in the seventh century.[25]

2.1.1.3 Tell Beit Mirsim (Stratum A2) Originally, Albright had determined Tell Beit Mirsim survived until the Babylonian destruction of the sixth century.[26] However, his dating has been shown to be flawed (and partially based on the earlier misdating of Lachish Level III to the Babylonian destruction instead of that of 701).[27] Aharoni redated the destruction to 701 BCE, followed by most, especially due to the four *lmlk* jar handles found on-site.[28] The fortress in the town was destroyed,

---

21. Oded Borowski, "Tell Halif—2009," *Hadashot Arkheologiyot/Excavations and Survey in Israel* 122 (2018).

22. Joe D. Seger, "Tel Halif," *NEAEHL* 558. For discussion of the pottery, see Jeffrey A. Blakely and James W. Hardin, "Southwestern Judah in the Late Eighth Century B.C.E.," *BASOR* 326 (2002): 24–34; Dever, *Beyond the Texts*, 562.

23. Israel Finkelstein and Nadav Na'aman, "The Judahite Shephelah in the Late 8th and Early 7th Centuries BCE," *TA* 31 (2004): 71; Stern, *Archaeology of the Land of the Bible*, 146.

24. This conclusion is based on the fact the pottery found is "identical to the Lachish III repertoire," which means "only a short period of time—no more than a decade or two—separated the destruction of the Shephelah by Sennacherib and the recovery." Cf. Finkelstein and Na'aman, "Judahite Shephelah," 72.

25. Stern, *Archaeology of the Land of the Bible*, 146. The date of the abandonment of the town has also been placed earlier in the seventh century. Cf. Seger, "Tel Halif," 558; Finkelstein and Na'aman, "Judahite Shephelah," 64. Borowski refers to the resettlement as the "Squatters Settlement" as he thinks it was only briefly resettled by "refugees from the previous stratum." Cf. Oded Borowski, "Sennacherib in Judah—The Devastating Consequences of an Assyrian Military Campaign," in *Lawrence E., Stager Volume* (Eretz-Israel: Archaeological, Historical and Geographical Studies; Jerusalem: Israel Exploration Society, 2018), 38*.

26. William Foxwell Albright, *The Excavation of Tell Beit Mirsim in Palestine* (AASOR 12; New Haven, CT: Yale University Press, 1932), xxi.

27. A seal impression found on-site was also dated incorrectly to the reign of Jehoiakim (ibid., 39, 66–8).

28. Aharoni and Aharoni, "Stratification of Judahite Sites," 73; Stern, *Archaeology of the Land of the Bible*, 10. Blakey and Hardin ("Southwestern Judah," 14–24) argue for two eighth-century destructions. But see Finkelstein and Na'aman, "Judahite Shephelah," 60–79, for a strong rebuttal.

along with the gates, though the entire site was not razed. In fact, Greenberg notes that "most of the town escaped destruction at this time."[29] Aharoni noted that part of the site (and a tower) was subsequently rebuilt in the seventh century.[30] Clearly, the town recovered following Sennacherib's invasion, but the recovery was perhaps limited.[31]

2.1.1.4 Timnah (Tel Batash) This Shephelah border town between Philistia and Judah had been fortified prior to Sennacherib's invasion with a double wall and a new gate.[32] Timnah (Stratum III) appears to have suffered partial destruction in 701 (with the dating aided by the eleven *lmlk* jar handles found therein).[33] The inner gate was destroyed, but not the outer gate. Some buildings show no destruction but evince continued use subsequent to 701.[34] The site shows Philistine material culture early on, but later evinces Israelite material culture.[35] Afterward, it appears that it may have returned to Philistine hegemony, with Ekron controlling the town,[36] perhaps in the reallotment of areas following the Assyrian withdrawal wherein Sennacherib claims to have redistributed part of Hezekiah's kingdom to

---

29. Raphael Greenberg, "Beit Mirsim, Tell," *NEAEHL* 66-7.

30. Aharoni and Aharoni, "Stratification of Judahite Sites," 73; Yohanan Aharoni, *The Archaeology of the Land of Israel: From the Prehistoric Beginnings to the End of the First Temple Period* (Philadelphia, PA: Westminster, 1982), 261-2, 266.

31. Yohanan Aharoni, "The Stratification of the Site," in *Beer-Sheba I: Excavations at Tel Beer-Sheba, 1969-1971* (Monographs of the Institute of Archaeology; Tel Aviv: Tel Aviv University, 1973), 6. Zimhoni argues that the town was *not* reoccupied following Sennacherib's campaign, contesting Aharoni's determination that the pottery found at Tell Beit Mirsim was contemporary with Level II of Lachish. Cf. Orna Zimhoni, "The Iron Age Pottery of Tel 'Eton and Its Relation to the Lachish, Tell Beit Mirsim and Arad Assemblages," *TA* (1987): 82-8. Most, however, find evidence of a limited recovery to be more convincing. Cf. Finkelstein and Na'aman, "Judahite Shephelah," 61-4; Stern, *Archaeology of the Land of the Bible*, 149; Raphael Greenberg, "Beit Mirsim, Tell," *OEANE* 1.295-7.

32. Bloch-Smith, "Assyrians Abet," 39.

33. Amihai Mazar, George L. Kelm, and Nava Panitz-Cohen, *Timnah (Tel Batash) II: The Finds from the First Millennium BCE (Text)* (Qedem, 42; Jerusalem: Institute of Archaeology, Hebrew University of Jerusalem, 2011); George L. Kelm and Amihai Mazar, "Three Seasons of Excavations at Tel Batash—Biblical Timnah," *BASOR* 248 (1982); Amihai Mazar, "Batash, Tel," *OEANE* 1.281-3.

34. George L. Kelm and A. Mazar, "Tel Batash (Timnah) Excavations: Second Preliminary Report (1981-1983)," in *Preliminary Reports of ASOR-Sponsored Excavations, 1981-83* (ed. Rast; BASORSup; Winona Lake, IN: Eisenbrauns, 1985), 104-5; George L. Kelm and A. Mazar, *Timnah: A Biblical City in the Sorek Valley* (Winona Lake, IN: Eisenbrauns, 1995), 119, 126-7, 131-5.

35. Dever, *Beyond the Texts*, 562.

36. Ibid; Nava Panitz-Cohen, "A Salvage Excavation in the New Market in Beer-Sheba: New Light on Iron Age IIb Occupation at Beer-Sheba," *IEJ* 55 (2005): 281-2.

Philistia.³⁷ Kelm and Mazar note that Timnah was "reclaimed" by Judah in the seventh century but say "it is impossible to state exactly when."³⁸ Stern thinks the hypothesis of Philistines controlling the town "appears to be unnecessary in view of the many official Judaean remains here."³⁹ Either way the town appears to prosper in the post-701 environment.⁴⁰

*2.1.1.5 Tell el Ḥesi (Substrata VIIIa)*⁴¹ Only partly excavated, some strata appear to show destruction that could be dated to 701 BCE, though no *lmlk* jar handles were found.⁴² Blakely and Hardin have suggested the destruction could go back to Tiglath-Pileser.⁴³ Most hold to it being destroyed in 701, with no recovery evident.⁴⁴

2.1.1.6 Tel 'Erani (Stratum VI) This walled city appears to have been something of a lookout point for Lachish.⁴⁵ The site (VIII and VII)⁴⁶ was apparently destroyed in 701 with Field I Areas 41 and 51 showing a destruction layer as dated by the *lmlk* jar handles found on-site.⁴⁷ Slingstones found on-site also witness the Assyrian attack.⁴⁸ Subsequently, the site recovered and was fortified with a wall and "four room" houses were found containing "large numbers of Judaean finds."⁴⁹ The town continues to be occupied into the sixth century.

2.1.1.7 Tel Beth-Shemesh (Stratum II) An administrative town in the Shephelah on the border with Philistia, excavations at Beth-Shemesh reveal a clear destruction layer dated to 701 BCE due to the *lmlk* jar handles found.⁵⁰ The city gate, along with

---

37. RINAP 3.1:176, 22.iii.31–34.
38. Kelm and Mazar, "Three Seasons," 248.
39. Stern, *Archaeology of the Land of the Bible*, 144.
40. As Stern writes, "Timnah of Stratum II was also a flourishing town." Ibid.
41. Formally referred to as Sub-stratum VIIa.
42. Lawrence E. Toombs, "Tell El-Ḥesi," in *Biblical Archaeology Today, 1990: Proceedings of the Second International Congress on Biblical Archaeology, Jerusalem, June-July 1990* (Jerusalem: Israel Exploration Society, 1993); Cf. Dever, *Beyond the Texts*, 560.
43. Blakely and Hardin, "Southwestern Judah," 33, 52.
44. Dever, *Beyond the Texts*, 560.
45. Stern, *Archaeology of the Land of the Bible*, 146.
46. Ibid.
47. Dever, *Beyond the Texts*, 562; Bloch-Smith, "Assyrians Abet," 40; Eliot Braun and Edwin C. M. van den Brink, "Tel 'Erani," in *Excavations and Surveys in Israel* (Jerusalem: Israel Antiquities Authority, 1997); Stern, *Archaeology of the Land of the Bible*, 10. As well a Hebrew ostracon and some Judahite clay figurines were recovered. Ibid., 146.
48. Z. Yeivin, "'Erani, Tel," *NEAEHL* 418–19, 421; B. Brandl, "'Erani, Tel," *OEANE* 2.257.
49. Stern, *Archaeology of the Land of the Bible*, 146.
50. Some early excavations dated the destruction layer to the Babylonian invasion of the sixth century; however, this was based largely on the misdating of the *lmlk* seals that was common at the time. Cf. Elihu Grant and G. Ernest Wright, *Ain Shems Excavations (Palestine): Part V (Text)* 8; Haverford, PA: Haverford College, 1931), 67–75. Bunimovitz

other public structures, was destroyed.⁵¹ Initially, there were no remains from the seventh century discovered besides some found in the water system.⁵² The lack of seventh-century pottery led excavators to conclude that there was a gap in settlement following 701 suggesting the area did not recover quickly afterward. Aharoni and Aharoni determined the site was not resettled based on the lack of pottery contemporary with Level II of Lachish.⁵³ Renewed excavations on the site led Bunimovitz and Lederman to conclude that only after the Assyrian hegemony was failing in the late seventh century were Judahites able to return to the Shephelah.⁵⁴ Fantalkin has offered an alternative historical reconstruction based on the archaeological evidence that suggests that the renewal of the Shephelah began in the early seventh century (as early as Manasseh) and that Judah and Ekron cooperated economically under both Assyrian and later Egyptian hegemony.⁵⁵

More recent work, however, has discovered the town expansion off the Tel, which was surprising to the excavators.⁵⁶ It now appears Beth-Shemesh was rebuilt shortly after 701 and was Judahite (as evinced by the Judahite jar handles found). Excavations of the expansion showed a lot of agro-industrial activity only a short time after the Assyrians returned home from the third campaign.⁵⁷ The production of olive oil so soon after the end of the Assyrian campaign of 701 suggests a rather quick recovery, rather than a large gap.

---

and Lederman date the end of Stratum 12 to 701 BCE. Cf. Shlomo Bunimovitz and Zvi Lederman, "The Final Destruction of Beth Shemesh and the Pax Assyriaca in the Judean Shephelah," *TA* 30 (2003): 5.

51. Bloch-Smith, "Assyrians Abet," 39.

52. Stern, *Archaeology of the Land of the Bible*, 148; Faust, "Settlement and Demography," 169. Bunimovitz and Lederman, "Final Destruction of Beth Shemesh."

53. Aharoni and Aharoni, "Stratification of Judahite Sites," 86–9. These findings were initially confirmed with renewed excavations at the site. See Shlomo Bunimovitz, Zvi Lederman, and Raz Kletter, "Tel Bet Shemesh–1990," *Excavations and Surveys in Israel* 10 (1991): 143. This conclusion was a bit tentative given the dearth of pottery found in the renewed excavations.

54. Bunimovitz and Lederman, "Final Destruction of Beth Shemesh," 3–26. They suggested that a small group of Judahites were stopped from reopening the reservoir at Beth Shemesh in the seventh century because of "the strength of the opposition of their Philistine neighbours and their Assyrian masters to any Judahite attempt to settle the Shephelah" (23). Cf. Shelomoh Bunimovits and Zvi Lederman, "The Archaeology of Border Communities: Renewed Excavations at Tel Beth-Shemesh Part I the Iron Age," *NEA* 72 (2009): 141.

55. Alexander Fantalkin, "The Final Destruction of Beth Shemesh and the Pax Assyriaca in the Judahite Shephelah: An Alternative View," *TA* 31 (2004): 245–61.

56. Personal communication with Dale Manor (2019).

57. Personal communication with Zvi Lederman (2019).

2.1.1.8 Azekah (Tel Zakariah) Excavated by Bliss and Macalister long ago in 1890, the stratigraphy is problematic, and it is difficult to determine the state of the site in the seventh-century BCE.[58] Many *lmlk* seals were found (in so-called periods B and C) along with Judahite figurines and weights. An inscription of Sennacherib was initially thought by Na'aman to refer to the Assyrian conquest of Azekah,[59] though others, and Na'aman himself now, have rejected this conclusion.[60] Its existence in the seventh century is suggested by a jar handle seal impression with a galloping horse found in Azekah, which is identical to one found at Ein Gedi clearly dating to the seventh century. Furthermore, a Lachish ostracon suggests that Azekah remained an important part of Judahite defense against Babylonian advances in 586 BCE.[61]

2.1.1.9 Tel Goded (Tell Judeideh) This site, on the main road from Beth-Shemesh and Azekah to Mareshah and Lachish, served as a lookout post warning of movements on the road. At least forty *lmlk* seals were found there, along with other personal seals.[62] Some have argued that this Iron Age site survived until the sixth century.[63] The most thorough examination of the data was done by Gibson, who concluded the city was destroyed in 701.[64] In light of the conflicting positions, Faust suggests the data "be treated with caution."[65] The site clearly existed in the seventh century with Judahite figurines and rosette seal impressions from this period found (though not many buildings).[66]

2.1.1.10 Mareshah Material remains suggest the site was destroyed in 701 based on a comparison of pottery discovered at Mareshah with that of Lachish.[67] Some concluded that it no longer existed afterward due to the fact that there was no extant pottery corresponding with Level II at Lachish.[68] More recent work has

---

58. Ephraim Stern, *Archaeology of the Land of the Bible*, 148. Cf. Ephraim Stern, "Azekah," *NEAEHL* 123–4.
59. Na'aman, "Letter to God," 25–39.
60. Na'aman, "Hezekiah," 235–54.
61. Stern, *Archaeology of the Land of the Bible*, 148.
62. Stern, *Archaeology of the Land of the Bible*, 148.
63. Dagan, "The Settlement in the Judean Shephela," 91–3; Oded Lipschits, *The Fall and Rise of Jerusalem: Judah under Babylonian Rule* (Winona Lake, IN: Eisenbrauns, 2005), 220.
64. Shimon Gibson, "The Tell ej-Judeideh (Tel Goded) Excavations: A Re-Appraisal Based on Archival Records in the Palestine Exploration Fund," *TA* 21 (1994).
65. Faust, "Settlement and Demography," 173.
66. Stern, *Archaeology of the Land of the Bible*, 148.
67. Vaughn, *Theology, History*, 27.
68. Yehudah Dagan, "The Shephelah During the Period of the Monarchy in Light of Archaeological Excavations and Surveys" (MA Thesis. Tel Aviv University, 1992) 47; Vaughn, *Theology, History*, 27.

discovered material evidence (an ostracon, pottery, walls, etc.) that suggest a continued existence into the seventh century.[69]

2.1.1.11 Tel 'Eton (Eglon) Most likely biblical Eglon, Tel 'Eton was a city in the Shephelah, near Tell Beit Mirsim. Limited excavations found Lachish-like pottery revealed a clear destruction dating to the Assyrian campaign of 701.[70] The limited excavations, which consisted largely of a small trench on the site, have found "no large-scale resettlement" in the seventh century.[71] Stern suggested the data are too limited for such conclusions (and thinks the trench excavated may have been past the town's borders).[72] More recent work has still to reveal any *lmlk* jar handles and while the pottery "is similar" to Lachish, it also shows "some differences between them."[73] However, most still attribute the destruction to Sennacherib's campaign in 701.[74] Stern suggests that the town was "renewed after Sennacherib's destruction and existed until the end of the Iron Age, as all the other towns in the region."[75]

As is well known, the Shephelah was the hardest hit region in Judah during the Assyrian campaign of 701 BCE. As our survey has noted, some sites did not recover or show only very limited recovery that was clearly diminished from their eighth-century peak (e.g., Lachish, Tell el Ḥesi, Tel 'Eton). Other sites suffered only partial destruction (Tell Beit Mirsim, Tel Batash), some showed a fairly quick recovery to prosperity (Tel Beth-Shemesh), some were renewed but only after a longer occupational gap (Tel 'Erani), while still others offer only ambiguous evidence (Mareshah, Azekah). Despite the recovery of some sites, the devastation of Sennacherib's invasion can be clearly seen in the archaeological remains of these eighth-century Shephelah sites. Yet the recovery of some sites should not be discounted when considering how Judahites assessed the events of 701 and the outcome of Hezekiah's rebellion. As we will see other areas of eighth-century Judah fared better than the Shephelah during the Assyrian campaign, though there is still evidence of destruction.

---

69. Amos Kloner, *Survey of Jerusalem: The Northeastern Sector, Introduction and Indices* (Jerusalem: Israel Antiquities Authority, 2003), 150.

70. Avraham Faust and Hayah Katz, "Tel 'Eton Cemetery: An Introduction," *Hebrew Bible and Ancient Israel* 5 (2016); Blakely and Hardin, "Southwestern Judah," 35; Dever, *Beyond the Texts*, 562; Orna Zimhoni, "The Iron Age Pottery of Tel Eton and Its Relation to the Lachish, Tell Beit Mirsim and Arad Assemblages," *OTA* 10 (1987).

71. Faust, "Settlement and Demography," 169; E. Ayalon, "Trial Excavation of Two Iron Age Stata at Tel 'Eton," *TA* 12 (1985): 54–62; Zimhoni, "Iron Age Pottery," 63–90.

72. Stern, *Archaeology of the Land of the Bible*, 150.

73. Avraham Faust and Hayah Katz, "A Canaanite Town, a Judahite Center, and a Persian Period Fort: Excavating over Two Thousand Years of History at Tel 'eton," *NEA* 78 (2015): 95.

74. Ibid. Cf. Faust and Katz, "Tel 'Eton Cemetery."

75. Stern, *Archaeology of the Land of the Bible*, 150.

2.1.2 Other Areas Showing Destruction

2.1.2.1 Khirbet Rabud (Stratum B-II) One of the few highland sites with damage dated to 701 BCE, Khirbet Rabud is usually identified as biblical Debir, a city 32 kilometers from Jerusalem, which was fortified with a surrounding wall 4 meters thick.[76] Its evident destruction layer is usually credited to the Assyrian invasion due to similar pottery to Lachish and an *lmlk* jar handle.[77] Some suggest it was the victim of an "additional incursion" of the army that approached Jerusalem (2 Kgs 18:17), but was not part of the main strategy of the Assyrian campaign.[78] The town appears to have been rebuilt in the seventh century with an expanded wall.[79]

2.1.2.2 Hebron (Al-Khalil) Eight *lmlk* jar handles were found here, indicating the 701 level.[80] A four-room house was excavated that was "violently destroyed and partially burnt."[81] Like Khirbet Rabud, its destruction may have been a more cursory incursion of the Assyrian army delegation that entered the highlands (2 Kgs 18:17).[82] Dever speculates Hebron may have only been "a market town in the southern Judean hills."[83] A settlement in the seventh century has been excavated.[84] In fact, Faust has suggested that its location on the site's slopes suggests a settlement of substantial size.[85]

2.1.2.2.1 Beersheba (Tell es-Saba' Stratum II) One of two key administrative sites outside of Jerusalem[86] (the other being Lachish), excavations of Beersheba (Stratum II) have determined that it was razed by fire and "was destroyed in a huge conflagration, whose evidence is recognizable everywhere."[87] The dating of the conflagration to 701 BCE is corroborated by pottery found on-site similar to that found in Lachish III.[88] Furthermore, excavators found a couple of *lmlk* handles

---

76. Borowski, "Sennacherib in Judah—the Devastating Consequences of an Assyrian Military Campaign," 36*.

77. Moshe Kochavi, "Khirbet Rabûd = Debir," *Tel Aviv* 1 (1974): 2–33; Moshe Kochavi, "Rabud, Khirbet," *NEAEHL* 1252; Moshe Kochavi, "Rabud, Khirbet," *OEANE* 4.401.

78. Faust, "Settlement and Demography," 183. Cf. Elayi, *Sennacherib*, 73.

79. Ibid., 178; Dever, *Beyond the Texts*, 560.

80. Emanuel Eisenberg and Alla Nagorski, "Tel Hevron (Er-Rumeidi)," *Hadashot Arkheologiyot* (2002): 91*–92*.

81. Ibid., 91*; Stern, *Archaeology of the Land of the Bible*, 10.

82. Faust, "Settlement and Demography," 183.

83. Dever, *Beyond the Texts*, 569.

84. Eisenberg and Nagorski, "Tel Hevron (Er-Rumeidi)," 92*.

85. Faust, "Settlement and Demography," 178.

86. A. de Groot, "Notes on the Development of Jerusalem," in *The Fifteenth Archaeological Conference in Israel* (Jerusalem: Israel Exploration Society, 1989), 21.

87. Yohanan Aharoni, ed., *Beer-Sheba I: Excavations at Tel Beer-Sheba, 1969–1971* (Monographs of the Institute of Archaeology; Tel Aviv: Tel Aviv University, 1973), 5.

88. Ibid., 107; Cf. Itzhaq Beit Arieh, "The Western Quarter," in *Beer-Sheba, Vol. 1, Excavations at Tel Beer-Sheba, 1969–1971 Seasons* (ed. Aharoni; Tel Aviv: Institute of Archaeology, Tel Aviv University, 1973), 31–7.

(admittedly less than expected), which tie it to the time of Hezekiah as well.[89] It does not appear that the entire city was rebuilt on-site in the seventh century.[90] Aharoni observed that "large parts of the city were never rebuilt"[91] and Dever notes only "a period of scant reoccupation" represented by Stratum II.[92]

2.1.2.2.2 Philistine Sites While our focus is on the devastation and recovery of Judah, it is worth noting the destruction left in Sennacherib's wake that is evident in Philistine border sites. For example, Tel Sera' (Stratum VI),[93] possibly biblical Ziklag, shows it was burnt in the late eighth century.[94] The destruction is usually dated to the third campaign in 701.[95] Similarly, the walled border town of Tell Jemmeh (Stratum CD)[96] evinces some eighth-century levels that may have been destroyed.[97] As Jemmeh is a "daughter town" of Gaza, and was apparently under its control, this site is Philistine.[98] A mud-brick vaulted building (either

---

89. Blakely and Hardin have argued that some of the destruction (Stratum III) attributed to Sennacherib's campaign actually was the result of earlier Assyrian campaigns. Blakely and Hardin, "Southwestern Judah," 11–64. But see Finkelstein and Na'aman, "Judahite Shephelah," 60–79, for a persuasive rejection of their theory.

90. Faust, "Settlement and Demography," 169. Aharoni, "Stratification," 6–7. Cf. Aharoni, *The Archaeology of the Land of Israel*, 261–6. Aharoni and Aharoni, "Stratification of Judahite Sites." Dever states that after Sennacherib's campaign it was "virtually abandoned." Dever, *Beyond the Texts*, 427.

91. Aharoni, "Stratification," 5.

92. Dever, *Beyond the Texts*, 559.

93. Eliezer D. Oren, "Sera', Tel," *NEAEHL* 1333; Bloch-Smith, "Assyrians Abet," 40.

94. Dever, *Beyond the Texts*, 439.

95. Oren, "Sera', Tel," *NEAEHL* 1332–1333; Oren, "Sera', Tel," *OEANE* 5.1.

96. William Matthew Flinders Petrie, *Gerar* (PERA, 43; London: British School of Archaeology in Egypt, 1928). Petrie identified the site with biblical Gerar (the identification originally made by W. J. Pithian-Adams of the Palestinian Exploration Fund). Benjamin Mazar later refuted this identification, instead arguing it should be identified with Yursa/Arsa, mentioned in the Egyptian Amarna Letters from 1350 to 1330 BCE. Cf. Gus W. Van Beek, "Digging up Tell Jemmeh," *Arch* 36 (1983): 12–19.

97. Dever, *Beyond the Texts*, 560. Regarding defensive structures, Van Beek notes that an eighth-century defensive casemate wall is the best preserved (17), and that the Assyrians built another casemate wall directly over the destroyed eighth-century one (18). The date of when the first casemate wall was destroyed is not clear. Sennacherib's successor, Esarhaddon plundered Arsa (Jemmeh) *c.* 679 BCE and took its king captive Hayim Tadmor, "Philistia under Assyrian Rule," *BA* 29 (1966): 97. It is possible the destruction is to be dated to Esarhaddon rather than Sennacherib and that the Assyrian palace and new casemate wall were constructed at that time. Tamor speculates that the campaign against Arsa (Jemmeh) "was a show of force demonstrating that Assyria alone ruled in Philistia and warning Tirhaka against any attempt to assert himself in that area," ibid., 98.

98. Van Beek, "Digging up Tell Jemmeh," 16.

a palace or large house) dating to the seventh-century level (Stratum AB) was found, along with Assyrian Palace Ware, suggesting a recovery but extensive Assyrian influence.[99] The border town Tell es-Safi (Gath)[100] appears to have been destroyed in 701, though it is not mentioned in Assyrian records.[101] Stern notes some have suggested it might be "the royal city of the Philistines" mentioned in Sennacherib's annals related to the 701 invasion and that some think it was captured by Hezekiah.[102] The town was clearly rebuilt subsequently. In fact, based on archaeological finds from the excavations that are similar to those of other Judahite towns, Stern suggests that after the third campaign, "Gath again became a part of the Judaean kingdom."[103]

2.2 Areas Showing No Destruction in 701 BCE[104]

While it is clear there was much destruction in Judah due to the Assyrian campaign of 701, particularly in, but not limited to, the Shephelah, in the survey that follows, we will see that the archaeological evidence does *not* support a conclusion of rampant destruction across the entire territory of Judah.[105] As noted

---

99. Dever, *Beyond the Texts*, 560.

100. Shawn Z. Aster, "The Historical Background of the Destruction of Judahite Gath in 712 BCE," in *Tell It in Gath: Studies in the History and Archaeology of Israel. Essays in Honor of Aren M. Maeir on the Occasion of His Sixtieth Birthday* (Münster: Zaphon, 2018), 436–44; Ephraim Stern, "Zafit, Tel," *NEAEHL* 1522–24. Contra. Lawrence E. Stager, "The Impact of the Sea Peoples in Canaan (1185–1050 BCE)." in *The Archaeology of Society in the Holy Land* (ed. Levy; London: Leicester University Press, 1995), 332–48.

101. Na'aman initially thought the name "Gath" should be reconstructed in Sennacherib's so-called letter to god (Na'aman, "Letter to God"), but later demurred Na'aman, "Hezekiah," 245–7, instead following Mittmann, "Hiskia und die Philister," 91–106, who instead reconstructed "Ekron" instead of "Gath."

102. Stern, *Archaeology of the Land of the Bible*, 145.

103. Ibid., 146. He notes Judahite rosette seal impressions found here and a *lmlk* seal on a jar handle found at nearby Tel Harasim, which he thinks was "on the same western line of defense" as suggesting it was again a Judahite town post 701 BCE.

104. Not covered in this survey is the ambiguous evidence of Tel Malhata, which shows continued existence after 701 BCE. Moshe Kochavi, "The Excavations at Tel Malhata—an Interim Report," *Qad* 115 (1998), 30–9. Furthermore, sites in Ammon, Moab, and Edom appear to have retained their independence with no discernable Assyrian presence recovered (Assyrian names, palace ware, imported pottery, Assyrian-type construction, etc.). Piotr Bienkowski, "Transjordan and Assyria," in *The Archaeology of Jordan and Beyond: Essays in Honor of James A. Sauer* (eds. Stager et al.; Sahl; Winona Lake, IN: Eisenbrauns, 2000), 52–3. Clearly, this undermines any supposition of near-universal Assyrian influence as the south remained independent even during Assyrian's zenith in the seventh century.

105. Faust, "Settlement and Demography," 182.

above, Assyrian strategy focused on the Judahite–Philistine border towns, which suffered the most. Yet, as we have seen, some sites even in the Shephelah recovered rather quickly after 701, and the highlands were apparently only victims of minor military incursions, and many other regions of Judah escaped without any destruction at all. In what follows, we will highlight sites that show no destruction layers connected to 701 BCE.

The partial nature of destruction in Judah is clearly supported by the archaeological evidence. Many sites were established, and others actually survived and peaked *after* the invasion of Sennacherib. While we will briefly survey those towns that survived the Assyrian invasion unscathed and continued to exist without disruption, it is likely this was simply due to Assyrian strategy wherein they targeted certain towns (along major roadways) and not others.[106] As studies have shown, smaller homesteads and farms escaped unscathed as well with none showing destruction at the time.[107] Clearly, all Judahites did not flee their farmsteads as a result of the Assyrian assault.[108] As Bloch-Smith observes, "These sites demonstrate some continuity in highland rural settlement from the eighth century to the sixth century."[109]

As is well known, Jerusalem suffered no destruction in Sennacherib's campaign, despite Sennacherib's boasts of restricting it, and Assyrian threats against it recorded in biblical texts. However, Jerusalem is not the only site to have escaped Sennacherib's campaign unscathed as many sites in the vicinity of Jerusalem remained untouched by the Assyrian invasion. Sites in Benjamin, just north of Jerusalem, show no signs of destruction from 701.[110] Some have suggested that Sennacherib actually did not send the army into the highlands of Judah at all,[111] though the accompanying force sent to Jerusalem may have made incursions into highland sites (as noted above in regard to Khirbet Rabud and Hebron).[112] This would make sense of the evidence of not only Jerusalem but Tell en-Naṣbeh,

---

106. Bloch-Smith, "Assyrians Abet," 40.

107. Faust, "Settlement and Demography." Cf. Avraham Faust, "The Farmstead in the Highlands of Iron Age II Israel," in *The Rural Landscape of Ancient Israel* (eds. A. Maeir et al.; Baris; Oxford: Archaeopress, 2003), 92, 94; Vaughn, *Theology, History*, 144–5; Nurit Feig, "New Discoveries in the Rephaim Valley, Jerusalem," *PEQ* 128 (1996); D. Amit, "Farmsteads in Northern Judea (Betar Area), Survey," *Excavations and Surveys in Israel* 10 (1991): 147.

108. As suggested by Baruch Halpern, "Jerusalem and the Lineages in the Seventh Century BCE: Kinship and the Rise of Individual Moral Liability," in *Law and Ideology in Monarchic Israel* (eds. Baruch Halpern and Deborah W. Hobson; JSOTSup, 124; Sheffield: JSOT Press, 1991), 27.

109. Bloch-Smith, "Assyrians Abet," 40.

110. As Faust writes, "It is important to note that not even in a single site [in Benjamin], urban or rural, was an Assyrian destruction observed." Cf. Faust, "Settlement and Demography," 177.

111. Bloch-Smith, "Assyrians Abet," 38.

112. Faust, "Settlement and Demography," 183.

Gibeon, and Ramat Raḥel as well, all of which evince no signs of destruction from Sennacherib's campaign.

2.2.1 Tell en-Naṣbeh Stratum III (Mizpah)

Located north of Jerusalem, Mizpah was a central settlement in the region that was settled throughout the time of the monarchy.[113] Stratum III (in which were found 87 *lmlk* seals) shows no signs of destruction from the eighth century up until the Babylonian period.[114] In fact, excavations reveal an uninterrupted existence from the tenth to the sixth century.[115] Clearly, this city survived Sennacherib's invasion unscathed.[116]

2.2.2 Gibeon

This site, near Tell en-Nasbeh and Jerusalem, evidently escaped the Assyrian invasion without any destruction.[117] Archaeological evidence suggests a continued existence for Gibeon beyond the Assyrian campaign of 701 with Pritchard concluding "the frequent invasions of the Assyrian kings in the eighth and seventh century apparently bypassed the city."[118] The excavators suggest that the peak of Gibeon actually came from the seventh rather than the eighth century.[119] Excavations have revealed continued use of the eighth-century installations at Gibeon (e.g., the winery, water system) from the eighth through to the seventh

---

113. Avraham Faust, *Judah in the Neo-Babylonian Period: The Archaeology of Desolation* (SBLABS 18; Atlanta, GA: SBL Press, 2012), 158; Chester Charlton McCown, Joseph Wampler, and William Frederic Badè, *Tell En-Nasbeh Excavated under the Direction of the Late William Frederic Badè* (Berkeley, CA: The Palestine Institute of Pacific School of Religion and ASOR, 1947); A. Mazar, "Three Israelite Sites in the Hills of Judah and Ephraim," *BA* 45 (1982): 174–6.

114. Jeffrey R. Zorn, "Nasbeh, Tell En-," *NEAEHL*, 1098–102. Avraham Faust, *The Archaeology of Israelite Society in Iron Age II* (Winona Lake, IN: Eisenbrauns, 2012), 72.

115. Zorn, "Nasbeh, Tell En-," *NEAEHL*, 1098–102. Jeffrey R. Zorn, "Nasbeh, Tell En-," *OEANE* 4.101–3. Faust, "Settlement and Demography," 176. Dever, *Beyond the Texts*, 557; Faust, *Archaeology of Israelite Society*, 72–7; Ze'ev Herzog, "Arad: Iron Age Period," *OEANE* 1.174–6.

116. In fact, as Faust states, "There is no reason to believe that the town of the seventh century was smaller than that of the eighth century." Cf. Faust, *Judah in the Neo-Babylonian Period*, 158.

117. In fact, Faust comments that "nothing of importance occurred at the sites in the late-eighth century." Faust, *Judah in the Neo-Babylonian*, 159.

118. James B. Pritchard, *Gibeon, Where the Sun Stood Still: The Discovery of the Biblical City* (Princeton, NJ: Princeton University Press, 1962), 161–2. See Faust, *Archaeology of Israelite Society*, 267; Vaughn, *Theology, History*, 37–8.

119. Pritchard, *Gibeon*, 162–163; Faust, "Settlement and Demography," 176.

centuries.¹²⁰ Abundant seventh-century pottery has been excavated at Gibeon, including rosette seals, Judahite figurines, weights, and so on.¹²¹

2.2.3 Ramat Raḥel (Hirbet Salih)

Located about 4 kilometers from both Bethlehem and Jerusalem, Ramat Raḥel appears to be an eighth-century palace with extensive fortifications.¹²² Level VB appears to have been besieged by the Assyrians.¹²³ There is much debate about the function and the putative destruction of the palace. The many *lmlk* seals discovered (c. 180) suggest an administrative role to the town, with some suggesting it should be identified with the previously unknown city, *mmšt*, referenced on the *lmlk* seal impressions (which list one of four cities, Hebron, Sokoh, Ziph, and *mmšt*,¹²⁴ which must have been Judahite administrative centers).¹²⁵ Others have

---

120. Dever, *Beyond the Texts*, 569.
121. Stern, *Archaeology of the Land of the Bible*, 139.
122. Yohanan Aharoni, "Ramat Rahel," in *The New Encyclopedia of Archaeological Excavations in the Holy Land* (eds. Stern et al.; New York: Henrickson, 1993), 1261–7; G. Barkay, "Royal Palace, Royal Portrait? The Tantalizing Possibilities of Ramat Rahel," *BAR* 32 (2006): 34–44. It is now suggested to have been a royal administrative center under Assyrian hegemony. Cf. Oded Lipschits, Yuval Gadot, Benny Arubas, and Manfred Oeming, "Palace and Village, Paradise and Oblivion: Unraveling the Riddles of Ramat Raḥel," *NEA* 74 (2011): 9. Cf. Oded Lipschits, Yuval Gadot, and Liora Freud, *Ramat-Raḥel III: Final Publication of Yohanan Aharoni's Excavations (1954, 1959–1962) 1–2* (Winona Lake, IN: Eisenbrauns, 2016); Oded Lipschits, Yuval Gadot, Benjamin Arubas, and Manfred Oeming, *What Are the Stones Whispering? Ramat Rahel: 3000 Years of Forgotten History* (Winona Lake, IN: Eisenbrauns, 2017).
123. Aharoni initially found only evidence of destruction he dated to the Babylonian destruction in the sixth century but suggested there had been an earlier palace on-site constructed by Hezekiah that accounted for the pottery assemblages found under the floors of the sixth-century palace. Cf. Yohanan Aharoni, Antonia Ciasca, Università di Roma and Universiṭah ha-ʿIvrit bi-Yerushalayim, *Excavations at Ramat Raḥel, Seasons 1961 and 1962* (SA, 6; Roma: Centro die studi semitici, 1964), 120. Subsequently, after Aharoni's death 170 jar handles with *lmlk* seals were discovered, which, along with other seal impressions matching Lachish III, suggest a palace dating to the late eighth century. Cf. J. P. Dressel, "Ramat Rahel," *OEANE* 4.402–4. As well, Lachish III-like pottery fragments suggest a late eighth-century date as well. Cf. Vaughn, *Theology, History*, 100. The palace Aharoni dated to Jehoiakim at the beginning of the sixth century is now seen to have been an early seventh century (re)construction. Cf. Barkay, "Royal Palace," 38. Though it met its end with the Babylonian conquest. Grabbe, "Introduction," 10.
124. Hebron is Jebel er-Rumeidah; Sokoh is likely Khirbet Shuweiket er-Ras; Ziph is south of Hebron at a site now known as Tel Ziph.
125. Barkay, "Royal Palace," 38. The Hebrew *mmšt* has been translated by some as "government" (Dever, *Beyond the Texts*, 553).

suggested the palace was an Assyrian fortress, and the many *lmlk* jars found therein evidence of its imperial function as a place for the collection of Assyrian taxes.[126] Regarding the question of its destruction, some have interpreted the evidence as it being destroyed in 701 BCE due to Sennacherib's invasion.[127] If it was destroyed in 701, most think it was rebuilt soon thereafter (e.g., Barkay suggested that Hezekiah rebuilt the site immediately after the Assyrian withdrawal).[128] Others suggest there was no destruction to be dated to Sennacherib's invasions but interpret the evidence as showing continued use of the site before and after the third campaign.[129] For the purposes of the present study, it is significant that both reconstructions of the evidence suggest the use of the site following 701, whether it was an immediate rebuilding or the fact that the site survived the Assyrian campaign unscathed.

2.2.4 Tel Haror

Often identified with biblical Gerar,[130] west of Beersheba, this is another border town near the Philistine coastal plain. Tel Haror shows no signs of destruction that could be associated with Sennacherib's campaign. It may, however, show evidence of some Assyrian occupation in the late eighth century.[131] Either way, it survived the Assyrian invasion and continued to function in the seventh century.

---

126. Lipschits et al., "Palace and Village," 20; Lipschits et al., *What Are the Stones Whispering?* Some suggest the Assyrians left some sites untouched like Ramat Raḥel, Megiddo, and so on "to be utilized by the Assyrians as administrative centers" (Bloch-Smith, "Assyrians Abet," 36). Cf. Lipschits, "Long Seventh Century," 27–9.

127. Faust, *Judah in the Neo-Babylonian Period*, 162; Barkay, "Royal Palace," 38; Grabbe, "Introduction," 9. Vaughn, *Theology, History*, 100; Stern, *Archaeology of the Land of the Bible*, 130.

128. Barkay ("Royal Palace," 44) writes, "It appears to have been rebuilt shortly after Sennacherib abandoned his siege of Jerusalem, most likely by Hezekiah himself in the later years of his reign, although his son Manasseh is another candidate." Cf. Aharoni, "Ramat Raḥel."

129. Dever, *Beyond the Texts*, 574; Lipschits et al., "Palace and Village," 10–20; Lipschits et al., *Ramat-Raḥel III*; Lipschits et al., *What Are the Stones Whispering?*

130. Dever, *Beyond the Texts*, 560. Petrie originally suggested Tell Jemmeh was Gerar Petrie, *Gerar*. Albright identified it with Tell Abu Hereirah. Cf. William Foxwell Albright, "Abram the Hebrew: A New Archaeological Interpretation," *BASOR* 163 (1961). See Yohanan Aharoni, "The Land of Gerar," *IEJ* 6 (1956). Dever rejected this claim. Cf. W. G. Dever, "Palestine in the Second Millennium BCE: The Archaeological Picture," in *Israelite and Judean History* (eds. Hayes and Miller; Philadelphia, PA: Westminster, 1977). Cf. Yohanan Aharoni, "Tel Haror," in *Moshé Stekelis Memorial Volume* (Jerusalem, 1977).

131. Dever, *Beyond the Texts*, 560.

2.2.5 Tel Gezer (Stratum V)

Gezer was conquered by Assyria under Tiglath-Pileser III sometime between 734 and 732.[132] After the fall of Samaria, Gezer appears to have been reckoned to be part of the kingdom of Judah.[133] Stern suggests Hezekiah annexed Gezer (as indicated by *lmlk* seals found[134]) in his preparation to rebel against Sennacherib.[135] Gezer appears to have survived Sennacherib's invasion unscathed.[136] Some suggest that Gezer found itself under direct Assyrian control after 701, given the Assyrian cuneiform tablets found there (Stratum V).[137] Interestingly, these legal documents are contracts of land purchases, mentioning a man with a Hebrew name, Natanyau, who was selling land. This is suggestive that Judahites who survived the Assyrian invasion retained legal land rights in the aftermath.[138] Stern suggests it again became Judahite territory, noting Dever's excavations that uncovered "a Judean character" to the seventh-century stratum.[139]

2.2.6 Tel el-Ful (Gibeah?)

This site, likely biblical Gibeah,[140] was occupied in the eighth century as evidenced by the eighth-century pottery types as well as the *lmlk* impressions found.[141] No signs of destruction have been found that can be tied to Sennacherib's campaign. In fact, the peak of the city appears to have been in the seventh century.[142]

---

132. See relief from Tiglath-Pileser's palace showing the conquest of the city, with the label "Ga-za-ra." See Tadmor, *The Inscriptions of Tiglath-Pileser III*, 210.

133. Ibid., 561.

134. H. Darrell Lance, "Royal Stamps and the Kingdom of Josiah," *HTR* 64 (1971): 330 n. 70; Hanan Eshel, "A lmlk Stamp from Beth-El," *IEJ* 39 (1989): 60–2.

135. Stern, *Archaeology of the Land of the Bible*, 140.

136. Ronny Reich and Baruch Brandl, "Gezer under Assyrian Rule," *PEQ* 117 (1985): 49–53.

137. Raz Kletter, "Pots and Polities: Material Remains of Late Iron Age Judah in Relation to Its Political Borders," *BASOR* 314 (1999): 26; Becking, *The Fall of Samaria*, 114–18. Some suggest the documents were originally part of an Assyrian administrative centre at Gezer, though the possibility they were a landholder's personal possession to show his property rights remains. Cf. Reich and Brandl, "Gezer under Assyrian Rule," 41.

138. Reich and Brandl, "Gezer under Assyrian Rule," 41.

139. Stern, *Archaeology of the Land of the Bible*, 140.

140. Dever, *Beyond the Texts*, 557.

141. Nancy L. Lapp, "Other Finds from the 1964 Campaign," in *Third campaign at Tell El-Ful: The Excavations of 1964* (Cambridge, MA: American Schools of Oriental Research, 1981), 111–12.

142. Faust, *Judah in the Neo-Babylonian Period*, 159; Faust, "Settlement and Demography," 176.

2.2.7 Beth-Zur (Stratum II)

This city appears to have been a prosperous community from the late eighth until the sixth centuries.[143] Ten *lmlk* handles were found here, but the destruction layer appears to date to the Babylonian rather than the Assyrian invasion.[144]

2.2.8 Arad (Stratum VIII)

This Judahite fort, excavated by Aharoni, shows Lachish-like pottery, and ten *lmlk* jar handles have been recovered there.[145] The excavator suggested Stratum VIII was destroyed by Sennacherib (supported by Herzog).[146] The stratigraphy of the site has been repeatedly challenged, undermining this conclusion.[147] Dever notes "the lack of clear evidence of a major destruction circa 701," though he notes there were clear "changes in the seventh century."[148] Stern notes that the entire fort at Arad "from its erection in the 10th to 9th centuries until its final destruction during the 6th century B.C.E., existed in its original form, i.e., square, surrounded by a solid wall."[149] Faust observes that it was rebuilt several times but showed continued use "until its destruction in the early-sixth century."[150] Thus, despite the putative Assyrian attack, the site continued to be used after 701 BCE.[151]

2.2.9 Khirbet el Kom (Biblical Makkedah)

This fortified town, west of Hebron, shows no destruction layer connected to Sennacherib's invasion. The pottery suggests the fortifications continued in the seventh century, and an *lmlk* seal has been found (along with a decanter with a Hebrew name incised on it, and Judahite weights).[152] Furthermore, the town was

---

143. Stern, *Archaeology of the Land of the Bible*, 164. Cf. Faust, *Judah in the Neo-Babylonian Period*, 162.

144. Dever, *Beyond the Texts*, 562. Contra. Stern, *Archaeology of the Land of the Bible*, 130.

145. Yohanan Aharoni, *Arad Inscriptions* (Jerusalem: Israel Exploration Society, 1981), 149; Miriam Aharoni, "Arad: The Israelite Citadels," *NEAEHL* 82.

146. Z. Herzog, "The Fortress Mound at Tel Arad: An Interim Report," *TA* 29 (2002): 98; Z. Herzog, "Beer-Sheba Valley: From Nomadism to Monarchy," in *From Nomadism to Monarchy* (eds. Finkelstein and Na'aman; Jerusalem: Biblical Archaeology Society, 1994), 122–49.

147. Finkelstein, "The Archaeology of the Days of Manasseh," 170.

148. Dever, *Beyond the Texts*, 563.

149. Stern, *Archaeology of the Land of the Bible*, 158–9. Regardless, Stern actually assumes an Assyrian conquest of the fort in 701.

150. Faust, *Judah in the Neo-Babylonian Period*, 156.

151. William G. Dever, "Qom, Khirbet El-," *OEANE* 4.391–2; Faust, "Settlement and Demography," 175.

152. Stern, *Archaeology of the Land of the Bible*, 165.

clearly expanded in the seventh century.[153] The site was finally destroyed during the Babylonian invasion of 586 BCE.[154]

2.2.10 Tel Malḥata

Tel Malḥata (Biblical Moladah[155]), located in the northeastern Negev in the Arad-Beersheba valley, shows continued existence from the eighth through to the sixth centuries.[156] This appears in keeping with other sites in the Negev, which appear to have largely survived Sennacherib's invasion unmolested. Again, this is possibly due to Assyrian strategy, but the survival of such areas may have encouraged the view of the success of the rebellion.[157]

2.2.11 Nebi-Samuel (Continuously Occupied)

The settlement was established prior to Sennacherib's invasion as evident in the Judahite pottery, rosette, and *lmlk*-stamped jar handles recovered there.[158] While not much more is known about the site, it clearly continued to be used until its destruction in 586 BCE.[159]

2.2.12 Tel Ira

This isolated city, on a large outcropping of flint jutting into the Beersheba-Arad valley from the Judahite hills, shows Lachish-like pottery and an *lmlk* jar handle.[160] However, the evidence shows continuous existence from the early

---

153. Faust, "Settlement and Demography," 178.

154. The town was not rebuilt thereafter, even into the Hellenistic period. Cf. Stern, *Archaeology of the Land of the Bible*, 324.

155. Cf. Josh 15:26; 19:2. This identification is held by Itzhaq Beit Arieh, Liora Freud, and Gregory H. Bearman (*Tel Malḥata Central City in the Biblical Negev* [Monograph Series 32; Winona Lake, IN: Eisenbrauns, 2015], 15) and others (e.g., Nadav Na'aman, "Ostracon 40 from Arad Reconsidered," in *Saxa loquentur: Studien zur Archäologie Palästinas/Israels: Festschrift für Volkmar Fritz zum 65. Geburtstag* (eds. Hertog et al.; AOAT, 302; Münster: Ugarit, 2003).

156. Kochavi, "Excavations at Tel Malhata," 39; Cf. Beit-Arieh et al., Tel Malḥata a Central City in the Biblical Negev.

157. Regarding Assyrian strategy, Elayi (*Sennacherib*, 75) suggests, "Destruction was not his objective, because he intended to leave loyal allies and vassals behind him, and not to create certain enemies."

158. Y. Magen and M. Dadon, "Nebi Samwil (Shmuel HaVani-Har Hasimha)," *Qadmoniot* 118 (1999): 62–3 (Hebrew); Faust, "Settlement and Demography," 176.

159. Stern, *Archaeology of the Land of the Bible*, 140. Faust, *Judah in the Neo-Babylonian Period*, 159.

160. Dever, *Beyond the Texts*, 563.

Iron Age until the Neo-Babylonian period.[161] The last city built on the site was in the mid-seventh century, which existed until its destruction in the early sixth century.[162]

In sum, contrary to assumptions of near-total devastation of Judah from the Assyrian invasion of 701 BCE, our survey has shown that the destruction was far from complete. In light of the somewhat partial destruction of Judahite sites, the question remains of how well Judah recovered from the war of 701 BCE.

2.3 The Recovery of Judah

The recovery of Judah after the Assyrian invasion of 701 has been the subject of much debate.[163] In the not too distant past, the mainstream consensus was that prior to Sennacherib's third campaign, Judah had reached its peak in terms of settlement and prosperity,[164] but that afterward Judah was completely devastated, lost its independence and much of its territory (as it was redistributed by Sennacherib), and had only a limited and very slow recovery in the next century.[165] Sennacherib's claims to have deported some 200,000 people from the area were taken at face value, with the conclusion that Judah faced a serious manpower problem in the aftermath of 701.[166] Sennacherib further boasted of destroying forty-six of Judah's fortified cities, which naturally suggests nearly complete devastation, given Judah's small size. Nadav Na'aman sums up this position:

> Large districts were destroyed and tens of thousands of people deported to distant places. There was a drastic reduction in settlement in the kingdom in the seventh century. Even in the late seventh century, following a hundred years of

---

161. Beit Arieh, "Ira, Tel," *NEAEHL* 644. Dever speculates that it "may have been destroyed, however, in 701" (*Beyond the Texts*, 563).

162. Faust, *Judah in the Neo-Babylonian Period*, 157.

163. See Ephraim Stern, "The Eastern Border of the Kingdom of Judah," in *Scripture and Other Artifacts: Essays on the Bible and Archaeology in Honor of Philip J. King* (eds. Coogan et al.; Louisville, KY: Westminster John Knox, 1994), 399–409; Finkelstein, "The Archaeology of the Days of Manasseh," 169–87; Stern, *Archaeology of the Land of the Bible*, 142–51; Finkelstein and Na'aman, "Judahite Shephelah," 60–79; Ido Koch and Oded Lipschits. "The Rosette Stamped Jar Handle System and the Kingdom of Judah at the End of the First Temple Period." *ZDPV* 129 (2013): 55–78.

164. As Na'aman writes, "In the late eighth century, Judah reached the height of its power and prosperity." Cf. Na'aman, "Let Other Kingdoms Struggle," 67.

165. Tadmor, "Sennacherib's Campaign," 76. Cf. Koch and Lipschits, "Rosette Stamped Jar Handle System," 55–78.

166. Nadav Na'aman, "Population Changes in Palestine Following Assyrian Deportations," *TA* 20: 114–15; Stern, *Archaeology of the Land of the Bible*, 11, 130.

recovery, the kingdom's settlement, population, and economy were considerably less than in the eighth century.[167]

As Faust sums up the consensus, "The view that Judah was devastated and did not fully recover is therefore shared by most scholars, and very few challenged it or attempted to refine it."[168]

More recent work has brought into question aspects of this reconstruction.[169] First, the number of deportees claimed in Sennacherib's annals has been called into question.[170] Broshi and Finkelstein suggest that the whole of Judah had only about 110,000[171] people at the time of the invasion, making the Assyrian claims impossible.[172] In his study, Ziony Zevit concludes that at minimum the number claimed by Sennacherib's scribes is more than double the historical

---

167. Na'aman, "Let Other Kingdoms Struggle," 70. Taken nearly verbatim from Herzog, "Beer-Sheba Valley," 248. Cf. Thomas L. McClellan, "Towns to Fortresses: The Transformation of Urban Life in Judah from 8th to 7th Century BC," *SBLSP* 13 (1978): 277–86. Halpern, "Jerusalem and the Lineages," 11–107.

168. Faust, "Settlement and Demography," 170. Other archaeologists have noted the seventh-century growth in Judah but did not take the evidence further to question the overall state of Judah following the Assyrian invasions. Cf. Finkelstein, "The Archaeology of the Days of Manasseh"; Israel Finkelstein, "Environmental Archaeology and Social History: Demographic and Economic Aspects of the Monarchic Period," in *Biblical Archaeology Today, 1990: Proceedings of the Second International Congress on Biblical Archaeology, Jerusalem, Je-Jl 1990* (Jerusalem, 1993), 59; Amihai Mazar, *Archaeology of the Land of the Bible: 10,000–586 BCE* (ABRL, 1; New Haven, CT: Yale University Press, 1990), 438.

169. As Bloch-Smith writes, "The scale of the conquest was more modest than the Assyrians claimed. Selected fortified cities and administrative centers were devastated, others were partially destroyed, and some capitulated; but sites in the central highlands around Jerusalem show no evidence of battle or submission." Cf. Bloch-Smith, "Assyrians Abet," 36.

170. Gallagher, *Sennacherib's Campaign*, 131–2; Marco De Odorico, *The Use of Numbers and Quantifications in the Assyrian Royal Inscriptions*; Helsinki: Neo-Assyrian Text Corpus Project, 1995); Zevit, "Implicit Population Figures"; Faust, "Settlement and Demography," 168.

171. Broshi and Finkelstein, "Population of Palestine," 54. Finkelstein ("Archeaology of the Days of Manasseh,"176) later estimated it at 120,000 "due to a better knowledge of the settlement pattern of the Shephelah." But still far from sizeable enough to support Sennacherib's claims.

172. Others continue to take the number at face value. For example, Borowski notes that the number deported by Sennacherib dwarfs the number Sargon deported from Samaria (he notes "it is almost 7.5 times larger") and that "the deportation from Judah amounts to a little less than half of the number of those deported by Sennacherib" throughout all his campaigns. Cf. Borowski, "Sennacherib in Judah—the Devastating Consequences of an Assyrian Military Campaign," 38*. Rather than showing how devastating the campaign

reality.¹⁷³ Second, the number of fortified cities claimed to have been destroyed is also suspect and thought to be exaggeration. As Dever writes, "There cannot have been any such number of fortified sites in the whole of Judah. Here we have been able to cite no more than a dozen or so late eighth-century destructions."¹⁷⁴ This discrepancy is significant as the previous consensus of scholars held to the accuracy of Sennacherib's claims.¹⁷⁵ This opinion was merely an assumption based on the widespread scholarly disposition to believe Assyrian texts. The conclusion was clearly not based on archaeological evidence or the witness of biblical texts (which were sometimes denigrated as if they were downplaying the destruction). Despite viewing these claims as exaggeration, Dever concludes, "Nevertheless, the reduction of Judah by Sennacherib in 701 was apparently devastating."¹⁷⁶ He further elaborates,

> The results must have been traumatic, with profound implications for most people's lives at every level of the new society. In the countryside, life may have gone on very much as usual, but elsewhere, especially in the urban centers, Assyrian values, lifestyles, culture, and economic measures prevailed.¹⁷⁷

However, some recent work has led others to argue that despite the hardships suffered, Judah actually grew after the invasion and actually reached its zenith demographically. Observing discrepancies between the surveys and excavations,

---

was, in my judgment these comparisons further undermine the credibility of Sennacherib's claims.

173. Zevit ("Implicit Population Figures," 364) thinks the actual population claimed by Sennacherib "is less than half of what Sennacherib's scribes recorded (or almost 100,000 short if Jerusalem and the southern hills are included)." He suggests that Sennacherib's annals do not claim to have deported but merely 'claimed' them as spoil, despite leaving them in the land to rebuild.

174. Dever, *Beyond the Texts*, 563. Similarly, Elayi (*Sennacherib*, 73) argues, "The figure of forty-six given for the fortified cities of Judah conquered was probably exaggerated, because it is doubtful that they were so numerous."

175. Even those doubting the number of deportees claimed in the Assyrian annals held to the general reliability of the claims of forty-six fortified cities. Cf. Rainey and Notley, *The Sacred Bridge*, 243, 245; Gallagher, *Sennacherib's Campaign*, 261; Mayer, "Sennacherib's Campaign," 177; Faust, "Settlement and Demography," 168. Of course, some recent work still assumes the accuracy of the claim. For example, Borowski writes, "When Sennacherib claimed in his Annals that he besieged and destroyed 'forty-six of [Hezekiah's] strong, walled cities, as well as the countless small towns in their vicinity,' he probably did not exaggerate. Almost every Judahite site that was occupied at the time shows signs of destruction." Cf. Borowski, "Sennacherib in Judah—the Devastating Consequences of an Assyrian Military Campaign," 35*.

176. Dever, *Beyond the Texts*, 563.

177. Ibid., 564.

Finkelstein was the first to suggest that the seventh century was one of demographic growth for Judah, outside of the Shephelah.[178] Faust took this position further, leveraging archaeological surveys, and argued persuasively that Judah's peak was in fact the seventh, not the eighth century.[179] Zevit, independent of Faust, has argued that the devastation was not as widespread as previously thought, suggesting Sennacherib captured many cities but did not destroy them.[180] His reconstruction suggests that the average Judahites were likely not that much affected by Sennacherib's campaign.[181] In Faust's view, "the gloomy description of that period is a result mainly of our biased perspective."[182]

As we have seen, it is clear that the entire country was not devastated by the Assyrians as some areas show signs of prosperous existence both before and after the 701 BCE invasion.[183] After the invasion, Jerusalem was left as a city with no rivals and was poised for success.[184] The capital expanded significantly, possibly due to the immigration from the Shephelah after the invasion.[185] The archaeological evidence does not suggest that Judah's territory was limited to the area around Jerusalem after the Assyrian invasion.[186] Evidently, Jerusalem continued to control the countryside.[187] As we will see, following the Assyrian withdrawal, settlements once again increased, with new towns and growth in rural areas.[188] In his study that looked at Judaean material culture (Judean Pillar Figurines [JPF], rosette stamps,

---

178. Finkelstein, "The Archaeology of the Days of Manasseh," 174–5.

179. Faust, "Settlement and Demography." More recently, in *Judah in the Neo-Babylonian Period*, 149–66.

180. Zevit, "Implicit Population Figures," 361.

181. Regarding the Judahites in 701 BCE he writes, "Not much happened to them personally." Ibid., 365. Master similarly concludes that "Judah's economy was shocked and diminished by Sennacherib's campaigns, but it was not radically altered." Cf. Daniel M. Master, "From the Buqe'ah to Ashkelon," in *Exploring the Longue Durée: Essays in Honor of Lawrence E. Stager* (ed. Schloen; Winona Lake, IN; Eisenbrauns, 2009), 313.

182. Faust, "Settlement and Demography," 11. Cf. Faust, "Shephelah in the Iron Age," 214–15.

183. Ofer, "Monarchic Period."

184. Lynn Tatum, "King Manasseh and the Royal Fortress at Horvat 'uza," *BA* 54 (1991): 141–2.

185. Faust, "The Settlement of Jerusalem's Western Hill." Cf. Magen Broshi, "Expansion of Jerusalem in the Reigns of Hezekiah and Manasseh," *IEJ* 24 (1974); Lester L. Grabbe, "The Kingdom of Judah from Sennacherib's Invasion to the Fall of Jerusalem: If We Had Only the Bible …," in *Good Kings and Bad Kings* (ed. Grabbe; JSOTSup, 393; ESHM, 5; New York: T&T Clark, 2005), 83.

186. Becking, "Chronology: A Skeleton without Flesh?" 69.

187. Helga Weippert, *Palästina in vorhellenistischer Zeit* (HdAr, 2; Munich: C. H. Beck, 1988), 559–681.

188. Finkelstein, "The Archaeology of the Days of Manasseh," 174–80; Tatum, "King Manasseh," 142.

inscribed scale weights, etc.) and their relation to what the borders of Judah were in the eighth-seventh century, Kletter concluded that Judah's borders remained basically the same throughout these centuries, at least until the Babylonian invasions of the sixth century.[189]

Archaeological excavations show Judah enjoying a time of "rebuilding and relative prosperity" after Sennacherib's withdrawal.[190] In fact, the rebuilding appears to take place rapidly following 701 BCE.[191] The return to prosperity occurred early in the seventh century.[192] Some scholars place the time of Judah's recovery and prosperity in Manasseh's reign.[193] However, the likely dates for Hezekiah's reign, 715–686 BCE, would actually place much of this progress still within Hezekiah's tenure.[194] The seventh century in Judah experienced extensive economic prosperity

189. Raz Kletter, "Pots and Polities: Material Remains of Late Iron Age Judah in Relation to Its Political Borders," *BASOR* 314 (1990) 28.
190. Stern, *Archaeology of the Land of the Bible*, 163.
191. Ibid., 130–1.
192. Finkelstein and Silberman, *The Bible Unearthed*, 265–9.
193. For example, some scholars have suggested that Manasseh reclaimed the territory lost after Sennacherib's invasion. E.g., Harold Lewis Ginsberg, "Judah and the Transjordan States from 734 to 582 B.C.E.," in *Alexander Marx Jubilee Volume* (ed. Lieberman; New York: The Jewish Theological Seminary of America, 1950), 349–5;. S. W Bulbach, "Judah in the Reign of Manasseh" (PhD Dissertation, New York University, 1981); Tatum, "King Manasseh"; Anson F Rainey, "Manasseh, King of Judah, in the Whirlpool of the Seventh Century B.C.E.," in *Kinattiltu Sa Ddirdti. Raphael Kutscher Memorial Volume* (ed. Rainey; Tel Aviv: Institute of Archaeology; Tel Aviv: Occasional Publications, 1993), 147–64.
194. See Na'aman, "Hezekiah," 236–9. Of course, the problems with dating Hezekiah's reign are well known and related to 2 Kgs 18:13, which puts Sennacherib's invasion of 701 BCE occurring in Hezekiah's fourteenth year (2 Kgs 18:13). This appears to contradict 2 Kgs 18:9-10, which informs us that Hezekiah was in his sixth year when Samaria fell to Assyria in 722 BCE. In order to solve the problem, some have suggested that 2 Kgs 18:13 originally referred to an earlier Assyrian invasion by Sargon *c*. 715 BCE (Becking, "Chronology: A Skeleton without Flesh?") or 713–11 BCE (Jenkins, "Hezekiah's Fourteenth Year"). However, this reconstruction is too speculative, and, as Matty (*Sennacherib's Campaign*, 127) opines, "It seems hazardous to infer a date of 715 for a first campaign on the basis of 18:13a alone, given that no details about the campaign are reported in either the Assyrian or the biblical records." A simpler solution to Hezekiah's fourteenth year would be to emend the text from Hezekiah's "fourteenth" year to his "twenty-fourth" or "twenty-seventh" year (Rawlinson, *The Five Great Monarchies*, II, 434 n.12) to make the date a better fit with the dating of the fall of Samaria. Of course, with no textual witnesses to support this emendation, this approach should be rejected. Alternatively, a plausible literary solution to the problem suggests that the reference to the fourteenth year was an invention of a later compiler who arrived at it by subtracting the fifteen-year extension of Hezekiah's life in 2 Kgs 20:6 from Hezekiah's twenty-nine-year reign. However, most studies conclude that the reference in 2 Kgs 18:13 is from archival material and not the work of a later compiler (Grabbe, "Reflections on the Discussion," 319; Cogan and Tadmor, *II Kings*, 288). Probably the

connected with not only agricultural and mineral production in the south but also extensive trade. Much of the south evinces increased settlement on a never-before-seen scale. As Stern writes, "The results, as reflected by archaeological evidence, were nonetheless immediately successful and the re-building process appears to have been rapid, starting perhaps *as early as the last days of Hezekiah* and certainly during the reign of Manasseh" [emphasis mine].[195] The development of the south was, some suggest, motivated by efforts to benefit from natural resources like bitumen.[196] Finkelstein suggested the expansion into the desert was to compensate for the agricultural loss of the Shephelah.[197] It is clear that many of these new sites produced grain,[198] with some suggesting the area became the center of grain production (some suggesting it became "the 'grain basket' of the entire region").[199] Archaeological evidence from Jerusalem evinces extensive trade from quite distant trading partners. For example, the fish bones and shells found in Jerusalem show evidence of trade from not only the Mediterranean but also the Red Sea and the Nile River.[200] Some inscriptions suggest trade with South Arabia and as far as

proposal most likely to solve the issue is one that accounts for years of co-regencies of Judahite kings (Edwin R. Thiele, *Mysterious Numbers of the Hebrew Kings: A Reconstruction of the Chronology of the Kingdoms of Israel and Judah* (Chicago, IL: University of Chicago Press, 1951). Egyptian evidence shows the practice of co-regencies (joint rule) of father and son was intended to secure the succession of the dynasty, and co-regencies may have been the norm in Judah since Athaliah nearly destroyed the Davidic dynasty (2 Kgs 11:1). Cf. Nadav Na'aman, "Historical and Chronological Notes on the Kingdoms of Israel and Judah in the 8th Century BC," *VT* 36 (1986): 91. If so, Hezekiah's accession to the throne in Hoshea's third year (2 Kgs 18:1) refers to when his co-regency with his father Ahaz began. The later synchronization with Hoshea's reign (2 Kgs 18:9-10) continues to reflect his co-regency. However, the twenty-nine years ascribed to Hezekiah in 2 Kgs 18:2 covered only Hezekiah's time as sole ruler (Na'aman, "Historical and Chronological," 89), as did the reference to Hezekiah's fourteenth year in 2 Kgs 18:13. Thus, the dates for Hezekiah's sole reign were *c.* 715–686. Cf. Na'aman, "Hezekiah," 236–9.

195. Stern, *Archaeology of the Land of the Bible*, 131.

196. Larwence E. Stager, "Farming in the Judean Desert During the Iron Age," *BASOR* 221 (1976); Beit Arieh, "The Dead Sea Region: An Archaeological Perspective," in *The Dead Sea, the Lake and Its Setting* (eds. Niemi et al.; Oxford: Oxford University Press, 1997).

197. Finkelstein, "The Archaeology of the Days of Manasseh," 169–87.

198. Stager, "Farming."

199. Avraham Faust and Ehud Weiss, "Judah, Philistia, and the Mediterranean World: Reconstructing the Economic System of the Seventh Century B.C.E.," *BASOR* 338 (2005): 80.

200. H. K. Mienis, "Molluscs," in *Excavations at the City of David 1978-1985, Vol. 3: Stratigraphical, Environmental, and Other Reports* (eds. de Groot and Ariel; Qedem; Jerusalem: Institute of Archaeology, Hebrew University of Jerusalem), 129; Faust and Weiss, "Judah, Philistia," 75.

Greece.²⁰¹ Jerusalem expanded and became a center of trade, described by Auld and Steiner as follows:

> Inhabited by rich merchants and artisans with their families and servants …
> Several inscriptions … may signify Arab traders living in the city … Luxury goods were imported into Judah. Excavations in and around the city have revealed the following imports: wood or wooden furniture from North Syria, ivory from Mesopotamia, decorative shells from the Red Sea, wine jars from Greece or Cyprus, fine pottery bowls from Assyria, scarabs from Egypt, and fish from the Mediterranean. Bronze ingots must have been imported from either Transjordan or Cyprus.²⁰²

As Holladay has concluded,

> Jerusalem itself withstood the Assyrian siege [sic], despite the loss of magnificently fortified Lachish and the destruction of virtually every other fortified settlement. And, clearly, Hezekiah and Jerusalem prospered and grew under the Assyrians, with every indication of an explosion in literacy and written legal documentation, to say nothing of unparalleled literary activity (the "Book found in the Temple" and Jeremiah's scroll, if nothing else).²⁰³

Thus, it seems clear that in the seventh century Judah expanded and prospered in mineral production, agricultural growth, as well as in extensive trade. This is clearly seen not only in Jerusalem but also in the wider kingdom of Judah that expanded and reached its demographic zenith in the seventh century.²⁰⁴ Even the Shephelah began to recover in the early seventh century.²⁰⁵ Furthermore, as Faust has underscored, the establishment of many new towns and/or settlement activity occurs after the Assyrian invasion (e.g., Ein Gedi,²⁰⁶ 'Aroer, Tel Mesos, Khirbet

---

201. Y. Shiloh, "South Arabian Inscriptions from the City of David," *PEQ* 119 (1987): 9–18; Benjamin Sass, "Arabs and Greeks in Late First Temple Jerusalem," *PEQ* 122 (1990): 59–61.

202. A. Graeme Auld and M. L. Steiner, *Jerusalem* (Cambridge: Lutterworth, 1996), 63–4.

203. John S. Holladay Jr., "Hezekiah's Tribute, Long-Distance Trade, and the Wealth of Nations ca. 1000–600 BC: A New Perspective," in *Confronting the Past: Archaeological and Historical Essays on Ancient Israel in Honor of William G. Devers* (eds. Gitin et al.; Winona Lake, IN: Eisenbrauns, 2006), 328.

204. As Stern (*Archaeology of the Land of the Bible*, 131) writes, "The result of this effort was a new, dense network of settlements, many more than during the period before the Assyrian conquest, while Jerusalem became a relatively large city, probably also much larger than before, and served as its capital."

205. Finkelstein and Na'aman, "Judahite Shephelah," 79.

206. Though Ein Gedi was possibly founded in the eighth century. See Finkelstein, "The Archaeology of the Days of Manasseh," 175; Vaughn, *Theology, History*, 72–4.

Radum; Ras el Kharrûbeh, Khirbet es Sid, Khirbet Shilhah, Mezad Michmas)[207] along with an unprecedented number of forts (e.g., fourteen new forts appear in Judah in the seventh century, compared to approximately five in the eighth century).[208] Furthermore, as we have seen, several sites grew after the Assyrian withdrawal.

2.3.1 Pax Assyriaca

The success and expansion of Judah in the seventh century have largely been explained by the theory of Pax Assyriaca.[209] The term Pax Assyriaca is commonly used for a period of "peace" and even prosperity that resulted from Assyrian rule *c.* 700–630 BCE.[210] (In my opinion, the term "peace" should be replaced by "pacification" with a sinister sense given to it by Pinker who describes it as "not just the bringing about of peace but the imposition of absolute control by a coercive government."[211] Judahites were less likely to die in a war during this period, but were under the thumb of the Assyrian tyrant.) It is widely held that the Assyrians used their military power to unite the disparate ancient Near Eastern culture into "single political structure."[212] The aim of their military conquest

207. Faust, "Settlement and Demography," 177.

208. Dever, *Beyond the Texts*, 578.

209. Dever (ibid., 580) opines, "The Pax Assyriaca was no doubt the reason for Jerusalem's continued growth and prosperity" and thinks this explains Faust's evidence of Judahite prosperity in the seventh century (620 n.20).

210. See Miller and Hayes, *History*, 365–70. Sometimes Pax Assyriaca is referred to as an Assyrian policy. E.g., Bunimovits and Lederman, "Archaeology of Border Communities," 140. Cf. Lipschits, "The Long Seventh Century" 24.

211. Steven Pinker, *The Better Angels of Our Nature: Why Violence Has Declined* (New York: Viking, 2011), 58.

212. Frederick Mario Fales, "On Pax Assyriaca in the Eighth-Seventh Centuries BCE and Its Implications," in *Isaiah's Vision of Peace in Biblical and Modern International Relations: Swords into Plowshares* (New York, 2008), 17. Cf. Oded Lipschits, "The Changing Faces of Kingship in Judah under Assyrian Rule," in *The Changing Faces of Kingship in Syria-Palestine 1500–500 BCE* (eds. Agustius Gianto and Peter Dubovský; AOAT, 459. Münster: Ugarit-Verlag, 2018) 119–21; Oded Lipschits, "The Long Seventh Century," 9–44. There are different theories regarding how Assyrian imperialism impacted annexed territories and vassals. Some see only economic impositions and contributions made by Assyria. E.g., Angelika Berlejung, "The Assyrians in the West: Assyrianization, Colonialism, Indifference, or Development Policy?" in *Congress Volume Helsinki 2010* (ed. M. Nissinen; Leiden: Brill, 2012), 21–60. Others suggest Assyrian imperialism entailed cultural, religious, and intellectual contributions. E.g., Simon Parpola, "Assyria's Expansion in the Eighth and Seventh Centuries and Its Long-Term Repercussions in the West," in *Symbiosis, Symbolism, and the Power of the Past* (eds. Dever and Gittin; Winona Lake, IN: Eisenbrauns, 2003) 99–111. Cf. Ariel M. Bagg, "Palestine under Assyrian Rule: A New Look at the Assyrian Imperial Policy in the West." *JAOS* 133 (2013): 119–44; Dever, *Beyond the Texts*, 584;

was not destruction but the subjection of other lands to their yoke and their incorporation into the Assyrian empire.[213] This incorporation was the result of the imposition of an Assyrian imperial ideology aimed at commercial exploitation benefiting Assyria.[214] Often this resulted in economic growth of one region, while causing economic deterioration in another.[215] As Angelika Berleung describes it, "[Assyrian] development policy and relief management were organized from the Assyrian side, but only according to the limited and pragmatic Assyrian interests. Minimum investments were made, where necessary for later exploitation."[216]

Pax Assyriaca is often leveraged to suggest that the reason for the recovery of Judah, and Jerusalem's growth, following the Assyrian invasions is due to their being part of the Assyrian economic machine.[217] Judah became part of the agricultural production that served Assyrian trading interests. Evidence for this "enforced peace" has been found in Philistine sites like Tel Miqne/Ekron (which showed significant growth post-701 and was the location of a well-developed olive oil industry).[218] Dever has also pointed to Ashkelon and Ashdod as benefiting

---

Bradley J. Parker, *The Mechanics of Empire: The Northern Frontier of Assyria as a Case Study in Imperial Dynamics* (Helsinki: Neo-Assyrian Text Corpus Project, 2001).

213. Though when describing the economic interrelationship between Assyria and their conquered lands Stern prefers the term "the period of Assyrian domination" and does not use the term Pax Assyriaca. Cf. Stern, *Archaeology of the Land of the Bible*, 147.

214. Seymour Gitin, "The Philistines in the Prophetic Texts: An Archaeological Perspective," in *Hesed Ve-Emet: Studies in Honor of Ernest S. Frerichs* (eds. Magness and Gitin; Brown Judaic Studies; Atlanta, GA: Scholars Press), 276–8. Cf. Seymour Gitin, "The Neo-Assyrian Empire and Its Western Periphery: The Levant, with a Focus on Philistine Ekron," in *Assyria 1995: Proceedings of the 10th Anniversary Symposium of the Neo-Assyrian Texts Corpus Project, September 7–11, 1995* (eds. Parpola and Whiting; Helsinki: University of Helsinki, 1997), 77–103.

215. For example, some think the Pax Assyriaca resulted in the flourishing of Philistine economy at the expense of the Judahite economy. Cf. Bunimovits and Lederman, "Archaeology of Border Communities," 140.

216. Berlejung, "The Assyrians in the West," 50.

217. As Lipschits ("The Long Seventh Century," 17) writes, "In the first two-thirds of the seventh century BCE, Judah enjoyed the economic prosperity of the entire region under Assyrian rule." For example, Knauf ("Sennacherib at the Berezina," 149) opines that "the growth of Jerusalem in the seventh century (up to 50–60 ha) was more due to Assyrian interests and 'aid in development' than to untraceable fugitives from the North."

218. Dever (*Beyond the Texts*, 581) suggests it produced up to 1,000 tons of oil each year. The excavator of the site, Gitin, argues that its prosperity was the "direct result of the stability produced by the pace enforced in Philistia and Judah by Assyria." Cf. Seymour Gitin, "The Effects of Urbanization on a Philistine City-State: Tel Miqne-Ekron in the Iron Age II Period," in *The Proceedings of the Tenth World Congress of Jewish Studies 1989* (ed. Assaf; Jerusalem: World Union of Jewish Studies, 1990), 280; Gitin, "Tel Miqne-Ekron in the Seventh Century B.C.; City Plan Development and the Oil Industry"; Seymour Gitin, "Philistines in the Books of Kings," in *The Books of Kings: Sources, Composition,*

greatly from Assyrian rule, as evinced in their growth in wine production, and also "large-scale weaving."[219] The economic growth of Philistia under Assyrian hegemony is widely held. Given the economic prosperity and expansion of Judah as well, it would seem that Pax Assyriaca was beneficial for the entire region.[220]

At the same time, Assyria in the early seventh century had to deal with continuous conflict away from the Levant. Sennacherib's fourth campaign began in 700 BCE against Babylon.[221] The fifth campaign began in 697 as regions in Anatolia to the northwest of Assyria rebelled (Mount Nipur[222] and Ukku).[223] As Elayi writes, "In other words, the Pax Assyriaca lasted two years."[224] Babylon (Assyria eventually destroyed Babylon in 689 BCE) and Elam, as well as the Arabs[225]

Historiography and Reception (eds. Halpern and Lemaire; VTSup; Leiden: Brill, 2010), 335-47. Cf. Avraham Faust, "The Interests of the Assyrian Empire in the West: Olive Oil Production as a Test Case," *JESHO* 54 (2011): 62-86. Finkelstein suggested Judah paid their tribute "in kind" was olives shipped to Tel Miqne. Cf. Finkelstein, "Archaeology of the Days of Manasseh," 180. Rather than seeing both Philistia and Judah as wholly serving Assyrian interests, Stern (*Archaeology of the Land of the Bible*, 112) suggests that "Philistine production was in competition with that of Judah, which also produced large quantities in surrounding settlements, such as Tel Batash (Timnah) and Gezer, where similar oil presses were uncovered, though, admittedly, not in such large numbers."

219. Dever, *Beyond the Texts*, 581. Dever notes Stager's suggestion that Ashkelon's difficulties in producing enough grain to feed its people was made up for by its commercial wine production. Cf. Stager, "Impact of the Sea Peoples," 332-48.

220. At times the supposed benefit of Assyrian hegemony forgets the nature of the enforced peace. While from a perspective of economic output the historian can view it this way, from the perspective of the conquered peoples at the time, it is questionable the extent to which the relationship was viewed positively. Some writers seem to suggest that these conquered kingdoms saw submitting to Assyria as entirely beneficial. For example, Stern (*Archaeology of the Land of the Bible*, 10) writes, "The kingdoms of Ammon, Moab, and Edom chose to surrender without a battle, willingly accepting Assyrian domination for the benefits it promised." It seems unlikely the people submitted due to "the benefits it promised" alone but was doubtless motivated by the "benefit" of not being the subject of Assyrian military action and destruction. Lipschits ("Long Seventh Century," 24) suggests Assyrian policy lasted so long in Judah because of "how well suited such systems were to the Judean elite and ruling classes." Of course, the elites participated in a rebellion under Hezekiah, making suspect such claims. Though some saw Assyrian policies as benefits, obviously these were viewed as detriments by others.

221. Elayi, *Sennacherib*, 89.
222. Modern Judi Dagh.
223. RINAP 3.1:134, 17.iv.18-51; RINAP 3.1:210, 26.i.14-18; RINAP 3.1:222, 34.16-18.
224. Elayi, *Sennacherib*, 94.
225. As Miller and Hayes note, a fragmentary inscription notes military action against Arab rulers, though it does not specify the nature of the problem or the location of the conflict. Cf. Miller and Hayes, *History*, 365.

caused much trouble for the Empire. Furthermore, hostility marked relations between Assyria and the Twenty-Fifth dynasty in Egypt (with the Ethiopian Pharaohs) who were consistent thorns on the Empire's side during the early seventh century.[226] Given the years without Assyrian aggression in the Levant (especially as they had their hands full with Anatolia, Elam, and Babylon), it seems likely that this absence of Assyrian aggression against Judah could have been interpreted as Assyrian weakness and the result understood by Judahites as due to the success of Hezekiah's rebellion. As mentioned earlier, Knauf goes so far as to suggest that "after his narrow escape at/from Eltekeh" in the 701 BCE campaign, Sennacherib "had no intention of returning to southern Canaan."[227] Of course, as noted in the biblical text, Sennacherib himself was murdered by his sons, which was followed by a short fraternal war for the throne.[228]

Despite Assyrian setbacks and wars elsewhere in the empire, most still hold that the seventh century represented a stronger Assyrian hold over Judah than ever.[229] As Miller and Hayes assert, "Probably during Manasseh's reign Assyria controlled the economic, religious, and political life of Judah with a strong hand."[230] This is argued on the supposition that the third campaign was utterly successful and resulted in Assyria placing more "stringent controls" on Judah following their rebellion.[231] They further assert, "Where the Assyrians had the opportunity to exercise firm control, as in Judah, they would certainly have done so."[232] The question, of course, is what opportunity they had to do so.[233] Given the serious rebellions with which Assyria was distracted in the early seventh century and the fact that Hezekiah remained on the throne, it is open to question whether or not the result of the third campaign was more control over Judah than before the rebellion.

226. Esarhaddon (680–669 BCE) and Assurbanipal (668–627 BCE) both campaigned against Egypt during the years 674–663 BCE. Cf. Stern, *Archaeology of the Land of the Bible*, 3; Miller and Hayes, *History*, 365.

227. Knauf, "Sennacherib at the Berezina," 149.

228. Cf. Luckenbill, *Annals of Sennacherib*, 161; *ANET* 289–90; Miller and Hayes, *History*, 365.

229. The greatest extent of the Assyrian empire followed Sennacherib's reign during the tenure of Esarhaddon and Assurbanipal. Stern (*Archaeology of the Land of the Bible*, 3) notes that Assyrian control of Palestine may have been lost sometime before Assurbanipal's death in 627 BCE as "we do not possess any documents attesting to Assyrian presence here after 645 BCE." In fact, Stern suggests that "Assyrian administration in Palestine collapsed totally around 640 BCE" (107).

230. Miller and Hayes, *History*, 370.

231. Ibid.

232. Ibid., 371.

233. Ibid.

We see more clearly the impact of Assyrian rule in Philistia, with Philistine sites held up by scholars, as the clearest examples of Assyrian management.[234] Along the Via Maris, Assyrian fortresses have been discovered (Rishon le-Zion, Tell Jemmeh, Sheikh Zuweid, Ruqeish, Tel Sera', Tel Haror, etc.),[235] providing the clearest evidence of Assyrian influence in Philistia. However, it is open to question whether Judah had the same amount of Assyrian management involved in their economy. Miller and Hayes speculate that the Assyrians may have appointed an "Assyrian high commissioner in Judah" to run things after Hezekiah's rebellion, though they note that "there is no reference to the appointment" but think "the practice of doing so elsewhere could suggest that this was the case here."[236] Should we assume the same level of economic management was held by Assyria in territories where they enforced regime change and placed a ruler of their choice on the throne (Philistia) as with a kingdom wherein the rebel king remained in place?[237] A higher degree of Assyrian involvement in Philistia seems logical given the fact Assyria had replaced

---

234. Dever (*Beyond the Texts*, 584) suggests, "By and large, however, the Assyrian-managed economy is currently best witnessed in the south at sites such as Ashkelon and Ekron."

235. Stern, *Archaeology of the Land of the Bible*, 3. Though some of these were built after the Egyptian conquest by the Assyrians and thus date quite a bit later.

236. Miller and Hayes, *History*, 371. The level of control assumed in Judah (which remained an independent state) should not be equated to that of Assyrian provinces. Eph'al looked at the titles of governors in Assyrian eponym lists and found that the only Assyrian provinces mentioned in Assyrian administrative texts are Megiddo, Samirina, and Dor, none of which include Judah's territory. Eph'al had pointed out that we only have evidence for Megiddo and Samirina as Assyrian provinces in western Palestine. Cf. Israel Eph'al, "The Assyrian Domination of Palestine," in *The World History of the Jewish People* (ed. Mazar; Jerusalem: Rutgers University Press, 1979). However, later Fales and Postgate published an Assyrian text that also mentions the province of Dor along with Megiddo and Samirina. Cf. Frederick Mario Fales and J. N. Postgate, *Imperial Administrative Records, II. Provincial and Military Administration* (SAAS, 11; Helsinki: Neo-Assyrian Text Corpus Project, 1995). The city of Dor was likely the provincial capital of the region that includes Phoenicia and the coast of western Galilee. Cf. Stern, *Archaeology of the Land of the Bible*, 12. Later, under Assurbanipal, an eponym list from 669 BCE notes that an Assyrian governor was appointed to oversee Gaza, Ashdod, and Ashkelon. Ibid., 106. No such reference to an Assyrian governor to oversee Judah is extant.

237. Some have suggested that because Hezekiah was the ringleader, he "suffered the most" as "much of his land was cut off and given away." Cf. Borowski, "Sennacherib in Judah," 36*. However, to what extent Hezekiah lost his own territory, and not just the Philistine territory he had annexed, is open to question. Besides this, Sennacherib obviously had a heavier hand with other rebel kingdoms taking direct control of their government by replacing their kings with puppet kings (Ashkelon, Sidon, kings of Shamsimurunu, Arvad, Gebal, Ashdod, Beth Ammon, Moab, and Edom). In this way, Hezekiah suffered the least of the rebels.

the Philistine rebel leaders with puppet kings. Clearly, they dominated Philistia more than Judah in the third campaign.

Judahite towns on the Judahite–Philistine border were hit hard by Sennacherib's invasion, but clearly some sites were being rebuilt.[238] Throughout Israel's history, the border between Judah and Philistia was somewhat fluid and moved back and forth somewhat throughout their coexistence.[239] Areas such as Beth-shemesh, Tell-Batash (Timna), Azekah, and others were likely claimed by both Judah and Philistia at different times, and the border probably fluctuated in accordance with power struggles and/or ecological necessity.[240] Stern suggests that the Judahite western border was "more elaborate" than the other Judahite borders and "it still faced Philistia in the first part of the 7th century B.C.E. and Egyptian Philistia in the second part of that century."[241] Alternatively, Dever suggests the Judahite–Philistine border became porous in the early seventh century with the areas becoming "a cosmopolitan mix that contained both Judahite and Philistine elements."[242] Nevertheless, the situation may have been viewed positively by Judahites as Dever notes that Judah did "retain some degree of self-identity, even a putative border with Philistia."[243]

Whether the prosperity of Judah was due to the Pax Assyriaca, as is widely held, or due to the fact that Assyria was distracted and less interested in Judah at the time (and Judah was emboldened by the Assyrian withdrawal that left their king on the throne), the nation clearly prospered and expanded in the seventh century. The question to be asked is how this prosperity would have been viewed by those within Judah. In what way did the economic prosperity that followed the withdrawal of Assyria and the aftermath of Hezekiah's rebellion shape their view (positively or negatively) of their leader and his leadership during the Assyrian crisis at the end of the eighth century? Did the recovery make up for the evident destruction and

---

238. Contrary to some who earlier argued that only 39 of the known 354 Judahite settlements were reestablished after 701 BCE. See. Y. Dagan, "The Shephelah." Archaeological evidence has continued to uncover more seventh-century settlements. Stern notes that "two sites on the extreme western border of Judah facing Philistia, Tell e-Safi and Tel Harasim, which are also located one beside the other, produced rosette seal impressions and a few Judaean clay figurines, which are the best chronological evidence for the existence of a 7th century BCE site." Cf. Stern, *Archaeology of the Land of the Bible*, 142.

239. See Dever, *Beyond the Texts*, 317–30.

240. Dever (*Beyond the Texts*) suggests that borders "were constantly shifting with changing environmental conditions" (223) and that "both the geographical and the psychological boundaries are always in flux" (224).

241. Stern, *Archaeology of the Land of the Bible*, 143. He concludes, "It is hard to believe, therefore, that behind such an elaborate system of defensive lines, the interior of the country remained deserted and unsettled!"

242. Dever, *Beyond the Texts*, 584.

243. Ibid.

devastation left in the wake of Sennacherib's campaign? Again, looking at the outcomes of conflicts from military history can be suggestive, if not instructive. However, before we turn to look at such examples from military history, we will first turn to other types of evidence relevant to historical reconstruction: Assyrian and biblical textual evidence.

Chapter 3

ASSYRIAN TEXTS

Many extant Assyrian texts reference the war of 701 BCE. The inscription on the Rassam cylinder dates to within one year of Sennacherib's third campaign and is the earliest witness to the events of 701 BCE. The text appears to have been "mass produced" as evidenced by the many extant copies, suggesting its importance to Assyrian interests at the time.[1] The first copy of the text discovered in modern history was the Taylor Prism[2] (written c. 691 BCE),[3] which is, likely for that reason, quoted more often than the Rassam cylinder.[4] It is thought these texts were part of a state archive.[5] The Chicago and Taylor Prisms and Bull 4 correspond so closely (other than orthographical and minor deviations) that they are often translated together.[6] The Rassam cylinder corresponds closely except in its more elaborate description of the tribute. Given the few deviations between the Rassam account and the Taylor inscription (and other copies), we will treat the annalistic accounts together but will note any substantive divergences. Historical reconstructions of the events on the basis of the inscription have not reached consensus. There is debate as to the extent it presents the events chronologically (or not), what omissions were made, to what extent hyperbole is employed, and to what extent events are shaped by political spin instead of a necessity to represent history.[7]

---

1. Luckenbill, *The Annals of Sennacherib*; Frahm, *Einleitung* 47–61; Eckart Frahm, *Historische und Historisch-Literarische Texte* (WDOG, 121; Wiesbaden: Harrassowitz, 2009), 79–80; Grayson and Novotny, *The Royal Inscriptions of Sennacherib*, 55–69.

2. Col. J. Taylor apparently acquired it at Nebi Yunus in 1830, and Sir Henry Rawlinson, on behalf of the British Museum, purchased it from his widow in 1855. First published by Rawlinson and Norris.

3. The Chicago Prism is similarly dated to c. 689 BCE, but its discovery was much later when it was purchased by J. H. Breasted in 1920.

4. Cogan, "Cross-Examining," 54.

5. Frahm, *Historische*, 9; Cogan, "Cross-Examining," 54.

6. E.g., "Sennacherib's Siege of Jerusalem," translated by Mordechai Cogan (COS 2.119B: 302–3).

7. As Cogan and Tadmor (*II Kings*, 250) write, "The richness of literary evidence for the events of 701, as conflicting as it is, is no different from the sometimes contradictory reports

3.1 Chronological Matters

The chronological intentions of the text have been viewed variously by scholars with literary analyses of the Assyrian account reading the structure of the inscription in different ways. Many point out the presentation is not strictly chronological.[8] Some[9] suggest that it is instead geographical, proceeding from North to South (which Knauf thinks has many parallels with chronology since the army came from the north).[10] Some think the Assyrian army split into contingents and attacked different cities at the same time, while others are not so sure. For example, Cogan acknowledges that "we cannot know whether the army fought as a single corps or was at times divided into separate military units."[11] Alternatively, Mayer asserts that it was "strategically impossible" for the army to have not "split up into divisions."[12] While sure answers to this question are unachievable at present, such knowledge would factor into any conclusions regarding the chronological order in which cities and areas were attacked.

Tadmor and Younger both view the text as presenting the military campaign in two parts.[13] Tadmor sees the first section depicting enemies surrendering without a battle and the second presenting the defeat of enemies after a battle.[14] Younger understands the first section to depict loyal kings of the West, while the second showed disloyal kings, with the first depicting easy conquests, and the latter more difficult victories.[15] Cogan discerns five sections in the Assyrian inscription that

---

that issue forth from modern-day battlefields and official government sources. Each report represents a partisan view and is grist for the historian's mill."

8. Elayi (*Sennacherib*, 52) confidently views the presentation in Sennacherib's annals as chronological, stating "as a matter of fact, this campaign comprised three phases: against Phoenicia, against Philistia, and against Judah." Matty (*Sennacherib's Campaign*, 42) similarly writes, "Sennacherib's third campaign had three phases: Phoenicia, Philistia and Judah."

9. Knauf, "Sennacherib at the Berezina," 142; Peter Dubovský, "Assyrians under the Walls of Jerusalem and the Confinement of Padi," *JNES* 75 (2016): 111.

10. Knauf, "Sennacherib at the Berezina," 142. Dubovský similarly thinks "the general outline … is most likely in chronological order." Cf. Dubovský, "Assyrians under the Walls of Jerusalem," 113. Elayi (*Sennacherib, King of Assyria*, 53) also views the geographical presentation as historical asserting that "Sennacherib followed a logical geographical route, and successively proceeded to Phoenicia, to Philistia southward, and to Judah eastward."

11. Cogan, "Cross-Examining," 72.

12. Mayer, "Sennacherib's Campaign," 175.

13. Tadmor, "Sennacherib's Campaign," 65–80; Younger, "Assyrian Involvement," 249.

14. Tadmor, "Sennacherib's Campaign," 71–3. Matty (*Sennacherib's Campaign*, 43) similarly notes that Sennacherib was not obviously engaged in military activities in the Phoenician phase of the campaign, as "according to the annals, in the first phase [Phoenicia] Sennacherib did not destroy, devastate or set cities on fire."

15. Younger, "Assyrian Involvement," 249. Similarly, Tadmor, "Sennacherib's Campaign," 71, 73; Gallagher, *Sennacherib's Campaign*, 117.

contrast rebellious and submissive vassals: (1) the escape of a rebellious vassal and submission of his nation; (2) submissive kings; (3) punishment of a rebellious vassal; (4) battles with rebellious vassals (and allies); and (5) the defeat of Hezekiah ("the most obstinate rebel").[16] All eventually submit to Sennacherib, as shown by gifts and tribute. Despite the variation in how the structure is understood, these studies viewed the inscription largely as chronological in its presentation, though each observed that some events were "presented out of order."[17] Gallagher detects a division into three sections, with the first concerning Phoenicia, the second Philistia, and the third Judah.[18] The following survey will adopt this structural view.

3.2 The Offensive against Phoenicia

The first section focuses on Sidon, and the king Lulî, referred to as the king of Sidon, when in fact he reigned from Tyre (Gallagher calls this "misleading"),[19] who fled from Sennacherib.[20] Mayer takes this initial focus on Sidon as chronologically historical, suggesting that Sennacherib bypassed "the mountains of Judah" to head straight for the coastal plain to begin his campaign.[21] Lulî is said to have fled from Sennacherib's "awesome splendor." His destination is not specified, with the text simply saying he went "overseas." We are not told why he feared Assyrian retribution.[22] Possibly he was a participant in the rebellion with Hezekiah and had withheld tribute, though nothing specific is said in that regard.[23] Later in the Rassam text, Ekron is said to have allied with Hezekiah, but no such alliance is intimated here.[24]

---

16. Cogan, "Cross-Examining," 55.
17. Younger, "Assyrian Involvement," 249.
18. Gallagher, *Sennacherib's Campaign*, 91–142. Followed by Dubovský, "Assyrians under the Walls of Jerusalem," 112. Matty (*Sennacherib's Campaign*, 42), as noted above, considers these "three phases" of the third campaign, "Phoenicia, Philistia and Judah."
19. Contra. Nadav Na'aman, "Sargon II and the Rebellion of the Cypriote Kings against Shilta of Tyre," *Or.N.S.* 67 (1998): 239–47. Cf. Gallagher, *Sennacherib's Campaign*, 96, 100. Elayi (*Sennacherib*, 55) suggests that "king of Sidon" simply meant that the king of Tyre "ruled over the double kingdom of Tyre and Sidon."
20. RINAP 3.1:4.32–34.
21. Mayer, "Sennacherib's Campaign," 175.
22. Cogan, "Cross-Examining," 58. Elayi (*Sennacherib*, 53) speculates that Sennacherib's priority was "the defeat of Lulî and the conquest of Tyre" because his father, Sargon, had been unable to take Tyre despite putting it to siege, though Sargon "boasted falsely of having conquered Tyre."
23. Mayer, "Sennacherib's Campaign," 175. Tyre was the capital of Phoenicia during Sargon's reign and contributed to Dur-Sharrukin as well as providing soldiers in the Assyrian forces. Gallagher, *Sennacherib's Campaign*, 92. They paid significant tribute and taxes, which likely led Lulî to join the rebellion—though this is not stated in the text.
24. Cogan, "Cross-Examining," 58.

Lulî flees and is never captured. Cogan points out that in the Rassam text Sennacherib "had failed to punish this unrepentant rebel personally" since he escaped overseas.[25] This is sometimes thought to bolster the credibility of the Rassam text since an enemy escaped Sennacherib's wrath.[26] However, probably to make up for that which might detract from Sennacherib's glory, later recensions of the story (Cylinder C) specify that Lulî died (that is he "disappeared forever" *šadašu ēmid*).[27] Since Rassam was written so soon after the battle, it is possible Lulî's location was unknown to the scribes who wrote (who were content to present his flight as cowardice) and that later recensions were not just making up his demise to make Sennacherib look good, but may have later learned of his fate and recorded it. If so, this would be an instance where later texts (e.g., Cylinder C) are in some respects actually more accurate than earlier texts (e.g., Rassam cylinder).[28] However, still later Assyrian texts (*c.* 694 BCE) make the claim that Lulî died "in that very year," that is, 701 BCE.[29] This, however, is likely *not* accurate given that Rassam did not mention it and it was written the following year (*c.* 700 BCE).[30] Gallagher considers this a "lie" that attempted to continue "an old Mesopotamian epic-heroic motif in which kings accomplish spectacular military feats within a single year."[31] Still, this embellishment may simply be an incident of editorial updating considered acceptable in ancient historiographic practice. Significantly, given this example of updating texts to the glory of Assyria, no later texts (as late as 684 BCE) mention the eventual death of Hezekiah, which may have implications regarding the dates of his reign (supporting our dates suggested earlier and discounting suggestions Hezekiah died in 698 BCE).[32]

25. Ibid. A later Bull inscription (RINAP 3.2:79, 46.18) puts Lulî's destination as "Iadnana" (Cyprus). Elayi (*Sennacherib*, 56) takes this at face value and further suggests that "he probably retired to his colony of Kition, where he could quietly continue to control Tyrian affairs, at least the island of Tyre."

26. Ibid., 72.

27. RINAP 3.1:95, 15.iii.5. Cf. *COS* 2.119B:302; Cogan, "Cross-Examining," 58; Frahm, *Einleitung* 66, T 10. Elayi compares the use of the phrase *šadašu ēmid*, "he disappeared" in Assurbanipal's annals and concludes it means "he died." See Elayi, *Sennacherib*, 57.

28. As Ben Zvi notes that such things "strongly undermine the principle that the closer to the events, the higher the historical accuracy of a document." Cf. Ben Zvi, "Malleability and Its Limits: Sennacherib's Campaign against Judah as a Case-Study," in *"Like a Bird in a Cage": The Invasion of Sennacherib in 701 BCE* (ed. Grabbe; JSOTSup, 363; ESHM, 4; London: Sheffield Academic Press, 2003), 96.

29. Bulls 2 and 3, Ins. 17–20.

30. Elayi (*Sennacherib*, 58) suggests Lulî "fled to Cyprus in 701 and died at some moment between 699 and 697."

31. Gallagher, *Sennacherib's Campaign*, 98.

32. Given that some think Hezekiah expired with a couple of years of the campaign in 701, it is significant that Assyrian recensions of the third campaign written after this date (up to 684 BCE) still refer to Hezekiah as if he was living, while his death would have made great fodder for divine punishment for his sin of rebellion. As Grabbe writes,

The summary inscription of 684 BCE on Bull colossus No. 2 expanded it further to explain Lulî's fleeing as due to his "fear" of battling Sennacherib, identifying his place of refuge explicitly as Cyprus, and attributing the cause of his death (he disappeared forever)[33] as due to "the terrifying appearance of the weapon of Assur."[34] Only Taharqo is said to have died in the exact way in Assyrian texts, leading Gallagher to suggest that Lulî died a natural death at Cyprus, just as Taharqo died "in the place where he had fled" away from the Assyrians.[35] Gallagher writes "the Assyrian scribes used a motif of the enemy being struck down by the flaming spendor [sic] of Assur's weapon when the enemy was too distant for the Assyrians to kill directly."[36] Interestingly, this more elaborate description of Lulî and his fate in the summary inscription of 684 BCE on Bull colossus No. 2 did *not* affect the later copying of the annalistic tradition that did not draw on it to expand its account despite the fact copies of the annals continued to be made.[37]

The annals boast of the entire Phoenician coast submitting to Sennacherib. How exactly did this occur? The submission of Sidon is said by the text to be due to "the terrifying nature of the weapon of Assur." Does this imply a peaceful submission by the rebels or does the expression attribute a victory in battle as due to the divine intervention of Assur (their god)? As Cogan has commented, this expression "hides more than it reveals because of its figurative nature."[38] Some have interpreted the phrase as indicating a peaceful surrender of Sidon and the surrounding towns.[39] The way the text is phrased may wish such a conclusion to

---

"Sennacherib's inscriptions continued to be revised at least until 691, yet Hezekiah's death is not mentioned, making it unlikely that he died in 698 as some have thought." Cf. Grabbe, "Introduction," 30. Surprisingly, perhaps in forgetting this evidence, elsewhere Grabbe writes, "If Manasseh's reign was anything like as long as portrayed in the biblical text, Hezekiah could not have lived much past 701 BCE." Cf. Grabbe, "The Kingdom of Judah from Sennacherib's Invasion," 101.

33. As seen in its use elsewhere, the phrase "indicates the death of its subject" (Gallagher, *Sennacherib's Campaign*, 94).

34. Cogan, "Cross-Examining," 59.

35. Elayi (*Sennacherib*, 57) also suggests Lulî "probably died of a natural death."

36. Gallagher, *Sennacherib's Campaign*, 99.

37. Cogan, "Cross-Examining," 59.

38. Ibid.

39. Knauf explicitly states that Sidon was captured "without a fight." Knauf, "Sennacherib at the Berezina," 142. Elayi (*Sennacherib*, 58) simply states that the cities "immediately submitted." Others do not reconstruct any battle. E.g., Gallagher, *Sennacherib's Campaign*, 104; H. Jacob Katzenstein, *The History of Tyre, from the Beginning of the Second Millennium B.C.E. until the Fall of the Neo-Babylonian Empire in 538 B.C.E.* (Jerusalem: Ben-Gurion of the Negev Press, 1997), 247. Mayer ("Sennacherib's Campaign," 175) seems to hold to a peaceful surrender as well, though he doesn't state it explicitly, writing, "The whole area … submitted and paid homage." Cogan and Tadmor (*II Kings*, 246) suggested all "the Phoenician coastal cities surrender to Sennacherib without a fight."

be drawn. A significant issue here is that Tyre ruled Phoenicia at the time, yet Sennacherib avoids mentioning the city.[40] Elayi explains this as due to the fact Sennacherib could not capture the city of Tyre, so "the Assyrian king denied its existence."[41] Gallagher speculates that Sidon may have been motivated to surrender in order to become the center of power instead of Tyre.[42] The reference to the splendor of the deity papers over what really happened in 701, but there is evidence that assumptions of a completely peaceful surrender are unlikely.

Ahlström suggested the expression inferred a battle with Tyre (the city from which Lulî ruled) after which Lulî fled.[43] Of course, as already mentioned, the Rassam text does not mention Tyre in the campaign, and no Sennacherib texts mention any Assyrian engagement with Tyre.[44] However, near the end of the Rassam text,[45] reference is made to the deportation of Tyrians, suggesting the Assyrian king did face resistance from the Phoenicians.[46] Other Phoenician cities are not mentioned here (perhaps because their surrender came more quickly?), so singling out Tyre would seem to betray that a military conflict did in fact occur in 701. Cogan cautions that we should not assume Sennacherib's time in Phoenicia "was a romp" and further points out that later Bull colossus inscription no. 2 also refers to Tyrian captives who built Sennacherib ships in preparation for war who most likely were captured during the third campaign.[47] However, the lack of reference to Tyre in the Rassam text may indicate that the city was *not* taken by Sennacherib[48] since the capture of the capital would have been a significant

---

40. This was observed long ago by Leo Lazarus Honor, *Sennacherib's Invasion of Palestine: A Critical Source Study* (COHP, 12; New York: Columbia, 1926), 19–22. Cf. Gallagher, *Sennacherib's Campaign*, 92.

41. Elayi, *Sennacherib*, 59.

42. Gallagher, *Sennacherib's Campaign*, 95. Elayi (*Sennacherib*, 58) similarly suggests Sennacherib's policy was "to take advantage of the rivalry between the two neighboring cities of Tyre and Sidon as a way of weakening the rebellious city and favoring the other city."

43. Gösta W. Ahlström, Diana V. Edelman, and Gary Orin Rollefson, *The History of Ancient Palestine from the Palaeolithic Period to Alexander's Conquest* (JSOTSup, 146; Sheffield: JSOT Press, 1993), 708.

44. Even though Tyre had been at war with Assyria under Shalmaneser. Cf. Cogan, "Cross-Examining," 59.

45. RINAP 3.1:67, 4.69.

46. Gallagher, *Sennacherib's Campaign*, 97; Cogan, "Cross-Examining," 60.

47. Cogan, "Cross-Examining," 60. See Frahm, *Sancherib-Inschriften*, 117.

48. In the past, some speculated that Tyre had been besieged by Sennacherib, but the siege was unsuccessful, thus explaining the omission of Tyre from the annals because "the annalist, not wishing to resort to falsehood, and at the same time not wishing to admit that Sennacherib had failed in something that he set out to do, thought it best to omit all reference to Tyre in his account." Cf. Honor, *Sennacherib's Invasion*, 20.

highlight for the inscription.[49] Sennacherib does emphasize the installation of Taba'lu as the king in Sidon, which likely acted to isolate Tyre (even if the island was not taken by the Assyrians).[50] Katzenstein[51] held that the hegemony of Tyre remained in place, even though Sennacherib claims to have installed a new king over these cities (Sidon to Acco).[52] Gallagher thinks Sennacherib made Sidon the new capital in Tyre's place in 701.[53]

All this to say that the Assyrian's omission of Tyre creates some ambiguity for the historian.[54] The Phoenician coast is said to submit but fails to mention the most prominent city. Mayer assumes that the submissive area "incorporated the coastal cities of Tyre and Acco."[55] It seems logical to conclude the city was not taken,[56] given its prominence and the glory its capture would bring to Sennacherib. Yet, despite failure to take the city, king Lulî abandoned it and eventually died (likely by 697 BCE and perhaps in Cyprus).

3.3 Eight Kings Submit

The next section lists kings who submitted (in contrast to the rebel Lulî) and the tribute/gifts they gave to Sennacherib. Rassam claims that eight western kings submitted to Sennacherib and the campaign against Phoenicia is presented as utterly successful. Conspicuous for their absence from this submission are the kings of Ashkelon, Gaza, Ekron, and Jerusalem.[57] The kings listed appears to have a geographical arrangement from north to south to southeast.[58] Curiously, the king *just installed by Sennacherib* in Sidon, Taba'lu, is mentioned in this list of submissive kings as well. Whether these kings are supposed to be understood as loyal or politically shrewd enough to submit early in the campaign so as to

---

49. Ben Zvi ("Malleability and Its Limits," 96) notes that the Assyrian annalist was constrained by the fact that Sennacherib did not take Tyre "despite the fact that such claims would have been supportive of the ideology and genre of the report."

50. Cogan, "Cross-Examining," 60; Cf. Katzenstein, *The History of Tyre*, 220–58.

51. Katzenstein, *The History of Tyre*, 251–2.

52. Gallagher, *Sennacherib's Campaign*, 95.

53. Ibid., 96.

54. Elayi (*Sennacherib*, 60) concludes that Sennacherib's failure to conquer Tyre was "a fact that was carefully concealed in the Assyrian royal inscriptions."

55. Mayer, "Sennacherib's Campaign," 175.

56. So Cogan, "Cross-Examining," 72; Gallagher, *Sennacherib's Campaign*, 104. Contra Mayer, "Sennacherib's Campaign," 175.

57. Mayer, "Sennacherib's Campaign," 175.

58. Cogan, "Cross-Examining," 61.

avoid Assyrian wrath is open to question.⁵⁹ The inclusion of Taba'lu undermines the hypothesis that these were all simply submissive kings.⁶⁰

Where these submissions took place is not indicated in the Rassam text (or the later Taylor and Chicago recensions). In the summary inscription of 694 BCE, it is said that the kings presented themselves at Ushu, which is on the Phoenician coast across from Tyre.⁶¹ Seeing as this information was not incorporated into later annalistic recensions, it is open to question whether it is accurate. Were it historical, it would have been known at the time, and this would not be an instance where later annalistic accounts were updated with the latest information. Was there a "group submission" at Ushu, or did Sennacherib receive the submission of the various kings in their respective regions during the campaign?⁶² The earliest texts claim no mutual submission ceremony, making later such claims suspect.⁶³

The annalistic account goes on to record the punishment of a rebel, Ṣidqâ of Ashkelon, who clearly did not go down without a fight. In the Rassam account, the punishment of Ṣidqâ is recounted *before* the conflict with Philistia itself. Knauf assumes a chronological progression, and the historicity of the "group submission" ceremony in Sidon, suggesting that Ṣidqâ "had not shown up at Sidon" for the submission ceremony (which he labels the "Sidonian congress of Syrian princes") leading Sennacherib to attack.⁶⁴ Aharoni also assumed a chronological sequence and went as far as to posit that Ṣidqâ submitted "as soon as the Assyrian army appeared in Palestine" right after the submission of the eight kings.⁶⁵ This interpretation of a chronological portrayal was rejected in the revision of Aharoni's work by A. F. Rainey on logical grounds "that Sennacherib could not have exiled Ṣidqâ, king of Ashkelon, before he arrived in Philistia."⁶⁶ As Gallagher points out,

---

59. Dubovský ("Assyrians under the Walls of Jerusalem," 111) suggests, "The Assyrian scribes depicted Padî as the only faithful man in the entire region, who preferred to suffer rather than to violate his treaty."

60. Elayi understands theses kings to be submissive, rather than rebellious because their revolt would have been explicitly mentioned otherwise (*Sennacherib*, 61). Realizing the problem of Taba'lu's mention, she thinks it is possible that the mention of Taba'lu (Ittobaal) along with these kings may have been "an error on the part of scribes."

61. Cogan, "Cross-Examining," 62.

62. Some take the later text at face value and hold to the group submission to Sennacherib at Ushu Mayer, "Sennacherib's Campaign," 175; Ahlström et al., *History of Ancient Palestine*, 708; Gallagher, *Sennacherib's Campaign*, 109. Cogan ("Cross-Examining," 62) thinks this is done "on questionable evidence."

63. As Dubovský ("Assyrians under the Walls of Jerusalem," 113) observes, "We cannot be sure whether the payments of tribute to Sennacherib by the kings listed … indeed took place at the end of the Phoenician phase—or during the later phases—or even at the end of the campaign."

64. Knauf, "Sennacherib at the Berezina," 142.

65. Aharoni, *The Land of the Bible*, 337.

66. Yohanan Aharoni, *The Land of the Bible: A Historical Geography* (London: Burns & Oates, 1979), 388. This was a revision of Aharoni (after his death) by Anson Rainey.

Jaffa is 48 kilometers north of Ashkelon, "so the Assyrians reached Jaffa before they did anything about Ashkelon."[67] The true chronology of Ṣidqâ's surrender in relation to other events recounted in Assyrian annals is unclear and open to multiple reconstructions, but it seems logical that Sennacherib's conquest of Philistine cities preceded the Philistine king's surrender.

3.4 The Offensive against Philistia

Sennacherib claims to have bested Philistia easily, conquering four cities north of Ashkelon. It is possible that the loss of these cities led Ṣidqâ to surrender.[68] Alternatively, the loss of these cities may have led Ṣidqâ's people to revolt and hand him over to the Assyrians.[69] The Philistine king may have held out even after the capture of the northern cities as he waited to see what success the coming Egyptian aid might find (as recounted in the battle at Eltekeh).[70] As noted above, some scholars think that rather than understanding the battles in the Assyrian annals as being presented in chronological order, the rationale for their order of presentation may be moving from easy to difficult battles.

The conquest of Ashkelon is not mentioned in the annals. This may be due to the fact that either the people revolted and surrendered their king to the Assyrians, or that the king surrendered himself to save the city or his family.[71] Either way, the submission/capture of the king meant the city did not need to be taken in battle.

Surprisingly, the annals fail to mention the status of Gaza and whether it had been part of the anti-Assyrian coalition and how it was brought back into the Assyrian fold. As noted above, the king of Gaza is not mentioned as one of the kings who "willingly" submitted to Sennacherib in the annals, which could imply Gaza's Assyrian loyalty even before Sennacherib's Philistine campaign.[72] Yet, it would seem certain that Gaza was among the rebels given the fact that the Nubian-Egyptian forces penetrated as far north as they did (all identifications of Eltekeh assume it being north of Gaza) and the other Philistine cities all were part of the

---

67. Gallagher, *Sennacherib's Campaign*, 117. Similarly Elayi, *Sennacherib*, 63.

68. Cogan ("Cross-Examining," 62) notes the possibility that "this defeat broke Ṣidqâ's resistance and he surrendered" but notes that there may also have been "resistance in Ashkelon after this defeat."

69. So Tadmor, "Philistia under Assyrian Rule," 97; Knauf, "Sennacherib at the Berezina," 142.

70. Gallagher (*Sennacherib's Campaign*, 117) suggests that it was not until after the battle of Eltekeh, which he thinks took place after the conquest of those Philistine cities, that Ṣidqâ may have been taken captive.

71. Ibid., 118; Tadmor, "Philistia under Assyrian Rule," 96–7; Elayi, *Sennacherib*, 64.

72. Elayi (*Sennacherib*, 61–7) speculates that Gaza may have "remained loyal to the Assyrian king and was left autonomous because it was useful for reasons of economic profit … and Assyrian strategy, as a buffer state adjoining Egypt."

rebellious coalition (and forced participation in such alliances was common).[73] As we will see in our next chapter, the biblical account in Kings (2 Kgs 18:8) references Hezekiah's attack on Gaza and its vicinity, which may have intended to force them into participating in the rebellion.[74]

The submission of Gaza is not mentioned in the annals. Perhaps Gaza's king had participated in the rebellion, then submitted, or the people of Gaza, like the Ekronites, deposed the king and imprisoned him. At the end of Sennacherib's annalistic account, it is said that Ṣil-Bēl, king of Gaza, is one of the recipients of Hezekiah's redistributed territory, along with the kings of Ekron and Ashdod.[75] The king of Ekron (Padî) had remained loyal to Assyria (as evinced by his being deposed by anti-Assyrian elements in Ekron and their turning him over to Hezekiah). The loyal/rebel status of Mitinti, king of Ashdod, is not clear, but he is listed among the eight kings who submitted to Sennacherib.[76] Perhaps the fact Ṣil-Bēl is one of the three recipients of redistributed territory reflects the fact he, like Padî, remained loyal and did not participate in the rebellion and had been deposed by his own people, perhaps with Hezekiah's backing (2 Kgs 18:8). Unfortunately, any details on Gaza or Ṣil-Bēl's role in the rebellion are omitted by the Assyrian scribes. No doubt this information did not for some reason fit with the Assyrian scribes' agenda to glorify Sennacherib and his campaign.

The annals next go on to chronicle the defeat and punishment of Ekron, another rebel city. In this account, the issue of chronology is brought to the fore again as Ekron's former king, Padî, had been deposed by an anti-Assyrian movement in Ekron and had been given as prisoner to Hezekiah in Jerusalem (cf. 2 Kgs 18:8).[77] In this section of the Assyrian annalistic account, however, well before recounting what happens with Hezekiah and Jerusalem, Padî is restored to the throne at Ekron. Logic would suggest that Padî was not released by Hezekiah before the Assyrians assaulted Judahite territory.[78] In what context Hezekiah released the Ekronite

---

73. As Ben Zvi ("Malleability and Its Limits," 95) writes, "It is unlikely that Gaza remained a pro-Assyrian island in the area" before Sennacherib's conquest.

74. Van der Brugge suggests Hezekiah attacked Gaza to control the entrance to the Via Maris to Egypt. Caroline Van der Brugge, "Of Production, Trade, Profit and Destruction: An Economic Interpretation of Sennacherib's Third campaign," *JESHO* 60 (2017): 306–7.

75. RINAP 3.1:176, 22.iii.32–34.

76. RINAP 3.1:175, 22.ii.54.

77. Mayer ("Sennacherib's Campaign," 175) thinks 2 Kgs 18:8 may refer to the time Padî was taken.

78. Cogan ("Cross-Examining," 66) has called this account an example of prolepsis wherein the eventual result is recorded out of order to bring an account to an appropriate conclusion. Gallagher (*Sennacherib's Campaign*, 123) thinks similarly and calls it a "topical arrangement."

king is open to speculation.[79] Clearly no conquest of Jerusalem is mentioned, so Sennacherib cannot have liberated Padî by breaching the walls of the city and taking him.[80] It seems clear Padî was released in a context of 'negotiations' with Hezekiah—negotiations that were likely closer to threats.[81] Most think Padî was released in connection to Hezekiah's submission to Sennacherib.[82] It could be the Ekronite king was used as a bargaining chip by Hezekiah in negotiating Jerusalem's indemnity, or the Judahite monarch was simply forced to release him due to the extreme military duress applied by Sennacherib's forces. It is possible Hezekiah's "submission" took place in stages, with the release of Padî representing one of several Judahite concessions.[83]

In the Assyrian annals, the Ekronites are explicitly said to have allied with the Egyptians and Cushites in their rebellion and called upon them for aid.[84] Sennacherib claims to have soundly defeated both the Egyptian and Philistine forces, taking Eltekeh, Timnah, and Ekron. Rebels from Ekron are said to have been impaled around their city to warn other potential rebels of the price of treachery. As noted, Padî is restored as king, having been emancipated from Hezekiah's custody in Jerusalem.

79. Dalley suggests that the fact that Sennacherib was able to procure from Hezekiah and reinstate him suggests "that Hezekiah was mainly regarded as a reliable ally of Assyria at that time." Cf. Dalley, "Yabâ, Atalyā and the Foreign Policy," 90.

80. Although Elayi (*Sennacherib*, 68), without explanation, speculates that Padî may have been repatriated from Jerusalem through "a commando operation." Apparently, this seems more likely to her than the Ekronite episode occurring after the attack on Judah.

81. Rainey and Notley, *The Sacred Bridge*, 241c; Ahlström et al., *History of Ancient Palestine*, 710. Cf. Frederick Mario Fales, "'To Speak Kindly to Him/Them' as Item of Assyrian Political Discourse," in *Of God(s), Trees, Kings, and Scholars. Neo-Assyrian and Related Studies in Honour of Simo Parpola* (eds. Lukko et al.; StudOr, 106; Helsinki: Finnish Oriental Society, 2009), 27–40.

82. Bright, A History of Israel, 286; Miller and Hayes, *History*, 419. Dubovský ("Assyrians under the Walls of Jerusalem," 125) suggest the negotiations for Padî took place "during the blockade of Jerusalem while the Assyrian troops were already stationed under the city walls."

83. Dubovský, "Assyrians under the Walls of Jerusalem," 125; Bustenay Oded, "'The Command of the God' as a Reason for Going to War in the Assyrian Royal Inscriptions," in *Ah, Assyria ... Studies in Assyrian History and Ancient Near Eastern Historiography Presented to Hayim Tadmor* (ScrHier, 33; Jerusalem: Magnes Press, 1991), 223–30.

84. Given the common hypothesis that Hezekiah was the ringleader in the rebellion, it is perhaps surprising that the Ekronites did not call on Judah for aid. Mayer ("Sennacherib's Campaign," 176) suggests that Ekron viewed Judah as an enemy, and they called on Egypt "to buffer their tight position between expected Assyrian aggression on one side and Judah's mounting onslaughts of Philistine cities on the other." However, in my opinion this is unlikely given the fact the pro-Assyrian Ekronites gave their king to Hezekiah for holding suggesting Hezekiah was an ally rather than enemy.

3.5 The Battle of Eltekeh

The Assyrian annals recount a battle at Eltekeh against a Nubian-Egyptian force. The annals describe the Nubian-Egyptian forces as "kings of Egypt"[85] and "Egyptian charioteers and princes"[86] along with the "archers, chariots and horses of the king of the land *Meluḫa* [Ethiopia]"[87] and the "charioteers of the king of the land *Meluḫa*."[88] Given the lack of explicit reference to the Nubian king's presence, some question the actual presence of the king of *Meluḫa*.[89] The account in Kings explicitly mentions Tirhakah (Taharqa/Taharqo) as the king of Cush who fought Sennacherib in 701 BCE (2 Kgs 19:9), but the name of the Ethiopian monarch is not mentioned in the Assyrian account.[90] Given that Taharqo later became famous as the king who resisted Assyria, it is understandable that the biblical account names him explicitly, since it was written after Taharqo's fame. However, at the time the Assyrian text was composed (*c.* 700 BCE), Taharqo had no recognizable currency, so the omission of his name from Assyrian texts is equally understandable. If, like the Kings account, it was written after Taharqo's famous battles with Assyria,[91] the

---

85. RINAP 3.1:176, 22.ii.79.
86. RINAP 3.1:176, 22.iii.3.
87. RINAP 3:1:176, 22.ii.79–80.
88. RINAP 3:1:176, 22.iii.4.
89. Matty (*Sennacherib's Campaign*, 174–5) observes, "No note about the presence of the king of *Meluḫa* is given in the episode." Though she goes too far when claiming, "According to the annals of Sennacherib, the Kushite king did not participate in the war" (180). The text does not explicitly say the king was absent. The soldiers and calvary of the Nubian king are mentioned, which may suggest the king was present.
90. There is some debate about whether the battle of Eltekeh was with the same Cushite force referenced in the "rumour/report" Sennacherib hears of in 2 Kgs 19:7. Na'aman and Gallagher think the biblical reference and the Eltekeh reference in the Assyrian annals are *not* to the same contingent. Cf. Na'aman, "Sennacherib's Campaign to Judah," 65. Gallagher suggests the second contingent was very far away when the rumor was heard (perhaps still in Egypt); Gallagher, *Sennacherib's Campaign*, 123–4. Mayer and Knauf seem to view both the biblical references to Cush and the Eltekeh contingents as one expedition. Cf. Mayer, "Sennacherib's Campaign," 177; Knauf, "Sennacherib at the Berezina," 141–9. Recently, Jordi Vidal argued for only one Egyptian–Cushite expedition. Cf. Jordi Vidal, "Some Remarks on the Battle of Altaqu," in *The Perfumes of Seven Tamarisks. Studies in Honour of Wilfred G.E. Watson* (eds. Lete et al.; AOAT, 394; Münster: Ugarit-Verlag, 2012), 77–8. Lacking explicit reference to a second Nubian Egyptian contingent and wishing to not multiply hypotheses, I hold to there being one contingent, represented in the biblical text in 2 Kgs 19:7 and the battle of Eltekeh as referenced in the Assyrian annals.
91. E.g., Taharqo defeated Assyrian forces in 674 BCE. See G. Goosens, "Taharqa Le ConquéRant," *ChrEg* 22/44 (1947): 239–44; Anthony Spalinger, "Esarhaddon and Egypt: An Analysis of the First Invasion of Egypt," *Or* 43 (1974): 295–326; Paul-Eugène Dion, "Sennacherib's Expedition to Palestine," *Egt* 20 (1989): 5–25.

account would surely have named him in order to glorify Sennacherib's battle at Eltekeh. This is another instance where a later account can actually include more accurate (or at least specific) information due to its later historical perspective.

The Eltekeh conflict is depicted as a resounding victory for Sennacherib in the annalistic account.[92] As Cogan notes, it is unclear why the Assyrian annals chose to recount the events at Eltekeh specifically (especially when he fails to mention the battle at Lachish, the depiction of which decorated Sennacherib's throne room).[93] The extent to which the battle at Eltekeh should be deemed an Assyrian victory has been the subject of much debate. Some have suggested that the language employed in the description of the battle suggest that the Assyrian "victory" was exaggerated.[94] Gallagher finds the Eltekeh account in Rassam "meager" when compared with the account of Sennacherib's battle with Merodach-Baladan, which raises doubts about an Assyrian success.[95] Knauf has argued it was "far from a glorious victory for the Assyrians and much more of a close run thing."[96] He notes that Sennacherib himself is said to join in the battle, which suggests the army was in "dire straits indeed."[97] Without discounting the possibility that Eltekeh was not a resounding victory for Assyria, the portrayal of a king's personal involvement in the battle was likely meant to glorify the king rather than give a reliable presentation of exactly how the battle went, making Knauf's suggestion that Sennacherib's participation was an indication that the Assyrians fared poorly unlikely.[98]

Knauf suggests that the Assyrian failure at Eltekeh was due to the fact their army was "severely diminished" by this point in the campaign, due to their many sieges[99] and fighting, obviating any need to postulate an "angel of the Lord" or

---

92. Mayer ("Sennacherib's Campaign," 177) takes this account at face value concluding that "the Egyptian unit of charioteers and archers engaged in battle with Assyrians at Eltekeh and was annihilated."

93. Cogan, "Cross-Examining," 66.

94. Tadmor, "Philistia under Assyrian Rule," 97; Gallagher, *Sennacherib's Campaign*, 121; Kitchen, *Third Intermediate Period*, 385, n. 822; Spalinger, "Foreign Policy," 36. Caroline van der Brugge suggests (with no textual evidence) that the battle of Eltekeh is pure fiction and that only trade negotiations took place. Cf. van der Brugge, "Of Production, Trade, Profit," 319–21.

95. Gallagher, *Sennacherib's Campaign*, 121.

96. Knauf, "Sennacherib at the Berezina," 147. Similarly, Israel Eph'al, "On Warfare and Military Control in the Ancient Near Eastern Empires: A Research Outline," in *History Historiography and Interpretation: Studies in Biblical and Cuneiform Literatures* (eds. Weinfeld and Tadmor; Jerusalem: Magnes, 1983), 98.

97. Knauf, "Sennacherib at the Berezina," 147.

98. As Fales ("The Road to Judah," 239) notes Eltekeh was "a battle Sennacherib claims to have won hands down. This victory was claimed thanks to Sennacherib's own personal, heroic, intervention on the battlefield."

99. Knauf ("Sennacherib at the Berezina," 147) suggests the army had put fifty cities to siege, apparently taking Sennacherib's claims at face value.

"an invasion of mice" to explain the outcome of the battle.[100] Gallagher notes the lack of any description of the Assyrians pursuing their enemies in the Eltekeh battle account suggesting it was "a stalemate" rather than an Assyrian triumph.[101] Knauf further points out that the text is silent about how Sennacherib treated the prisoners he claims to have taken in battle at Eltekeh[102] and suggests the battle led to "Sennacherib's retreat to Ekron."[103] Redford has suggested the Assyrian account is a complete misrepresentation and that the battle of Eltekeh "was an unexpected and serious reverse for Assyria [sic] arms."[104]

Kitchen suggested that after the initial battle, the Egyptian/Cushite force regrouped for an additional attack on Sennacherib's forces, perhaps represented by 2 Kgs 19:8-9, which notes the approach of Tirhakah, news of which caused Sennacherib to leave his base of operations at Lachish to fight elsewhere.[105] As is well known, Herodotus gives an account of an Egyptian victory over Sennacherib (Herodotus *Hist.* 2.141). In this account, the Assyrians reach as far south as Pelusium, a fortress on Egypt's frontier. Some have held the Herodotus account as relevant for historical reconstructions,[106] whereas other think there is no connection.[107] Through a detailed literary analysis, Grabbe has demonstrated the independence of the

---

100. Ibid.

101. Gallagher, *Sennacherib's Campaign*, 121.

102. Knauf suggests they were sent back to Egypt as intermediaries, based on the parallel of Napoleon sending back Meerveldt, an Austrian general, after the Battle of Dresden. Cf. Knauf, "Sennacherib at the Berezina," 148. Karen Radner has suggested a house-sale document from Nineveh (*c.* 692) that mentions some Egyptians may be the Egyptian prisoners from the battle of Eltekeh, with the future Pharaoh Shoshenq being one of them. See Karen Radner, "After Eltekeh: Royal Hostages from Egypt at the Assyrian Court," in *Stories of Long Ago: Festschrift für Michael D. Roaf* (eds. Baker et al.; AOAT, 397; Münster: Ugarit-Verlag, 2012), 473–9. So Kahn, *Sennacherib's Campaign*, 115–16. Elayi has undermined this conclusion by pointing out that the text in question mentions Egyptian ship captains, but Eltekeh is not near the sea, and there is no mention of ships in any source for the campaign. See Elayi, *Sennacherib*, 67.

103. Ibid.

104. Redford, *Egypt, Canaan, and Israel*, 353.

105. Kitchen, *Third Intermediate Period*, 385; Kenneth A. Kitchen, "Egypt, the Levant and Assyria in 701 BC," in *Fontes Atque Pontes: Eine Festgabe Für Hellmut Brunner* (ed. Görg; Wiesbaden: Otto Harrassowitz, 1983), 243–53. Similarly, Rainey and Notley, *The Sacred Bridge*, 244; Mario Liverani, *Israel's History and the History of Israel* (London: Equinox, 2005), 148.

106. E.g., James A. Montgomery and Henry S. Gehman, *A Critical and Exegetical Commentary on the Book of Kings* (Edinburgh: T&T Clark, 1951), 497–8; John Gray, *1 & 2 Kings* (Philadelphia, PA: Westminster, 1970), 694.

107. E.g., Cogan and Tadmor (*II Kings*, 251) assert, "It is clear that Herodotus's account has nothing to do with Sennacherib's invasion of Judah." Cf. Bright, *History*, 288. Elayi (*Sennacherib*, 82) suggests connecting the Herodotus and biblical account can only be done through "circular reasoning."

Herodotus text.[108] Similarly, Kahn has concluded the biblical and Herodotus account are "totally independent" and further argued that there were only minor "adaptions" of the Egyptian story made for Herodotus's Greek audience.[109] Mayer suggests the Greek story was based on a tradition "that confused the fight between Sennacherib and Egyptian troops at the Judaean city of Eltekeh with an invasion of Egypt."[110]

If Assyrian claims of victory at Eltekeh were an exaggeration, it would not be the first time that Assyrian texts claimed total victory when reality was less than this. Similar embellishments are found with Shalmaneser III's claims of victory at Qarqar (853 BCE) and Sargon II's claims to victory at Der (720 BCE).[111] Of course, reconstructions of an Assyrian defeat cannot be based solely on the Assyrian annals but must rely on other evidences.[112] Some have attempted to correlate this

---

108. Grabbe, "Of Mice and Dead Men," 119–40, esp. 136–7. Similarly, Dan'el Kahn, "The War of Sennacherib against Egypt as Described in Herodotus II 141," *JAEI* 6 (2014): 28. Contra, Brent A. Strawn, "Herodotus' History 2.141 and the Deliverance of Jerusalem: On Parallels, Sources, and Histories of Ancient Israel," in *Israel's Prophets and Israel's Past: Essays on the Relationship of Prophetic Texts and Israelite History in Honor of John H. Hayes* (eds. Kelle and Moore; LHBOTS, 446; New York: T&T Clark, 2006), 210–38.

109. Kahn ("War of Sennacherib," 28) writes, "It seems impossible that [Herodotus] had access to the biblical account or was influenced by it." Kahn suggests that the Herodotus text reflects "a failed campaign by Esarhaddon (680–669 BCE) to conquer Egypt in 673 BCE." See Kahn, *Sennacherib's Campaign*, 123.

110. Mayer, "Sennacherib's Campaign," 171. Lloyd suggests the Herodotus account "inserted Pelusium into the narrative mix simply because that was the classic entry point into Egypt." Cf. Alan B. Lloyd, "The Siege of Jerusalem by Sennacherib," in *Jerusalem's Survival, Sennacherib's Departure, and the Kushite Role in 701 BCE: An Examination of Henry Aubin's Rescue of Jerusalem* (ed. Bellis; PHSC, 32. Piscataway: Gorgias Press, 2020), 215.

111. Albert Kirk Grayson, "Problematic Battles in Mesopotamian History," in *Studies in Honor of Benno Landsberger on His Seventy-Fifth Birthday, April 25, 1965* (eds. Güttersbock and Jacobsen; AS 16; Chicago, IL: Chicago University Press, 1965), 337–42; Ben Zvi, "Malleability and Its Limits," 97 n. 69; Cogan, "Cross-Examining," 65.

112. Dan'el Kahn suggests that Egypt also claimed victory at Eltekeh, noting that Shebitku (who had called on Taharqo to fight against Sennacherib) "adopted expansionistic imperial titles" suggesting that "the Kushite propaganda also claimed victory." Cf. Dan'el Kahn, "Taharqa, King of Kush and the Assyrians," *JSSEA* 31 (2004): 109. Kahn also points out that Taharqo did not attempt to hide his involvement in the battle (as he notes Shabatako recruited him to fight in it), which suggests it was not an Egyptian defeat. Of course, if the reversal of the succession of Shabako and Shabatako is accepted, this means that the calling of Taharqo from Kush to Egypt cannot have been in order to participate in the campaign of 701, since it occurred in 712 BCE. Cf. Bányai, "Ein Vorschlag zur Chronologie," 46–129; Payraudeau, "Retour Sur La Succession," 115–27; Broekman, "The Order of Succession," 17–31. Bányai, "Die Reihenfolge der kuschitischen Könige," 115–80; Jurman, "The Order of the Kushite Kings," 124–51. Pope, "Sennacherib's Departure" 147–51. Dodson, "Rescue of Jerusalem," 167–88; Dodson, *The Royal Tombs of Ancient Egypt*, 115–49.

with the Herodotus text and the biblical account of the destroying angel (e.g., that both refer to a plague),[113] or simply hold that the fact that a tradition of an Assyrian defeat under mysterious circumstance is referred to in two different accounts, coming from two disparate groups, may indicate that it is a genuine historical memory.[114]

Questions of chronology for the Eltekeh battle are important in reconstructing the Assyrian campaign. Some have suggested the battle with Egyptian forces may have been the impetus for the Assyrian withdrawal, connecting it to the reference to Tirhakah in 2 Kgs 19:9, which is the last time the Assyrian army is mentioned as being near Jerusalem in the biblical account.[115] Gallagher has argued against this suggestion on the basis of the basic chronology of the Assyrian account.[116] While acknowledging nonchronological elements (like mentioning the reinstallation of Padî in Ekron before recounting Hezekiah's surrender wherein Padî would have been acquired), Gallagher holds that if the battle of Eltekeh took place *after* the action against Jerusalem, the Assyrian scribes would have had to "drastically altered" the chronology, and suggests that no sufficient explanation has been offered to account for this.[117] This argument, however, seems weak given his

---

113. Becking ("Chronology: A Skeleton without Flesh?" 70) allows that "a suddenly spreading lethal disease could explain the tradition." Cf. Gallagher, *Sennacherib's Campaign*, 241–52. See Radner, who points out how often Assyrian armies were ravaged by epidemics. Cf. K. Radner, "The Assyrian King and His Scholars: The Syro-Anatolia and the Egyptian Schools," in *Of God(s), Trees, Kings, and Scholars: Neo-Assyrian and Related Studies in Honour of Simo Parpola* (eds. Luukko et al.; StudOr 106; Helsinki: Finnish Oriental Society, 2009), 230. Similarly, Antti Laato, *Who Is Immanuel? The Rise and the Foundering of Isaiah's Messianic Expectations* (Åbo, Finland: Åbo Akademy press, 1988), 270; Gray, 1 & 2 Kings, 694.

114. As Ben Zvi ("Malleability and Its Limits," 103) writes, "Shared perceptions or representations by diametrically separate groups must point to something that stands beyond or outside their own perceptions or representations, although these perceptions or representations surely point at it. If these perceptions or representations are independent, this 'something' is likely to be what we usually call the historical event." (Of course, Ben Zvi is writing in particular about correspondences between the Assyrian annals and the book of Kings, not Herodotus and Kings.) Based on the structural similarities of the stories in Herodotus's account and 2 Kings 18–19, Strawn asserts that the former account is based on an oral version of the latter (Strawn, "Herodotus' History 2.141," 210–38), though he does not offer a plausible scenario wherein the Kings account could have been communicated to the Egyptian priests (who were Herodotus's source). While anything is possible a simpler explanation is that both rely on a historical memory of a defeat of Sennacherib in his 701 BCE campaign.

115. See my earlier monograph, *Invasion of Sennacherib*, 192. Others put the battle of Eltekeh at the end of the campaign as well. E.g., Knauf, "Sennacherib at the Berezina," 144. Redford, *Egypt, Canaan, and Israel*, 351–3.

116. Gallagher, *Sennacherib's Campaign*, 123.

117. Ibid.

admission that the Ekronite account already contains nonchronological elements. Furthermore, a rationale for not placing it last in the Assyrian account seems obvious if the battle was indeed more of a stalemate or setback for Assyria. The annalistic account would never conclude on a negative, or even a muted, note but on a glorious one for Sennacherib.

Gallagher further objects to the battle being after Assyrian movements against Judah on the basis of its geographical location.[118] Of course, the location and identification of Eltekeh is uncertain, with some suggesting its strategic importance,[119] necessitating its conquest before Ekron could fall, while others think it was an "unimportant town."[120] Gallagher posits it is Tell esh-Shalaf, northwest of Judah, based on Mazar's identification.[121] However, Mazar's identification actually depends upon the Assyrian annals depicting a chronological campaign. Gallagher, thus, supports the chronology in the annals because rejecting it necessitates identifying a new location for Eltekeh.[122] This objection, however, is not logically sound. The fact that the identification is based on assumptions of chronology is not an argument for the chronology, but simply an observation of the shaky ground on which the identification of Tell esh-Shalaf as Eltekeh rests. Mayer suggests Eltekeh was one of "the group of 46 Judaean sites Sennacherib conquered" and "may have been located far south of Ekron."[123] Similarly, Knauf suggests the Egyptian forces were "probably concentrated around Ashdod."[124]

3.6 The Offensive against Judah

The final section of the Rassam cylinder recounts the assault on Judah and Hezekiah. Based on the space given to narrate the assault on Judah, some think Sennacherib was presenting Hezekiah as "public enemy number one."[125] In the earliest Assyrian account (the Rassam cylinder of 700 BCE), Hezekiah's crimes are not mentioned, other than the imprisonment of Padî of Ekron. This was similar to Lulî, whose crimes were not elaborated. However, in subsequent recensions of the

---

118. Ibid.
119. Tadmor, "Sennacherib's Campaign," 73.
120. Gallagher, *Sennacherib's Campaign*, 121.
121. B. Mazar, "The Cities of the Territory of Dan," *IEJ* 10 (1960): 72-7. So Elayi, *Sennacherib*, 64.
122. Gallagher, *Sennacherib's Campaign*, 124.
123. Mayer, "Sennacherib's Campaign," 177.
124. Knauf, "Sennacherib at the Berezina," 148.
125. Younger, "Assyrian Involvement," 253; Cogan, "Cross-Examining," 66. Contra. Elayi (*Sennacherib*, 84) who opines that attack on Hezekiah was "a routine military operation" that is "put on the same level as the attack against of Lulî of Tyre, which is even more developed." Given the way Hezekiah is described and how he concludes the narration of his campaign with Hezekiah, I disagree with her characterization.

annals (e.g., Cylinder C 697 BCE), it is explicitly stated that Hezekiah did not submit to the Assyrian yoke.[126] This expression made Hezekiah similar to Ṣidqâ who is said to have "not submitted to me quickly."[127] Dubovský sees this as an example of "the tendency of the Assyrian scribes to vilify Hezekiah."[128] The infamy of the rebel is accentuated in the later summary inscription of the bull colossi, which describes Hezekiah (or his land) as "strong and powerful" (*šēpṣu mit-ru*).[129] Gallagher points out that this goes against usual scribal Assyrian practice that sought to undermine the strength of their enemies rather than underscore it.[130] Doubtless, the addition was to make Sennacherib's victory look like a greater accomplishment than it would otherwise have appeared (given that Jerusalem did not fall and Hezekiah did not personally bow in submission, as we will discuss below).[131]

Sennacherib famously boasts that he locked up Hezekiah "in Jerusalem, his royal city, like a bird in a cage."[132] While this used to be thought to refer to Jerusalem being put to siege by the Assyrians, it is now widely understood that in fact no siege occurred.[133] Two statements in the Assyrian texts had been thought to refer to a siege of Jerusalem: (1) "like a bird in a cage" and (2) "I laid out *earthworks/forts* [URU.ḪAL-ṢU.MEŠ] against him." Mayer has pointed out that the first phrase is often used to describe a "cornered position" rather than a military siege.[134] Tadmor has called this phrase "hyperbole ... a face-saving device to cover for a failure to

---

126. Cogan, "Cross-Examining," 67.

127. RINAP 3.1:175, 22.ii.71.

128. Dubovský, "Assyrians under the Walls of Jerusalem," 118.

129. Luckenbill translated this as describing Hezekiah. Cf. *The Annals of Sennacherib*, 77 (Lines 20–22). Gallagher (*Sennacherib's Campaign*, 142) also sees it as "a label for Hezekiah." Contra. RINAP 3.2:69, 20b–22a, which translates it as describing Judah, not Hezekiah. Cf. similarly RINAP 3.2:49.10b–11a. Cf. *CAD* M/1, 140a, which defines *mitru* as "strength, power" and translates "I destroyed Judah ... a strong kingdom." Either way, it depicts Hezekiah as powerful since it is his "strong kingdom." This goes against normal Assyrian propaganda that as a rule belittled their opponents. See Frederick Mario Fales, "The Enemy in Assyrian Royal Inscriptions: 'The Moral Judgment," in *Mesopotamien und seine Nachbaren* (eds. Nissen and Renger; XXV Rencontre Assyriologique Internationale; Berlin: Deitrich Reimer, 1982), 425–35.

130. Gallagher, *Sennacherib's Campaign*, 142.

131. Cogan similarly suggests this addition was to "enhanced Sennacherib's victory over [Hezekiah]" Cogan, "Cross-Examining," 67.

132. RINAP 3.1:176, 22.iii.27. Cf. *COS* 2.119B, 303.

133. E.g., Evans, *Invasion of Sennacherib*, 17–19, 161–2, 191; David Ussishkin, "Sennacherib's Campaign to Philistia and Judah: Ekron, Lachish, and Jerusalem," in *Essays on Ancient Israel in Its Near Eastern Context: A Tribute to Nadav Na'aman* (Winona Lake, IN: Eisenbrauns, 2006), 352. Tadmor, "Sennacherib's Campaign," 65–80; Mayer, "Sennacherib's Campaign," 168–200; Mayer, *Politik und Kriegskunst Der Assyrer*, 360–1; Knauf, "Sennacherib at the Berezina," 145.

134. Mayer, "Sennacherib's Campaign," 179.

take the enemy's capital and punish the rebellious king."[135] Mayer[136] has pointed out that the verb used (*esēru*) in this phrase means to "enclose, confine"[137] and is not the normal Assyrian verb for besieging, *lamû*,[138] which is never applied to Jerusalem. Pointing to the use of the phrase by Tiglath-Pileser in his assault against Damascus, D. Nadali identifies this as an Assyrian strategy of blockade but similarly concludes: "the simile [like a bird in a cage] can be seen as an indirect declaration that the city was not captured."[139]

For the second statement in question, Mayer translates the Akkadogram URU.ḪAL---ṢU.MEŠ as "forts" rather than the common translation "siege walls" rendered in several older translations.[140] Some have translated these as "earthworks"[141] suggesting perhaps embankments used as field fortifications. Gallagher understands these as "garrison forts which ensured control of an area."[142] Nadali suggests it was an Assyrian strategy of blockade used against larger cities that were difficult to put to siege.[143] So it would seem that Sennacherib blockaded Jerusalem but did not put it to an actual siege.[144] No siege language is used of Jerusalem, which contrasts with the descriptions of the siege tactics used against other Judahite cities in the campaign (cf. RINAP 3.1:176, 22.iii.6–7, 19–23). As Knauf writes, "There never was a siege of Jerusalem—all Sennacherib's verbiage implies no more than that he had picketed the, or some, gates of Jerusalem with one or more cavalry troops, one of which might have dug itself in."[145]

The Rassam text concludes its account with an extensive list of tribute given by Hezekiah, the longest such list from the third campaign (later recensions shortened the list considerably).[146] Surprisingly, the tribute is said to have sent to

---

135. See Tadmor, *Tiglath-Pileser III*, 79, n. 11.

136. Mayer, "Sennacherib's Campaign," 179.

137. See AHw: 252; CAD E: 334–335.

138. See AHw: 541; CAD L: 69–77.

139. Davide Nadali, "Sieges and Similes of Sieges in the Royal Annals: The Conquest of Damascus by Tiglath-Pileser III," *KASKAL* 6 (2009): 140.

140. See AHw: 313–314; CAD H: 51–52. Uehlinger suggests that these "forts" are depicted as low-siege walls on Sennacherib's reliefs from his palace. See Christoph Uehlinger, "Clio in a World of Pictures—Another Look at the Lachish Reliefs from Sennacherib's Southwest Palace at Nineveh," in *"Like a Bird in a Cage": The Invasion of Sennacherib in 701 BCE* (ed. Grabbe; JSOTSup, 363; ESHM, 4; London: Sheffield Academic Press, 2003), 295–6.

141. Luckenbill, *The Annals of Sennacherib*, 33. ANET 288a.

142. Gallagher, *Sennacherib's Campaign*, 133 n. 32.

143. Nadali, "Sieges and Similes of Sieges," 145. So Fales, "The Road to Judah," 245–6.

144. Tadmor, "Sennacherib's Campaign," 653–75.

145. Knauf, "Sennacherib at the Berezina," 145. These forts are claimed by Sennacherib to have prevented Jerusalem's inhabitants from leaving the city gate. Cf. Kooij, "Das Assyrische," 97–8; Ernst Vogt, *Der Aufstand Hiskias und die Belagerung Jerusalems 701 V. Chr* (Rome: Biblical Institute, 1986), 63–7.

146. RINAP 3.1:177, 22.iii, 41–49. The list in Rassam is the second longest list of tribute known in Assyrian annals. The first is the tribute list from Sargon's eighth

Sennacherib *after* his return to Nineveh. This text thus suggests that Sennacherib's army did *not* take the tribute as booty during their campaign. This is in contrast to what the annals already noted in this campaign, where the other rebel kings bowed in submission and personally presented gifts. In a thorough examination of Assyrian military campaigns (both Sennacherib and other Assyrian kings), Matty has observed a pattern that successful battles invariably end with the enemy monarch submitting by coming out of his city to pay tribute or allowing the Assyrian king into the city to receive the tribute.[147] She writes, "In no case other than the 701 campaign of Sennacherib is an Assyrian king described as receiving a tribute without the inclusion of a description of the submission of the enemy king at the location of the battle."[148] In the account of the third campaign, how the chief rebel himself is permitted to pay his indemnity through a third party (rather than in-person with a formal act of submission)—and only at a later date—is left unsaid, though the account is still written as if it was a positive development.[149]

Mayer has suggested that the only reason it is stated that Hezekiah's tribute arrived after Sennacherib was already in Nineveh is because Sennacherib and his entourage travelled quicker than a caravan bringing tribute.[150] However, given that other kings presented tribute to Sennacherib not only *during* the campaign but also *in person*, this explanation is undermined. Some have also viewed the extensive nature of the tribute list as compensating for the lack of a clear-cut victory of Hezekiah.[151] After all, the fact Hezekiah is left on the throne is in contrast to the picture of Sennacherib's policy earlier in the annalistic account wherein Sennacherib deposed unfaithful vassal kings and replaced them with new pro-Assyrian monarchs.[152] In sum, Hezekiah remained in power, his kingdom did not become an Assyrian province, as had Samaria, and the tribute was not collected

campaign. Cf. F. Thureau-Dangin, *Une relation de la huitième campagne de Sargon (714 av. J.-C.)* (TCL, 3; Paris: P. Geuthner, 1912), 52–65, Ins. 352–406. Gallagher, *Sennacherib's Campaign*, 133.

147. Matty, *Sennacherib's Campaign*, 192.

148. Ibid.

149. Matty underscores the ambiguity of Hezekiah's tribute, writing, "The way this tribute was delivered is rather obscure; the text does not say that it was imposed, nor does it say it was sent as a gift" (ibid., 58).

150. Mayer, *Politik und Kriegskunst Der Assyrer*, 361–2.

151. Tadmor, "Sennacherib's Campaign to Judah," 670. Cf. Millard, "Sennacherib's Attack on Hezekiah," 72. Gallagher, *Sennacherib's Campaign*, 132–3.

152. Elayi (*Sennacherib*, 83) suggests leaving Hezekiah on the throne has precedent in the reign of Sargon, where the king of Mannea was left on the throne after his submission. She quotes the text (*ARAB* 2.10) as saying "Ullusunu, the Mannean … seized my feet. I had mercy upon them. I forgave his transgression, on the royal throne [I placed him]." However, I do not find this to be an equivalent situation. Here the king personally submits (seizing Sargon's feet), whereas Hezekiah does *not* come out to submit and only sends his payment via a messenger. Marvin A. Sweeney suggests that Sennacherib left Hezekiah in office due to military pressure applied simultaneously by the Babylonian ruler Merodach-Baladan

during the campaign (as booty collected from the other kings mentioned in the Assyrian text). Still, from the Assyrian perspective, tribute was collected, so they could still see this as a clear-cut victory regardless.

It is debated whether Sennacherib's original intention was to take Jerusalem or not.[153] As noted in our chapter on archaeological remains, many have suggested that the Assyrian strategy was to focus on the border cities (Philistine and Judahite) mainly in the Shephelah, rather than the highlands and Jerusalem.[154] In contrast, the biblical texts would suggest that Sennacherib's aims, as outlined by the speeches of the Rabshakeh (2 Kgs 18:19-35), was to capture Jerusalem. The Rabshakeh speaks of a long siege of Jerusalem (18:27) and the deportation of its inhabitants (18:32), neither of which was accomplished. Of course, this may have been more intimidating rhetoric than official policy, but the contrast between how Hezekiah is treated compared with his fellow conspirators is striking and suggestive that not all went perfectly as planned. As Cogan writes,

> Hezekiah should have personally presented himself before Sennacherib and the army should have taken the booty as it departed Judah to return home. This was not a "typical victory" and so the scribes made up the difference by detailing the pain and damage inflicted on Judah and including one of the longest booty lists in Sennacherib's inscriptions.[155]

Of course, from an Assyrian perspective, Hezekiah submitted and paid tribute, so regardless of allowing him to remain enthroned, the campaign was a victory. In later Assyrian Bull inscriptions, Sennacherib intimates a more public submission of Hezekiah, writing: "The recalcitrant (and) strong land Judah (and) I made Hezekiah, its king, bow down at my feet."[156] Coming as it was from a much later date, with no acknowledgment or reference to any literal bowing of Hezekiah in

---

(Marduk-apla-iddina II), who is connected to Hezekiah in 2 Kings 20. See Marvin A. Sweeney, *I & II Kings: A Commentary* (Louisville; Westminster John Knox, 2007), 413.

153. Mayer ("Sennacherib's Campaign," 184) opines that "from the Assyrian point of view, launching a full-scale offensive against the capital of Jerusalem would have been superfluous and even senseless." Knauf ("Sennacherib at the Berezina," 146) suggests that "nobody wanted Jerusalem" at that point. Clements (*Deliverance of Jerusalem*, 62) opines that leaving Jerusalem intact was not due to "unexpected leniency" or the Assyrians being under pressure but was within the range of normal "Assyrian policy."

154. Of course, the problem with Hezekiah being able to take refuge in his capital city is that elsewhere in the annals, enemy capital cities were not safe havens, with Lulî fleeing, Ṣidqâ taken prisoner, and rebellious Ekronites punished. Cf. Gallagher, *Sennacherib's Campaign*, 132. Matty (*Sennacherib's Campaign*, 40) points out that in all of Sennacherib's campaigns, Hezekiah "is the only king who did not come out of his city and show submissive behaviour, flee, or get taken from Jerusalem to Assyria."

155. Cogan, "Cross-Examining," 70.

156. RINAP 3.2:69, 20b–22a. Cf. similarly RINAP 3.2:49.10b–11a.

earlier texts, this is obviously either a deceptive embellishment or should be taken to refer to a metaphorical "bowing" as evinced by the Judahite paying of tribute.

Instead of being focused on Jerusalem, Assyrian texts themselves seem content with their isolating Hezekiah in his capital and taking action against his fortified cities instead.[157] The extent of the Judahite damage is put at forty-six fortified cities and "innumerable" other towns in the annals. None of the cities are named, even Lachish, which became the subject of the magnificent artwork that would decorate Sennacherib's throne room in Nineveh. The omission of the names of the cities contrasts other conquests in the Assyrian text like Ṣidqâ's towns that are explicitly named on the Rassam text. Gallagher suggests the names were not included "for reasons of space,"[158] which, if we assume literally forty-six towns were to be named makes sense, and many scholars *have* taken the number of Judahite towns claimed at face value.[159] Cogan suggests the number relied upon lists of conquered cites kept by scribes in the Assyrian army.[160] However, as noted earlier, archaeological evidence suggests there were not that many fortified cities in all of Judah at the time, making this a clear instance of exaggeration.[161] Some allow the number listed to include any type of Judahite town "whether town, fortress or city"[162] though it seems clear it refers to forty-six fortified cities, claiming the other types of sites were "without number." As mentioned above, explicit siege language is used in providing details of the various ways in which the Assyrians molested Judahite towns. The siege of Lachish is, of course, famously depicted on the relief from Sennacherib's throne room, complementing the Assyrian annals in that way (though the annals strangely omit any mention of Lachish).

What caused Hezekiah to pay tribute is not clear. As Matty writes, "One cannot decide from the context if it was surrender tribute, annual tribute, or even peace-time tribute."[163] The Assyrian text claims it was the "terrifying splendor/radiance" of Sennacherib's majesty (*pulḫi melamme bēlūteya isḫupušuma*)

---

157. While acknowledging that Sennacherib did not put Jerusalem to siege, Elayi (*Sennacherib*, 76) suggests this was only because he chose not to, opining that "it seems likely that Sennacherib could have done the same for Jerusalem as he did for Lachish, both cities being strong Judean fortified cities." Most scholars, however, would not agree with Elayi in equating the difficulty of taking Jerusalem with Lachish.

158. Gallagher, *Sennacherib's Campaign*, 131.

159. For example, Borowski ("Sennacherib in Judah," 35*) writes, "When Sennacherib claimed in his Annals that he besieged and destroyed 'forty-six of [Hezekiah's] strong, walled cities, as well as the countless small towns in their vicinity,' he probably did not exaggerate. Almost every Judean site that was occupied at the time shows signs of destruction." Cf. Rainey and Notley, *The Sacred Bridge*, 243, 245; Gallagher, *Sennacherib's Campaign*, 261; Mayer, "Sennacherib's Campaign," 177; Faust, "Settlement and Demography," 168.

160. Cogan, "Cross-Examining," 67.

161. Dever, *Beyond the Texts*, 563.

162. Mayer, "Sennacherib's Campaign," 175.

163. Matty, *Sennacherib's Campaign*, 58.

that led to Hezekiah's payment.[164] Shawn Aster has argued that the Akkadian "splendor/radiance" (*melammu*) when followed by the word "terror" (*pulḫi*) usually means "the force that causes people in one land to submit to the king, while the king is in another land. Although the king is not physically present, his powerful reputation causes the inhabitants of a particular area to submit to him."[165] Based on Aster's observations, Matty has argued that Hezekiah sent the payment later (after Sennacherib returned to Nineveh) because "Hezekiah was still threatened after Sennacherib went back to Nineveh."[166] That is, Matty suggests some Assyrian forces may have still been left in Jerusalem's vicinity after Sennacherib had left and Hezekiah sent the payment to have them withdrawn,[167] or the payment was to prevent Sennacherib from invading once again in the future.[168] Regardless of the specifics, the payment of tribute indicated Judah was under duress and was in some way forced to pay their way out of a crisis (whether present or future).

The tribute listed in the Assyrian annalistic account is exceptionally large and claims to have deported 200,150 captives from Judah.[169] As noted above, this number is implausible and cannot be taken at face value.[170] The number of captives claimed likely exceeded the entire population of Judah. Mayer has suggested it reflects the number not of people only but of the combination of people and animals taken as booty in the entire campaign.[171] However, people and animals usually appear separate in Assyrian lists, as Mayer notes in the same article.[172] Others have suggested the number should be read as 2,150 rather than 200,150.[173] The hypothesis seems dubious and appears simply to be an attempt to harmonize the Assyrian data with what could be seemed historically plausible (as his statement in his conclusion suggests "Eine solche Zahl hat weder das Odium

---

164. As Knauf ("Sennacherib at the Berezina," 145) writes, "It was not exactly Sennacherib's splendour that turned Hezekiah's Arab allies away from him … but rather a lack of further funds and means." Similarly, Cogan, "Cross-Examining," 67.

165. Shawn Zelig Aster, *The Unbeatable Light: Melammu and Its Biblical Parallels* (AOAT, 384; Münster: Ugarit-Verlag, 2012), 86.

166. Matty, *Sennacherib's Campaign*, 60.

167. Ibid., 61, 168, 187.

168. Ibid., 64.

169. RINAP 3.1:176, 22.iii.24.

170. Broshi and Finkelstein ("Population of Palestine," 54) suggest that the whole of Judah had only about 110,000 people at the time of the invasion, making the Assyrian claims impossible.

171. Mayer, "Sennacherib's Campaign," 182.

172. Ibid. Cogan, "Cross-Examining," 67 n. 71.

173. As Arthur Ungnad concludes, "Unter diesen Umständen halte ich es für sicher, daß die Zahl der gefangenen und deportierten Judäer nicht 200150. sondern 2150 gelesen werden muß." Cf. Ungnad, "Die Zahl der von Sanherib deportierten Judäer," *ZAW* 59 (1942): 202.

der Ungenauigkeit noch das der Vertreibung, die man ihr sonst zu- schreiben müßte").[174]

Rather than attempting to substantiate this number, De Odorico suggests Sennacherib's claim should be understood as "an example of propagandistic inflation."[175] This reading of the large number seems justified in light of the more modest (but still very large!) numbers of conscripts listed at the end of the Rassam cylinder (Lines 59–60), which claims a mere 20,000 soldiers taken from "all the lands" Sennacherib conquered.[176] While, from an Assyrian perspective, the inflated number reflected the gist of the extent of the victory, perhaps, as Zevit has suggested, the Assyrian scribes were really claiming not to have "deported" 200,150 people but that the Judahites were merely "claimed" as spoil; that is, from an Assyrian perspective the conquered people were "claimed" (*šallālu*) but actually were left in the land to rebuild.[177] Of course, inflated numbers were part of the genre of a victorious battle account, and from the Assyrian view it was a victory indeed.

The Assyrian annalistic account claims to have redistributed much of Judahite territory[178] in the aftermath of the conflict as punishment for Hezekiah's rebellious ways. The exact cities turned over are not named, and it is not clear if this might be "re-patriated" territory rather than Judahite territory proper. The Judahite territory in question is said to be given to Philistine vassals, Mitinti of Ashdod, Padî of Ekron, and Ṣillibel of Gaza.[179] Later recensions (Bull 4) add Ashkelon to this list, possibly referring to subsequent rearrangements of the territory.[180] The taking of territory is a clear indication of victory, and from the Assyrian perspective the mention of the redistribution of Hezekiah's land is a clear statement of Sennacherib's triumph.

In sum, the Assyrian annalistic accounts consider the third campaign a grand success. It is recounted in many copies of the annalistic account and in different

---

174. Ibid.

175. De Odorico, *The Use of Numbers*, 114–15. De Odorico notes that the specificity of the number (200,150 rather than 200,000) attempts "to associate the sense of emphasis given by the 'high round number'… with the (appearance) of truthfulness given by their 'exact' form" (172).

176. Cf. Frahm, *Einleitung* 105.

177. Zevit, "Implicit Population Figures," 364. Some have suggested the number of captives (200,150 may have been denoting the entire population of Judah. Cf. Francolino J. Gonçalves, *L'expédition de Sennachérib en Palestine dans la littérature hebraïque ancienne* (Ebib, 7; Paris: Gabalda, 1986), 115; A. R. Millard, "Large Numbers in the Assyrian Royal Inscriptions," in *Ah, Assyria … Studies in Assyrian History and Ancient Near Eastern Historiography Presented to Hayim Tadmor* (eds. Cogan and Ephàl; ScrHier 33; Jerusalem: Magnes Press, 1991), 221-2; Herbert Sauren, "Sennachérib, les Arabes, les déportés Juifs," *WO* 16 (1985): 84-9.

178. RINAP 3.1:176, 22.iii.31.

179. RINAP 3.1:176, 22.iii.32–34.

180. Cogan, "Cross-Examining," 68; Gallagher, *Sennacherib's Campaign*, 135.

recensions. The Assyrian success is partially attributed to divine intervention, with the "weapon of Assur" being appealed to frequently to explain the victory. On the other hand, the text glosses over parts of the campaign that from a historian's perspective may not have been ideal: the fact Lulî successfully fled and escaped punishment; the possible rebellious status of Gaza; the setback, or failure, at Eltekeh; the survival of Jerusalem and other highland Judahite cities unscathed; Hezekiah's remaining in power without reference to his ultimate fate; and failure to have Hezekiah come out of his city and pay tribute (or Sennacherib entering Jerusalem and the king paying tribute in his palace), instead, receiving Hezekiah's tribute *after* the campaign. As we will see in subsequent chapters, helpful perspectives on how Assyria could consider the campaign successful despite these drawbacks can be gained by an examination of outcomes of conflicts in military history. As we will see, a victory did not have to be utterly complete to be a victory still.[181] But before we look at examples from more recent history, we will first examine the biblical account of Sennacherib's invasion in 2 Kings 18–19.

---

181. Cogan further argues that Sennacherib was simply not "an expansionist" like his father. Cf. Cogan, "Cross-Examining," 71. That is, he did not care to make the Western states into provinces as evinced by his leniency on Hezekiah. This, of course, may have been the case, though whether the policy was the planned policy or a policy of necessity given the way things went in the campaign is open to question. Cogan supposes, "It does not seem to have been in Assyria's interest to pursue further military action against Jerusalem," but the evidence upon which this assumption rests is circular. Assyria did not besiege Jerusalem, so they must not have wanted to do so. Alternatively, it could be they did not besiege Jerusalem because they were unable to do so, due to setbacks at Eltekeh, and so on.

Chapter 4

BIBLICAL NARRATIVE ACCOUNTS

Three biblical narratives are concerned with the invasion of Judah by Sennacherib in 701 BCE during Hezekiah's regency. The fullest account is found in 2 Kings 18–19, though it is paralleled very closely (nearly verbatim) with the narratives in Isaiah 36–37.[1] The Chronicler also recounts the story again, in an abbreviated version (2 Chronicles 32). Given that the account in Chronicles is dependent upon the Kings account (or perhaps Isaiah 36–37), we will not focus on its account to discern its

---

1. The main difference between the Isaiah and Kings accounts of the Assyrian invasion is the omission in Isaiah of the capitulation of Hezekiah's to Sennacherib and his payment. Both the Kings and Isaiah narratives of the Assyrian invasion begin similarly, noting the invasion in Hezekiah's fourteenth year and Sennacherib's capture of all the fortified cities (2 Kgs 18:13; Isa 36:1). However, the Isaiah account then skips the account of Hezekiah's negotiations with Sennacherib at Lachish and the payment made (2 Kgs 18:14–16). Seeing as Hezekiah took the precious metals from the Jerusalem temple, it is possible the reason for the omission of the payment of tribute in Isaiah was in order to present the image of Hezekiah as a faithful king who trusts Yahweh rather than rely upon human resources to deliver Judah. Cf. Johannes Meinhold, *Die JesajaerzäHlungen, Jesaja 36–39: Eine Historisch-Kritische Untersuchung* (Göttingen: Vandenhoeck und Ruprecht, 1898), 18. I have argued elsewhere that the Judahite king could appropriate temple treasures without censure in the monarchic period and that it was only in later postexilic literature where such actions were viewed negatively. Cf. Paul S. Evans, "The Function of the Chronicler's Temple Despoliation Notices in Light of Imperial Realities in Yehud," *JBL* 129 (2010): 31–47. See also my discussion in Evans, *Invasion of Sennacherib*, 127–9. Childs (*Assyrian Crisis*, 69–70 n. 1) suggested that the omission of Hezekiah's capitulation was unintentional and due to haplography "caused by the recurrence of the identical verb at the beginning of vv. 14 and 17." Seitz has argued that the story of capitulation was an addition to the Kings narrative, though few have followed him. Cf. Seitz, *Zion's Final Destiny*, 51–61; Seitz, "Account A and the Annals of Sennacherib: A Reassessment," *JSOT* 58 (1993): 47–57. Recently Kahn has argued for new source critical delineations and for the priority of the Isaiah text over the Kings version. See Kahn, *Sennacherib's Campaign*, with the source-critical conclusions summarized on pp. 68–72 and then elaborated on for the rest of the monograph.

historical claims.[2] Due to the near-verbatim similarity between the accounts in 2 Kings 18–19 and Isaiah 36–37, we will not treat the Isaiah narratives separately, but focus on the narrative from Kings. This chapter seeks to provide a survey of what events the respective biblical narratives purport to describe. Questions asked will be similar to those posed to the Assyrian texts in the Chapter 3. A wealth of scholarship exists for these biblical narratives, and this brief chapter will not attempt to represent it in a complete way. Instead, the narrative will be read with a view to what its claims are and how they have been understood by historians (as to how the biblical narrative relates to real events external to the text).

4.1 2 Kings 18–19 (Isaiah 36–37)

As noted in the introduction, many assessments of the Hezekiah–Sennacherib narrative begin with a determination of what sources were actually used in the construction of the narrative. However, recent work and my previous monograph in particular have undermined the matrix of sources as traditionally perceived by historical critical biblical scholars.[3] In my judgment, it is impossible to definitively determine the sources that underlie the present narrative in 2 Kings 18–19, though I have no doubt that sources were used.[4] The current state of affairs must conclude that such sources are ultimately *unidentifiable*. Thus, our reading of the text will not assume speculative source-critical delineations (e.g., the Stade–Childs source-critical hypothesis).[5] Rather than assume that the narrative describes the same event thrice (in the putative sources many have held to in the past—sources A, B1, and B2), we will take the narrative as it is and take into account the intended claims of the text as relevant to our research questions.

Another aspect of 2 Kings 18–19 that is held by a significant consensus is that these narratives are part of the so-called Deuteronomistic History. Despite the

---

2. Paul S. Evans, "Historia or Exegesis? Assessing the Chronicler's Hezekiah-Sennacherib Narrative," in *Chronicling the Chronicler: The Book of Chronicles and Early Second Temple Historiography* (eds. Evans and Williams; Winona Lake, IN: Eisenbrauns, 2013), 103–20.

3. Paul S. Evans, "Sennacherib's 701 Invasion into Judah: What Saith the Scriptures?," in *The Function of Ancient Historiography in Biblical and Cognate Studies* (eds. Kirkpatrick and Goltz; JSOTSup/LHBOTS, 489; London: T&T Clark, 2008), 39–63. As Sweeney writes of the source-critical conclusions of Stade and Childs, "It is based largely on the limited presuppositions of late-nineteenth-century source-critical exegesis that failed to consider the literary relationships between materials that it identified as discrete literary sources." Cf. Sweeney, *I & II Kings*, 411. Cf. Smelik, "King Hezekiah," 93–128.

4. Yet it seems clear that the author of the narrative must have had access to sources that gave him information concerning the events he describes. If we posit the author living over a century later than Sennacherib's invasion, there is no other way to account for the correspondences we find between his narrative and Assyrian accounts of the same events.

5. For a thorough debunking of this hypothesis, see Evans, *Invasion of Sennacherib*, 39–63.

consensus that Deuteronomy–2 Kings are part of one extended narrative, there is no longer a consensus concerning when its composition should be dated. Noth's position of an exilic Deuteronomist still has adherents, while others hold to the double redaction promulgated by the Harvard School.[6] Still others hold to a multiple redaction theory theorized by the Göttingen school.[7] Alternatively, some simply posit it, along with Chronicles, as competing postexilic histories.[8] Regardless of which hypothesis one chooses, all hold the narratives to be completed much later than the events recounted—perhaps a century later, if not more. However, despite the late date of its final compilation, we will assume it is reliant on earlier sources, though unidentifiable, and approach the story as more than pure fiction but wary of the passage of time and its later historical perspective.

4.1.1 The Regnal Resume (2 Kgs 18:1-8)

The narrative account in 2 Kings 18 begins with an introduction of Hezekiah, which assesses him very positively (this is especially underscored when assessments of other monarchs in the narratives of Kings are taken into account, given they are nearly always negative). Besides genealogical information and his length of

---

6. Frank Moore Cross, "The Themes of the Book of Kings and the Structure of the Deuteronomistic History," in *Canaanite Myth and Hebrew Epic* (Cambridge, MA: Harvard University Press, 1973), 274–89; Richard D. Nelson, *The Double Redaction of the Deuteronomistic History* (JSOTSup, 18; Sheffield: JSOT Press, 1981); Steven L. McKenzie, *The Chronicler's Use of the Deuteronomistic History* (HSM, 33; Atlanta, GA: Scholars Press, 1985). Richard E. Friedman also argued for a two-stage composition. Cf. *The Exile and Biblical Narrative: The Formation of the Deuteronomistic and Priestly Works* (Chico, CA; Scholars Press, 1981). Brian Peckham held to a two-stage compositional theory, but one that was very different from others in specifics. Cf. *The Composition of the Deuteronomistic History* (Atlanta, GA: Scholars Press, 1985). Others not associated with Harvard also have argued for the theory. A. D. H. Mayes, *The Story of Israel between Settlement and Exile: A Redactional Study of the Deuteronomistic History* (London: SCM Press, 1983); Iain W. Provan, *Hezekiah and the Books of Kings: A Contribution to the Debate about the Composition of the Deuteronomistic History* (Berlin: de Gruyter, 1988).

7. Rudolf Smend, "Das Gesetz und die Völker: Ein Beitrag zur deuteronomistishen Redaktionsgeschichte," in *Probleme Biblischer Theologie: Festschrift Gerhard Von Rad* (ed. Wolff; Munich: Chr. Kaiser, 1971); Walter Dietrich, *Prophetie und Geschichte; eine redaktionsgeschichtliche Untersuchung zum deuteronomistischen Geschichtswerk* (FRLNT, 108; Göttingen: Vandenhoeck & Ruprecht, 1972); Timo Veijola, *Die ewige Dynastie: David und die Entstehung seiner Dynastie nach der deuteronomistischen Darstellung* (AASF, 193; Helsinki: Suomalainen Tiedeakatemia, 1975).

8. Raymond F. Person, *The Deuteronomic School: History, Social Setting, and Literature* 2 (Atlanta, GA: Society of Biblical Literature, 2002); Thomas Römer, *The So-Called Deuteronomistic History: A Sociological, Historical, and Literary Introduction* (London: T&T Clark, 2005).

reign, a key event for our research question that is referenced in this section is Hezekiah's military action against Philistia (2 Kgs 18:8). Here Hezekiah is said to have attacked the Philistine city of Gaza and its territory (גְּבוּלֶיהָ). As noted in the previous chapter, the defeat of Gaza by anti-Assyrian forces is not mentioned in Assyrian annals, and Ṣil-Bēl, King of Gaza, is not among those kings who "willingly" submitted to Sennacherib.[9] The Kings account claims Hezekiah's attack on Philistia was not limited to Gaza, but that he attacked it and its vicinity "from watchtower to fortified city" (2) (מִמִּגְדַּל נוֹצְרִים עַד־עִיר מִבְצָר Kgs 18:8). This phrase is used only one other time in the OT/HB, in 2 Kgs 17:9 wherein it denotes the ubiquity of the unorthodox cultic practices of the northern kingdom that were being widespread from "watchtower to fortified city" (מִמִּגְדַּל נוֹצְרִים עַד־עִיר מִבְצָר).[10] Thus, its use in 18:8 clearly implies Hezekiah had military success beyond Gaza itself.

As noted in our treatment of Assyrian texts, neither Gaza's status as a rebel city nor its conquest by Assyria is mentioned in Sennacherib's annals, though it is most likely that they, like other Philistine cities, participated in the rebellion. Therefore, it seems likely that Hezekiah's attack on Philistine Gaza referenced here in 2 Kgs 18:8 was to secure its participation in the rebellion. Mayer has suggested that this Judahite attack on Philistia was the occasion for the capture and imprisonment of Padî, King of Ekron.[11] If so, it is interesting that there is no mention of it here, with the focus being on Gaza instead. Whether Ṣil-Bēl, King of Gaza, was taken prisoner by Hezekiah, like Padî, is open to question. No such action is referenced in biblical or Assyrian texts. Perhaps Gaza's king under Judahite military duress eventually agreed to participate in the rebellion, or the people of Gaza kept the king imprisoned themselves without handing him to Hezekiah. Regardless, it is noteworthy that Kings fails to mention Ekron, while Assyrian texts fail to mention Gaza. Both traditions focus on different aspects of the geopolitical situation. Perhaps in some way Gaza was an embarrassment for Assyria (Gaza and its king may have rebelled, yet Sennacherib later gives land grants to the king), but an occasion to boast for Hezekiah (as victory against Philistines shows a David-like quality). Similarly, Sennacherib's focus on Ekron, and the liberation of Padî, was an important aspect of Sennacherib's achievements,[12] but could have been an

---

9. Ben Zvi, "Malleability and Its Limits," 95.

10. This suggests either conscious redactional efforts to connect the Hezekiah macronarrative with what went before or the purposeful work of the author of *both* narratives.

11. Mayer, "Sennacherib's Campaign," 176.

12. Dubovský has argued that from the Assyrian perspective, the Padî incident was "one of the most important events of Sennacherib's campaign." Sennacherib's liberation of Padî presented a clear "political message: the vassals loyal to Assyria, such as Padî, should not be afraid; they would be saved from the clutches of rebels, despite being imprisoned in fortified enemy headquarters such as Jerusalem." Cf. Dubovský, "Assyrians under the Walls of Jerusalem," 114.

embarrassment for Hezekiah (since it entailed surrendering a guilty Philistine king to the enemy). Thus, the biblical texts do not mention Ekron, or Padî, despite the extensive Assyrian threats and "negotiations" recounted.

The Assyrian texts seem to imply cooperation between Hezekiah and Philistia, but the Kings text does not. The Assyrian annals clearly present Hezekiah in collusion with Philistine Ekron as the Ekronites handed over their deposed pro-Assyrian king to Hezekiah in fetters.[13] In contrast to the sense of the Annalistic account, the Kings account presents Hezekiah's action in Philistia as hostile. Rather than working with Philistia to form a rebel alliance to oppose Assyria, Hezekiah attacks the Philistines (הִכָּה אֶת־פְּלִשְׁתִּים) and prevails (יַשְׁכִּיל) (2 Kgs 18:7-8). This presentation is in keeping with traditional Judahite ideology wherein Philistia is the enemy and Hezekiah's success against this ancient foe is likely meant to cast him positively and in a similar light as the founder of the dynasty, King David (e.g., 2 Sam 8:1). Significantly, in biblical accounts, only David and Hezekiah are said to have had success against Philistia. If in fact Hezekiah was allied with the Philistines, this would not reflect well on him in regard to traditional Judahite ideology. Therefore, Hezekiah's alliances in the rebellion go unmentioned. This also explains the omission of Padî and his imprisonment in Jerusalem.

This omission of the acknowledgment of Hezekiah's involvement with other rebel states is underscored with the use of the phrase in 2 Kgs 18:8 from "watchtower to fortified city" (מִמִּגְדַּל נוֹצְרִים עַד־עִיר מִבְצָר), which clearly connects with the story of Samaria's fall to Assyria in the previous chapter (2 Kgs 17:9). In 2 Kings 17, it is recounted that the king of Samaria both rebelled against Assyria and made an alliance with Egypt (2 Kgs 17:4). Since such actions by Samaria in 2 Kgs 17 led to the destruction of Samaria, it is understandable that the presentation of Hezekiah in ch. 18 would avoid showing Hezekiah undertaking similar actions. The account of Samaria's fall is actually re-narrated within the Hezekiah narrative itself (2 Kgs 18:9-12) so the omission of Hezekiah's foreign alliances fits with the goal of presenting Hezekiah as distinct from the Israelite monarchs of the former northern kingdom.

4.1.2 The Assyrian Crisis (2 Kgs 18:13–19:37)

4.1.2.1 Sennacherib's Initial Success The narration of Sennacherib's invasion begins by recounting the widespread military success of the Assyrian campaign as Sennacherib is said to have "seized" (תפש) all the fortified cities (2 Kgs 18:13). The verb תפש denotes "to seize, take possession of" and with the accusative being a town or city; "to seize possession" or "to conquer."[14] Clearly, this describes more than an attack on these cities, but a successful assault that resulted in the "capture" of the said municipalities. As we have seen in the Assyrian texts, Sennacherib boasts of capturing forty-six of Hezekiah's fortified cities along with innumerable

---

13. RINAP 3.1:175, 22.ii.74. Cf. Luckenbill, *The Annals of Sennacherib*, 31.
14. תפש *HALOT*.

other Judahite sites.[15] The Kings account offers no contrast to this accounting, being willing to acknowledge the capture of "all" (כָּל) such cities by the Assyrians. As noted previously, archaeological evidence suggests there were not forty-six fortified cities in all of Judah at the time, making the Assyrian claims a clear instance of exaggeration.[16] Similarly, the recounting of the loss of "all" fortified cities here in the Kings' text appears also to be an exaggeration. As we have seen in the earlier chapter on archaeological evidence, not all fortified cities were actually taken by the Assyrians with notable exceptions being untouched by Assyrian aggression (e.g., Mizpah, Gibeon, Ramat Raḥel, Gerar, Gezer, Gibeah, Beth-Zur, Makkedah, Moladah, Nebi-Samuel). It is possible the Kings account would exaggerate in this regard in order to accentuate the surprise of the final outcome (Assyria had taken every city but Jerusalem, but still failed to conquer the land) as well as make sure to attribute Judahite success to reliance on Yahweh, and not fortifications.

4.1.2.1.1 Hezekiah's Submission Following the acknowledgment of the Assyrian success against his Judahite cities, Hezekiah's submission to Sennacherib is recounted (18:14). In fact, according to this text, Hezekiah's submission occurred *before* any military action took place against Jerusalem itself. This seems to contrast the Assyrian presentation, which only mentions Hezekiah's capitulation after action is taken against Jerusalem.[17] While Sennacherib was at Lachish, Hezekiah "sent (וַיִּשְׁלַח) to the king of Assyria ..." (v. 14). This verb has no explicit direct object but probably implies the ellipsis of the object, "messengers." Thus, like in the Assyrian annals, Hezekiah does *not* present himself in person and submit to Sennacherib, as do the eight submissive kings mentioned in Assyrian texts.[18]

Sennacherib is said to have demanded a heavy tribute of Hezekiah during his meeting with Hezekiah's messengers at Lachish (2 Kgs 18:14). We may speculate that, historically, a demand for Padî's release may have been part of the demands made of Hezekiah here, but as we have already noted, Padî and Hezekiah's cooperative involvement with Philistia is omitted from Judahite texts. Regarding the amount of tribute demanded, as is well known, there are some close correspondences with the amount of gold listed here and in the Assyrian annals. Assyrian texts claim a payment of 30 talents of gold and 800 talents of silver,[19] whereas the Kings account records a demand of 30 talents of gold and 300 talents of silver. Various scenarios and explanations have been offered to explicate the discrepancy between the amounts of silver mentioned in each,[20] but more remarkable is their close agreement in regard to the gold.

15. RINAP 3.1:176, 22.iii.19–21.
16. Dever, *Beyond the Texts*, 563.
17. RINAP 3.1:176, 22.iii, 28–30.
18. RINAP 3.1:175, 22.ii.50–58.
19. RINAP 3.1"177, 22.iii.41–42.
20. Harold Henry Rowley suggested that the Assyrian talent and the Judahite talent were of different sizes. Cf. Rowley, "Hezekiah's Reform and Rebellion," *BJRL* 44 (1962): 432. Cogan and Tadmor (*II Kings*, 229) suggested the larger amount of silver recorded in the

What is more of a contrast than the amount of tribute paid is *when* each text claims payment was delivered. Hezekiah is said "at that time" (בָּעֵת הַהִיא) to have taken precious metals from the temple and paid them to Sennacherib (2 Kgs 18:15-16). In contrast, the Assyrian account records that tribute was sent to Sennacherib only *after* he had returned to Nineveh.[21] As we have noted, the acknowledgment that tribute was not collected during the campaign is often seen as a detail that may disguise the fact that not all went perfectly for the Assyrians in the campaign. But what do we make of the note about tribute being paid earlier in the campaign, before Sennacherib's withdrawal? Gallagher has suggested, "Sennacherib initially rejected Hezekiah's offer, but later accepted it."[22] In the Kings account, subsequent to the payment of tribute Sennacherib sends an army ("חֵיל כָּבֵד") to Jerusalem to demand its total surrender (2 Kgs 18:17-37). It seems likely that the payment to Sennacherib is recorded as being delivered before the Assyrian demands for surrender in order to vilify the Assyrian king.[23] Sennacherib is presented as dishonorable and going back on his word. Hezekiah had agreed to payment on condition that Sennacherib withdraw from him (שׁוּב מֵעָלַי) (2 Kgs 18:14), yet despite Hezekiah living up to his end of the bargain, Sennacherib takes the payment but does not withdraw. This vilification of the enemy king is not unique to the biblical text. Dubovský has observed of Assyrian accounts "the tendency of the Assyrian scribes to vilify Hezekiah."[24] Both sides sought to present the enemy in a negative light.

4.1.2.1.2 The Assyrian Delegation to Jerusalem In the Kings account, after accepting payment from Hezekiah, Sennacherib sends an army and demands the total surrender of Jerusalem as the text narrates a long confrontation (18:17-37). The Assyrians are said to send a "חֵיל כָּבֵד" to Jerusalem to demand its surrender.

Assyrian annals included the silver from the temple doors, while the biblical amount did not, which is an ironic suggestion given that it is only the biblical account that mentions precious metals being taken from the temple doors in the context of the tribute (2 Kgs 18:16). In fact, it does not note what precious metal came from these doors, though most translators add the word "gold" to explain (probably to make it conform to the Assyrian demand in v. 14). Mayer suggests the larger number (800) in the Assyrian texts includes not only the 300 talents of silver mentioned in the biblical account but also the other goods mentioned in the Assyrian inscription (silver, antimony, carnelian, ivory beds etc.). Cf. Mayer, *Politik und Kriegskunst Der Assyrer*, 360–3.

21. RINAP 3.1:177, 22.iii.47–49.
22. Gallagher, *Sennacherib's Campaign*, 257.
23. As Sweeney (*I & II Kings*, 412) writes, the placement of Hezekiah's submission "at the outset of the narrative highlights Sennacherib's despicable character as an arrogant and unjust enemy of YHWH by portraying his demands for Hezekiah's surrender and the deportation of the population even after Hezekiah had already submitted to his authority." Cf. Ben Zvi, "Malleability and Its Limits," 82.
24. Dubovský, "Assyrians under the Walls of Jerusalem," 118.

There have been various suggestions regarding how to understand this phrase in the Kings account. A standard translation of "חַיִל כָּבֵד" here is "a great army." In the past, when the Assyrian siege of Jerusalem was read into this account "חַיִל כָּבֵד" was often understood to be a besieging army. Given the consensus that Jerusalem was not besieged in 701 BCE, this understanding of "חַיִל כָּבֵד" is unlikely. Elsewhere in the book of Kings "חַיִל כָּבֵד" is used of an Aramean army that "encircles" the city of Dothan (וַיַּקִּפוּ עַל־הָעִיר) but is later led away by Elisha the prophet and brought into the city of Samaria (2 Kgs 6:19-20). In this instance, the "חַיִל כָּבֵד" appears small enough to not only enter the city with ease but also to be destroyed by the inhabitants (2 Kgs 6:21). Thus, "it would appear from the context in 2 Kings 6 that 'חַיִל כָּבֵד' is used to denote a small military force appropriate for attacking a small city in order to capture an individual but inappropriate for the task of defeating a larger city like Samaria—despite the fact they successfully entered through the city walls."[25] The use of the "חַיִל כָּבֵד" here may denote a similar-sized military contingent that supported the rhetorical mission of the Assyrian emissaries.

Dubovský has argued the "חַיִל כָּבֵד" must have been significant enough to support the intimidation strategy being used to negotiate Padî's extradition.[26] However, it does not seem necessary to posit that a major Assyrian military contingent was present at the time, as the Judahites knew how the nearby Shephelah was being devastated by Assyrian armies. Grabbe suggests that "the nearest Assyrian army [to Jerusalem] seems to have approached no closer than Ramat Raḥel" and that "no Assyria troops were camped outside the city's walls."[27] While Sennacherib does not acknowledge the rhetorical mission, he does assert that he blockaded Jerusalem, which could be the same occasion remembered here by the biblical text, though the "blockade" contingents were not necessarily close to the city. Mayer suggests Sennacherib had "forts built around Hezekiah's territory" to "control access routes."[28] Knauf notes that Sennacherib's forts were not necessarily near the city, as Sennacherib's annals do not state their distance from Jerusalem (he questions whether they were "100 m, 1 km or 10 km" from Jerusalem's gate).[29]

As noted above, the Kings account presents the rhetorical mission as negotiations between Hezekiah's and Sennacherib's officials—neither king is present.[30] What is significant in our work here is that no such negotiations are mentioned in the Assyrian texts. Of course, as noted, it seems "negotiations" of some kind must have taken place, at minimum to secure the extradition of Padî from Hezekiah's

---

25. Evans, *Invasion of Sennacherib*, 153.
26. Dubovský, "Assyrians under the Walls of Jerusalem," 125.
27. Lester L. Grabbe, "Israelite Interaction with Egypt During the Monarchy: A Context for Interpreting 2 Kings 19:8–13," in *Jerusalem's Survival, Sennacherib's Departure, and the Kushite Role in 701 BCE* (ed. Bellis; PHSC, 32; New Jersey: Gorgias Press, 2019), 201.
28. Mayer, "Sennacherib's Campaign," 181.
29. Knauf, "Sennacherib at the Berezina," 145.
30. The main Assyrian negotiator is referred to as the Rabshakeh, though he is accompanied by the Tartan and the Rabsaris (2 Kgs 18:17).

custody.³¹ There have been various suggestions regarding how to understand the content of the Assyrian "negotiations" in Kings.³² While it appears evident that the Rabshakeh's speeches comprise common biblical language and even resemble prophetic language,³³ it is unlikely they are created out of whole cloth as they also must have been constrained somewhat by the historical event and likely represent Judahite memories of the occasion.³⁴ In favor of their historicity is the fact that the main speaker is the Rabshakeh, rather than a more important official (like the Tartan) or Sennacherib himself.³⁵ As Ben Zvi concludes, they represent "some collective memory about an Assyrian Rabshakeh, who came to Jerusalem at that time with a message from the Assyrian king."³⁶

Several times in the Kings account of the Assyrian speeches it seems clear the demand is for total surrender of the city (2 Kgs 18:30, 35), with a lengthy siege threatened (18:27) and deportation promised (18:32).³⁷ Besides the problematic nature of the use of common biblical language in the Rabshakeh's speeches, the Assyrian demand for Jerusalem's total surrender is potentially problematic historically. As we have seen, many reconstructions of Sennacherib's campaign and his war aims exclude the goal of taking Jerusalem.³⁸ Of course, the Assyrian

---

31. See my arguments for the historicity of the Assyrian rhetorical mission in Evans, *Invasion of Sennacherib*, 179–81. An example of similar negotiations is found in the Nimrud letters, where the Assyrians send emissaries to the city of Babylon, which was in rebellion against their suzerain. The parallels between the 2 Kings account and the Nimurd letters have been dealt with at length in earlier studies. Cf. Childs, *Assyrian Crisis*, 80–2.

32. Weinfeld, "Cult Centralization," 202–12; Childs, *Assyrian Crisis*, 78–93; Ben Zvi, "Who Wrote the Speech," 79–92; Smelik, "King Hezekiah," 93–128; Rudman, "Is the Rabshakeh Also among the Prophets," 100; Steven W. Holloway, "Harran: Cultic Geography in the Neo-Assyrian Empire and Its Implications for Sennacherib's 'Letter to Hezekiah' in 2 Kings," in *The Pitcher Is Broken: Memorial Essays for Gösta W. Ahlstrom* (eds. Holloway and Handy; JSOTSup, 190; Sheffield: Sheffield Academic Press, 1995), 276–314. Machinist, "The Rab Saqeh," 151–68; Cohen, "Neo-Assyrian Elements," 32–48; Gallagher, *Sennacherib's Campaign*.

33. Paul S. Evans, "The Hezekiah-Sennacherib Narrative as Polyphonic Text," *JSOT* 33 (2009): 335–58; Rudman, "Is the Rabshakeh Also among the Prophets," 100; Ben Zvi, "Who Wrote the Speech," 79–92.

34. Ben Zvi, "Who Wrote the Speech," 79–92; Cohen, "Neo-Assyrian Elements," 32–48; Machinist, "The Rab Saqeh," 151–68; Weinfeld, "Cult Centralization," 202–12.

35. As Ben Zvi ("Who Wrote the Speech," 92) suggests, "The theological importance of the message that the biblical writer(s) put in [Rabshakeh's] mouth is more appropriate for the king of Assyria. If the literary features of the piece required a messenger, as it seems, the more suitable messenger would be a high-ranking Assyrian officer, like Tartan."

36. Ibid.

37. The Rabshakeh actually claims he has a divine mandate to "destroy" (לְהַשְׁחִתוֹ) the entire "land" (עֲלֵה עַל־הָאָרֶץ הַזֹּאת וְהַשְׁחִיתָהּ) of Judah (2 Kgs 18:25).

38. E.g., Mayer, "Sennacherib's Campaign," 184; Knauf, "Sennacherib at the Berezina," 146; Clements, *Deliverance of Jerusalem*, 62.

texts do not even refer to any negotiations taking place, so what war aims were communicated to the enemy is open to question. It seems unnecessary to exclude the Assyrian demand for surrender from being part of the rhetorical strategy of the Assyrians, even if in reality they were prepared to accept less than total surrender. This is part and parcel of how negotiations work. Large demands begin negotiations, with the final agreement being presented as a huge concession—even if the negotiator was prepared to concede this from the beginning. In other words, from the Assyrian viewpoint, demands of total surrender of Jerusalem may have been mostly a rhetorical strategy and not an essential element of their war aims. However, from the Judahite perspective, demands for total surrender were made. The war aims communicated by the Assyrian negotiators included the taking of Jerusalem (2 Kgs 18:30) and the deportation of its inhabitants (2 Kgs 18:32). When this did not occur, the Judahites could understand that the Assyrian conquest was unsuccessful. From a Judahite perspective, Assyria had failed and Judah had prevailed.

4.1.2.1.3 The Nubian Egyptian Expedition In response to the threats of the Rabshakeh, Hezekiah sends officials to the prophet Isaiah who delivers a prophecy that Sennacherib will hear a report, return to his land, and be killed (19:7). This apparently begins to be fulfilled in 19:8 where the Rabshakeh hears a report that Sennacherib had left Lachish to fight Libnah, causing the Rabshakeh to "withdraw." Possibly (presumably?) the "חַיִל כָּבֵד" that accompanied the Assyrian emissaries would have gone with the Rabshakeh (though they may have remained "dug in" in order to blockade routes to the city). The clear fulfillment of the first part of the Isaianic prophecy is seen in 19:9 as Sennacherib himself hears a report about the advance of Tirhakah, King of Cush, necessitating that Sennacherib make plans to deal with the Egyptian incursion.[39]

Much has been written about whether Tirhakah (Taharqo) could have been present in Palestine in 701 BCE as it was once thought he was too young in 701 BCE. As noted in the introduction, more recent work, however, has confirmed Taharqo was old enough to lead the army at Eltekeh, and he may have even been King of Cush (though not King of Egypt) at the time. Thus, as Young writes, "although Taharqo was not yet a Pharaoh, ruler of Egypt, there is no reason to doubt that he was both a skilled military leader and 'the king of Kush' in 701 B.C.E."[40] As to whether any battle occurred between the Assyrians and the Nubian Egyptian forces, the biblical account is silent. As we have seen the Assyrian accounts focus on the battle at Eltekeh, and consider it a major victory for Sennacherib, even noting his personal contributions to the fighting ("The Egyptian charioteers

---

39. Regarding Sennacherib's response to the report of the Nubian incursion, Younger notes, "The Assyrian king took action based on this report (at least in the first instance, sending a message to Hezekiah to persuade him to surrender)." Cf. Younger, "Aubin's the Rescue of Jerusalem," 243.

40. Young, *Hezekiah in History and Tradition*, 76.

and princes, together with the charioteers of the Ethiopians, I personally took alive in the midst of battle").⁴¹ The Kings account, however, does appear to leave room for a Nubian Egyptian contribution. After Sennacherib hears the report about Tirhakah's approach, the Assyrians no longer approach Jerusalem, sending threatening letters (19:14) and not their army. In fact, the geographic location of the angelic attack (2 Kgs 19:35) that concludes the Assyrian crisis in the Kings account is ambiguous. Though many have supposed the narrative presenting this action to have taken place at "the walls of Jerusalem," the narrative last presents the Assyrian army hearing of Tirhakah, and presumably moving to stop the incursion.

If the battle of Eltekeh was either a Nubian Egyptian victory or a stalemate, it is easy to see why Assyrian scribes would not include this in their text as it would counter Assyrian ideology and expectations. However, the biblical scribes would be equally unlikely to acknowledge the positive contribution of an Egyptian contingent in the withdrawal of Sennacherib as it would be counterideological to the biblical narrative. Biblical texts assert that only Yahweh can be relied upon for success, not foreign powers like Egypt. In fact, Egypt is singled out as an unreliable agent many times (e.g., 2 Kgs 17:4; Hos 12:2; Isa 30:1-7; 31:1, 3; Jer 37:6-8; 46:25; Ezek 29:6-7). Yet, the reference to Tirhakah and his distracting effect upon Sennacherib is included in the Kings account. Acknowledgment by the Kings text that the Egyptian army was effective against the enemy of Judah is remarkable in light of many references to the impotence of Egyptian allies.⁴²

4.1.2.1.4 The Assyrian Letter Threat In the Kings text, following the Rabshakeh's withdrawal from Jerusalem and Tirhakah's approach leading Sennacherib to deal with the Nubian Egyptian forces, threatening letters are sent to Jerusalem (2 Kgs 19:14). The content of the letters is similar to the Rabshakeh's threats in the previous chapter, except this time they address the king. While the Rabshakeh warned the Jerusalemites not to let Hezekiah deceive them (2 Kgs 18:29), the letter threat warns Hezekiah not to let his god deceive him (2 Kgs 19:10). Again, no mention is made of Padî or his extradition. Dubovský has noted that in Assyrian practice "negotiations aimed at getting hold of a wanted person were mainly conducted by means of messengers and letters."⁴³ Of course, Padî may have already been freed along with the initial tribute offered by Hezekiah at Lachish, but the use of a letter here makes it possible that the issue of the extradition of Padî was also addressed in the correspondence.

Dubovský has further noted Assyrian practice was usually to employ psychological warfare in letters first, then in face-to-face negotiations. He writes,

---

41. Cogan's translation (*COS* 2.119B). Cf. RINAP 3.1:176, 22, iii, 3–5.
42. Evans, *Invasion of Sennacherib*, 178–9.
43. Dubovský, "Assyrians under the Walls of Jerusalem," 120. Cf. Peter Dubovský, *Hezekiah and the Assyrian Spies: Reconstruction of the Neo-Assyrian Intelligence Services and Its Significance for 2 Kings 18–19* (BibOr 49; Rome: Pontifical Biblical Institute, 2006), 80–3.

The Assyrians, in order to get hold of a wanted person, first sent letters and messengers. If such peaceful diplomatic missions failed, they next employed threats and paramilitary operations. But if even these failed, and the person was important enough, the Assyrians would bring military units to devastate the region.[44]

This appears to be the very opposite of the presentation of events in the Kings account. Perhaps this might suggest the Kings account is dischronologized.[45] As we have seen above, it is widely acknowledged that the Assyrian annals is not chronological, for example, recounting the reinstallation of Padî before the Judahite phase of the campaign. Perhaps the letter threat was sent first, to demand Padî's release and Jerusalem's surrender. When Hezekiah did not comply, the Rabshakeh was sent with some military forces (חַיִל כָּבֵד). The final stage of the Assyrians devastating a region did not occur in Jerusalem's case as the city and the highlands remained unmolested. If the account is dischronologized, the payment of tribute by Hezekiah (18:13-16) may have been sent after Sennacherib's withdrawal as is the case in the Assyrian annals.[46] Regardless, the lack of an Assyrian implementation of a full siege of Jerusalem may have led to the Judahite perspective of failed war aims for Sennacherib.

4.1.2.1.5 The Angelic Assault on Assyrian Forces The climax of the Kings account of Sennacherib's invasion is found when an angel assaults the Assyrian camp nocturnally and claims "185,000" casualties (19:35). This devastating loss of soldiers leads Sennacherib to withdraw (וַיָּשָׁב) to Nineveh and "dwell" (וַיֵּשֶׁב) there. Thus, the text ends the Assyrian crisis with a clear loss for Sennacherib's army. Despite early success and the taking of all the fortified cities, what mattered to the Kings' scribe was that the final battle was a loss, and Sennacherib returned home without achieving his stated war aims of taking Jerusalem and deporting its inhabitants. What is more, the text, written well after the fact, claims that Sennacherib did not return to Judah but instead stayed (וַיֵּשֶׁב) in Nineveh.

Needless to say, this claim of the text is the most disputed historically. The number, 185,000, seems indefensible, and a clearly exaggerated number given that, as Broshi and Finkelstein's have estimated, Palestine had a total population of only around 400,000 at the time.[47] That an army of this size was moving around Palestine is not possible. What is more, the size of the army is greater than the number of

---

44. Dubovský, "Assyrians under the Walls of Jerusalem," 121.

45. Cf. W. J. Martin, "'Dischronologized' Narrative in the Old Testament," in *Congress Volume Rome 1968* (VTSup 17; Leiden: Brill, 1969), 179–86.

46. As Lloyd writes, "It is impossible not to suspect that this latter payment has been transposed in Kings to the location before the siege so that YHWH could have a free hand in delivering Jerusalem by His intervention." Cf. Lloyd, "The Siege of Jerusalem by Sennacherib," 216.

47. Broshi and Finkelstein, "Population of Palestine," 47–60.

casualties, since the survivors woke in the morning to see their dead comrades. It is clear that both Judahite and Assyrian traditions employ exaggerated numbers in their account. Sennacherib's annals also exaggerated numbers greatly, claiming to have deported 200,150 people from Judah, when in reality Judah only had a population of about 110,000 in total.[48] Inflated numbers do not require a necessary rejection of a historical kernel behind the claim.[49] Lloyd suggests the number be "treated as impressionistic, meaning no more than 'a very large number of men.'"[50] As we noted above, Sennacherib's deportation numbers are thought by some to be merely a "claim" on the Judahites as spoil rather than a claim that they were actually deported (though the number claimed still exceeds the actual population of Judah by a 2:1 margin).[51]

More at issue than the remarkably large number is the recording of an Assyrian defeat at all in the third campaign. As we have seen, Sennacherib's annals present the campaign as an unqualified victory.[52] Of course, the recounting of the Eltekeh battle has suggested to some that the success of Assyria here is exaggerated.[53] Some think it might hide an Assyrian setback,[54] a stalemate,[55] if not outright loss.[56] Since the last time the Assyrian army was mentioned in the Kings account before the angelic attack is in the context of the Nubian Egyptian approach, it is possible that what historically lay behind the Assyrian defeat at the hands of the angel was the battle of Eltekeh. Regardless of exaggerated numbers, divine causation of the defeat, or the exact location, from a Judahite perspective the Assyrians lost their last battle and had to retreat. Sennacherib abandoned his stated war aims of taking Jerusalem and returned to Nineveh, never to return.

The presentation of the perceived Assyrian defeat at Eltekeh as a defeat at Yahweh's hands is usually understood by scholars to be a much later theologizing of the event.[57] For example, Clements asserts that the attribution of Jerusalem's

---

48. Ibid., 54. Or, alternatively, 120,000 as Finkelstein ("Archeaology of the Days of Manasseh," 176) later estimated.

49. As Elayi (Sennacherib, 73) opines, "Exaggerating the number of conquered cities, prisoners of war, items of booty was part of the propaganda in the royal inscriptions."

50. Lloyd, "Siege of Jerusalem," 217.

51. Zevit, "Implicit Population Figures," 364.

52. Mayer, "Sennacherib's Campaign," 177.

53. Tadmor, "Philistia under Assyrian Rule," 97; Gallagher, *Sennacherib's Campaign*, 121; Kitchen, *Third Intermediate Period*, 385, n. 822; Spalinger, "Foreign Policy," 36.

54. Knauf, "Sennacherib at the Berezina," 147; Eph'al, "On Warfare," 98.

55. Gallagher, *Sennacherib's Campaign*, 121.

56. Redford, *Egypt, Canaan, and Israel*, 353.

57. It is commonly held this part of the narrative had to come from a much later time period. E.g., Sweeney, *I & II Kings: A Commentary*, 412; Na'aman, "Updating the Messages," 213; Machinist, "The Rab Saqeh," 151–68; Alexander Rofé, *The Prophetical Stories: The Narratives about the Prophets in the Hebrew Bible, Their Literary Types and History* (Jerusalem: Magnes Press, Hebrew University, 1988), 88–95; Vogt, *Der Aufstand Hiskias*, 50–8; Childs, *Assyrian Crisis*, 94–103.

deliverance to the angel of Yahweh had "only been introduced into the narrative of the events of that year at a comparatively late stage."[58] However, this supposition is unnecessary. The Judahite perspective of the eighth century was not less theological than later generations. The events of Eltekeh would likely have been understood as Yahweh's victory immediately by the people of Judah. We need not posit centuries in between to explain the interpretation. It is not as if the people in 701 BCE Judah were Rankean and only wanted to record history *wie es eigentlich gewesen*, but later came to embellish and mythologize. We have no reason to believe that eighth-century Judahites were any less theological in their worldview than sixth-century Judahites.[59] The positing of the interval of a century or more before such an interpretation was invented seems like a scholarly attempt to isolate the historical in the story and cut out the miraculous as a late addition. Besides which, history shows that *contemporary* mythologizing occurs even in wars as recent as the War of 1812. Even contemporary words, actions, and events may be commemorated and mythologized during the same war. After all, as we have seen in Assyrian texts, divine intervention is appealed to in their initial accounts of the campaign with the frequent reference to the "weapon of Assur" being responsible for victorious battles. There is no need to posit a gulf of years to allow for such interpretations to arise.

4.1.2.1.6 The Death of Sennacherib The account in Kings concludes recounting Sennacherib's assassination at the hand of his sons, which occurs while he is worshipping in the temple of his god (19:37). It is possible to consider this reporting somewhat deceptive given that Sennacherib's murder did not occur until *c.* 680 BCE, some twenty years after the third campaign.[60] Doubtless, this telescoping was employed to associate the death of Sennacherib in his own god's temple with the prophecy about his death uttered by Isaiah (19:7) and to underscore the irony of its circumstances given that Sennacherib had boasted about being more powerful than Israel's God, yet his own god cannot save him. As we have seen, the telescoping of events to bolster the account of the defeat of the enemy is also employed in Sennacherib's annals. In the Rassam account, the rebellious Phoenician king, Lulî, is said to have fled Sennacherib's advance and escaped overseas. However, later recensions of the annals claim Lulî died.[61] In fact, the Kings account is less

---

58. Clements, *Deliverance of Jerusalem*, 60-1.

59. This type of thinking seems evident in reconstructions like that of John Gray who suggests that in Account B1 "the Deuteronomistic compiler has elaborated on *historical tradition*" while in Account B2 "the redactor" has elaborated "on an *edifying legend* (emphasis mine)." Cf. Gray, *I & II Kings*, 688.

60. As the Babylonian Chronicle notes, "On the twentieth day of the month of Tebet Sennacherib, king of Assyria, was killed by his son." Cf. Albert Kirk Grayson, *Assyrian and Babylonian Chronicles* (TCS, 5; Locust Valley, NY: J. J. Augustin, 1975), 81. Cf. (*ANET*, 309).

61. With the Assyrian annalistic recension text of 697 (Cylinder C) adding "and disappeared forever." Cf. Cogan, "Sennacherib's Siege of Jerusalem," 302; Cogan, "Cross-Examining," 58; Frahm, *Einleitung* 66, T 10.

deceptive than later Assyrian texts (c. 694 BCE), which explicitly make the claim that Lulî died "in that very year," that is, 701 BCE.[62] Given that the Rassam account, written the following year, did not mention his demise, this dating seems unlikely. The Kings account, on the other hand, does not suggest Sennacherib died that very year, but actually states that he dwelt in Nineveh (וַיֵּשֶׁב בְּנִינְוֵה) first.[63]

4.2 Summary

Like the Assyrian annals, the Kings account of the events of 701 BCE is selective. Regarding Hezekiah's interaction with Philistine states, the focus is on Gaza, and his interactions are presented as hostile. The account is silent regarding any alliance with Philistia or Ekron, and the imprisonment and subsequent release of their pro-Assyrian king, Padî. The presentation of Hezekiah's success against Gaza was likely to present Hezekiah similar to David, the dynasty's founder, who was famous for defeating Philistines. The omission of any cooperative action with Ekron was likely due to the desire to distinguish Hezekiah from the kings of Samaria whose foreign alliances are said to have been their downfall in the previous chapter.

The Kings account presents Sennacherib as having widespread military success, to the point of exaggeration, claiming he captured "all" Judah's fortified cities, though archaeological evidence suggests less cities were captured. Hezekiah's submission to Sennacherib and payment of tribute are presented before Assyrian action against Jerusalem, likely to vilify Sennacherib by presenting him as double-crossing Hezekiah.

In the Kings account, Assyrian threats make no mention of negotiations for Padî's release. Instead, Assyrian threats demanded the total surrender of Jerusalem, threatening a long siege and the deportation of Jerusalem's inhabitants. Given that the stated war aims were not accomplished the Assyrian campaign could be viewed as unsuccessful by Judahites. The defeat at the hands of the angel, which is presented as the culminating event in the campaign, may be Judahite interpretation of the Assyrian setback or defeat at Eltekeh (as implied by reference to the approach of Tirhakah's forces in 19:9a). The account concludes with the assassination of Sennacherib at the hands of his sons, apparently telescoping the event since the intervening decades are not explicitly acknowledged.

While these narratives clearly give a positive portrayal of Jerusalem's survival in the face of the Assyrian war machine, and view Hezekiah positively as one who trusted Yahweh, and was for that reason successful, not all biblical texts remember

---

62. Bulls 2 and 3, Ins. 17–20.
63. Honor understood "and he lived in Nineveh" (וַיֵּשֶׁב בְּנִינְוֵה) as implying a passing of time between Sennacherib's retreat and his assassination. Cf. Honor, *Sennacherib's Invasion*, 72, n. 21.

the Assyrian crisis as fondly. Prophetic oracles from the book of Isaiah often provide a different perspective, not only of the events but also of the leadership of Jerusalem during the Assyrian crisis of the late eighth century. In our next chapter, we will survey Isaianic oracles and determine their perspective on Hezekiah's rebellion and the resulting Assyrian invasion.

Chapter 5

TEXTS FROM THE BOOK OF ISAIAH

Many texts in the book of Isaiah are thought to be relevant to the historical reconstruction undertaken here. Most obviously, Isaiah 36–37 are a synoptic version of the events of Sennacherib's invasion that parallel the text in 2 Kings 18–19 quite closely. However, besides this historiographic/prophetic account, there are prophetic oracles that scholars have often suggested were genuine to the prophet Isaiah and were directed toward Hezekiah and/or his policies and involvement in the rebellion leading up to the Assyrian invasion of 701 BCE.[1] In many Isaianic passages, scholars have observed a contrast between the prophetic promises of Yahweh's protection of Jerusalem, with the prophetic condemnation of Judah's trust in her alliance with Egypt and forecast the concomitant disaster.[2] Many question how the contrasting prophetic promises of assurance could be authentic if the oracles critiquing Judahite leadership are original to Isaiah. Some speculate they may have been uttered in relation to a different historical context[3] or else argue they were written sometime after the Assyrian crisis had ended when the events had been reevaluated from a later perspective. In this chapter, we will look at the disparate texts, surveying scholarly opinions on their relevance in order to be prepared to then read them in light of insights from the study of military

---

1. As Laato bluntly puts it, "It is also often stressed that the picture of Hezekiah in [Isaiah 36–37] ... is completely different to the image of the historic Hezekiah, who has been regarded as the wicked king by Isaiah, because of his planned rebellion which was not according to Yahweh's will (see Is 30,1–5.15–17; 31,1–3)." Antti Laato, "Hezekiah and the Assyrian Crisis in 701 BC," *SJOT* 2 (1987): 49. E.g., Gonçalves sees the book of Isaiah as diametrically opposed to the historical prophet Isaiah of Jerusalem. Cf. Francolino J. Gonçalves, "Isaïe, Jérémie et la Politique Internationale de Juda," *Bib* 76 (1995): 282–98.

2. Of course, some have speculated that Isaiah supported the rebellion but opposed alliances with Egypt. Walther Zimmerli, "Jesaja und Hiskija," in *Wort und Geschichte: Festschrift für Karl Elliger Zum 70. Geburtstag* (eds. Gese and Rüger; AOAT, 18; Kevelaer: Neukirchen-Vluyn, 1973), 201–7. Cf. Gonçalves, "Isaïe, Jérémie," 282–91. The debate over the interpretation of the passages is not new. Cf. Kemper Fullerton, "Viewpoints in the Discussion of Isaiah's Hopes for the Future," *JBL* 41 (1922): 1–101.

3. For example, Bright (*History*, 308) argued for the necessity of two different invasions by Sennacherib on the basis of the dichotomous perspectives found in Isaiah.

history. Rather than following a canonical order, the study will divide the oracles into those that are understood to condemn Hezekiah's policies and predict disaster and those that appear to favor him and forecast deliverance. In the end. we will assess how they fit within the reconstruction offered in the present study.

5.1 Texts Critical of Hezekiah

Besides the obvious positive portrayal of Hezekiah in the story of Sennacherib's invasion, there remains both subtle and overt critiques of the King and his policies in oracles from the book of Isaiah. In the texts that follow, a different view of Hezekiah and his governance is detected by many scholars.

5.1.1 Isaiah 39

A text synoptic with 2 Kings 20, most scholars hold it to be drawn from the Deuteronomistic History, although some suggest the opposite origins.[4] In this text, Hezekiah's entertaining of Babylonian envoys is usually understood to be in the context of an alliance between the nations with Assyria as their shared enemy. The prophet Isaiah explicitly condemns Hezekiah's actions in this regard.[5] Some suggest that although the "original" account was purely condemnatory of Hezekiah, the extant Isaianic account is favorable to Hezekiah and exonerates him from accusations of Babylonian collaboration.[6] However,

---

4. Klaas A. D. Smelik, "Distortion of Old Testament Prophecy: The Purpose of Isaiah XXXVI and XXXVII," *OtSt* 24 (1986): 70-93; Jacques Vermeylen, "Hypothèses sur l'Origine d'Isaïe 36-39," in *Studies in the Book of Isaiah* (eds. Ruiten and Vervenne; Leuven: Leuven University Press and Peeters, 1997), 95-118.

5. Isaiah 39 places blame on Hezekiah for revealing all that was his, which is a sign that the king trusted and boasted in his riches rather than his God. It also suggested that he sought to impress the Babylonian envoy. Cf. Otto Kaiser, *Isaiah 13-39* (OTL; Philadelphia, PA: Westminster Press, 1974), 410-11. Motyer suggests that "in very truth, Hezekiah, by refusing the way of faith, had thrown in 'his lot' with Babylon ... Hezekiah looked to collective strength of alliance with Babylon and forgot where real power lay." Cf. J. A. Motyer, *The Prophecy of Isaiah: An Introduction & Commentary* (Downers Grove, IL: InterVarsity Press, 1993), 297.

6. Blenkinsopp suggests that the narrative as it stands portrays Hezekiah as "hospitable to Merodach-Baladan's envoys, who had come a great distance on a courtesy visit during his convalescence, and he could be accused of nothing worse than naïveté for his "show and tell" display." Cf. Joseph Blenkinsopp, "Hezekiah and the Babylonian Delegation: A Critical Reading of Isaiah 39:1-8," in *Essays on Ancient Israel in Its Near Eastern Context: A Tribute to Nadav Na'aman* (eds. Amit et al.; Winona Lake, IN: Eisenbrauns, 2006), 117. Oswalt mitigates Hezekiah's blame here somewhat, writing, "We should not think that this one sin of Hezekiah's pride doomed Judah to Babylonian captivity. Rather, this sin is illustrative of the kind of pride and refusal to trust that the entire nation would

even in the canonical version, Hezekiah's actions are criticized clearly, and it is suggested they had long-lasting negative ramifications for Judah.[7] While it could present Hezekiah as having a momentary lapse of judgment, but overall being a good king,[8] in my judgment, it is undeniably at least a partly negative portrayal.[9] Isaiah's hostility and suspicion directed at Hezekiah in this short narrative aligns with the other condemnations in the broader literary context of first Isaiah.[10]

---

manifest and that would ultimately result in the captivity. Thus, this act is not causal but typical." John N. Oswalt, *The Book of Isaiah: Chapters 1–39* (NICOT; Grand Rapids, MI: Eerdmans, 1986), 696. Watts sees the passage as both affirming and critiquing of the Judahite monarch in that "Hezekiah's piety is demonstrated in his acceptance of YHWH's word. His weakness is implied when no political decisions to reverse his course are recorded." Cf. John D. W. Watts, *Isaiah 1–33* (WBC, 24; Nashville, TN: Word Books, 1985), 600.

7. See Sehoon Jang, "Is Hezekiah a Success or a Failure? The Literary Function of Isaiah's Prediction at the End of the Royal Narratives in the Book of Isaiah," *JSOT* 42 (2017): 117–35. Using a synchronic approach, Jang argues that the oracle following the descriptions of Hezekiah's storehouse in Isaiah 39 reveals a portrait of a failed king. The prediction in Isa 7:18-25 follows an expression of false piety by Ahaz, implying the coming destruction is a result of Ahaz's lack of faith in requesting foreign military aid (130). A similar pattern appears in Isaiah 39, where Hezekiah asks for aid from Babylon. Isaiah's oracle in 39:5-8, which tells of the impending Babylonian campaign, is the "inevitable result of his actions" (131). The nonchronological order of Isaiah 36–39 then reveals that Hezekiah is a failed king who was formerly faithful (132-3). As a result, Isaiah 40 continues the critique of Hezekiah as a failed king by showing the results of his faithlessness (134). The whole of Isaiah 36–39 is a "negative example to warn the [exilic] community not to repeat their ancestors' failure to place their whole trust in God" (134).

8. Peter R. Ackroyd, "An Interpretation of the Babylonian Exile: A Study of II Kings 20 and Isaiah 38–39," in *Studies in the Religious Tradition of the Old Testament* (ed. Ackroyd; London: SCM, 1987), 152–71. Cf. Marvin A. Sweeney, *Isaiah 1–39: With an Introduction to Prophetic Literature* (FOTL, 16; Grand Rapids, MI: Eerdmans, 1996), 510.

9. Some think it emphasizes Hezekiah's humanity and presents him as a complex rather than ideal character. Motyer, *The Prophecy of Isaiah*, 290.

10. Joseph Blenkinsopp, *Isaiah 1–39* (AB, 19; New York: Doubleday, 2000), 488. Fales ("The Road to Judah," 243) offers a unique interpretation suggesting Hezekiah's illness was "a metaphoric rendering for a serious political perturbation which had struck Hezekiah after Sargon's demise" as Hezekiah was torn between whether he should rebel against Assyria or not. He points out that Isaiah's response to Hezekiah is political, promising Yahweh will deliver the city from Assyria (20:6). These words steeled Hezekiah's nerves into revolting against his suzerain, leading him to ally with Babylon. Thus, in Fales view, Isaiah encouraged the rebellion, but not the alliance with Babylon.

5.1.2 Isaiah 1:4-26

Most commentators have found the historical context of the Assyrian invasion of Judah to be behind the opening prophetic oracles of ch. 1, especially vv. 4-9.[11] In this chapter, Judah is devastated by a foreign invader with its cities burned and its capital "like a city besieged" (1:8).[12] The critique of the temple cult in the same oracle (1:11-17) has been read as critical of its support of Hezekiah's policies regarding the rebellion and alliances with foreign lands.[13] Blenkinsopp suggests the oracle dates to shortly after Sennacherib's withdrawal and understands the prophet's critique of the "rulers of Sodom" as including Hezekiah.[14]

5.1.3 Isaiah 18:1-2[15]

This passage appears to picture emissaries going to the Nubian court in Cush (or emissaries from Cush coming to Jerusalem).[16] Many scholars have understood the historical background as the time of rebellion planning wherein negotiations were taking place between Egypt and Judah (which at the time had a Nubian Pharaoh, Shebitku).[17] The passage is usually understood to refer sarcastically

---

11. John A. Emerton, "The Historical Background of Isaiah 1:4-9," in *Studies on the Language and Literature of the Bible: Selected Works of J. A. Emerton* (eds. Davies and Gordon; VTSup, 165; Leiden: Brill, 2015), 537-47; Blenkinsopp, *Isaiah 1-39*, 176-88; Sweeney, *Isaiah 1-39*, 67; Ronald E. Clements, *Isaiah 1-39* (Grand Rapids, MI: Eerdmans, 1980), 32, 34-36; Childs, *Assyrian Crisis*, 20-2. Some have cautioned against assigning these verses to 701 BCE, arguing they could also fit with other historical situations. Cf. Ben Zvi, "Isaiah 1:4-9, Isaiah, and the events of 701 BCE in Judah: A Question of Premise and Evidence," *SJOT* (1991): 95-111; Ulrich Berges, *The Book of Isaiah: Its Composition and Final Form* (Sheffield: Sheffield Phoenix Press, 2012), 50-2.

12. See Reinhard Müller, *Ausgebliebene Einsicht: Jesajas "Verstockungsauftrag" (Jes 6,9-11) und die judäische Politik am Ende des 8. Jahrhunderts* (BThS 124; Neukirchen-Vluyn: Neukirchener Verlag, 2012), 80-4.

13. Blenkinsopp, "Hezekiah and the Babylonian Delegation," 119.

14. Ibid. Cf. John T. Willis, "An Important Passage for Determining the Historical Setting of a Prophetic Oracle: Isaiah 1:7-8," *ST* 39 (1985): 151-69.

15. Although not covered in the survey of relevant oracles in the present study, some scholars have seen Isa 2:6-17 as originally critiquing Hezekiah's foreign alliances in his anti-Assyrian rebellion. So Eric Ortlund, "Reversed (Chrono-)Logical Sequence in Isaiah 1-39: Some Implications for Theories of Redaction," *JSOT* 35 (2010): 209-224. Cf. Marvin A. Sweeney, *Isaiah 1-4 and the Post-Exilic Understanding of the Isaianic Tradition* (BZAW 171; Berlin: Walter de Gruyter, 1988), 177.

16. Alternatively, Wildberger reads this as "a delegation from Cush" arriving in Jerusalem. He thinks the occasion was "to forge a political-military alliance." Cf. Hans Wildberger, *Isaiah 13-27* (Minneapolis, MN: Fortress Press, 1997), 212.

17. E.g., Wildberger writes of Isaiah 18 that it is "most likely from the time immediately preceding Hezekiah's revolt against the Assyrians, chronologically very soon after the death

to the emissaries' mission and hold a skeptical view of its viability and success. The message appears to be one of warning not to participate in plans with the Cushite envoys.[18] Thus, the prophecy is a critique of Judahite leadership, no doubt including Hezekiah, for considering foreign alliances as backing for the rebellion against Assyria.[19] This is the first of several passages in Isaiah that appear to denounce Hezekiah's putative pro-Egyptian policies (or alliances with any foreign powers).[20] Some think it also evinces a prophetic critique of Judah's anti-Assyrian policies as well.[21]

5.1.4 Isaiah 21:1-10

Many scholars hold to a sixth-century provenance for this passage.[22] In it, the prophet predicts the fall of Babylon, which many think is a reference to Cyrus's conquest of the city in 539 BCE.[23] However, some have argued for an eighth-century

---

of Sargon." Ibid., 218. Cf. Blenkinsopp, "Hezekiah and the Babylonian Delegation," 119; Na'aman, "Let Other Kingdoms Struggle," 69. Alternatively, Sweeney suggests the passage reflects "the historical situation of Hoshea's embassy to King So of Egypt to gain support for his revolt against the Assyrian empire in 724 (2 Kgs 17:4)." Cf. Sweeney, *Isaiah 1–39*, 261.

18. Clements, *Isaiah 1–39*, 165. John H. Hayes and Stuart A. Irvine, *Isaiah, the Eighth Century Prophet: His Times and His Preaching* (Nashville, TN: Abingdon Press, 1987), 256.

19. E.g., J. J. M. Roberts, "Egypt, Assyria, Isaiah, and the Ashdod Affair: An Alternative Proposal," in *Jerusalem in Bible and Archaeology: The First Temple Period* (SBLSymS, 18; Atlanta, GA: SBL Press 2003), 283.

20. Herbert Donner, *Israel unter den Völkern: die Stellung der klassischen Propheten des 8. Jahrhunderts v. Chr. zur Aussenpolitik der Könige von Israel und Juda* (VTSup, 11; Leiden: Brill, 1964), 169–71; Zimmerli, "Jesaja und Hiskija," 207; Walter Dietrich, *Jesaja und die Politik* (BEvT, 74; Münich: Kaiser, 1976), 222. Friedrich Huber, *Jahwe, Juda und die anderen Völker beim Propheten Jesaja* (BZAW, 137; Berlin: de Gruyter, 1976), 211. Wildberger, *Isaiah 13–27*, 225–6.

21. Jesper Høgenhaven, "The Prophet Isaiah and Judaean Foreign Policy under Ahaz and Hezekiah," *JNES* 49 (1990): 351–4.

22. E.g., Wildberger, *Isaiah 13–27*, 310–311. For a good survey of scholars holding this position, see A. A. Macintosh, *Isaiah XXI: A Palimpsest* (Cambridge: Cambridge University Press, 1980), 63–75. Some date the passage even later. E.g., Otto Kaiser, *Der Prophet Jesaja; Kapitel 13–39* (ATD, 18; Göttingen: Vandenhoeck & Ruprecht, 1973), 97–105; Benjamin Uffenheimer, "The 'Desert of the Sea' Pronouncement (Isaiah 21:1–10)," in *Pomegranates and Golden Bells: Studies in Biblical, Jewish, and Near Eastern Ritual, Law, and Literature in Honor of Jacob Milgrom* (Winona Lake, IN: Eisenbrauns 1995), 681–682.

23. E.g., Clements, *Isaiah 1–39*, 176–7; Kaiser, *Isaiah 13–39*, 120–2; Hans Wildberger, *Jesaja 13–27*; reason g (BKAT, 10/2; Neukirchen-Vluyn: Neukirchener, 1978), 770–1; Bernard Gosse, *Isaïe 13,1–14,23: Dans La Tradition Littéraire Du Livre d'Isaïe et dans la Tradition des Oracles Contre Les Nations: Étude de la Transformation du Genre Littéraire* (OBO, 78; Göttingen: Vandenhoeck & Ruprecht, 1988), 43–67.

date instead.²⁴ In this passage, the prophet laments the fall of Babylon, which would not fit a sixth-century date when Babylon was Judah's main enemy, but does fit with an eighth-century date when Babylon was Judah's putative ally (Isa 39:1-8).²⁵

24. E.g., William Henry Cobb, "Isaiah XXI. 1-10 Reëxamined," *JBL* 17 (1898): 40-61; Willliam Barnes, "A Fresh Interpretation of Isaiah 21:1-10," *JTS* 1 (1900): 583-92. P. Dhorme, "Le Désert de la Mer (Isaïe, XXI)," *RB* 31 (1922): 403-6; Seth Erlandsson, *The Burden of Babylon: A Study of Isaiah 13:2-14:23* (ConBOT 4; Lund: CWK Gleerup, 1970), 81-92; Hayes and Irvine, *Isaiah*, 272-4; Gallagher, *Sennacherib's Campaign*, 21-38. Gallagher has convincingly argued for an eighth-century date for ch. 21 based on the following evidence: (1) The Medes in this chapter are called "treacherous" or "traitors" (בֹּגֵד 21:2) (וגֹד), which would not fit an exilic context wherein the Medes were the exiles hope for deliverance and would not be described as treacherous. (2) The mention of "Elam" here would not fit an exilic context because Elam had been subsumed by the Persian empire long before the attack on Babylon (and Elam had an important role in Babylon in the eighth century). As Gallagher points out, "Babylonia constantly depended on Elam for military aid against Assyria." Ibid., 26. Cf. J. A. Brinkman, "Elamite Military Aid to Merodach-Baladan," *JNES* 24 (1965): 161-6. (3) The prophet's apparent distress at the fall of Babylon does not fit with an exilic date as a Judahite would have welcomed Babylon's punishment. However, in the eighth century, Babylon was a Judahite ally as evidenced by the Babylonian emissaries hosted by Hezekiah (2 Kings 20/Isaiah 39). Of course, Isaiah clearly opposed this alliance, but the elaborate description of the prophet's pain and empathy at Babylon's demise (e.g., "At this my body is racked with pain, pangs seize me, like those of a woman in labor; I am staggered by what I hear, I am bewildered by what I see. My heart falters, fear makes me tremble; the twilight I longed for has become a horror to me." Isa 21:3-4) does not seem to fit with an exilic date where Babylon was public enemy number one to Judah. (4) Isa 21:5-6 appears to address Judahites to prepare for war ("oil the shields" "post a lookout," etc.), which would make no sense in an exilic context but fits with an eighth-century setting where the fall of Babylon would mean certain invasion of Judah by the Assyrians. Some have argued that it is the Babylonians who are summoned to fight, but as Gallagher (*Sennacherib's Campaign*, 25) writes, "Nothing in 21:6-10 provides a reason why the supposedly Babylonian rulers should prepare for a war. The announcement of Babylon's fall in vs. 9b shows that it would be too late for the Babylonians to even fight." What is more, during Isaiah's lifetime, Babylon fell twice to the Assyrians in 710 and 704 BCE. Some have argued that the lack of an explicit mention of Assyria here militates against an understanding of the oracles being in the eighth century. However, as Gallagher has argued, the majority of oracles against the nations in Isaiah do not explicitly mention the enemy. He writes, "Is. 22:1-14 portrays a major military crisis, yet no enemy is named. This also applies to the Arabian Oracles (21:11-17). The oracles on Philistia (Is. 14:28-32), Moab (15, 16), Damascus (17), and Egypt (18, 19) relate military disasters, but again no enemy is named" (ibid., 28).

25. As Sweeney (*Isaiah 1-39*, 279) points out, if it is a sixth century oracle, "it is difficult to understand why the author would react to the news of an assault against the oppressor of Judah with pain and sickness (vv. 3-4)." Sweeney, however, holds to an early seventh-century date that presupposes Sennacherib's destruction of Babylon in 689 BCE (ibid., 282).

Babylon fell to Assyria in 704, shortly before Sennacherib's campaign to Judah, which would explain Isaiah's distress (Isa 21:3-4) at Babylon's loss.[26] The prophet would personally be affected by the fallout of the Babylonian loss. The picture of the feasting in this passage may depict Judahite leaders (though those who hold to a sixth-century date posit the feasters to be Babylonian leaders).[27] This feasting shows how unaware Judahite leadership is of the reality of the situation facing them. This critique may be similar to the hedonistic activities alluded to elsewhere in the face of the Assyrian threat (Isa 22:13).[28] If this is the historical setting of this negative prophetic appraisal, then clearly Hezekiah is among those to whom it is directed. The lament over the fall of Hezekiah's putative ally (Babylon) also evinces a negative attitude by the prophet regarding his anti-Assyrian coalition.

5.1.5 Isaiah 22:1-14

Many scholars set these oracles in the time of the Assyrian crisis during Hezekiah's regency and understand it to evince the prophet Isaiah's critical (if not embittered) stance toward the people before and after the Assyrian assault of 701 BCE.[29] Most

However, due to the fact that "Judah was never oppressed by Babylon" during Isaiah's tenure, Wildberger suggests that "there would have been no reason for him to predict its ruin when he was still alive." Cf. Wildberger, *Isaiah 13-27*, 310. Wildberger's position seems to assume such a prediction would be in keeping with the prophet's own disposition toward the city rather than simply taking into account political realities. That is, the prophet may predict coming doom without personally desiring it.

26. Gallagher, *Sennacherib's Campaign*, 36. Wildberger (*Isaiah 13-27*, 317), on the other hand, discounts the description of the prophet's "psychological experiences" connected to this prophesied downfall of Babylon he attributes it to simply underscoring "the severity of the events that have been predicted" and discounts any possible personal "sympathy for Babylon" as "out of the question." This judgment appears entirely based on an a priori decision that the oracle stems from the time of the Babylonian exile.

27. Some consider Daniel 5 as helping to explain this picture. Cf. Wildberger, *Jesaja 13-27*, 778; George Buchanan Gray, *A Critical and Exegetical Commentary on the Book of Isaiah, I-XXXIX* (New York: C. Scribner, 1912), 353.

28. Judahites are also negatively pictured as feasting elsewhere in the book (Isa 5:11-12, 22-3), and Judahite rulers criticized (Isa 1:23 and 3:14). For this reason, Gallagher (*Sennacherib's Campaign*, 25) concludes the picture here is of Judahite rulers feasting.

29. Blenkinsopp, "Hezekiah and the Babylonian Delegation," 119; Hoffmeier, "Egypt's Role," 230-2; Wildberger, *Isaiah 13-27*, 358; Peter Machinist, "Assyria and Its Image in the First Isaiah," *JAOS* 103 (1983): 722, n. 12. Several hold that vv. 1-4 and vv. 12-14 date to 701 BCE with subsequent verses being additions made after the fall of Jerusalem in 587 BCE. E.g., Karl Marti, *Das Buch Jesaja; Erklärt* (KHC, 10; ed. Marti; Tübingen: Mohr, 1900); Kaiser, *Isaiah 13-39*; Clements, *Deliverance of Jerusalem*, 33-4. Wildberger (*Isaiah 13-27*, 357) argues that the intervening verses must also be attributed to Isaiah on both formal and thematic grounds. The association of these verses with the Assyrian crisis of 701 BCE is somewhat disputed. For consideration of several historical occasions for the oracles related

view it as a prophetic critique of the Judahite response to the Assyrian military action against Jerusalem.[30] While Judahites are rejoicing, the prophet argues it is instead an occasion for mourning and lament.[31] Isaiah argues it is actually Yahweh behind the Assyrian attack, and he castigates the people for not recognizing Yahweh's hand.[32]

This text is often juxtaposed with the narrative account of the Assyrian assault in Isaiah 36–37 where the prophet Isaiah is sympathetic of the people, encourages them, and brings oracles of salvation.[33] The oracle depicts Jerusalem in turmoil

to the events of 701 BCE, see Honor, *Sennacherib's Invasion*, 104–8. Some have pointed out the affinity between this passage and Isaiah 21. Gallagher has also drawn attention to these similarities. Formally, both begin with a superscription, followed by the statement of the crisis (Isa 21:1b-2, 22:1b-3), then a lament beginning with "therefore" (עַל־כֵּן) (21:3-4, 22:4). Both oracles have a כִּי clause (21:6; 22:5) and conclude with an emphasis on the oracle's divine origins (21:10, 22:14). Cf. Gallagher, *Sennacherib's Campaign*, 47. Both passages emphasize Isaiah's distress (Isa 21:3-4, 22:4). Elam is also mentioned in both (and hardly ever elsewhere in the book). Both mention a "vision" (Isa 21:2; 22:5). Eating and drinking are mentioned in both (Isa 21:5; 22:13) with nearly verbatim wording. Both reference horses and chariots (Isa 21:7, 9; 22:6, 7). For more detailed comparison of the two chapters, see Gallagher, *Sennacherib's Campaign*, 47–50. Others have held that the oracles date from earlier in 701. E.g., Otto Eissfeldt, *The Old Testament, an Introduction: Including the Apocrypha and Pseudepigrapha, and Also the Works of Similar Type from Qumran: The History of the Formation of the Old Testament* (Oxford: Blackwell, 1965), 314. Childs (*Assyrian Crisis*, 26) warned against being too specific in dating of the oracle due to lack of specific information.

30. Sweeney, *Isaiah 1–39*, 289; Kaiser, *Isaiah 13–39*, 140–1. Gallagher argues that the oracles date to 704 BCE or early 703 rather than 701 BCE and thinks this explains Isaiah's different approach here than in the historical account of 2 Kings 18–19. He writes, "The three years between this oracle and the Assyrian invasion of Judah also allow time for a development in Isaiah's thought." Cf. Gallagher, *Sennacherib's Campaign*, 60–1. Despite the difficulties in dating Isaian oracles with certainty, the present study allows for such development in Isaiah's thinking regarding the Assyrian crisis and the policies of Hezekiah.

31. Motyer (*The Prophecy of Isaiah*, 181) suggests that the Judahite's "choice of a militarist, self-sufficient solution (8–11) had put them beyond divine forgiveness."

32. As Kaiser (*Isaiah 13–39*, 142) writes, "They had failed to hear the voice of their almighty God who has spoken to them in the defeat they had just suffered."

33. In fact, Oswalt rejects dating of Isaiah 22 to the time of Sennacherib's invasion in 701 due to the contrary presentation of Hezekiah in Isaiah 36–37, which depicts Hezekiah trusting in Yahweh in 701. Oswalt alternatively understands the passage to refer to Jehoiachin or Zedekiah because of the references to exile. Cf. Oswalt, *The Book of Isaiah*, 407–8. Alternatively, Watts reconciles these oracles with Hezekiah's willingness to pray in the narrative accounts of Isaiah 36–37 by suggesting that "Hezekiah's appeal to Isaiah and prayer to YHWH followed a long period in which no such advice or assurance was sought." Cf. Watts, *Isaiah 1–33*, 341.

with their army and leadership having abandoned them, leaving Judah without defense and a foreign army approaching. The apparent abandonment of the city by its soldiers finds an interesting parallel in Sennacherib's annals, which similarly claims the loss of military forces through desertion (ANET 288).[34]

In this passage, the prophet takes issue with the disposition of the city's residents who are not penitent but instead have chosen in despair to enjoy themselves hedonistically before their coming doom (22:1-2, 13).[35] The historical context is further bolstered by the description of the preparations for the coming foreign attack that are thought to parallel those found elsewhere (2 Kgs 20:20; 2 Chr 32:3-5, 27-30).[36] The prophet's critique of those making preparations but not looking to Yahweh ("the one who planned it long ago," Isa 22:11) suggests a critique of Hezekiah for his lack of trust in Yahweh and instead relying on his defensive building program.[37]

5.1.6 Isaiah 22:15-25

Scholars have also viewed the historical background of these oracles as being during the Assyrian crisis under Hezekiah.[38] For example, Sweeney understands

---

34. Gallagher points out that the abandonment in Isaiah 22 does not appear to fit with Sennacherib's claims but depicts all the city's leadership abandoning the city. He writes, "No records at our disposal indicate that any leaders of Jerusalem or Judah fled from their posts during Sennacherib's invasion" Cf. Gallagher, *Sennacherib's Campaign*, 60-1.

35. Kim argues that the fact that Hezekiah is not explicitly named in Isaiah 22 is the result of editorial activity to "diminish any possible faults in the reign of Hezekiah," though the oracle certainly would have condemned the king for his actions. Cf. Hyun Chul Paul Kim, "Isaiah 22: A Crux or a Clue in Isaiah 13-23?" in *Concerning the Nations: Essays on the Oracles against the Nations in Isaiah, Jeremiah and Ezekie* (ed. Mein; LHBOTS, 612; London: Bloomsbury, 2015), 10-12.

36. Blenkinsopp, "Hezekiah and the Babylonian Delegation," 119; Wildberger, *Isaiah 13-27*, 370.

37. As Wildberger writes, "Without a doubt, [Isaiah] opposed the decision to break off their subservient relationship with Assyria by joining with the Philistines who had issued a plea to Ethiopia/Egypt, hoping to get a promise of help." Wildberger, *Isaiah 13-27*, 376-7. Similarly, Shawn Zelig Aster, "Isaiah 31 as a Response to Rebellions against Assyria in Philistia," *JBL* 136 (2017): 356, n. 27; John Barton, "Ethics in Isaiah," in *Writing and Reading the Scroll of Isaiah: Studies of an Interpretative Tradition, Volume 1* (eds. Boyle and Evans; VTSup, 70/1; Leiden: Brill, 1997), 70. Contra. Clements (*Deliverance of Jerusalem*, 33-4) who holds the description of the preparations as a later redactional addition to the story after Jerusalem had been destroyed in 586 BCE. However, the description of the preparations with their focus on the water supply provide a nice parallel to Hezekiah's preparations as described elsewhere (2 Kgs 20:20; 2 Chr 32:3-5, 27-30), which more likely means it is original to the oracle from 701 BCE. So Blenkinsopp, "Hezekiah and the Babylonian Delegation," 119.

38. E.g., Sweeney, *Isaiah 1-39*, 298; Watts, *Isaiah 1-33*, 337.

it to be critical of the negotiations with the Assyrians and its condemnation of Shebna to be a reference to the payment delivered to Sennacherib to end the hostilities, speculating that Shebna was the official sent to deliver the monies.[39] The oracle asserts that Yahweh was behind the Assyrian siege of the city and that the deity was threatening the Davidic house (Hezekiah) along with the people who recklessly were celebrating defiantly.[40] The removal and deportation of Shebna serve as a warning for the Davidic dynasty and Jerusalemites that their security based on Yahweh's promises is not guaranteed.[41] Thus, the prophet appears hostile to Hezekiah and his rebellion, attributing its failure to Yahweh's direct actions against the city and the dynasty.[42]

5.1.7 Isaiah 28–31

A broad scholarly approach to these chapters understands them as relating to the Assyrian crisis while Hezekiah is on the throne. Hezekiah is not explicitly mentioned therein, but the consistent negative view of the political leadership in this section must imply a culpability of the Davidide along with the rest of Judahite leadership.[43] Of course, consensus also holds that later material was added to these sections, usually thought to help in bringing a later perspective to the events and apply them to a later time period.[44] In their final form, there

---

39. Sweeney, *Isaiah 1–39*, 298.

40. Wildberger speculates that Shebna "was pressing Hezekiah to make dangerous, if not suicidal, decisions." Cf. Wildberger, *Isaiah 13–27*, 390. However, he thinks the passage shows Isaiah's support for Hezekiah.

41. Some hold that Isaiah had a change of attitude regarding the Assyrian crisis at this point when Shebna and "the pro-Egyptian party" were displaced and that the prophet supported his replacement (Eliakim). E.g., Honor, *Sennacherib's Invasion*, 103.

42. Interestingly, Shebna is said to be a "disgrace" to his "master's house" (בֵּית אֲדֹנֶיךָ) in v. 18. The fact that "Hezekiah is not named" could imply the critique is not on Hezekiah at all, but "Shebna is acting like a king with his own military forces." Cf. Peter D. Quinn-Miscall, *Isaiah* (Sheffield: Sheffield Phoenix Press, 2006), 78. Watts (*Isaiah 1–33*, 342) suggests that the accusation's address to the government officials includes Hezekiah, but that the exclusion of his name suggests that "it implies that they [Eliakim, Shebna, and Joah] must bear responsibility for the policies that they had persuaded the king to follow (cf. prophecies in 3:4, 12)."

43. As Blenkinsopp (*Isaiah 1–39*, 381) writes, "There can be no doubt that the attitude to the political and religious leadership is overwhelmingly negative in this section, and since the sense is being conveyed that policies pursued at the court are dangerous, misguided, and foolish, the diatribe must also take in Hezekiah, even though he is not named." Na'aman suggests the lack of explicit mention of the king is due to "editors who worked the original prophecies in a way that cleared the king from the blame." Cf. Na'aman, "Let Other Kingdoms Struggle," 69.

44. Clements, *Jerusalem and the Nations*, 83; Sweeney, *Isaiah 1–39*, 367.

are warnings against trusting foreign powers along with prophetic assurance of a coming glorious future for Jerusalem.[45] The warnings appear to predict a future doom, while the assurances predict Yahweh's intervention and deliverance. Some suggest that the juxtaposition of these two perspectives is based on their historical setting in relation to the events of 701. Oracles genuinely coming from the period of the Assyrian crisis condemned the rebellion and pictured a coming doom. Those originating from the later period, after subsequent interpretations viewed the outcome as a Judahite triumph, predict a positive result.[46]

5.1.8 The Five Woe Oracles

This series of woe oracles in Isaiah 28–31 warns against any reliance upon Egypt for its military support of the rebel alliance in which Hezekiah had joined. They forecast a disastrous result for those foolish enough to rely on the Egyptians for defense. The oracles presuppose that change was still possible and that Judah could still back out of the alliance with Egypt. The disaster they predict had not yet come to pass. Dating them precisely is not possible but most think their provenance to be from the years leading up to Sennacherib's attack upon the Levant.[47]

5.1.8.1 Isaiah 28:1-4 This oracle condemns the "drunkards of Ephraim" (v. 1), and thus does not appear to be concerned with Judah. However, some think Ephraim is referenced to accentuate Hezekiah's regional activities; that is, his alliance includes cities from not only Judah but surrounding areas.[48] Furthermore, the return to the drunkenness motif in v. 7—this time regarding the leadership of Judah—may evince that the initial reference to the "drunkards of Ephraim" was solely for the benefit of the negative comparison with Judah's leaders and to show

---

45. Wagner, following Barth, holds that redactional layers of Isa 28:1-4, 29:1-8, 30:1-5, and 31:1-3 are all directed to the Davidic royalty encouraging them not to seek the help of Egypt. Cf. Thomas Wagner, "From Salvation to Doom: Isaiah's Message in the Hezekiah Story," in *Prophecy and Prophets in Stories: Papers Read at the Fifth Message of the Edinburgh Prophecy Network, Utrecht, October 2013* (eds. Becking and Barstad; OtSt, 65; Leiden: Brill, 2015), 96.

46. Seitz (*Zion's Final Destiny*, 79) argues against the consensus that Isaiah of Jerusalem was critical of Hezekiah, pointing out Hezekiah is never explicitly named in chs. 28–31 and that when "king" (*melek*) is mentioned it is not in the context of criticism but instead is "found among those the prophet had contrasted with the unfaithful." Thus he concludes there is no evidence that Isaiah was critical of Hezekiah (80).

47. Clements, *Jerusalem and the Nations*, 86; Sweeney, *Isaiah 1–39*, 356. Of course, the chapter as it stands is understood to be a composite text. E.g., ibid., 361; Hans Wildberger, *Jesaja 28–39* (BKAT, 10/3; Neukirchen-Vluyn: Neukirchener, 1982), 1041–96. Clements, *Isaiah 1–39*, 223-4.

48. See Clements, *Jerusalem and the Nations*, 87.

how their actions are consistent with those of the Northern Kingdom before its fall to Assyria.[49]

Yahweh's sending one "mighty and strong" (חָזָק וְאַמִּץ) to wrack devastation like a storm or flood, resulting in the trampling of the drunkards "under foot" (בְּרַגְלָיִם) is usually understood to be speaking about Assyria. For those understanding the reference to come from the historical period near the end of the Northern Kingdom, some think the campaigns of Tiglath-Pileser are referenced.[50] To others, who think the point of the entire oracle is to critique Hezekiah and his anti-Assyrian policies, the mighty one may be Sennacherib himself.

Somewhat surprisingly, following this vision of coming doom, the subsequent oracle (v. 5) pictures a time (בַּיּוֹם הַהוּא) when Yahweh supports the "remnant" (לִשְׁאָר) of his people. This view of future hope is usually understood to come from a later period after the devastation left only a remnant.

5.1.8.2 *Isaiah 28:14-22* This condemnatory oracle levels judgment on the leaders of Judah (אַנְשֵׁי לָצוֹן מֹשְׁלֵי הָעָם הַזֶּה).[51] There has been much discussion concerning the nature of the "covenant with Death" and the historical background alluded to here.[52] Most view it as a reference to Judah's alliance with other nations (like Egypt)[53] through which the nation hopes to survive the "overwhelming

---

49. As Sweeney (*Isaiah 1-39*, 361) concludes, "The passage is not directed to announce the fall of the northern kingdom, but to wain the southern kingdom of potential disaster based on the example of the north." Oswalt reads this as critiquing Judahite "cynical, faithless leadership drunk on its own power and privilege." Cf. Oswalt, *The Book of Isaiah*, 504. Although he does not single out Hezekiah in this passage, he does mention "the highest authorities" (516) who model faithlessness, which results in the same attitude among the people.

50. E.g., Walter Brueggemann, *Isaiah 1-39* (Louisville, KY: Westminster John Knox Press, 1998), 221.

51. Kaiser places this oracle within 703–701 during Hezekiah's diplomatic decisions that reflect that "the people were seeking help not from Yahweh but from earthly forces," which is making them believe or act as though they are immortal. Cf. Kaiser, *Isaiah 13-39*, 251–2.

52. John Day who dates the oracle to the time of Ahaz instead of Hezekiah, suggests it refers to the god Molek, although without using the name specifically. Cf. Day, *Molech: A God of Human Sacrifice in the Old Testament* (UCOP, 41; Cambridge: Cambridge University Press, 1989), 58–64.

53. E.g., Marti, *Das Buch Jesaja; Erklärt*, 207; Johann Fischer, *Das Buch Isaias* (Bonn: P. Hanstein, 1937), 188; Donner, *Israel Unter Den Völkern*, 153. Some think it is specifically about reliance on Egypt Clements, *Isaiah 1-39*, 230; Roberts, "Egypt, Assyria, Isaiah," 282. Sweeney (*Isaiah 1-39*, 367) thinks it "a more general indication of the futility of entering into political alliances against the Assyrians." Cf. Kaiser, *Isaiah 13-39*, 250–2. Similarly, Blenkinsopp refers to "negotiations between Hezekiah and Merodach-baladan II in Babylonia and between the courts of Jerusalem and Napata during the early years of Sennacherib's reign." Cf. Joseph Blenkinsopp, "Judah's Covenant with Death (Isaiah XXVII 14–22)," *VT* 50 (2000): 474. J. J. M. Roberts holds that vv. 1-4 originally date to the

scourge"—presumably Assyria— (cf. v. 2) that is coming. The oracle underscores the futility of the Judahite policies, with Yahweh promising to "sweep away" their refuge with hail, and their "hiding place" with a flood, so that their covenant is annulled and the "scourge" beating them down (v. 18). If coming from the period of the Assyrian crisis under Hezekiah, the oracle vehemently rejects his policies that depend upon foreign alliances for the success of the rebellion.[54]

5.1.8.3 Isaiah 29:1-10 A second woe oracle (vv. 1-4) pronounces judgment on Jerusalem, referencing a siege of the city (vv. 2-3) and though alluding to David's capture of Jerusalem, boasts not of the city's inviolability, but warns of its vulnerability.[55] As David laid siege to and captured Jerusalem in the past, now Yahweh will be the besieger and Jerusalem will fall. The prophet clearly lays the blame for the crisis at the feet of Jerusalem itself and depicts Yahweh as its enemy (v. 3).

Following the pattern seen in the first woe oracle, the subsequent verses predict a miraculous deliverance by Yahweh (vv. 4-10).[56] It could be understood that the former oracle comes from the time of the Assyrian crisis, and the latter verses from a later period when it is remembered more triumphantly. As it stands, even read together as genuine eighth-century oracles, the deliverance is not connected to the city's leadership in any way, and the critique of the government (particularly in its cultic activities; v. 1) implicates Hezekiah (who is known for his cultic reforms).[57]

5.1.8.4 Isaiah 29:15-16[58] This third woe oracle castigates those who think their policies (עֵצָה) can be hidden from Yahweh. It further critiques them for thinking

---

Syro-Ephraimite War and were directed against northern Israel, but that Isaiah "reused" it during the Assyrian crisis under Hezekiah's tenure "to introduce his oracle against the Judahite leaders, who were just as irresponsible as the northerners had been (28:7-13)." Cf. J. J. M. Roberts, "Yahweh's Foundation in Zion (Isa 28:16)," *JBL* 106 (1987): 37.

54. Barton, "Writing and Reading the Scroll of Isaiah," 70.

55. Clements, *Jerusalem and the Nations*, 84.

56. Blenkinsopp includes this in his list of passages critical of Hezekiah for his part in the anti-Assyrian rebellion. Cf. Blenkinsopp, "Hezekiah and the Babylonian Delegation," 121.

57. Alternatively, Routledge argues that the context of Isa 29:1-8 is the attack of 701, and that Sennacherib is driven away (theologically) because of his own pride and partly as a result of Hezekiah's repentance and renewed faith in Yahweh. However, Routledge holds that elsewhere in the book, Hezekiah is condemned by Isaiah in Isa 30:2 and 31:1 Robin L. Routledge, "The Siege and Deliverance of the City of David in Isaiah 29:1-8," *Tyndale Bulletin* 43 (1992): 185-6.

58. Most view these verses as independent of those that follow. Clements, *Deliverance of Jerusalem*; Clements, *Isaiah 1-39*, 240; Kaiser, *Der Prophet Jesaja; Kapitel 13-39*, 218-24; H. G. M. Williamson, *The Book Called Isaiah: Deutero-Isaiah's Role in Composition and Redaction* (Oxford: Oxford University Press, 1994), 58. Some see vv. 15-24 as one unit. W. A. M. Beuken, "Isa 29,15-24: Perversion Reverted," in *The Scriptures and the Scrolls: Studies in Honour of A.S. van der Woude* (eds. Martinez et al.; VTSup, 49; Leiden: Brill, 1992), 43-64; Sweeney, *Isaiah 1-39*, 408; Blenkinsopp, *Isaiah 1-39*, 407-8.

they—the creatures—can independently act without consulting God (the potter).⁵⁹ Read in the context of Hezekiah's rebellion, it would appear to critique the political machinations that led to the rebellion. The previous verses (v. 13) critique those who "honour" Yahweh with their lips, but their "worship" (יִרְאָתָם) is disingenuous. If stemming from the period of the Assyrian crisis under Hezekiah, it could be a critique against the king who famously reformed cultic worship but was pursuing foreign policies that precluded reliance upon Yahweh.⁶⁰

5.1.8.5 Isaiah 30:1-5 This fourth woe oracle is usually understood to have a similar historical background to that of Isa 18:1-2 with Judahite envoys seeking Egyptian aid for their planned rebellion.⁶¹ The oracle criticizes the rebellious Judahites for neglecting Yahweh's counsel and trusting in Egypt, reliance upon whom will bring shame on them.⁶² The words "*his* officials" (שָׂרָיו) and "*his* messengers" (מַלְאָכָיו) are usually thought to refer to Hezekiah.⁶³ It represents a clear condemnation of Hezekiah's anti-Assyrian policies that rely on Egyptian backing for their success

---

59. August Dillmann, *Der Prophet Jesaia* (Leipzig: Hirzel, 1890), 266; Wildberger, *Jesaja 28-39*, 1129-31; Clements, *Isaiah 1-39*, 240.

60. In keeping with the pattern seen thus far, the woe oracle is followed (vv. 17-21) by a promise of assurance to be fulfilled "on that day" (v. 18). The reference to the "words of the scroll" suggest to most that this was redactionally added by later scribes. Cf. Clements, *Jerusalem and the Nations*, 94.

61. E.g., Childs, *Assyrian Crisis*, 32-3; Arthur Sumner Herbert, *The Book of the Prophet Isaiah, Chapters 1-39* (CBC; Cambridge: Cambridge University Press, 1973), 180; Kaiser, *Isaiah 13-39*, 283-4. Clements, *Isaiah 1-39*, 243; Klaus Koch, *The Prophets: Volume 1: The Assyrian Period* (Philadelphia: Fortress, 1983), 128-9; Høgenhaven, "The Prophet Isaiah and Judaean Foreign Policy," 351-4; Seitz, *Zion's Final Destiny*, 75-81; Sweeney, *Isaiah 1-39*, 397; Blenkinsopp, *Isaiah 1-39*, 411-2; Na'aman, "Let Other Kingdoms Struggle," 69. Others have disputed the dating of these oracles to the Assyrian crisis of 701 BCE. Cf. James K. Hoffmeier, "Egypt as an Arm of Flesh: A Prophetic Response," in *Israel's Apostasy and Restoration: Essays in Honor of Roland K Harrison* (Grand Rapids; Baker Book House, 1988), 88-9. Hayes and Irvine, *Isaiah*, 338-48.

62. Høgenhaven, "The Prophet Isaiah and Judaean Foreign Policy," 351. Sweeney (*Isaiah 1-39*, 399) suggests the embassy to Egypt is further condemned because it "relies on the Egyptian gods" as well. Kaiser (*Isaiah 13-39*, 284) suggests a possible reason for this condemnation is the king's decision to seek Egyptian help without consulting a Yahwistic prophet. He notes that "in a few intense words Isaiah states that the plan has not come from Yahweh, and that the treaty is neither in accordance with his will nor derives from him, cf. 34.16" (285).

63. Blenkinsopp, "Hezekiah and the Babylonian Delegation," 120. Sweeney (*Isaiah 1-39*, 358) sees the audience as "King Hezekiah and his advisors." Oswalt (*The Book of Isaiah*, 544) proposes that Hezekiah is not mentioned by name here because the decision to rely in Egypt may have been forced on him by his advisors. Clements (*Isaiah 1-39*, 243) similarly comments that "Isaiah appears surprisingly restrained in not singling out Hezekiah for individual condemnation, whilst correspondingly sharply condemning the political leaders

and predicts disastrous results (לְבֹשֶׁת וְגַם־לְחֶרְפָּה).[64] Contrary to the pattern we have seen thus far, there is no subsequent oracle of assurance immediately following.

5.1.8.6 Isaiah 30:15-17 Isaiah's critical perspective on Judahite policy continues here.[65] The oracle contrasts trust in Yahweh with relying on military preparedness. The prophet declares that salvation would be in their "trust" in Yahweh, but the oracle declares they are unwilling to adhere to the prophetic word.[66] In this instance, the people's hope of a last-ditch escape on horses is referenced and belittled (v. 16), and it predicts the abandonment of Jerusalem will leave it in a precarious situation (v. 17). Some have seen in this a reflection of the historical situation referenced in Sennacherib's annals that claims Hezekiah's elite troops defected and fled the city.[67]

5.1.8.7 Isaiah 30:31-32 The chapter concludes with an explicit mention of Assyria, predicting its doom (vv. 31–33). It draws on the imagery from Isaiah 9 referencing both the "staff" (מַטֶּה) and "rod" (שֵׁבֶט) in both (Isa 9:4; 30:31-32) and the enemy becoming fuel for a fire (9:5; 30:33). Most suggest this oracle of punishment against Assyria comes from a later time period,[68] with perhaps Assyria being a cipher for later enemies.[69]

5.1.8.8 Isaiah 31:1-3 This last woe oracle contrasts seeking Yahweh with seeking a foreign alliance with Egypt and is usually dated to the time of Hezekiah. Most understand it as an authentic Isaianic critique of Hezekiah and his attempt to secure support from Egypt for his anti-Assyrian coalition.[70] There is some debate over whether the addressee is actually going to Egypt to seek aid or is planning

of Jerusalem. This may well indicate the pressure exerted by the pro-Egyptian party, which Hezekiah may have endorsed only reluctantly."

64. Clements (*Jerusalem and the Nations*, 90) argues this suggests more than embarrassment, "foretells a consequence far more serious than 'loss of face' and implies ultimate failure and ruin."

65. Barton, "Writing and Reading the Scroll of Isaiah," 70.

66. Kaiser, *Isaiah 13–39*, 287–97.

67. Blenkinsopp, "Hezekiah and the Babylonian Delegation," 121.

68. Sweeney, *Isaiah 1–39*, 392.

69. Clements, *Jerusalem and the Nations*, 90; Sweeney, *Isaiah 1–39*, 408.

70. Clements, *Isaiah 1–39*, 254; Høgenhaven, "The Prophet Isaiah and Judaean Foreign Policy," 351–4; Sweeney, *Isaiah 1–39*, 407; G. C. I. Wong, "Isaiah's Opposition to Egypt in Isaiah XXXI 1-3," *VT* 46 (1996): 395; Barton, "Writing and Reading the Scroll of Isaiah," 70; Blenkinsopp, "Hezekiah and the Babylonian Delegation," 120–1; Na'aman, "Let Other Kingdoms Struggle," 69. Alternatively, Aster ("Isaiah 31 as a Response," 347–61) argues that the oracle is a response to a conflict around 713 BCE where the king of Ashdod invited Hezekiah to join a rebellion. de Jong doubts whether this reflects Isaiah's message before 701 BCE because he thinks it draws on earlier prophecies. Cf. Matthijs J. de Jong, *Isaiah among the Ancient Near Eastern Prophets: A Comparative Study of the Earliest Stages of the Isaiah Tradition and the Neo-Assyrian Prophecies* (VTSup, 117; Leiden: Brill, 2007), 94–7.

on such a mission. The way it is phrased, with a third person "the ones who go to Egypt for help" (31:1), suggests it is not addressing those who have already appealed to Egypt, but is presenting those who have already done so as a "countertype" to the audience.[71] That is, the oracle is attempting to persuade its audience not to be like those who rely on Egypt (perhaps the Ekronites, who Sennacherib claims called on Egyptian aid).[72] As Clements summarizes,

> [It] expresses a summary of the consistent message of Isaiah regarding the Egyptian link which fostered Hezekiah's choice of rebellion. It conveys an appropriate condemnation of the king's willingness to join the alliance that rejected Assyrian hegemony in the region. Throughout these condemnatory oracles there is a consistent prophetic warning by Isaiah that dependence on Egyptian military support would prove to be fatally misplaced and would lead to a disastrous result.[73]

As with the first three woe oracles, the subsequent oracle is one of assurance of Yahweh's protection of Jerusalem (31:4-6). This is often understood to come from a later historical perspective. The authentic message of Isaiah from the time period of the buildup to rebellion and Sennacherib's invasion is understood to be hostile to the rebellion and consistently warning Judah of the dangers of reliance upon Egypt for security. Some scholars have read both the warning and deliverance portions as authentically Isaianic. For example, Sweeney suggests,

> Isaiah had a role in the debate over Hezekiah's decision whether to ally with Egypt against the Assyrian empire. The best policy, Isaiah argued, would be to avoid a useless and costly confrontation in favor of waiting patiently for YHWH to complete the punishment that required the presence of the Assyrians in the first place. Once the punishment was completed, YHWH would act to destroy the Assyrian oppressors.[74]

In other words, the Assyrian crisis was prophetically explained as Yahweh's punishment, but the prophetic perspective also predicted that Jerusalem would not fall ultimately, as Yahweh would preserve his city after punishing it with the rod of his anger (Assyria).

To Kaiser (*Isaiah 13-39*, 318), it seems evident that a later redactor removed some of the historical details from this account.

71. Sweeney, *Isaiah 1-39*, 402.
72. RINAP 3.1:176, 22.ii.79.
73. Clements, *Jerusalem and the Nations*, 91.
74. Sweeney, *Isaiah 1-39*, 408. Motyer (*The Prophecy of Isaiah*, 255) understands the message similarly: "Thus, if his people see the dreaded Assyrians on the march, the Lord is in it in all his wisdom, and the way of trust and obedience will carry them through (*cf.* Dt. 8:2-4)."

The downfall of Assyria described here is violently described ("sword" is mentioned three times) but is ascribed to Yahweh's direct intervention rather than that of humans (בְּחֶרֶב לֹא־אִישׁ וְחֶרֶב לֹא־אָדָם) (31:8). If this comes from a post-701 date, it may be a reflection on what was understood to be a miraculous conclusion to Sennacherib's campaign wherein he returned to Assyria without claiming Jerusalem.[75] From a later perspective, at the time of Josiah, when Assyria actually did fall (to Babylon), these prophecies would have been seen as fulfilling these eighth-century prophecies from Isaiah.[76] Still later perspectives may have seen Assyria typologically stand for the enemy empires threatening Judah/Yehud at the time.[77]

5.1.9 Isaiah 33:7-9

The historical background Isaiah 33 has elicited varied scholarly opinions. Some have held it authentically from Isaiah ben Amoz,[78] from Josiah's time,[79] from the Babylonian exile,[80] from the Persian period,[81] or even the Hellenistic period.[82] Verses 7-9 depict the brave men of Jerusalem crying in the streets due to the horrible situation wherein the "highways" (מְסִלּוֹת) are deserted with no travelers (עֹבֵר).[83] The situation is vague enough to refer to any of the putative historical periods suggested by scholars. If coming from the Assyrian crisis under Hezekiah, it may perhaps reflect the historical situation behind Sennacherib's having isolated Jerusalem "like a bird in a cage." The reason for this loathsome state of affairs is said to be a "broken treaty/covenant" (הֵפֵר בְּרִית מָאַס עָרִים). Some have suggested this refers to Hezekiah's breaking of the treaty (described by Hezekiah as "sin" in 2 Kgs 18:13) with Assyria.[84] If so, it would

---

75. Brueggemann (*Isaiah 1–39*, 252) thinks it is a reflection on the fall of Assyria to Babylon, who is theologically "only an instrument of Yahweh."

76. Sweeney, *Isaiah 1–39*, 408.

77. Sweeney similarly suggests that "later editions of the book of Isaiah in the 6th and 5th centuries would have seen the passage largely in typological terms, insofar as the fall of Assyria would have symbolized the fall of the major empires that threatened Judah's existence: Babylon in the 6th century and the Persian-Median empire in the 5th century." Ibid.

78. J. J. M. Roberts, *First Isaiah: A Commentary* (Minneapolis, MN: Fortress Press, 2015).

79. Sigmund Mowinckel, *Psalmenstudien* (Amsterdam: P. Schippers, 1966), II.235 n. 1.

80. Clements, *Isaiah 1–39*, 265.

81. Wildberger, *Jesaja 28–39*, 1288; Sweeney, *Isaiah 1–39*, 429.

82. Kaiser, *Isaiah 13–39*, 342.

83. Motyer (*The Prophecy of Isaiah*, 264) understands Isaiah's rebuke to include Hezekiah, writing as follows: "The *brave men* are the military leaders coming belatedly, like Hezekiah (37:3), to a realization of their ineffectiveness."

84. Blenkinsopp understands the "witnesses" (reading with 1QIsa^a rather than the MT "cities") to the treaty who are despised as Hezekiah's God because "his oath confirmed by

evince a contrary opinion to the account in 2 Kings 18 that viewed Hezekiah's rebellion positively (18:7).

5.2 Texts Viewing Hezekiah Positively

5.2.1 Isaiah 36–37

This text needs little separate comment from its Vorlage in 2 Kings. In this text, Hezekiah is described very positively. Hezekiah goes to the temple in time of need, prays, utters a psalm, and receives signs from Isaiah. His trust in Yahweh is underscored and appears to exonerate him from charges of reliance upon Egypt leveled by the Assyrian Rabshakeh.[85] This positive tradition regarding Hezekiah is clear in the Deuteronomistic History as well. Hezekiah's rebellion against the Assyrians is presented as due to his piety and zeal for the purity of his Yahwistic faith (2 Kgs 18:7). Furthermore, in the Isaianic synoptic text, in distinction from its Vorlage, Hezekiah does not even turn to the temple to utilize its treasures to buy off the invading Assyrians.

5.2.1.1 Problems of Dating Oracles A broad scholarly consensus views Isaiah as consistently warning against reliance on Egypt and implicitly critiquing Hezekiah's policies in regard to his anti-Assyrian coalition that depended upon Egyptian support. This leads to the problem of how to understand the oracles of assurance that frequently accompany such warnings in the final form of the book. As noted by Childs, some scholars held that "Isaiah spoke only words of judgment" and that "oracles of promise play a subordinate role in the primary Isaianic tradition."[86] While this is no longer a scholarly consensus, the difficulties of interpreting the various oracles of judgment and promise continues to be a challenging undertaking. As Clements writes, "In the light of the decisiveness of [Isaiah's] warnings it is difficult to understand how they could have been accompanied by messages of assurance which contrasted with this."[87] Could prophecies of warning and prophecies of support be issued during the same time period? Could a prophetic voice at one point oppose the king's policies but shortly after support them? In light of these difficulties, the oracles of Isaiah 28–32 are often held to originate in different periods of time, with some oracles (those seen to oppose the rebellion) coming from Isaiah ben Amoz in the period prior to 701 BCE, and the others postdating the Assyrian invasion. In what follows, we will survey the oracles of assurance and promise that appear to some to be related to the Assyrian crisis. This survey will keep in mind the question of these "difficulties" in understanding the relation of oracles of warning and promise. Are these only difficulties or do they prove the oracles of assurance must come from a later period?

appeal to Yhwh, his own deity, as witness." Cf. Blenkinsopp, "Hezekiah and the Babylonian Delegation," 121.

85. And possibly the prophet Isaiah in chs. 30 and 31. Cf. Seitz, *Zion's Final Destiny*, 75–81.
86. Childs, *Assyrian Crisis*, 63.
87. Clements, *Jerusalem and the Nations*, 93.

5.2.2 Isaiah 8:23–9:6 (ET 9:1–7)

This prophecy has been variously interpreted as referring to Hezekiah or, through a later Josianic redactional stage, Josiah.[88] Some recent scholarship has again made the case for a Hezekian referent and posits its composition c. 734–720 BCE.[89] Given that Hezekiah's accession year appears to be within this range some suggest that Hezekiah was the subject of the oracle. As Young writes, "The Judean king is seen as a reason for the troubled house of Israel to rejoice, and his rule is hyperbolically described as increasing without end."[90] Furthermore, this "prince of peace" Hezekiah would not remove the imperial yoke himself, as it will be a work of Yahweh himself as "the zeal of Yahweh will accomplish this" (Isa 9:6, ET 9:7). Of course, dating the oracle precisely has been a matter of some debate. Its optimistic character has been thought to contrast the pessimism of Isaiah 22 so that it seems unlikely the prophet "would have spoken in such hopeful tones so soon after 701."[91] Therefore, some suggest dating it to the time of Hezekiah's preparations for the rebellion (c. 705–701).[92] If so, this would evince support for Hezekiah's anti-Assyrian policies and high hopes for its success.[93] If so, how could it correlate with the oracles that appeared to oppose Hezekiah's anti-Assyrian aspirations?

5.2.3 Isaiah 10:24-34

This prophecy predicts the defeat of an army before Zion and is often understood to imply a miraculous defeat.[94] There is no consensus on its dating, however, with some dating it to the period of the Assyrian crisis,[95] some dating

---

88. Some good reviews of scholarly opinions can be found in Paul D. Wegner, *An Examination of Kingship and Messianic Expectation in Isaiah 1–35* (Lewiston, NY; Edwin Mellen, 1992), 139–40; Laato, *Who Is Immanuel?* 173–96.

89. Young, *Hezekiah in History and Tradition*, 163.

90. Ibid.

91. Hans Wildberger, *Isaiah 1–12* (Minneapolis, MN: Fortress Press, 1991), 393.

92. Hans Walter Wolff, *Frieden Ohne Ende: Jesaja 7, 1–17 und 9, 1–6 Ausgelegt* (BibS(N), 35; Neukirchen Kreis Moers: Neukirchener Verlag des Erziehungsvereins, 1962), 62.

93. Wildberger (*Isaiah 1–12*, 393) finds this problematic as it would "mean that Isaiah was chiefly to blame for Hezekiah's rebellion against Assyria" and he therefore dates it earlier, understanding it to be Isaiah's prediction of the emancipation of the northern territories from Tiglath-Pileser. Høgenhaven alternatively suggests that Isa 8:11-18 may be condemnation of Hezekiah's involvement in conspiratorial efforts to overthrow the Assyrian yoke. Cf. Høgenhaven, "The Prophet Isaiah and Judaean Foreign Policy," 353. This seems quite speculative and, in my judgment, should not be followed.

94. E.g., Young writes, "The promise that the cloak of every warrior would be rolled in blood, and that all the trees of the enemy king's forest would be chopped down." Cf. Young, *Hezekiah in History and Tradition*, 84.

95. E.g., Laato, *Who Is Immanuel,* 67–8; Kirsten Nielsen, *There Is Hope for a Tree: The Tree as Metaphor in Isaiah* (JSOTSup, 65; Sheffield, England: JSOT Press, 1989), 129. Georg

it earlier,⁹⁶ and others dating it after the end of the Assyrian empire.⁹⁷ Some have argued that the prophecy cannot refer to Sennacherib's invasion because the direction from which the attackers advance does not correlate with what we know of the Assyrian advance in 701. For example, Wildberger considers the identification of the invaders as Sennacherib's advance "impossible" "since that offensive against Jerusalem did not come from the north, but from the southwest, from the coastal region."⁹⁸ Of course, others suggest the passage does not attempt to describe the actual route that Sennacherib's offensive took, but that it is implying the enemy's advance is subsuming the entire land of Judah.⁹⁹ Thus, numerous scholars have insisted that we are not to understand Isaiah as seeking to delineate the actual route by which the Assyrians would come, but rather we must see here an ideal picture, designed to express the thought that the enemy, when he comes, will take over the whole land. The intent of the present study is not to argue conclusively for one dating scheme over the other but to consider whether the possibility of the referent being Sennacherib's campaign could be better understood in light of our gleanings from military history.

Fohrer, *Das Buch Jesaja* (ZBK, 3 vols; Zürich; Stuttgart: Zwingli Verlag, 1960), 1:162–3; Otto Kaiser, *Isaiah 1–12* (Philadelphia, PA: Westminster Press, 1972), 245–51.

96. Some date it to the Sargon II's campaign, *c.* 712–711 BCE. E.g., Hans Wildberger, *Jesaja 1–12* (BKAT 10/1; Neukirchen-Vluyn: Neukirchener, 1972), 427; Clements, *Isaiah 1–39*, 117–19; Jacques Vermeylen, *Du prophète Isaïe à l'apocalyptique: Isaïe, I-XXXV, miroir d'un demi-millénaire d'expérience religieuse en Israël* (Paris: J. Gabalda, 1978), 276; Sweeney, *Isaiah 1–39*, 204; Nielsen, *There Is Hope for a Tree*, 137. Others dated it even earlier it to the period of the Syro-Ephraimite war. E.g., Childs, *Assyrian Crisis*, 62; Donner, *Israel Unter Den Völkern*, 30–8; Stuart A. Irvine, *Isaiah, Ahaz, and the Syro-Ephraimitic Crisis* (ed. Petersen; SBLDS, 123; Atlanta, GA: Scholars Press, 1990), 274–9.

97. E.g., Wildberger (*Isaiah 1–12*, 440) concludes, "It is not likely … that this section was written during the Assyrian era." Machinist views the Isaianic hope for Assyrian downfall as authentic. He writes, "I maintain, with a number of older commentators, that this hope is authentic to Isaiah, even though such a position has been revised recently by those who suppose that it developed mostly later, during the Josianic period at the end of the seventh century B.C. and was then reflected in additions and revisions to the book of Isaiah" Cf. Machinist, "Assyria and Its Image in the First Isaiah," 736.

98. Wildberger, *Isaiah 1–12*, 451. Cf. Duane L. Christensen, "March of Conquest in Isaiah 10:27c–34," *VT* 26 (1976): 385–99.

99. E.g., Alexander writes, "We may conceive the prophet standing in vision on the walls of Jerusalem, and looking toward the quarter from whence the invasion was to come, numerating certain intervening points, without intending to predict that he would really pass through them." Quoted by Edward J. Young, *The Book of Isaiah* (NICOT; Grand Rapids, MI: Eerdmans, 1965), 374.

5.2.4 Isaiah 11:1-9

There are many scholarly opinions regarding the setting of this prophecy and its authorship. Its prophecy has variously been understood to come from Isaiah himself,[100] from the time of Josiah's enthronement in 639 BCE.,[101] or be an exilic or postexilic prophecy composed after the fall of the house of David, but predicting the resurrection of the Davidic monarchy.[102] If the oracle is to be dated to the eighth-century BCE, Hezekiah is the most likely candidate for being the "shoot" from the "root of Jesse" (11:1), and "Isaiah was not speaking abstractly of a theoretical ruler reigning at some indefinite time."[103] The shoot of Jesse was seen to have the potential to restore the Israelite kingdom with the remnant (11:11-16), since the northern kingdom had now fallen (in 722 to Assyria).[104] If Hezekiah *was* the original referent, this could be further evidence of support for the monarch and optimism for the success of his policies.

5.2.5 Isaiah 7:10-17

Despite the plethora of interpretations surrounding the identification of the infant Immanuel, strong arguments favor him being Hezekiah. In 2 Kgs 18:7, it is said of Hezekiah that Yahweh was "with him," which seems to be a play on the name "Immanuel/God with us" (and only he and David are ever said to have God "with" them).[105] Some have objected that Hezekiah must have been born before this prophecy (which took place during the Syro-Ephramite war), but a good case can be made that Hezekiah was born during this crisis (*c.* 735 BCE), making him about ten years old when he became king in 725. After a co-regency with his father for three years, Hezekiah then took the throne on his own at the age of thirteen, *c.* 722 BCE (with Samaria falling to Assyria in his "fourth year" [2 Kgs 18:9]).[106] Thus Immanuel could have been his given name, and Hezekiah his throne name.[107] Of course, there will not be widespread agreement on this identification, but *if* authentic it would be another positive passage supporting the king.

---

100. E.g., Hugo Gressmann, *Der Messias* (FRLANT, 43; Göttingen: Vandenhoeck & Ruprecht, 1929), 247. Gerhard von Rad, *Old Testament Theology* (2 vols.; New York: Harper & Row, 1962), II.169-75; Laato, *Who Is Immanuel?* Nielsen, *There Is Hope for a Tree*, 141.

101. E.g., Vermeylen, *Du Prophète Isaïe*, 274, 282.

102. E.g., Mowinckel, *Psalmenstudien*, II.308. Sigmund Mowinckel, *He That Cometh* (Oxford: Blackwell, 1959), 17.

103. Young, *Hezekiah in History and Tradition*, 180.

104. Ibid.

105. Ibid., 187.

106. Ibid., 189.

107. Ibid. Contra. Laato who argued that the identification of Hezekiah with Immanuel was only a later interpretation based on the story in Isaiah 36-38. Laato, "Hezekiah and the Assyrian Crisis," 67-8. Cf. Laato, *Who Is Immanuel?*

5.3 Summary

While there is not a complete scholarly consensus in regard to the historical referent for all of these texts from the book of Isaiah, as the above survey has shown, there is a broad consensus that Isaiah 1–39 contain some oracles critical of Hezekiah's leadership and/or his anti-Assyrian coalition.[108] Of course, it is also clear that some oracles from Isaiah that likely refer to Hezekiah are more positive toward the king, either setting up high expectations for the monarch's reign or are later theological reflections on the successful nature of Hezekiah's reign, the highlight of which was the Assyrian withdrawal and Jerusalem's survival. Usually the supposition that these contrasting perspectives on Hezekiah and his policies could possibly come from the same person is deemed unlikely or impossible by scholars. In Blenkinsopp's words, "the differences between the two profiles of Isaiah in the book of Isaiah are not merely perspectival; they are irreconcilable."[109] Some have even suggested that Isaiah ben Amoz opposed Hezekiah's anti-Assyrian policies altogether and supported his father, Ahaz's, pro-Assyrian policies.[110] This supposition has led to some rejecting the presentation of the prophet Isaiah in the historiographical sections as inauthentic due to Isaiah's seemingly positive working relationship with the king during the crisis. As Høgenhaven concludes, "No historical significance can be ascribed to the Deuteronomistic presentation, for it contradicts the evidence of the primary Isaiah traditions."[111] However, it is the position of the current study that this conclusion is unnecessary. Even if there were prophetic indictments castigating Judahite foreign policy before the Assyrian invasion, a change from opposition to support during a military crisis is consistent with what we see in military history, as we will see in our study of the War of 1812, to which we now turn.[112]

108. Bright (*History*, 283) represents a consensus when he writes, "In spite of the earnest warnings of Isaiah, who branded the whole thing folly and rebellion against Yahweh, Hezekiah joined in and sent envoys to Egypt to negotiate a treaty."

109. Blenkinsopp, "Hezekiah and the Babylonian Delegation," 121. Similarly, Laato, "Hezekiah and the Assyrian Crisis," 49, 66.

110. As Høgenhaven writes, "The prophet Isaiah, however, seems to have maintained the view on foreign policy advocated by King Ahaz. The Isaiah prophecies may indeed be seen as evidence of the existence of a pro-Assyrian party, the views of which must have been pushed aside at the Judaean court when the anti-Assyrian party took the lead." Cf. Høgenhaven, "The Prophet Isaiah and Judaean Foreign Policy," 354.

111. Ibid.

112. Na'aman accounts for Isaiah's actions during the Assyrian threats to Jerusalem as merely the prophet doing his duty. He writes, "[Isaiah's] encouragement of the king during the blockade of the city by the Assyrian army is what one expects from a man in his position, and in no way reflects his attitude in the debate on a suitable policy toward Assyria." Cf. Na'aman, "Let Other Kingdoms Struggle," 69–70. Darr suggests Isaiah's change in approach was due to Hezekiah's change of attitude. Cf. Katheryn Pfisterer Darr, "No Strength to Deliver: A Contextual Analysis of Hezekiah's Proverb in Isaiah 37:3b," in *New Visions of Isaiah* (JSOTSup, 214; Sheffield: Sheffield Academic Press, 1996), 232–45.

Chapter 6

DISPUTED VICTORY IN THE WAR OF 1812

Approaching the assessment of an ancient war and why its outcome may have been perceived and remembered so differently from participants may be aided by consideration of another war in military history with a disputed outcome that has been perceived differently by the participants. As Martin van Creveld reminds us,

> However much economic, social, technological and other circumstances may have changed, history and particularly military history remains the record of the thoughts and actions ... of men [sic] whose basic needs, drives and passions have not changed since time immemorial.[1]

While there is a vast difference between ancient cultures and the modern varieties that are in view when comparing wars from different eras, the nearly universal characteristics shared by humanity make it plausible that similar factors might be involved in the divergent assessments of a war in ancient and more recent history.

In this chapter, the war selected for comparison with the war of 701 BCE is the War of 1812 between the United States and the United Kingdom of Great Britain and its dependent colony, Canada. One of the most well-known aspects of the memory of the War of 1812 is the fact that both sides claim victory. The Americans tend to think they won the war, while Canadians consider themselves the victors of the conflict. It is not only participants and contemporary entities who have varying opinions as to who the victor was. Scholarly opinions to this day vary on who should be considered the winner of the war. In fact, both sides of the conflict have developed "widely divergent national and local historiographies about the War of 1812."[2] Americans often consider it a US victory, while others have later judged it to be either an American defeat or a draw.[3] As one historian writes, "Although

---

1. Martin van Creveld, "Thoughts on Military History," *J. Contemp. Hist.* 18 (1983): 560.
2. Timothy S. Forest, "Epic Triumph, Epic Embarrassment, or Both? Commemorations of the War of 1812 Today in the Niagara Region," *Ont. Hist.* 104 (2012).
3. As the Hiedlers opine, "Nobody won the War of 1812." David Stephen Heidler and Jeanne T. Heidler, *The War of 1812* (Westport, CT: Greenwood Press, 2002), 123. Forest ("Epic Triumph," 96) similarly characterizes the war "from a military and a diplomatic perspective—as a stalemate."

most Americans pretended that they had won the war, they were hard-pressed to identify any concrete gains."[4] Canadian historians often view it as a clear Canadian victory ("the war that Canada won, or to put it more precisely *did not lose*").[5]

Despite the millennia separating the Assyrian invasion of 701 BCE and the War of 1812 and the obvious differences in cultures, a comparison between the two can be most fruitful and will offer some helpful insights with implications for debates surrounding the war of 701 BCE.

As one might expect, the extant ancient sources for the war of 701 BCE are dwarfed by the available sources for 1812. This study will draw on the work of historians who have meticulously studied the available sources and drawn out themes, propaganda, and the diverse opinions contained therein. This chapter will compare reasons for the divergent opinions with the diverse opinions on the Assyrian invasion of Judah in 701 BCE and the affinities between the comparison will become evident and instructive.

6.1 Origins of the War of 1812

Causes for war are always complex, and that is true for this conflict. Background to the war buildup was the Jay Treaty, a 1794 agreement between Britain and the United States, that regulated commerce and national rites for both parties.[6] Federalists in the United States supported the treaty, which went along with their "pro-British" foreign policies, whereas Republicans, very Anglophobic, "denounced the Jay Treaty as a one-sided sellout of American interests."[7] However, historians viewed the treaty as serving US interests in keeping peace with the nation that could destroy US trade, due to their naval power (the Mistress of the Seas), and also for beginning an era of friendly relations with Britain that allowed US trade to nearly triple (from its signing to 1801).[8] The treaty was set to expire in 1803 whereupon a new trade agreement was to be negotiated.[9]

Despite the treaty, British practices on the open seas were what fomented war motives in the United States. First, due to their war with France, British

---

4. Donald R. Hickey, *The War of 1812: A Short History* (Urbana, IL: University of Illinois Press, 2012), 3.

5. Pierre Berton, *The Invasion of Canada, 1812–1813* (Toronto: McClelland and Stewart, 1980), 19. Cf. Wesley B. Turner, *The War of 1812: The War That Both Sides Won* (Toronto: Dundurn Press, 2000), 131.

6. Heidler and Heidler, *The War of 1812*, 21.

7. Hickey, *The War of 1812*, 6. However, the treaty "also required the British to abandon all their military posts on the American side of the Great Lakes." Cf. Walter R. Borneman, *1812: The War That Forged a Nation* (New York: HarperCollins, 2004), 27.

8. Hickey, *The War of 1812*, 6.

9. Murray Polner and Thomas E. Woods, *We Who Dared to Say No to War: American Antiwar Writing from 1812 to Now* (New York: Basic Books, 2008), 263.

restrictions were placed on US trade with continental Europe (the "Orders-in-Council") with a naval blockade enforced by the Royal Navy.[10] The United States objected to the trade restrictions, which they deemed illegal and a slight on their sovereignty. Second, Americans objected to the British practice of "impressment" of American sailors. As a way of making up for manpower shortages during their ongoing war with France, "impressment" entailed recruiting sailors to the Royal Navy by force. Some 15,000 American sailors are thought to have been forcibly taken off of American merchant vessels and made to serve in the Royal Navy in the fight against France. The United States had had enough and was moving toward war over these issues.

Another motivation for war with Britain was related to desires to maintain US honor and its reputation. As some have observed, "An America that would meekly submit to the abuse of its neutral rights would prove itself to the rest of the world as worthless and weak. These square-jawed pioneers were not weak. They would kill to prove they were not worthless."[11] Others have suggested that politics was the material reason for US aggression, with Republicans attempting "to use war as a vehicle to forge party unity, preserve national power, and silence their Federalist critics."[12] Clearly, significant considerations regarding whether to wage war were political and ideological. War was a means to restore US honor and its reputation. The *National Intelligencer* compared the Twelfth Congress that declared the War of 1812 with that of 1776 of the American war of independence, opining that with the War of 1812 the United States "will have been preserved from disgraceful recolonization."[13] Thus, for many Americans this war was a second war of independence. Likely, all were factors in the start of the war, but restoring American honor may have topped the list as ironically, the peace treaty that formally ended the war did not actually deal with any of the other issues that caused the war in the first place.[14] As Berton concludes, "America went to war as a last resort because her leaders felt that the nation's honour had been besmirched to a point where any other action would be unthinkable."[15]

Although the Jay Treaty seemed beneficial to the United States in historical perspective, support for the treaty dissipated in 1800 when Federalists were voted out amid widespread dislike of Britain in the United States and opposition to Federalist pro-British policies. The election resulted in the Republicans winning both Congressional houses and the presidency.[16] Once in office, they repealed

---

10. Hickey, *The War of 1812*, 2.
11. Heidler and Heidler, *The War of 1812*, 5.
12. Hickey, *The War of 1812*, 2.
13. Ibid., 18.
14. Ibid., 2. As Polner and Woods (*We Who Dared to Say No*, 3) write, the "Treaty of Ghent … included not a single word about any of the grievances for which the U.S. government had allegedly fought."
15. Berton, *The Invasion of Canada*, 24.
16. Hickey, *The War of 1812*, 6.

previous party's policies. In 1807, Congress (at the behest of President Thomas Jefferson) passed the Embargo Act, which forbid any American exports. The goal was to pressure the British, but the impact was chiefly on America itself, with exports dropping from $108 million to $22 million in one year.[17] The extent to which Congress was willing to "cut off its nose to spite its face" in the Embargo Act showed the American frustration with British policies at the time.[18]

With the election of James Madison in 1810, the "war hawks" took important positions and began an economic and military buildup.[19] There was broad support for the buildup but the support "masked deep-seated differences."[20] Some supported it as a prelude to war, others wanted it for defensive measures only, whereas some hoped the British would see the buildup and make economic concessions. Even pro-Britain American elements supported the buildup. As Hickey writes,

> The Federalists offered little resistance to the war measures and even supported some of them. They were eager to avoid the charge that they were pawns of Great Britain, and they had long favored military and naval preparedness.[21]

As some have observed, "Opposition among the people to the War of 1812 matched that toward any war in American history, even U.S. involvement in Vietnam."[22]

Even when war bills were being written, studied, and emended, support was divided, with some wanting only a maritime war, and others wanting a full-scale war that would include the invasion of Canada. The divisive nature of national support can be seen in that the final bill for full-scale war was nearly changed to a "limited maritime war" on June 12, 1812, except that the modified bill failed to pass due to a *tied* vote, leaving the full-scale war bill to go forward. After further debate, the war was eventually declared on June 18, 1812. However, not even the Republicans were united on the issue with a quarter of them opposed to the war or having abstained from voting.[23] The vote for the final bill was 79 to 49, which is the closest vote for war in US history with only 61% support from members.[24] Due to the evident opposition, the war was often disdainfully referred to as "Mr. Madison's War."[25]

---

17. Borneman, *1812: The War That Forged a Nation*, 39.
18. Ibid., 40.
19. Ibid., 28–9.
20. Hickey, *The War of 1812*, 12.
21. Ibid.
22. Heidler and Heidler, *The War of 1812*, 37.
23. Ibid., 43.
24. Hickey, *The War of 1812*, 17. As some have commented, the close vote "exposed a disturbing lack of backing for this dangerous endeavor." Cf. Heidler and Heidler, *The War of 1812*, 5.
25. Kelly King Howes and Julie Carnagie, *War of 1812* (Detroit, MI: UXL, 2002), 31.

The United States declared war in June 1812 in concert with the French Revolutionary and Napoleonic Wars between Britain and France (which was nearly a world war), which was thought to weaken British response to US aggression.[26] Significant difference of opinion on the war persisted even after war was declared. In Baltimore, the fourth largest city in the United States, a newspaper, the *Federal Republican*, condemned the war and the president's leadership.[27] This angered many Republicans in Baltimore who thought that the war effort should be supported now that war had been declared.[28] In response to the newspaper's position on June 22, 1812, a mob destroyed the newspaper's offices and burned Federalist ships and property in what became known as the "Baltimore Riots."[29] When the newspaper attempted to reopen in July, its buildings were destroyed, and the violent mob ended up killing two people and permanently injuring others, including the newspaper editor (who never fully recovered from his injuries).[30] The riots illustrate the strong loyalty to the nation's cause felt by some and strong opposition felt by others.[31]

As military history reveals, after a war has begun, "the perception of winning becomes far more important to the public. Citizens turn abruptly on any leader deemed culpable for losing."[32] President Madison, unlike most wartime presidents around whom most people rally, experienced dwindling support in his 1812 wartime election. He won the previous election 122 to 47 (with 175 members of the electoral college at that time), but this lead shrunk to 128 to 89 (with 217 members of the electoral college at that time) in the wartime election. Support for Republicans in the House and Senate also diminished during the war. These election results reveal opposition to the war during the conflict, though this was not popular following the war.[33] Interestingly, opposition to the war helped originate the figure of "Uncle Sam" during this time. A food inspector named Samuel "Uncle Sam" Wilson, who worked for the army, stamped inspected meat containers with a "US." Due to the problematic nature of food supplies for the army during this period, opponents to the war claimed the letters "US" stood for Uncle Sam as "a way of mocking the government."[34] Later, Uncle Sam became a

---

26. So connected are the Napoleonic wars in Europe with the War of 1812 that some have said "the War of 1812 was the North American phase of the Napoleonic Wars." Cf. Turner, *War of 1812*, 11.

27. Heidler and Heidler, *The War of 1812*, 39.

28. Howes and Carnagie, *War of 1812*, 34.

29. Also known as the "Baltimore Massacre" (ibid., 35).

30. Heidler and Heidler, *The War of 1812*, 39.

31. Robert Malcomson, *Historical Dictionary of the War of 1812* (HDWRCU, 31; Lanham, MD: Scarecrow Press, 2006), 20.

32. Hanson, *Father of Us All*, 22.

33. Hickey, *The War of 1812*, 120.

34. Miriam Greenblatt, *War of 1812* (ed. Bowman; New York: Facts on File, 2003), 62.

way of referring to the nation itself, one of several mythic elements originating in the War of 1812.

Opposition to the war was fiercest in New England. The *Connecticut Courant* captured some public sentiment when they wrote that the war "was commenced in folly, it is proposed to be carried on with madness, and (unless speedily terminated) will end in ruin."[35] Such opposition to the war reached a peak with the Hartford Convention (December 1814 to January 1815). Federalists in New England called the convention to discuss their discontent with the war crisis, meeting in secret.[36] The Massachusetts governor is even said to have "secretly explored a separate peace settlement with the British."[37] The New England press had openly opposed the current presidential administration and had suggested that their states might "secede (separate themselves) from the United States."[38] Some newspapers reported that the Hartford Convention similarly was seeking to negotiate peace with Britain and withdraw from the union of the United States, though it is clear that the report of Hartford Convention did not support such action. They did call for amendments to the US Constitution that, among other things, called for a requirement of a vote of two-thirds to declare war and limiting presidents to a single term.[39] They sent envoys to Washington but arrived only after the victory at New Orleans and news of the peace of Ghent arrived and nothing became of their work.[40] The convention is significant in showing the ongoing opposition to the government and the war. However, in the long run, the legacy of the convention was not to highlight problems with the government and its war policies. As Hickey writes,

> The Hartford Convention was the climax of Federalist opposition to the War of 1812 ... the Hartford Convention became a synonym for treason, and all of the shortcomings of the war were blamed on the Federalists. People forgot that both parties were involved in [debate and critiques regarding the war] and that Republicans no less than Federalists deserved a share of the blame for the misfortunes of the war.

---

35. Connecticut Courant (Hartford), June 30, 1812. Quoted in Borneman, *1812: The War That Forged a Nation*, 254.

36. Hickey, *The War of 1812*, 101. The secrecy led to suspicions "that rebellion and treason were on the agenda." Cf. James H. Ellis, *A Ruinous and Unhappy War: New England and the War of 1812* (New York: Algora, 2009), 244; Borneman, *1812: The War That Forged a Nation*, 254.

37. Ellis, *A Ruinous and Unhappy War*, 2.

38. Howes and Carnagie, *War of 1812*, 130.

39. Hickey, *The War of 1812*, 102.

40. Regarding American attitudes toward the convention, the Heidlers write, "The rest of the country was in no mood to tolerate such behavior while celebrating the victory at New Orleans and the achievement of peace." Cf. Heidler and Heidler, *The War of 1812*, 102.

Though there was debate on both sides during the war, after the war, the Hartford Convention was remembered as treasonous as most Americans felt the war had been "both justified and successful."[41]

The US president did not have a stellar reputation as a war leader, and during the British occupation of Washington, DC, it "virtually collapsed."[42] The loss of Washington led to criticism of the American president with graffiti on the Capitol's burned walls reading "George Washington founded this city after a seven years' war with England—James Madison lost it after a two years' war."[43] Yet things turned around for Madison with the successful peace negotiations in the fall of 1814 and the victory in New Orleans in early 1815. Public perception of a victory following a war goes a long way to secure support for wartime leaders.

6.2 US War Aims

As we noted above, Americans went to war in 1812 due to economic, diplomatic, political, and ideological reasons. Judging by the debates in and out of Congress in 1812, American aims were primarily to stop British restrictions placed on US trade with continental Europe (the "Orders-in-Council") and British "impressment" of American sailors.[44] The United States also sought to end British influence over indigenous peoples who threatened American independence and expansion. Given that the war bill was not limited to maritime conflict, it is clear that the US war aims also included the conquest of Canada with a view to gaining their farmland.[45]

Canada was seen as an easy target, with the famous quote from Thomas Jefferson saying that "the acquisition of Canada" would be "a mere matter of marching."[46] The United States had a much larger population than Canada (7.7 million to 500,000, respectively) and many thought Canadian loyalty was divided, with the French showing antipathy to Britain, and many Canadians being Americans who immigrated simply to gain land. This confidence of victory can be seen in war hawk Henry Clay's words to Congress in 1810: "The conquest of Canada is in your power. I trust that I shall not be deemed presumptuous when I state that I verily

---

41. Howes and Carnagie, *War of 1812*, 131.
42. Heidler and Heidler, *The War of 1812*, 53.
43. Hickey, *The War of 1812*, 74.
44. Ibid., 17.
45. Howes and Carnagie, *War of 1812*, 18; Hickey, *The War of 1812*, 1.
46. This confidence in the ease of Canada's capture can be seen Henry Clay's proclamation to Congress, "The conquest of Canada is in your power. I trust I shall not be deemed presumptious [sic] when I state that I verily believe that the militia of Kentucky are alone competent to place Montreal and Upper Canada at your feet." Quoted in Greenblatt, *War of 1812*, 64.

believe that the militia of Kentucky are alone competent to place Montreal and Upper Canada at your feet."[47]

Whether the conquest of Canada was a significant war aim is debatable. The antiwar critic, John Randolph clearly states that expansion into Canada was a main war aim, claiming "Agrarian cupidity, not maritime right, urges the war. Ever since the report of the Committee on Foreign Relations came into the House, we have heard but one word—like the whip-poor-will, but one eternal monotonous tone—Canada! Canada! Canada!"[48] Other primary sources disagree, with Henry Clay opining, "Canada was not the end but the means ... the object of the war being the redress of injuries, and Canada being the instrument by which that redress was to be obtained."[49] However, recruitment for the war was often made on the basis of these ends. Andrew Jackson, for example, claimed the fight was

> for the establishment of our national character ... for the protection of our maritime citizens impressed on board British ships of war ... to seek some indemnity for past injuries, some security against future aggression by *the conquest of all the British dominions upon the continent of North America* [emphasis mine].[50]

As Greenblatt explains, "Many Americans sincerely believed that only by conquering Canada would the British once and for all be removed as a threat to the United States. And only by conquering Canada would the Indians be removed as a threat on the western frontier."[51] Whether an end or a means, the conquest of Canada appears to be at least part of American war aims. Once conquered, it is possible the plan was to return Canada to Britain for concessions regarding the trade and maritime concerns, but this is not clear.[52] Some held the grievances expressed (impressment and trade restrictions) were only "a mask for the war's real purpose of territorial expansion."[53]

What war aims were communicated may have varied from official doctrine. The US War Department told its field commanders "to promise Canadians nothing more than protection for their persons, property, and rights."[54] However, the commanders did not always follow these instructions but instead "issued

---

47. Borneman, *1812: The War That Forged a Nation*, 57.
48. Quoted in Hickey, *The War of 1812*, 19.
49. Quoted in ibid.
50. Greenblatt, *War of 1812*, 63.
51. Ibid.
52. Borneman notes that several options were considered regarding Canada's fate once conquered: (1) Canada's annexation into the Union; (2) Canada becoming a colony with lesser rights; (3) Canada to be used as a bargaining chip to force concessions from Britain. Cf. Borneman, *1812: The War That Forged a Nation*, 58.
53. Heidler and Heidler, *The War of 1812*, 43.
54. Hickey, *The War of 1812*, 20.

proclamations that spoke openly of annexation."[55] In other words, although it is possible US war aims were really all about maritime concessions, the war aims communicated to Canadians on the front lines proclaimed that Canada would be annexed by the United States. This is a good reminder that war aims communicated to an enemy need not reflect actual war aims.[56] Conversely, perceived war aims may be based upon communicated war aims but still not be an accurate perception.

Some who voted for war, Republicans from the so-called Scarecrow faction, actually hoped the declaration of war would lead to concessions from Britain and that there would be no actual fighting or bloodshed. Antiwar critic John Randolph asserted that taking Canada would entail "no expense of blood, or treasure, on our part—Canada is to conquer herself—she is to be subdued by the principles of fraternity."[57] However, American strategy morphed as war realities sunk in. It quickly became clear that the acquisition of Canada was not going to be as easy as previously thought. The United States had not realized the logistical problems involved or the significant preparations of the enemy. British regulars were well trained and veterans of combat (unlike US forces) and also were allied with indigenous forces who were skilled trackers and had a ferocious reputation that "could tip the balance in any battle by panicking enemy soldiers."[58] As has Polner and Woods comment, "There was to be no cakewalk in Canada, as it turned out."[59]

6.3 US Opinion on the Outcome of the War

6.3.1 Memorable (and Memorialized) Victorious Battles

Americans of early 1815 (when the war ended) considered themselves the victors over their enemies for several reasons. First, victory was perceived due to American privileging (and sometimes mythologizing) the memory of certain successful battles over other less successful battles. In April 1813, the Americans captured the provincial capital of Upper Canada, York (modern Toronto), and burned the legislative building and other government buildings there.[60] Although

---

55. Ibid.
56. In peace negotiations, Americans denied their aim to conquer Canada to which the British pointed to Hull's proclamation of Canada's annexation in his attack from Detroit in 1812. The American negotiators rebutted that it was "not really government-sanctioned." Cf. Borneman, *1812: The War That Forged a Nation*, 268. Cf. Donald R. Hickey, *The War of 1812: A Forgotten Conflict* (Urbana, IL: University of Illinois Press, 2012), 284.
57. Hickey, *The War of 1812*, 20.
58. Ibid., 23.
59. Polner and Woods, *We Who Dared to Say No*, 2.
60. Carl Benn, *The Battle of York* (Belleville: Milan, 1984). Though Americans actually had a higher casualty count due to an explosion in the ammunition storeroom that caused 300 deaths, including the US commander Pike. Cf. Greenblatt, *War of 1812*, 74–5.

they withdrew several days later, it was a clear American victory with symbolic significance given they had taken the provincial capital.

Early on in the war, the Americans remember their victories in the September 1813 Battle of Lake Erie (aka Battle of Put-in-Bay).[61] In this battle, six ships of the Royal Navy were taken by nine better prepared US vessels, giving the Americans control of the lake for the duration of the conflict.[62] Earlier in the year, the American ship, the *Chesapeake*, commanded by James Lawrence had been taken by the British in a mere fifteen-minute battle. When Lawrence was mortally wounded and before the ship was boarded by the British, Lawrence told his crew "Don't give up the ship."[63] Despite the loss of the ship, the words became a rallying cry for the nation.[64] Significantly, the symbolic mythologization of these words took less than two months as by the time of the Battle of Lake Erie, "Don't give up the ship" was put on a flag and raised on an American vessel, the *Lawrence*, commanded by Oliver Hazard Perry.[65] In battle with two larger ships, most of Perry's crew was slaughtered and the *Lawrence* was nearly destroyed, but Perry was undaunted. He commanded the flag be brought down from the *Lawrence*, and he brought it via row boat in the midst of heavy gun fire, to the nearby US vessel, the *Niagara*.[66] Amazingly, Perry was untouched in his trip to the *Niagara*, and he took command of the fleet there and led them to victory in about an hour.[67] His initial report of the victory famously stated, "We have met the enemy and they are ours."[68] The strategic ramifications for the victory were great, as it gave the US command of Lake Erie, the first of two lakes they would control in the war.[69] The victory also was important in providing a boost to US morale "at a time of growing doubt, hardship, and danger."[70] However, the symbolic and mythic ramifications may have been greater still. The flag Perry had embroidered with Lawrence's last words ("Don't give up the ship") became something of a "sacred relic" and is still displayed today at the US Naval Academy in Annapolis, Maryland.[71]

---

61. Turner, *War of 1812*, 131; John Hattendorf, "The Naval War of 1812 in International Perspective," *Mar.'s Mirror* 99 (2013): 7.

62. Carl Benn, *The War of 1812* (New York: Routledge, 2002), 46. British casualties included forty-one killed and ninety-four wounded compared to US casualties that included twenty-nine killed and ninety-six wounded. Cf. Theodore Roosevelt, *The Naval War of 1812* (New York: Modern Library, 2004), 148–9.

63. Roosevelt, *The Naval War*, 182.

64. Heidler and Heidler, *The War of 1812*, 68.

65. Ellis, *A Ruinous and Unhappy War*, 143.

66. Heidler and Heidler, *The War of 1812*, 78.

67. Ibid.

68. Ellis, *A Ruinous and Unhappy War*, 143; Heidler and Heidler, *The War of 1812*, 78.

69. The second being Lake Champlain.

70. Ellis, *A Ruinous and Unhappy War*, 143.

71. Heidler and Heidler, *The War of 1812*, 85.

This victory on Lake Erie led to the United States taking Fort George in Upper Canada, as well as retaking Fort Detroit. Furthermore, they also were victorious in the Battle of the Thames (aka Battle of Moraviantown) on October 3, 1813, where the famous British indigenous ally Tecumseh and his confederation were broken due to a successful US cavalry charge (and Tecumseh himself was killed in the battle). In the end US forces had twenty-nine casualties compared to forty-three British and had taken more than 600 British soldiers prisoner, as well as a million dollars' worth of weapons.[72] The battle was a distinct American victory, which, along with the victory on Lake Erie, won back the Northwest for the United States once again.[73]

The bloodiest theatre in the war was the battle for control of the Niagara peninsula in 1814. During this time, the Napoleonic wars were nearly finished, and Britain began sending more regulars to the American theatre. The Niagara operations began with the Americans taking Fort Erie on July 3. The fort fell easily to the US brigade as it offered very little resistance.[74] On July 5, the Americans led 2,000 men against an equal-sized British force. The Americans had their soldiers dressed in gray instead of blue due to a cloth shortage. Due to the incorrect color, the British commander assumed they must be militia but was impressed at their discipline and is quoted as exclaiming "Why, those are regulars!" which became a famous element of American military lore.[75] In the end, the British lost 500 men to the US 325. It was the first American victory against an equal-sized British army. The use of the gray uniforms was later connected to the gray uniforms worn by West Point cadets with the claim that West Point Academy wore gray to honor the brave US soldiers fighting in the Niagara peninsula in 1814. Of course, gray uniforms were worn by West Point cadets before these events, making this an example of an anachronistic myth.

The bloodiest conflict of the war was the six-hour Battle of Lundy's Lane on July 25, 1814, where nearly 900 casualties were sustained on each side.[76] Notwithstanding the near parity in casualties, the American deaths were double that of their enemy (174 to 84) due to British artillery fire.[77] Despite having more men die in the battle, it was the Americans who initially forced a British retreat. Key to the battle had been the high ground held by the British and their artillery placed there.[78] After several attempts, the Americans eventually took the hill and captured the British guns. As Adams writes, "When the firing ceased, Ripley's brigade held the hill-top

---

72. Greenblatt, *War of 1812*, 78.
73. Hickey, *The War of 1812*, 45.
74. Ibid., 62.
75. Ibid.
76. Turner puts it as "almost 900 Americans and over 800 British soldiers were killed, wounded, or missing." Cf. Turner, *War of 1812*, 99. Hickey records 880 British to 860 American casualties. Cf. Hickey, *The War of 1812*, 63.
77. Hickey, *The War of 1812*, 63.
78. Howes and Carnagie, *War of 1812*, 104.

with the British guns, and the whole length of Lundy's Lane to the high-road."[79] This American achievement also resulted in an enduring memory that became another part of US military lore. When American Major General Jacob Brown ordered Lieutenant Colonel James Miller to capture the British guns on the high ground, he famously replied, "I'll try, Sir."[80] Miller's memorable reply became the regimental motto of the fifth US infantry.

Despite a major loss in late August 1814 with the occupation and burning of Washington, DC, Americans recall their success in the subsequent battle at Baltimore. Baltimore was more well prepared than the capital to defend itself.[81] Fort McHenry sat in front of the city on the peninsula with 1,000 men in its garrison. The commander of the forces Major George Armistead had previously demanded "a flag so large that the British will have no difficulty in seeing it from a distance."[82] Such a flag flew over the fort, one that measured 42 feet by 30 feet, with red and white stripes with white stars. The British bombarded the fort with Congreve rockets and cannon balls from their ships, but did minimal damage to Fort McHenry. On September 14, seeing their attack was not breaching the defenses, the British withdrew.[83] American opinion relished the rebuff, with the *Weekly Register* opining that "the enemy precipitately retired. Never was the mortification of an invader more complete."[84] In fact, this success has been enshrined in a national anthem, written during the British bombardment of Baltimore, recalling " 'the rockets' red glare' that showed that the flag was still there at Baltimore."[85]

Another success remembered was in August 1814 when the British besieged American-held Fort Erie, where, despite the British having significantly more troops than the Americans, the British failed to take the fort. The first failure came in a sneak attack on August 15 launched by the British. To safeguard the surprise, the soldiers were told to remove their flints from their muskets, which meant they could not return fire quickly when they reached the fort. What is more, when they reached the fort their ladders turned out to be too short to get over the wall, causing them to retreat. The British then attacked the north end of the fort, but an unexpected explosion turned the tide as a large gunpowder stockpile detonated devastating many of the British besiegers. As it turned out, most of the Americans "were behind barracks that protected them from the blast."[86] Thus "the British

---

79. Henry Adams, *The War of 1812* (ed. DeWeerd; New York: Cooper Square Press, 1999), 185–6.

80. John Robert Elting, *Amateurs, to Arms! A Military History of the War of 1812* (MBC 4; Chapel Hill, NC: Algonquin Books of Chapel Hill, 1991), 193.

81. Greenblatt, *War of 1812*, 106.

82. Ibid.

83. Ibid., 109.

84. Ibid.

85. Hattendorf, "The Naval War of 1812," 7.

86. Turner, *War of 1812*, 99.

attack ended ignominiously, as the troops fled back to their camp north of Fort Erie."[87] As a result, the Americans only had 85 casualties compared to the 900 British.[88] A clear victory for the United States.

In the following month, the British set up guns within half a kilometer of Fort Erie, when on September 17 the Americans (with 2,000 militia reinforcements having just arrived) surprised the British by storming the batteries at night in a rainstorm in what became known as the "Sortie from Fort Erie" where the British lost 720 men to 510 for the United States. This was later remembered by some Americans as perhaps "the most splendid achievement" of the war.[89]

The failed British invasion of New York under Sir George Prevost is also remembered as an outstanding American victory. Prevost led the largest British force seen in the war with some 10,000 men with him from Montreal as he crossed the border on August 31, 1814, heading for Plattsburgh, a significant US stronghold.[90] The British objective was to take American territory that could be used as a bargaining chip in ongoing peace negotiations that had begun earlier that month in Europe. The US stronghold was undermanned with only 3,400 men, as many troops had been sent to the Niagara front and an assault on Plattsburgh was unexpected.[91]

Some 8,000 British troops arrived in Plattsburgh on September 6. Prevost, however, decided to wait for naval support. The US and British Navies on Lake Champlain (on the coast of which Plattsburg was situated) were evenly matched, but on September 11 the US naval forces prevailed over the British, winning the Americans control of a second lake in the war (Erie being the first), a point of pride for the US memory of the war.[92] Theodore Roosevelt would later claim the battle on Champlain to be "the greatest naval battle of the war."[93] Prevost, though commanding a massive force who had been quite successful in the campaign thus far, ordered all to retreat when news of the British defeat in the naval battle reached him. They destroyed their supplies and returned to Canada "virtually unharmed."[94] Prevost was criticized for his actions as many thought this massive force was large enough to take Plattsburg without naval support. In order to defend himself, Prevost was set for an army court martial, which he hoped would vindicate him, but he died before the court was to convene.[95] In American perspective, it

---

87. Ibid.
88. Hickey, *The War of 1812*, 64; Turner, *War of 1812*, 99.
89. Hickey, *The War of 1812*, 64. Some report the date as September 15. Cf. Benn, *War of 1812*, 10.
90. Hickey, *The War of 1812*, 66.
91. Ibid.
92. Turner (*War of 1812*, 131) suggests that the United States having "won control of two lakes" contributed to the American opinion that they won the war.
93. Roosevelt, *The Naval War*, 2:108; Ellis, *A Ruinous and Unhappy War*, 205.
94. Turner, *War of 1812*, 104.
95. Hickey, *The War of 1812*, 66; Turner, *War of 1812*, 105.

was remembered as a grand victory as they bested a British naval squadron and defended their stronghold against a much larger British force.

6.3.2 No Loss of Land

An American victory was perceived due to the fact that the Americans did not lose any land in the war. While the British occupied Washington, DC, for a time, they eventually abandoned it. By the end of the war, all American territory held by the British was returned when peace was declared.[96] Similarly, in the fighting at the western end of Erie (the Old Northwest),[97] despite some early success in early 1813, the British and their indigenous allies eventually retreated to Canada after suffering some serious losses, never to return to Ohio. While at times Americans had to withdraw from positions held due to British aggression, the border lines were unchanged following the war. While the United States did not gain land, there were much worse outcomes that could be envisioned than retaining the status quo. The British had first demanded that an Indian state be established to prevent American expansion and that American ships be banned on the Great Lakes. Returning to antebellum borders could be viewed as victory in American perspective.

6.3.3 The United States Won the Final Battle in the War

An American victory was perceived due to the fact that the last conflict in the war, the famous Battle of New Orleans, was an American victory (over which future president Andrew Jackson presided). Even though the peace treaty of Ghent was signed well before the battle, the news of the US victory at New Orleans arrived in Washington ten days before news of the peace treaty. This sequence of events left Americans with the impression that the battle was a key catalyst in ending the war.[98] What is more, as Hickey writes, "in the years that followed, memories faded, and the link between the victory at New Orleans and honorable peace terms became ever more pronounced."[99] Americans came to believe they "virtually dictate[d] the Treaty of Ghent."[100]

6.3.4 Regained American Prestige

The situation after the war is positive in the American memory. After what had been a period of "partisan politics and troubled diplomacy" in the United States,

---

96. Benn, *War of 1812*, 47. Turner (*War of 1812*, 100) notes that although the British held Fort Niagara, they "could not advance any further."
97. Modern Michigan, Ohio, and Indiana.
98. Hickey, *The War of 1812*, 121.
99. Ibid.
100. Ibid.

the aftermath of the war resulted in "the Era of Good Feelings and a period of sustained and prosperous isolationism."[101] The war left the nation more self-confident and led to increased prosperity for the country. Postwar Americans believed they were now more respected having demonstrated their strength and independence.[102] It was widely thought that through the war the United States enhanced their reputation in European eyes. They had come out of the conflict intact and held their own both in naval conflicts and land maneuvers against the great power of Britain. In British official Augustus J. Foster's words, "The Americans have had the satisfaction of proving their courage—they have brought us to speak of them with respect."[103] The Americans had come out of the war with memorable victories, without losing territory, winning the final battle, and regaining respect and prestige. In some perspectives, these accomplishments by any other name mean an American victory.[104]

Perhaps more important, the War of 1812 left Americans with enduring symbols and military lore. Victorious American battles are immortalized with pithy names like the "Sortie from Fort Erie." The rebuff of the British bombardment at Fort McHenry, with its waving flag, is remembered as a glorious achievement. The creation of Uncle Sam as representing the nation stems from this war, as do the immortalized sayings like "Why, those are regulars!" "I'll try Sir," "Don't give up the Ship," and "We have met the enemy and they are ours." Even more significant is the writing of the national anthem, "The Star-Spangled Banner" inspired by the bombardment of Fort McHenry and its gigantic flag that withstood the worst Britain could throw at it. The anthem became an important part of the American psyche and self-definition.[105] The war is remembered through the connecting of the gray worn by West Point cadets to the US victory at Chippawa where the troops wore gray. The victorious battles created enduring American heroes and mythologized traditions and military lore that contributed to American prestige gained from the war.

Furthermore, the war became the seedbed for an ideology of American calling and purpose that became known as America's "Manifest Destiny."[106] This became an enduring cultural belief in the United States holding that God had destined America to expand and spread its dominion across all of North America. This

---

101. Ibid., 3–4.
102. Turner, *War of 1812*, 131. Turner further writes that the result of the war was an "increased pride in the nation and a feeling of greater security because both the British and the Indian threats had been eliminated from the northeast." Ibid., 120.
103. Adams, *The War of 1812*, 185–6.
104. Though some historians deem the War of 1812 as where "America was neither the victor nor the vanquished." Cf. William Weber, "Dueling Narratives: Henry Adams's Alternative History of the War of 1812," in *Neither Victor nor Vanquished* (Washington, DC: Potomac Books, 2013), 99.
105. Hickey, *The War of 1812*, 4.
106. Ibid., 118.

philosophy was behind the rapid expansion of US territory and the removal of indigenous peoples who stood in their way. The vestiges of the war also included increased hatred of Great Britain in the United States, an antipathy that had already begun with the American Revolution.[107] Soon after the War of 1812, Americans published a study criticizing Britain for its brutalities in the war and ill-treatment of American prisoners that affected popular opinion. This tradition of criticism of the British continued long afterward and became an enduring part of the war's legacy.

Finally, the War of 1812 was thought to renew American patriotism. Albert Gallatin, one of the American negotiators at Ghent, wrote in 1816:

> The war has been productive of evil and of good, but I think the good preponderates ... The war has renewed and reinstated the national feelings and character which the Revolution had given, and which were daily lessening. The people have now more general objects of attachment, with which their pride and political opinions are connected. They are more American; they feel and act more as a nation.[108]

In the United States, the War of 1812 was widely seen as a second war for independence that consolidated what had been started in 1775.

6.4 Canadian Opinion on the Outcome of the War

6.4.1 The Failure of US War Aims to Conquer Canada

Canadians considered themselves victorious in the conflict for several reasons. First, since they believed the goal of the Americans was to conquer Canada, their failure suggested a Canadian victory. "Simply, the fact that Canada survived is an argument that the defenders won."[109] As we have seen, whether or not the conquest of Canada was a true war aim for the United States is debated, but such war aims were explicitly communicated to Canadians (e.g., Hull's proclamation during his foray from Detroit).[110] While from an American perspective failure to take Canada may have primarily meant failure to gain the leverage they wanted to force Britain's hand on maritime concessions, failure is failure.[111] This war aim was *not* achieved. The Americans failed to take even a small part of Canada.[112] In fact, at war's end in

---

107. Ibid.

108. Cited in Captain A. T. Mahan, *Sea Power in Its Relations to the War of 1812* (London: S. Low, Marston, 1905, 2 vols., II, 436.

109. Turner, *War of 1812*, 131.

110. James Laxer, *Tecumseh and Brock: The War of 1812* (Berkeley, CA: House of Anansi Press, 2013), 139–42; Hickey, *The War of 1812*, 20.

111. Hickey, *The War of 1812*, 117.

112. Greenblatt, *War of 1812*, 81.

1815 it was only Canada that still occupied enemy territory (nearly 40,000 square kilometers of territory near Lakes Superior, Michigan, Maine, and Fort Niagara), although it was returned after the Treaty of Ghent brought peace.

6.4.2 Memorable Victorious Battles

Canadians viewed the war as a Canadian triumph because, like the Americans, Canadians privilege certain memories over others. Canadians remember the defeat of larger numbers of American troops by smaller Canadian forces.[113] They remember spectacular American failures in attempts to take Upper Canada, Lower Canada, and capture Montreal.

Early in the battle for Upper Canada, Canadians remember victory at the Siege of Detroit in July 1812. The Siege of Detroit began with American General William Hull bringing 2,000 men to Detroit with a plan to cross the Detroit River and besiege the Canadian Fort Malden. The British discovered his plans when they seized a schooner with Hull's papers on board. What is more, some of Hull's men refused to cross into Upper Canada at all but would only remain on US soil. Nevertheless, Hull proceeded with his plan, first issuing a proclamation to the Canadians telling them that with the annexation of their lands they would "be emancipated from tyranny and oppression" with his campaign, evincing some American thoughts that Canadians would view them as liberators.[114] Hull's siege of Fort Malden was brief and unsuccessful and resulted in him and his army retreating to Fort Detroit. In August 1812, the British, led by Isaac Brock, crossed the Detroit River unmolested and launched cannon fire at the fort.[115] Hull worried about the superior numbers of the British and was aware of his lack of gunpowder and cannonballs to survive the siege.[116] Brock arranged for Hull to receive a false document claiming 5,000 indigenous allies of the British were approaching the fort and then sent a demand for surrender, warning that he could not control these indigenous allies in a fight.[117] This psychological tactic led Hull, who had seen the horrors of indigenous warfare in the Revolutionary War, to surrender the entire army (for which he was later court-martialed for cowardice in 1814).[118]

---

113. Turner, *War of 1812*, 59. Berton, *The Invasion of Canada*, 26, which promotes the "underdog" myth prevalent in Canadian recounting of the war. Cf. Forest, "Epic Triumph," 98.

114. Laxer, *Tecumseh and Brock*, 139–42.

115. Heidler and Heidler, *The War of 1812*, 60; LeRoy Barnett and Roger L. Rosentreter, *Michigan's Early Military Forces: A Roster and History of Troops Activated Prior to the American Civil War* (Detroit, MI: Wayne State University Press, 2003), 74.

116. Barnett and Rosentreter, *Michigan's Early Military Forces*, 73.

117. He wrote, "It is far from my intention to join in a war of extermination, but you must be aware, that the numerous bodies of Indians who have attached themselves to my troops, will be beyond control the moment the contest commences." Cf. Greenblatt, *War of 1812*, 68.

118. Barnett and Rosentreter, *Michigan's Early Military Forces*, 75.

Canadians also remember victory in the battle of Queenston Heights on the Canadian side of the Niagara River in October 1812. The US invasion was delayed when an officer had taken all of the US boats' oars.[119] In the battle, the Americans initially took the high ground briefly, but they were subsequently repelled back down and captured when the New York militia that was to support them refused to cross into Canadian territory.[120] Some 300 US casualties were sustained compared with 100 for the British. By December, "the 1812 campaign on the Niagara frontier was over."[121]

Canadians also remember the US failure to take Montreal in November 1812. US General Henry Dearborn had over 6,000 men at his disposal for the campaign, but the American militia again refused to cross into Canadian territory. In the following battles, Americans reportedly shot at each other at night and eventually retreated without even entering Canadian soil. American assaults in the first six months of the war were remembered by Canadians as utter failures.[122] Their failure was widely acknowledged, with an American newspaper concluding the campaigns against Canada in 1812 had brought "disaster, defeat, disgrace, and ruin and death."[123]

Shortly following the American conquest of Fort George on May 27, 1813, the British had abandoned Fort Erie and retreated, but the US forces did not pursue them in time.[124] This allowed a successful British counteroffensive in a surprise attack in the middle of the night in the Battle of Stoney Creek on June 5, 1813. It was a confused battle, with Americans firing on their own in the dark. Two US brigadier-generals even walked right into the hands of the enemy because they could not differentiate red uniforms from blue in the darkness.[125] This was a key victory for Britain as it halted the US advance into Upper Canada.[126] They retreated to Fort George, thinking they were outnumbered (though, in fact, they were not).[127]

A key aspect of the end of American offensives into Upper Canada remembered by Canadians involve the bravery of Laura Secord.[128] The Americans had sent

---

119. It is not clear whether it was deliberate or accidental. Cf. Greenblatt, *War of 1812*, 72.

120. Heidler and Heidler, *The War of 1812*, 61. It appears it was the presence of Iroquois warriors fighting with the British that led to the militiamen's refusal to cross the Niagara River into Canadian territory. Cf. ibid., 102.

121. Ibid., 62.

122. Ibid., 63.

123. Hickey, *The War of 1812*, 39.

124. As Polner and Woods note, the failure to capture the enemy forces meant that "For the Americans, the battle failed to achieve complete success." Cf. Polner and Woods, *We Who Dared to Say No*, 207.

125. Benn, *War of 1812*, 40.

126. Ibid; Heidler and Heidler, *The War of 1812*, 80.

127. Benn, *War of 1812*, 41.

128. Heidler and Heidler, *The War of 1812*, 81.

troops from Fort George to launch a surprise attack at British positions near Beaver Dams.[129] En route, the Americans stayed the night in Queenston, Laura Secord's village, which was under American occupation. On June 21, 1813, after overhearing the Americans talk of their plan, she set out to warn the British, undertaking a long and arduous 27-kilometer journey through the woods. Due to the advance warning provided by Secord, the British and their indigenous allies were able to ambush the US contingent, which led to their surrendering to a much smaller British force.[130] Over five hundred American prisoners were taken after the battle, including fifty wounded, with twenty-five men killed beside.[131] Laura Secord's heroic deed was not well known during her lifetime, and was largely forgotten until 1860 when the Prince of Wales (and future King Edward VI) visited Canada and rewarded her, now a poor widow, with one hundred pounds for her service.[132] She lives on in Canadian memory today mostly associated with a chocolate company named after her, though Secord herself had nothing to do with it. Nevertheless, she is remembered as a key heroine of the war and her story has become something of a Canadian myth[133] that has been retold with much embellishments in literature and the theatre. Canadian schools have been named after her, stamps and coins issued with her likeness, and monuments erected in her honor.

Following this, the Americans were largely limited to Fort George, with the British blockading them (hoping the winter would end the American incursions).[134] Subsequently, the Americans could no longer make headway in the Niagara Peninsula as most of their men had been sent to join the offensive against Montreal, which became "the largest American operation of the war" and was "a most dangerous threat to the survival of Upper Canada."[135] Canadians remember the campaign to take Montreal as a colossal American failure. In late October 1813, American Major General Wade Hampton crossed the border en route Montreal but 3,564 of his men were defeated by 339 "well-positioned" Canadian and indigenous defenders at Chateaugay.[136] The battle has been characterized as "a

129. Benn, *War of 1812*, 41.
130. Heidler and Heidler, *The War of 1812*, 81.
131. Joseph H. Eaton, *Returns of Killed and Wounded in Battles or Engagements with Indians and British and Mexican Troops, 1790–1848, Compiled by Lt. Col J. H. Eaton* (Washington, DC: National Archives and Records Administration Microfilm Publications, 2000), 10.
132. Polner and Woods, *We Who Dared to Say No*, 513.
133. Some historians have undermined the historicity of her contribution and argued the story was mostly myth. Cf. W. Stewart Wallace, *The Story of Laura Secord: A Study in Historical Evidence* (Toronto: Macmillan, 1932). But FitzGibbon, the British commander who she warned, twice wrote of her contribution, backing up her account.
134. Benn, *War of 1812*, 44.
135. Heidler and Heidler, *The War of 1812*, 82; Benn, *War of 1812*, 45.
136. Benn, *War of 1812*, 45; Greenblatt, *War of 1812*, 78.

more comical than deadly affair."[137] In fact, the smaller force of French Canadians managed to repulse the American incursion "with shouting and bugle calls," which the Americans believed were the sound of "an enormous host" and led them to retreat.[138] The American brigade "dissolved into chaos" and "scattered as it withdrew" with some officers even abandoning their men.[139]

Canadians remember another defeat of a large American force by a much smaller group of Canadian defenders, which followed on the heels of the battle at Chateauguay. In November 1813, American Major General James Wilkinson led a 7,300-man army in another thrust toward Montreal but 3,050 of his men were defeated by 1,169 Canadian defenders in the Battle of Crysler's Farm on the St. Lawrence River on November 11.[140] The Americans ended their expedition and withdrew to winter camp in New York.[141] As Heidler comments, "The last year of the war [1814] would see the United States abandoning the idea of conquering Canada and instead facing the stark possibility of military defeat on its own soil."[142]

Regarding the battle of Lundy's Lane on July 25, 1814, where Americans remember their success and valor, although the Americans captured the high ground and British guns, American actions afterward did not suggest an American victory. As Turner writes,

> Although the Americans had prevailed in the struggle for the guns, they did not act like victors. The next morning … on seeing British troops ahead [they] pulled back to Chippawa … Almost as if they were a beaten army, the Americans prepared to abandon their camp: they threw baggage, camp equipment, and provisions into the Niagara River, burned Street's Mills, and destroyed the bridge over the Chippawa.[143]

Despite the setback of losing the high ground artillery, Canadians remember the retreat of US forces.[144] In fact, strategically the American withdrawal

137. Heidler and Heidler, *The War of 1812*, 84.
138. Ibid.
139. Polner and Woods, *We Who Dared to Say No*, 87.
140. Benn, *War of 1812*, 45; Hickey, *The War of 1812*, 50.
141. The battle is said to have "indisputably put an end to Wilkinson's dream of attacking Montreal." Cf. Polner and Woods, *We Who Dared to Say No*, 131.
142. Heidler and Heidler, *The War of 1812*, 85.
143. Turner, *War of 1812*, 97. As Hiedler notes, "Withdrawal of the mangled American army drew criticism, but the British did not molest his retreat. Everyone had seen enough killing for a while." Cf. Heidler and Heidler, *The War of 1812*, 108.
144. The retreat actually violated explicit orders by American Major General Brown to Brigadier General Eleazar Ripley to hold his position. Cf. Richard V. Barbuto, *Niagara, 1814: America Invades Canada* (Lawrence, KS: University Press of Kansas, 2000), 227–8. Brown had ordered Ripley to retake the British guns, but after seeing the British had reoccupied the high ground, retreated. The US forces "never advanced in force north of Lundy's Lane again." Cf. Malcomson, *Historical Dictionary of the War of 1812*, 300.

had a significant outcome on the war. The high casualties left the Americans outnumbered. As Barbuto writes,

> On 26 July, Brown's plan to advance on Burlington Heights was irretrievably shattered. Drummond had secured the forts at the northern end of the Niagara, and he had blunted an American advance. Although there was still a lot of fight in both forces, the balance of combat power on the Niagara Peninsula had swung from the invaders to the defenders.[145]

Despite Miller's memorable saying ("I'll try, Sir") in the battle, Lundy's Lane was no American victory.

Regarding the battle for Fort Erie in August–September 1814, where Americans remember stopping the besiegers (and memorialized the "Sortie from Fort Erie" on September 17), on November 5, 1814, due to the fort being very difficult to keep supplied, the United States chose to blow up the fort and return to Buffalo, New York.[146] These were the last of the US troops to be on Canadian soil in the war. Despite the "victory" at Lundy's Lane, and the successful staying off British besiegers at Fort Erie, the Americans retreated and the British retained the Niagara Peninsula.[147]

Significantly, Canadians remember that they successfully invaded and occupied the US capital, Washington, DC, in August 1814. American successes of 1813 in York, with the burning of government buildings, were avenged in this campaign as the British burned the Capitol (with the Supreme Court and Library of Congress)[148] as well as other public buildings (the State Department, the Treasury, the War Department, the Navy building, and the Post Office). What is more, they even burned the presidential palace. When the president's home was rebuilt, they painted the exterior walls white in order to cover over the burnt marks, thus it was called the White House.[149] As Greenblatt writes, "The razing of a capital city in Europe would have marked the final blow to national pride and would probably have ended the war."[150] As Snow comments, "The raid on Washington had achieved its purpose; decisive defeat and utter humiliation of the enemy, the proudest monuments of America's capital devastated."[151] Taking the capital city of the enemy is symbolically important and is remembered by Canadians as a clear sign of a Canadian victory. In fact, peace negotiations in Ghent, United

---

145. Barbuto, *Niagara*, 229.
146. Hickey, *The War of 1812*, 64.
147. Ibid., 65.
148. Greenblatt, *War of 1812*, 13–14.
149. Turner, *War of 1812*, 101. The name became official in 1902 as President Roosevelt used it on his stationery. Cf. Greenblatt, *War of 1812*, 14.
150. Greenblatt, *War of 1812*, 104.
151. Peter Snow, *When Britain Burned the White House: The 1814 Invasion of Washington* (New York: Thomas Dunne Books, 2014), 145.

Netherlands (modern Belgium), were already underway in August 1814 when the Battle of Bladensburg led to the occupation and destruction of Fort Washington, DC, giving the impression that the British had gained the upper hand in the conflict.

The embarrassing US surrender of Alexandria, an affluent city upriver from Washington, is remembered by Canadians as a significant victory for British forces and "another humiliating setback" for the United States.[152] The townspeople allowed the "seizure of merchantmen and goods" in order to prevent the destruction of the city.[153] Having surrendered all Alexandria's wealth, the British left with twenty-seven ships full of booty. The success of this mission is recalled by the British as "as brilliant an achievement ... as grace the annals of our naval history."[154]

The bombardment of Fort McHenry in September 1814 is remembered differently by Canadians than Americans. As noted above, the survival of the fort despite extensive British assaults led to the event being immortalized by Americans in their national anthem, "The Star-Spangled Banner." However, the British view was tantamount to a job well done. After the success in Washington, having accomplished their objectives, the royal fleet was nearly to move to the Gulf of Mexico to support campaigns there, when the admiral, Cochrane, was persuaded by some of his generals to instead move against Baltimore. The British found Baltimore a much more well-defended city than the capital, but bombarded Fort McHenry, the main defensive structure there, for twenty-five hours straight on September 13 to 14. In the end, Admiral Cochrane decided they had "accomplished what they wanted and that it was not worth heavy losses to try to capture the city."[155] The British returned to their original plan to move to support the planned campaign in the Gulf of Mexico. What is taken for a major victory by the Americans is viewed as a successful bombardment (or show of force) by the British.[156] In fact, the British retreat did not mean an abandonment of the area as they retained control of an island in Chesapeake Bay until January 1815.[157]

---

152. Hickey, *The War of 1812*, 75.

153. Polner and Woods, *We Who Dared to Say No*, 5.

154. Hickey, *The War of 1812*, 75.

155. Turner, *War of 1812*, 110.

156. Swanson suggests that if the British had really wanted to take Baltimore, the British would have committed troops to an overland attack as well. He writes, "Had it [an overland attack on Baltimore] been risked, and had the fleet made a simultaneous move up the bay, there is little doubt that Baltimore would have capitulated." Cf. Neil Harmon Swanson, *The Perilous Fight, Being a Little Known and Much Abused Chapter of Our National History in Our Second War of Independence and a True Narrative of the Battle of Godly Wood and the Attack on Fort Mchenry, More Suitably Described as the Battle of Baltimore ... To Which Is Added Some Notice of the Circumstances Attending the Writing of the Star Spangled Banner ... Recounted Mainly from Contemporary Records by Neil H. Swanson* (New York: Farrar and Rinehart, 1945), 334.

157. Turner, *War of 1812*, 111.

Finally, Canadians disregard the US victory in New Orleans, which was so celebrated by the Americans because the war had actually ended *before* the battle was fought. The peace treaty at Ghent was agreed to and signed by both British and American diplomats on December 24, 1814, though it took time for news of it to cross the Atlantic and reach the United States.[158] The key moment in the battle of New Orleans that led to the British defeat was the poorly executed British frontal assault against American positions on January 8, 1815, some *two weeks after* the peace treaty was signed by both sides.[159] While the battle was the worst defeat for the British in the entire war, it was fought by both sides in ignorance of the peace treaty. In Canadian perspective, winning a battle after the war was over and the peace treaty decided upon hardly shows victory in the war. The Battle of New Orleans doesn't count. Furthermore, in reality the final conflict of the war was *after* the Battle of New Orleans with the successful British assault against Fort Bowyer on February 11, 1815. The day after capturing the Fort, the British were preparing to attack Mobile Point when word of the ratification of Ghent's peace treaty arrived, ending the war. But technically, if final battles indicated victory, the British had the last successful conflict in the war.[160]

6.4.3 A Shared Common Tradition for Canadians

The War of 1812 had a unifying effect upon Canada. The tiny population of Upper Canada was quite diverse, with immigrants from the British Isles, Ireland, and settlers from the United States who came to Canada largely for land grants. They had less patriotism than their southern neighbors and could be described as largely indifferent or even disgruntled without a strong identity and shared tradition.[161] The war, however, changed Canadians from "a loose aggregation of village states into something approaching a political entity."[162] Canadian historian Pierre Berton suggests that it was not so much the war but "the *myth* of the war" that gave Canadians a new awareness of community. He writes,

> In the end, the myth became the reality … As the years went by and memories dimmed, as old scars healed and old grudges evaporated, as aging veterans

---

158. As Turner writes, "By the time it was fought, the two countries were making peace in Europe, but there was no way for the British government to call it off" (ibid., 106).
159. Heidler and Heidler, *The War of 1812*, 10.
160. Another measure of victory could be deaths suffered by either side. The final mortality count in the War of 1812 is estimated around 20,000 US deaths compared to 10,000 Canadian, with another 7,500 indigenous fighters as well. Cf. Hickey, *The War of 1812*, 117. While Canadians could boast of less casualties, the indigenous forces were vital to the war effort and their combined totals are fairly similar to American deaths—though the Canadian side still suffered over 2,000 less deaths.
161. Berton, *The Invasion of Canada*, 28.
162. Ibid.

reminisced and new leaders hyperbolized, the settlers began to believe that they had repelled the invader almost single-handed. For the first time, Upper Canadians shared a common tradition.[163]

While Canadians lack the enduring symbols (Laura Secord perhaps?) and do not emphasize the mythological military lore as do Americans from this war, Canadians, particularly Ontarians, take pride in their having prevented the American invasion of Canada. Interestingly, in the Niagara peninsula, where the worst of the fighting occurred, Canadians in Ontario have commemorated the war much more than the American's across the border in New York. Americans in Niagara, United States, and the Buffalo area seem to almost "conspicuously downplay or outright ignore the fact a war was even waged there."[164] The war plays an important part in Ontarian consciousness, but evidently not for those in New York. In the Canadian Niagara region, there are at least twenty-two commemorations of the war in both national and provincial parks, the latter of which has fifty-three "plaques, markers and monuments" dedicated to the war.[165] Conversely, all of Western New York has only twelve commemorations "marked only by state historical plaques."[166]

This dichotomy has been explained as due to the way in which Canadian identity is often defined in contradistinction to the United States. What it means to be Canadian is often defined by what Canadians are not—they are not American. The shared tradition of Upper Canadians that grew out of this war was largely established on rejecting American principles and ideals.[167] As Forest observes, "Significant aspects of the Canadian national identity centre on a repudiation of many things American. The War of 1812 is a very physical and visible (and successful) rejection of the United States."[168] Thus, as Canadian Historian Pierre Berton writes, "The Canadian 'way'—so difficult to define except in terms of negatives—has its roots in the invasion of 1812–14." The enduring legacy of the War of 1812 for Canadians was in creating a common tradition that unified its diverse population. In this way, one could say Canadians were the real winners of the war.[169]

---

163. Ibid.
164. Forest, "Epic Triumph," 98.
165. Ibid.
166. *Guidebook to the Historic Sites of the War of 1812* (Toronto: Dundurn Press, 1998); Forest, "Epic Triumph," 98.
167. Berton, *The Invasion of Canada*, 28.
168. Forest, "Epic Triumph," 98.
169. A religious perspective can be seen in the famous Canadian Anglican priest John Strachan, who saw some spiritual good come from the war, saying, "Since the return of Peace, a great change is observable among our inhabitants, many are desirous of religious instruction who used to be cold and indifferent." Cf. Benn, *War of 1812*, 80.

This brings us to the end of our discussion of the War of 1812. We have seen the differing perspectives on who the victor in the war was and how such victory is determined or perceived by each side. In the next chapter, we will undertake a comparative reading bringing our discussion regarding the War of 1812 into conversation with the war of 701 BCE. As we shall see, there are many valuable insights gained by the comparison, to which we now turn.

Chapter 7

DISPUTED VICTORY IN THE WAR OF 701 BCE

In our earlier survey of Assyrian and biblical texts, it was evident that the assessment of the war of 701 BCE and its outcome have been perceived and remembered quite differently by Assyrian and Judahite sides to the conflict.[1] Having considered the similar phenomena with the War of 1812, we now turn to compare our findings with the war of 701 BCE.

7.1 Origins of the War of 701 BCE

As we have seen, the origins of the War of 1812 were in concert with Britain's Napoleonic war with France. Similarly, the origins of the war of 701 were in concert with a larger conflict.[2] It seems clear that the rebellion of Judah and others in the Levant was in concert with the much larger Assyrian war with Babylon under Merodach-Baladan. An alliance with Babylon is implied in the biblical texts, with Hezekiah's hosting a Babylonian embassy in 2 Kings 20 at which time Hezekiah showed the Babylonians, among other things, his treasury (נְכֹתֹה אֶת־הַכֶּסֶף וְאֶת־הַזָּהָב), armory (כֵּלָיו), and storehouse (בְּאוֹצְרֹתָיו), which suggests the reason for the visit was to assess Judah's military preparedness.[3] Just as American war hawks hoped that British problems with Napoleon would mean a weakened response to the US aggression, so Judahite leaders doubtless hoped that Assyrian problems

---

1. As P. R. Davies has opined, "Even if the Assyrians and Judaeans had agreed exactly on the 'pure facts' of what had happened, each might disagree on the 'fact' of who had won or what the episode proved or meant. These things depend on one's view of the world, the strategic interests of each side, the definition of what counts as a success and what [does] not" (Grabbe, "Reflections on the Discussion," 314).

2. As Fales ("The Road to Judah," 224) notes, "Sennacherib's ascent to the throne is nowadays reconstructed as marked by an inner ideological crisis of no small import, due to the untimely and inauspicious death of his father Sargon, which bore immediate consequences in foreign policy—namely, local rebellions in diverse but equally sensitive theaters, of which the Levant was one of the most important, all of which needed to be faced and put down as soon as possible."

3. Gallagher, *Sennacherib's Campaign*, 271.

with Babylon would mean a weakened response to a Judahite rebellion. Of course, unforeseen to Judah was the collapse of Babylon and Sennacherib's strong response to the rebellion in the West.

7.2 Diverse Opinion of the War and the War Leader

As we have seen in our discussion of the origins of the War of 1812, there were significant differences of opinion even within the United States regarding the decision to go to war. Opposition to the war was voiced before and during the war, but not as much afterward. Commonly, people rallied around wartime leaders (as can be seen in the Baltimore riots), though in the wartime election of 1812, President Madison did see his support drop. But after the war was over Madison's political party was unrivalled and began a reign of hegemony that extinguished the opposition party entirely.[4] Similarly, as we have seen in our earlier chapter on prophetic texts, it is clear that Hezekiah's rebellion was not viewed positively by all in Judah. Isaiah 1-39 clearly contain some oracles that are critical of Hezekiah's leadership and his anti-Assyrian coalition, these likely originating before the invasion of Sennacherib. Our study of Isaian prophetic texts also made it clear that some oracles (which likely refer to Hezekiah) are more positive toward the king.

Furthermore, Isaiah was likely not alone in critiquing Hezekiah's policies. Other contemporary negative attitudes toward Hezekiah may be implied in the Rabshakeh's speech wherein he gives voice to those who objected to his reform and suggests that Yahweh was actually angry at Hezekiah for removing altars from the high places (2 Kgs 18:22). The voice of the Rabshakeh here may represent the opinion of the people at the popular level or the opinions of Israelite prophets/priests who did not approve of the reforms.[5] As Young suggests, the Rabshakeh's critique of the reforms with "its rationale for removing Yahwistic places of worship is such an important differentiator from Deuteronomic thought and the reforms of Josiah that it should properly be seen as evidence of national memory."[6] As Peter Machinist posits, "There clearly must have been Judaeans who had doubted or came to doubt the efficacy and correctness of the Judaean theology and, more particularly, Hezekiah's actions.[7]

In light of military history, this inconsistent support or opposition to Hezekiah and his policies should not be unexpected.[8] As is the case with many wartime

---

4. Hickey, *The War of 1812*, 120.
5. Evans, "Hezekiah-Sennacherib," 349; Weinfeld, "Cult Centralization," 202-12 (209).
6. Young, *Hezekiah in History and Tradition*, 121.
7. Machinist, "The Rab Saqeh," 163. Alternatively, Hans Wildberger (*Jesaja 28-39*, 1387) has suggested that this passage was a later addition written by an opponent to the Josianic cultic reform.
8. Nielson reconstructs the evolving Isaian opinion of Assyrian involvement in the crisis, suggesting "as the situation evolves towards 701 the Assyrians' role in Yahweh's plan must become increasingly uncertain. Although the leaders in Jerusalem do not heed

leaders, their popularity can wax and wane. For example, before the Japanese attack on Pearl Harbor, President Roosevelt's support for Britain's war effort was heavily criticized by Americans.[9] History shows that once a war starts, unless the public perceives imminent victory, citizens often quickly turn on their leader if he is deemed culpable for the conflict.[10] In the Second World War, Winston Churchill was taking the blame for apparently losing the war with Germany after the fall of France, the defeat at Dunkirk, and losses to the RAF Bomber Command, along with the U-boat rampage (never mind the fall of Greece and Singapore).[11]

Many leaders during wartime have either ended up becoming so unpopular or discredited that they were forced to leave office. This was true of Winston Churchill, Harry Truman, and Richard Nixon. With Churchill and Truman, this was after wars that were widely perceived to be victorious.[12] All this to say that divergent views of the wartime king need not be decisive in our assessments. Churchill's unpopularity after the war should not lead us to denigrate his achievements and leadership during the war which led to its victory. It should also caution us against viewing a leader negatively simply because citizens protested the conflict. Here it is possible that modern protest against America's wars are coloring our assessment of ancient war. Since some clearly protested Hezekiah's war, does that mean we should assess him negatively?

Significantly, the contrasting perspectives on Hezekiah and his rebellion within the book of Isaiah find some parallels with the views of American leadership we have seen in the War of 1812. Similar to the War of 1812, where opposition was expressed before and during the conflict, but not after the war's end, there appears to be little critique of Hezekiah's leadership after the conclusion to the war. This can be seen in the texts that appear to be later theological reflections on the successful nature of Hezekiah's reign (e.g., 2 Chronicles 29–32).

Isaiah's warnings to keep quiet and to abstain from political transactions in the form of alliances against the Assyrians, and although Isaiah still has something to say to his countrymen about this, *the events of 701* must have caused a *change* in attitude towards Assyria. The king of Assyria's siege is and remains an insult against Yahweh himself, and this cannot go unpunished. Isaiah must therefore curse the king of Assyria, who did not understand that he was only an axe in Yahweh's hand, and believed that he himself was the hand (Isa. l0:5ff)." Cf. Nielsen, *There Is Hope for a Tree*, 137.

9. "The Conservative Case against War," *Wilson Quarterly* 38 (2014).

10. Hanson, *Father of Us All*, 22.

11. Ibid., 23.

12. Such divergent public opinion of the wartime leader may be due to the use of "contemporary wisdom or innate logic to try to make sense of impending conflicts, rather than look to the history of past wars, which are frequently unpredictable and nearly inexplicable." Ibid., 38.

7.3 Judahite Opinion: Judah Won the War

7.3.1 Failure of Assyrian War Aims

Similar to the War of 1812, who won the war depends upon who you ask. Just as Canadians view themselves as victors in the war because the United States failed in its war aim of conquering Canada, so, from the Judahite perspective, which believed the Assyrian goal was to conquer Judah, take its capital, and replace its king, Assyria clearly failed, implying that Judah had prevailed. As we have seen, it is debated whether US war aims were really to conquer Canada and annex it into the Union or whether the goal was to gain it as a bargaining chip to force British concessions on maritime issues (whereupon any gained territory would be returned). Similarly, it is debated as to whether it was a true Assyrian war aim to conquer Jerusalem and replace Hezekiah.[13] However, it is vital to remember here that we are talking about Judah's perception of Assyrian goals. Judahite perception may have been based on the threats uttered against them by Assyria. The speeches of the Rabshakeh in 2 Kgs 18:19-35 suggest as much. In 2 Kgs 18:25, the Assyrian messenger claims that Assyria had come to "destroy" Judah. Clearly, the taking of Jerusalem was their goal as the Rabshakeh boasted, "How then can the Lord deliver Jerusalem from my hand?" (2 Kgs 18:35). The Rabshakeh promises a long siege if Jerusalem does not surrender, warning the people that they "will have to eat their own filth and drink their own urine" (2 Kgs 18:27). Furthermore, the Rabshakeh promises the deportation of the Judahites to a new land saying, "until I come and take you to a land like your own, a land of grain and new wine, a land of bread and vineyards, a land of olive trees and honey" (2 Kgs 18:32).

Judahite perceptions of Assyrian goals were likely also informed by known Assyrian policy to depose rebel rulers and to place a new pro-Assyrian king on the throne. For example, in Sennacherib's annals he describes how he replaced Lulî, the king of Sidon, with a new king, Taba'lu.[14] Sennacherib also deposed king Ṣidqâ, king of Ashkelon who had "not bowed down to my yoke"[15] and replaced him with

---

13. Some think the lack of conquest of Jerusalem shows failure of some sort. E.g., Baruch A. Levine, "Assyrian Ideology and Israelite Monotheism," *Iraq* 67 (2005): 417; Grabbe, "Of Mice and Dead Men," 138-9. Others have suggested that Assyrian war aims did not include the conquest of Jerusalem. E.g., "The submission of Hezekiah had been complete ... It does not seem to have been in Assyria's interest to pursue further military action against Jerusalem" (Cogan, "Cross-Examining," 71). Similarly Mayer, "Sennacherib's Campaign," 184; Knauf, "Sennacherib at the Berezina," 146; Clements, *Deliverance of Jerusalem*, 62; Zevit, "Implicit Population Figures," 361-2. Of course, others think Assyrian war aims were frustrated. E.g., Gallagher, *Sennacherib's Campaign*, 132.

14. RINAP 3:1:175, 22.ii.47.

15. RINAP 3:1:175, 22.ii.60-62.

a new king, Šarru-lū-dāri.¹⁶ Sennacherib not only deposed the king but completely destroyed Ṣidqâ's dynasty, claiming to have deported not only the king but also "his wife, his sons, his daughters, his brothers (and other) offspring of his father's house."¹⁷ Given that Hezekiah is similarly said to have "not submitted to my yoke,"¹⁸ one might expect similar treatment. As Levine writes, "It was not Assyrian policy to leave the capital of an insurrectionist kingdom standing on its tell."¹⁹ What is more, many scholars think Hezekiah was the ringleader of the rebellion, which would logically call for even harsher treatment.²⁰ From a Judahite perspective, the fact that Hezekiah and his dynasty remained on the throne showed Assyrian failure.

Despite the Rabshakeh's communication of Assyrian war aims, in reality it may be that official Assyrian goals were different for different parts of the Levant. As we have seen, some have suggested that the Assyrian strategy may have been to focus on fortified border cities (both Philistine and Judahite) mainly in the Shephelah and not the highlands and Jerusalem.²¹ Here the parallel with the War of 1812 is helpful as we have seen that war aims communicated to the enemy may vary from official doctrine. Despite directives from the US War Department that its field commanders were not to promise more than protection to Canadians who surrendered, some commanders did not always follow these instructions but instead "issued proclamations that spoke openly of annexation."²² War aims communicated to an enemy need not reflect actual war aims.²³ In other words, although it is possible that Assyrian war aims did not

---

16. RINAP 3:1:175, 22.ii.65. In his text regarding the fight with Babylon he boasts, "I installed Bel-ibni, son of a building inspector, a native-born Babylonian, who was raised in my palace like a young puppy" (COS 2.119A:302).

17. RINAP 3:1:175, 22.ii.62–63.

18. RINAP 3:1:176, 22.iii.19.

19. Levine, "Assyrian Ideology," 417. Fales ("The Road to Judah," 241) similarly observes, "From the viewpoint of the political-ideological tenets espoused in Sennacherib's annals, it seems clear that Hezekiah of Judah was a prime candidate for punishment on more than one count. Not only had he relinquished his previous status as loyal vassal, but he actively supported the anti-Assyrian revolt in Ekron by holding Padî as a captive in his capital city."

20. E.g., Young writes, "The invasion was a forceful reprisal against the coalition of western states, with *Judah as its particular target*" [emphasis mine]. Cf. Young, *Hezekiah in History and Tradition*, 65.

21. Aharoni, *The Land of the Bible*, 392; Rainey and Notley, *The Sacred Bridge*, 243; Bloch-Smith, "Assyrians Abet," 36; Zevit, "Implicit Population Figures," 362; Cf. Dever, *Beyond the Texts*, 578.

22. Hickey, *The War of 1812*, 20.

23. As noted in the previous chapter, during negotiations at Ghent after the British pointed to Hull's proclamation of Canada's annexation, Americans denied their aim to conquer Canada claiming Hull's offer was "not really government-sanctioned." Cf. Borneman, *1812: The War That Forged a Nation*, 268. Cf. Hickey, *1812: A Forgotten Conflict*, 284.

require the taking of Jerusalem, the entire conquest of Judah, or the deposing of its king, the war aims actually communicated by the Rabshakeh to Judahites on the walls of Jerusalem proclaimed that Jerusalem and its nation would be annexed by the Assyrians.[24] Conversely, perceived war aims may be based upon communicated war aims but still not be an accurate perception. Nevertheless, since Hezekiah remained king in Judah despite his rebellion, the capital city of Jerusalem remained unmolested, and the people were not exiled to Assyria, the Judahites thought they won.

7.3.2 No Loss of Land

Second, like the American perspective in the War of 1812, a Judahite victory may have been perceived because the Judahites did not lose any land in the war. While as we have seen, although Americans lost all territorial gains made during hostilities, in the end of the war, the land they owned before the conflict remain their own. Of course, as we saw in our survey of Assyrian texts, Sennacherib claims to have redistributed much of Hezekiah's territory as punishment for Hezekiah's rebellious ways.[25] Despite this claim, the extent of this loss of territory is unclear. The Assyrian texts do not list the exact cities, and it is not clear if this might be "re-patriated" territory rather than Judahite territory proper. The Judahite territory in question is said to be given to Philistine vassals in Ashdod, Ekron, and Gaza.[26] The biblical account extols Hezekiah for expanding his kingdom at Philistia's expense, as 2 Kgs 18:8 reads: "From watchtower to fortified city, [Hezekiah] defeated the Philistines, as far as Gaza and its territory." Since the king of Gaza is mentioned as one of the recipients of Hezekiah's cities that Sennacherib's claims to have despoiled, it is possible that the cities in question were none other than Philistine cities.[27] In other words, some of the territory put under Philistine control in the aftermath of Sennacherib's campaign appears to have been more of a restoration of Philistine territory rather than loss of Judahite territory proper.[28]

---

24. As Pope ("Sennacherib's Departure," 141) writes, "We also do not need to assume that the inhabitants of Jerusalem were aware of Assyrian grand strategy; if they dreaded the fate of Samaria and believed the *rab-šaqê*'s threats of deprivation (2 Kgs 18:27), then the subsequent lifting of the Assyrian blockade might very well have appeared to them a *deus ex machina*."

25. RINAP 3.1:176, 22.iii.31.

26. RINAP 3.1:176, 22.iii.32–34. Later recensions (Bull 4) add Ashkelon to this list, possibly referring to subsequent rearrangements of the territory. Cf. Cogan, "Cross-Examining," 68; Gallagher, *Sennacherib's Campaign*, 135.

27. Knauf ("Sennacherib at the Berezina," 148 n. 22) opines that "Sennacherib is explicit in stating that he redistributed only the part of Hezekiah's kingdom which he had conquered."

28. Gallagher *Sennacherib's Campaign*, 110. As Na'aman puts it, Sennacherib "also removed territory from Judaean control." Cf. Grabbe, "Reflections on the Discussion," 323.

From a Judahite perspective, if the territory in question was originally Philistine, its return to Philistine hands would not indicate defeat in the same way.

What is more, as seen in our review of archaeological remains, material evidence from Judahite sites suggests Judahite cities did *not* become Philistine territory. As Becking writes,

> The archaeological evidence hints at a continuation of Jerusalemite control over the Judaean countryside. The evidence of the palaeo-Hebrew inscriptions excavated at various Judaean sites (e.g., Tel Arad, Khirbet Beit Lei, Khirbet el-Qom, Mesad Hashabjahu) stands contrary to the idea that the area was Philistine territory.[29]

It appears that Jerusalem continued to control the countryside.[30] Settlements increased after Sennacherib's withdrawal, with new towns and growth in rural areas.[31] Study of Judaean material culture (JPF, rosette stamps, inscribed scale weights, etc.) and their relation to what the borders of Judah were in the eighth–seventh century, suggest that Judah's borders remained largely unchanged after the Assyrian invasion.[32]

Of course, we noted earlier, it is likely that the border between Judah and Philistia was somewhat in flux and moved back and forth all through their history of coexistence.[33] There is evidence that although many border towns were destroyed in 701, this border area was subsequently resettled with much of it becoming Judahite again.[34] But given the situation of somewhat fluid borders, the (likely) loss of some of the border towns would not have been viewed as reason to perceive a loss, but more of a return to normality.

The terms of the Assyrian withdrawal may have been similar to the terms proposed by the British at Ghent in 1814. Initially, the negotiators favored *uti possidetis*—a Latin expression meaning "that each side would keep whatever territory it held when the treaty went into effect."[35] This *uti possidetis* part of the agreement was eventually dropped from the final peace treaty from Ghent and territory lines were unchanged from the start of the war: the *status quo ante*

---

29. Becking, "Chronology: A Skeleton without Flesh?" 69.
30. Weippert, *Palästina*, 559–681.
31. Finkelstein, "The Archaeology of the Days of Manasseh," 174–80; Tatum, "King Manasseh," 142.
32. Kletter, "Pots and Polities," 28.
33. Dever, *Beyond the Texts*, 584.
34. See, for example, the building of Lachish II, which stood till 586 BCE, or the fort at Metsad Hashavyahu near Yavne, which stood in the same period, which were certainly Judahite.
35. Hickey, *The War of 1812*, 109. Furthermore, this agreement was "subject to such modifications as mutual convenience may be found to require."

bellum. This may have been similar to the situation after the Assyrian withdrawal for Judah. Judah's gains were returned, but their *ante-rebellion* territory remained in Judah.

Another parallel from the War of 1812 might be a helpful comparison. Just as the Americans had initial success at Lundy's Lane and had taken the high ground and the British guns, in the end, US forces retreated and abandoned their gains. Similarly, the Assyrians captured Judahite fortified cities, but ultimately withdrew without taking Judah itself. While the Americans remembered Lundy's Lane as a victory due to the taking of the British guns on the high ground, Canadians remember it as a Canadian victory since US forces withdrew and Canadians regained the high ground. Similarly, from a Judahite perspective, Sennacherib's taking of the Judahite fortified cities does not indicate an Assyrian victory because they subsequently withdrew and Judah regained possession of the cities.[36]

As we saw in our previous chapter, in the aftermath of the War of 1812, while the United States did not gain any territory, a positive US view of the war was enabled due to the fact that there were much worse outcomes that could have been envisioned than retaining the status quo. In initial talks at Ghent, the British had demanded that an Indian state be established to prevent American expansion, that British territorial gains in Maine and Minnesota be acceded to Canada, and that American war ships be banned on the Great Lakes.[37] In light of these possible outcomes, returning to antebellum borders was viewed as a victory in American perspective. Similarly, from a Judahite perspective there were worse possible outcomes from the rebellion that could be envisioned. Obviously, the Davidic dynasty may have come to an end if Hezekiah was deposed and a puppet king put on the throne (as we see Sennacherib do with Phoenician and Philistine rebel kings). Furthermore, Jerusalemites could have been deported, as threatened by the Rabshakeh. Finally, Judah could have been annexed into the Assyrian empire as was Samaria and the Northern Kingdom of Israel some twenty years before. Regardless of any negative aspects of the rebellion, the Assyrian army never ravaged Judah again. While territory previously occupied was returned or lost, there were far worse outcomes that could be envisioned, allowing the final situation to be viewed as a Judahite victory.

---

36. This may be the perspective found in the later account in Chronicles that claims Sennacherib "came against" Judahite fortified cities, aspiring (or thinking to) "to conquer them" for himself (וַיֹּאמֶר לְבִקְעָם אֵלָיו) in 2 Chr 32:1. Rather than suggesting the Chronicler is contradicting 2 Kgs 18:13, which claims Sennacherib did "capture" the cities, from a later historical perspective the Chronicler could have understood them not to be captured after all given the Assyrian withdrawal and the return to ante-bellum borders. Cf. Evans, "Historia or Exegesis?" 108–9.

37. Hickey, *The War of 1812*, 107; Turner, *War of 1812*, 116.

7.3.3 The Assyrians Lost the Final Battle in the War

Similar to the American perspective with the victory at New Orleans, an Assyrian loss may have been perceived by Judah due to their understanding the last conflict in the war to have been concluded with Assyrian losses sustained in conflict with a Nubian-Egyptian force. Of course, Sennacherib's annals claim to have bested this Cushite force, writing as follows:

> In the plain of the city Eltekeh, they sharpened their weapons while drawing up in battleline before me. With the support of the god Aššur, my lord, I fought with them and defeated them. In the thick of battle, I captured alive the Egyptian charioteers and princes (lit. "the sons of the king"), together with the charioteers of the king of the land Meluḫḫa [Ethiopia].[38]

However, as we noted in our earlier chapter, many do not take this victory at face value and see the phraseology employed therein as indicating it was not a clear Assyrian victory,[39] or perhaps that it was basically a defeat.[40] Some hold that the battle with Nubian-Egyptian forces was the impetus for the Assyrian withdrawal, connecting it to the reference to Tirhakah in 2 Kgs 19:9, which is the last time the Assyrian army is mentioned as being near Jerusalem in the biblical account.[41] While not necessarily an outright defeat, many scholars hold that the battle was something of a stalemate.[42]

Of course, for our purposes here the extent of "success" achieved by the Nubian-Egyptian forces should be viewed in light of a Judahite perspective. This "success" need not imply a complete victory by the Egyptians. In fact, all that may have been needed by Judah was a distraction to delay the military action against their land. The Assyrian army was somewhat restricted in their campaigns by time and space. In fact, Eph'al explains,

> If the rebels were able to hold out longer than the time which the imperial army could allocate for action against them, there was a reasonable chance that the emperor would either not send his army against them or that he would have

---

38. RINAP 3.1:176, 22.ii.82–iii.5.

39. Knauf, "Sennacherib at the Berezina," 148.

40. Redford, *Egypt, Canaan, and Israel*, 353.

41. See my earlier monograph (Evans, *Invasion of Sennacherib*, 192). Others put the battle of Eltekeh at the end of the campaign as well. Cf. Knauf, "Sennacherib at the Berezina," 144; Redford, *Egypt, Canaan, and Israel*, 351–3.

42. For example, Fales ("The Road to Judah," 239) writes, "Sennacherib claims to have won hands down [the battle at Eltekeh] thanks to Sennacherib's own personal, heroic, intervention on the battlefield, but nevertheless probably resulted in a stalemate, in the light of indirect evidence from the Egyptian sources." Cf. Kahn, "The Inscription of Sargon II at Tang-i Var," 2, ns. 10–11; D. Kahn, "Taharqa, King of Kush and the Assyrians," *JSSEA* 31 (2004): 109.

to stop fighting against them because the action extended beyond its allocated time.[43]

If the incursion of the Nubian-Egyptian army was not in the purview of the Assyrian battle plan, it may have been enough to cause the Assyrians to move on and abandon any planned action against Jerusalem.[44]

Whether large losses were incurred or not, if the Assyrians returned to Nineveh following the battle without launching an assault on Jerusalem, Judahite perception could have been that Sennacherib's army was defeated and his return to Nineveh a sign that Assyria had lost the war.[45] Judahite (2 Kgs 19:35) and Egyptian (*Hist.* 2.141) traditions of Sennacherib's unexpected miraculous defeat suggests such perceptions of the conflict endured.

7.3.4 Regained Judahite Prestige

Finally, despite what historians think of the conflict, the Americans in the War of 1812, believed that their nation "was more respected as a result of the war, that it proved its strength and independence."[46] This American perspective may have been similar to the Judahite perspective after the war of 701 BCE. In the biblical account, Hezekiah was viewed as a hero because he "rebelled against the king of Assyria and would not serve him" (2 Kgs 18:7). Sennacherib's annals acknowledge that Hezekiah himself did not bring the tribute to Nineveh or do obeisance himself. Instead, Sennacherib notes, "He sent a mounted messenger of his to me to deliver (this) payment and to do obeisance."[47] Thus, from Judahite perspective, Hezekiah did not serve Assyria. What is more, after Hezekiah's story, the Assyrians do not factor again in the book of Kings. While this absence has been denigrated by some

---

43. Eph'al, "On Warfare," 98.

44. Matty (*Sennacherib's Campaign*, 182) has argued that the archaeological evidence suggests the Egyptian–Cushite contingent was irrelevant to the conclusion of the campaign. She writes, "Because of the devastating action of Sennacherib in the southern Levant and the catastrophic condition he left Judah with, one can safely say that even if the Egyptian-Kushite army came to confront Sennacherib, it did not cause Sennacherib to return." In my opinion, this is a weak argument and lacks a certain logic. Just because Sennacherib had success in the Shephelah and in quelling the revolt (and this is even acknowledged in the biblical text), it does not follow that the Egyptian–Cushite force was irrelevant or could not have led to his return to Nineveh.

45. Of course, many have suggested that the Assyrians had no plans to take Jerusalem. E.g., "The submission of Hezekiah had been complete … It does not seem to have been in Assyria's interest to pursue further military action against Jerusalem." Cogan, "Cross-Examining," 71.

46. Turner, *War of 1812*, 131.

47. RINAP 3.1:177, 22.iii.49.

scholars as lacking historicity,[48] the Assyrian army never again campaigned against Judah, so from a Judahite perspective this was the essential history.

7.3.5 A Shared Common Tradition for Jerusalem

As noted in Chapter 6, the War of 1812 spawned important American symbols and military lore, a national anthem, and led to the belief in the "Manifest Destiny" of America to expand and spread its dominion across North America. Similarly, the survival of Jerusalem in 701 BCE is connected to important Zion traditions about the inviolability of Zion in the face of military threat. Some scholars think Jerusalem's survival in 701 inspired Zion psalms and originated these traditions of the Zion's inviolability.[49] Others think the preexistent Zion traditions colored the ancient Judahite interpretations of the war of 701 BCE.[50] Some attribute these Zion traditions to the prophet Isaiah who prophesied during Hezekiah's reign.[51] Others believe it did not originate from prophet Isaiah himself but developed directly from the Assyrian failure to take Jerusalem in 701 BCE.[52] As Clements writes, "The Zion tradition, as it emerged after 701 BCE, appears as a cluster of beliefs that drew

---

48. E.g., Grabbe ("The Kingdom of Judah from Sennacherib's Invasion," 113), who considers this absence as a "deliberate attempt by the compiler [of the book of Kings] to mask" Assyria's ongoing role as suzerain. Similarly Holloway, writes, "Geo-political reality is utterly silenced for ninety years in the service of the theological agenda of the writers of Kings." "Harran: Cultic Geography," 309–10 (note 121).

49. E.g., A. F. Kirkpatrick, *The Book of Psalms* (Cambridge: Cambridge University press, 1902), 253–5; Gunther Wanke, *Die Zionstheologie Der Korachiten in Ihrem Traditionsgeschichtlichen Zusammenhang* (BZAW 97; Berlin: Töpelmann, 1966).

50. E.g., Mowinckel, *Psalmenstudien*. The old consensus placed the origins of Jerusalem's invioability as a pre-Israelite tradition appropriated by Israel after the conquest of Jebusite Jerusalem. Cf. Edzard Rohland, "Die Bedeutung der Erwählungstraditionen Israels für die Eschatologie der alttestamentlichen Propheten" (PhD diss., Heidelberg, 1956). It has been speculated at times that the theology traces its origins to the Jebusite city and its belief evinced in their rhetorical bluster against David's attempt to take the city in 2 Sam 5:6, though the theory is want of clear evidence. Cf. A. A. Anderson, *2 Samuel* (WBC 11; Dallas, TX: Word, 1989), 84; John Haralson Hayes, "The Tradition of Zion's Inviolability," *JBL* 82 (1963): 424 n. 32. J. J. M. Roberts, while allowing the influence of an ancient pre-Israelite (Canaanite) tradition, argues that Israel's Zion tradition was "geneuinely Israelite" and places its origins in the period of the United Monarchy (and that Isaiah's use of the Zion tradition shows "he was making use of a preexisting tradition"). Cf. J. J. M. Roberts, "Solomon's Jerusalem and the Zion Tradition," in *Jerusalem in Bible and Archaeology: The First Temple Period* (eds. Vaughn and Killebrew. SBLSymS 18; Leiden: Brill, 2003), 169.

51. Hayes and Irvine, *Isaiah*, 54–6; Jon Douglas Levenson, *Sinai and Zion: An Entry into the Jewish Bible* (Minneapolis, MN: Winston Press, 1985), 156–65; Ben C. Ollenburger, *Zion: The City of the Great King* (JSOTSup, 41; Sheffield: JSOT Press, 1987), 107–29.

52. Clements, *Deliverance of Jerusalem*, 72–89; Clements, *Jerusalem and the Nations*, 143.

on a variety of sources and used the city's escape from destruction as a catalyst to fuse them together."[53] Without settling the question of origins here, it is widely acknowledged that Jerusalem's survival in the face of the Assyrian war machine at least strengthened the popular Judahite theology of Zion's inviolability, whether the historical event initiated it or whether the theology was part of the reason for the positive interpretation of Jerusalem's survival of the Assyrian campaign.[54]

Another vestige of the War of 1812 in America was increased hatred of Great Britain, with studies published criticizing Britain for its brutalities and ill treatment of Americans that affected popular opinion. Similarly, the war of 701 BCE led to increased hatred of Assyria in Judahite opinion. This can be seen in texts like Nahum, which chronicle the destruction of Nineveh, and such opinion can be seen in the character of the prophet Jonah.[55] Oracles against Assyria abound and chronicle how they went beyond their divine mandate (a rod of chastisement in Isa 10:5) and had now come under Yahweh's judgment (Isa 10:12).

The survival of Jerusalem further validated Yahwism. Hezekiah's father had embraced a more polytheistic worship and Assyrian vassaldom. He famously rejected the call by the prophet Isaiah to "trust" Yahweh rather than appeal to Assyria (cf. Isaiah 7 and 2 Kings 16) leaving Judah ill prepared to retain its independence. Hezekiah, conversely, centralized worship of Yahweh alone, is said explicitly to have "trusted" Yahweh (2 Kgs 18:5) and refused to be the vassal of Assyria as his father had. With Jerusalem's survival in the face of the Assyrian war machine, trust in Yahweh was perceived to have been vindicated.

Furthermore, Hezekiah is remembered, despite his shortcomings, as one "did what was right in Yahweh's eyes, just like his ancestor David did" (2 Kgs 18:3). Like David, Yahweh is said to be "with" Hezekiah (2 Kgs 18:7). He is remembered for his trust in Yahweh (18:5) rebelling against Assyria (18:7) and defeating the Philistines (18:8). Memories of the Assyrian invasion appear overwhelmingly positive, despite the atrocities suffered in the Assyrian campaign. Just as America could pride itself on having defied the great British Empire and the Mistress of the Seas, retaining its independence and strengthening its reputation, so the Assyrian withdrawal validated Hezekiah's leadership as he rebelled against the Empire and still retained his monarchy.

Furthermore, subsequent to the withdrawal of Sennacherib began a new period of Judahite prosperity (where Assyria was never to return to attack again). As discussed in Chapter 2 on archaeological evidence, many scholars hold that the

---

53. Later in Israel's history, in the face of the Babylonian threat, the prophet Jeremiah argued against this popular view of Zion's inviolability (e.g., Jer 7:1–15; 26:1–6) leading some to suggest that Zion theology became problematic as "at a later time, the popularity of such beliefs did foster reckless and irresponsible policies." Cf. Clements, *Jerusalem and the Nations*, 143.

54. Hayes, "Zion's Inviolability"; Bright, *History*, 288.

55. Though the book may argue against such a view by showing God predisposed to forgive the Assyrians of their crimes.

prosperity of Judah post-701 was due to the development of the area due to Assyrian interests (the so-called Pax Assyriaca). For example, Dever writes that the evident Judahite prosperity after 701 reflects "the beneficial aspects of reconstruction under the *Pax Assyriaca*."[56] That is, Judah's economy and security were increased due to their being part of the economic machine that was the Assyrian empire.[57] Alternatively, Judahite prosperity could be understood as partially due to the fact Assyria was afterward distracted (by Babylonian, Elamite, Arabian, and Egyptian problems) and had less interest in Judah and caused less problems for her. Either way, whether it was due to Assyrian interests being fostered in the area or Assyria's disinterest in Judah, all agree there is clear evidence of Judahite prosperity. Whether to ascribe this prosperity to Judahite leadership or Assyrian investment is a matter of perspective. Given that the years following rebellion were prosperous, any politician worth his salt could convince his electorate that his policies were the reason for the prosperity. Given the years without Assyrian aggression in the Levant (especially as they had their hands full with Anatolia, Elam, and Babylon), it seems likely that this absence of Assyrian aggression against Judah could have been interpreted as Assyrian weakness and the result understood by Judahites as due to the success of Hezekiah's rebellion. Zion did not fall and it now prospered. The war of 701 BCE was a resounding Judahite victory.

7.3.6 Victory Despite Hardship

Despite who "won the war," in the end wars leave devastation. As we saw in Chapter 2, the situation in Judah after the war of 701 BCE left devastation. Given the devastation, we might question how Judahites could remember the war as beneficial to Judah and glorifying Hezekiah? Here the comparison with the War of 1812 is instructive. The War of 1812 brought difficult times of hardship for both Americans and Canadians. American fishermen and sea merchants were particularly hit hard as they could not sail due to the British blockade. This further led to dockworkers becoming unemployed as they would have been servicing the fishing boats and commercial fleets. Even American farmers suffered major losses due to the lack of access to foreign markets. As Hickey writes, "For most people ... the war brought hard times."[58] The devastating aspects of the battles themselves hit farmers and agriculturalists especially hard. In Canada, west of the Grand River, American incursions "destroyed virtually all of that area's resources."[59] An

---

56. Dever, *Beyond the Texts*, 620 n. 20.

57. Knauf ("Sennacherib at the Berezina," 149) characterizes Assyria's role as "aid in development" for Jerusalem, which is more charitable than realistic. As mentioned in the introduction in my view, Pax Assyriaca would more accurately be rendered *Pacification by Assyria* connoting a sinister sense of not the bringing of peace but the imposing of control by a coercive Assyrian hegemony.

58. Hickey, *The War of 1812*, 69.

59. Turner, *War of 1812*, 111.

American travelling in the region in 1816 writes, "I was most sensibly struck with the devastation which had been made by the late war, [farms] formerly in high cultivation, now laid waste; houses entirely evacuated and forsaken; provisions of all kinds very scarce; and, where peace and plenty abounded, poverty and destruction now stalked over the land."[60] The destruction left in the wake of the battles led to food shortages in both the Niagara region and western Upper Canada. The food that was available was needed to feed combatants. As Turner writes, "Homes and barns, livestock and crops, mills, businesses of various kinds, and even furniture and clothing were lost."[61] Berton records the effects of the war in Canada as "family farms are overrun, crops despoiled, homesteads gutted, livestock dispersed."[62] The war further caused significant inflation, which "caused hardships for the poor."[63] Yet, despite these devastating effects, the war became a rallying point for Canadian identity. The war brought unity to the diverse population and the myth of the war gave Canadians a new awareness of community wherein they took pride in having "repelled the invader almost single-handed."[64]

From this comparative perspective, then, we can see that devastation and economic hardship are part and parcel of war but are not necessarily a barrier to seeing a conflict as having a positive outcome. In light of this reality, the notion that the war of 701 BCE, despite the hardships suffered, the towns destroyed, and the people lost, may yet have functioned to stir up a patriotic nationalistic perspective in Judah is more understandable. Besides which, as we saw in our survey of archaeological evidence, Judah enjoyed a time of "rebuilding and relative prosperity" after Sennacherib's withdrawal,[65] with the rebuilding taking place rapidly following 701 BCE.[66] Jerusalem and much of Judah recovered quickly from the economic degradations of the war. While some understand this discovery to be due to the Pax Assyriaca,[67] from a Judahite perspective this is a moot point. Recovery is recovery. Prosperity is prosperity. In Judahite perspective, Hezekiah's bold rebellion paid off. Judah won the war.

7.4 Assyrian Opinion: Assyria Won the War

7.4.1 Memorable (and Memorialized) Victorious Battles

Though some scholars (and with good reason) have questioned the extent of the Assyrian victory over Judah in 701 BCE, as Cogan has argued, this depends

---

60. Morris Zaslow, *The Defended Border* (Toronto: Macmillan, 1964), 240.
61. Turner, *War of 1812*, 111.
62. Berton, *The Invasion of Canada*, 28.
63. Benn, *War of 1812*, 78.
64. Berton, *The Invasion of Canada*, 28.
65. Stern, *Archaeology of the Land of the Bible*, 163.
66. Ibid., 130–1.
67. E.g., Knauf, "Sennacherib at the Berezina," 149.

upon whether "ancient reality conflicted with Assyrian ideological rhetoric."[68] In Assyrian perspective, Sennacherib's third campaign was utterly successful.[69] The West was won and the rebellion squelched. Widespread success was evident with the sacking of so many cities and the submission of prominent kings. The Phoenician and Philistine vassals were again faithfully aligned, with loyal kings installed, setting the stage for prosperity though tribute and economic investment in these areas (as evinced in the growth of sites like Ekron shortly following the third campaign).[70] Hezekiah's territory had been diminished and his kingdom chastened. The Assyrian king brought home glorious tribute and booty from the campaign.[71] Assyrian historiography recounts the victories with flourish, presenting the enemy as being overwhelmed by the Assyrian's weapon of Assur and willingly surrendering and offering gifts as a result.[72] Sennacherib himself heroically partook in battles and personally captured other kings.[73]

The Assyrian scribes even used epic language with religious undertones to accentuate Sennacherib's achievements. Sennacherib's annals used mythological language to describe Ekron's treachery in rebelling against its Suzerain. Ekron commits an abomination (Akkadian *anzillu*)[74] a word usually used in magical texts. Gallagher suggests a connection to the Legend of Etana where an eagle and a snake swore an oath to aid each other, but the eagle commits *anzillu* by eating the serpent's young.[75] He concludes that the Assyrian text "took this meaning-laden word *anzillu* from their religious and literary texts" to underscore the villainy of Ekron.[76] Similarly, when Sennacherib recounts his battle with the Nubian-Egyptian force, he notes the Egyptians "sharpened their weapons" before their battle (*uša"alu kakkīšun*), which is a phrase used in Enuma Elish IV to describe the actions of Tiamat's army, thus presenting Sennacherib in Marduk's place. As Gallagher observes, "The undertones of the king fighting against the forces of chaos were thus clear to those who knew Mesopotamian literature."[77] The victory in the third campaign had cosmological significance in Assyrian presentation.

68. Cogan, "Cross-Examining," 71.
69. Fales, "The Road to Judah," 248.
70. See Chapter 2 on archaeological evidences.
71. As Matty (*Sennacherib's Campaign*, 47–8) writes, "For Sennacherib, mention of the spoils taken during the campaign was an occasion for boasting and showing supremacy and domination." Cf. Maximilian Streck, *Assurbanipal und die letzten assyrischen Könige bis zum Untergange Ninivehs* (VAB, 7; Leipzig: J. C. Hinrichs, 1916), 12 I–116.
72. RINAP 3.1:177, 22.iii.37–48.
73. RINAP 3.1:176, 22.iii.3–5.
74. See *CAD* A II, p. 153.
75. J. V. Kinnier Wilson, *The Legend of Etana: A New Edition* (Warminster: Aris & Phillips, 1985).
76. Gallagher, *Sennacherib's Campaign*, 120.
77. Ibid., 121.

The third campaign was clearly a highlight of Sennacherib's reign as evidenced by the multiple copies of the events that have been found. Some are well known, such as the Rassam cylinder, the Chicago Prism, the Taylor Prism, and the Jerusalem Prism. However, these Assyrian accounts were also clearly mass-produced ("Massenproduktion")[78] with Frahm noting seventy-four copies of the Rassam Cylinder having been produced "possibly within a few days."[79] The conquests of the third campaign are clearly viewed positively in Assyrian perspective. Furthermore, Sennacherib's third campaign was memorialized by the commissioning of a massive relief depicting the siege and conquest of Lachish to decorate Sennacherib's throne room. The sculpture is an artistic account that clearly glorifies the third campaign. As Laylard has observed, "In no other [Assyrian] sculptures were so many armed warriors seen drawn up in array before a besieged city."[80] The image shows Sennacherib in his full attire sitting on his throne, while the accompanying epigraph explicitly states that it is Sennacherib sitting on the throne. As Uehlinger suggests, "One wonders whether the epigraph's main purpose in this respect was not after all to state that the king had been there himself."[81] Some have suggested that the emphasis on Lachish in the relief is there to make up for Sennacherib's not taking Jerusalem, though this is likely reading in too much of the Judahite perspective into this piece of art.[82] Besides which, as Matty points out, "Lachish is not the only conquered city depicted in the reliefs whose name is not mentioned in the annals."[83] Uehlinger has pointed out that various aspects of the Assyrian campaign could have been represented in the relief: "long-distance siege, surrender without defence or battle, ranged battle or pursuit in open countryside, and other situations" but that the Assyrian

78. Frahm, *Einleitung* 50. He writes, "Rass. ist aus verschiedenen Gründen von besonderem Interesse. Zunächst einmal wurden von keinem Sanherib-Text derartig viele Exemplare gefunden wie von dieser Edition."

79. Ibid., 51. He states, "Alle der hier angeführten 74 Textvertreter der Edition Rass. scheinen im Monat Ajjar des Jahres 700 entstanden zu sein, womöglich innerhalb weniger Tage."

80. Uehlinger, "Clio," 295.

81. Ibid., 240.

82. Amihai Mazar, "The Divided Monarchy: Comments on Some Archaeological Issues," in *The Quest for the Historical Israel. Debating Archaeology and the History of Early Israel* (eds. Finkelstein and Mazar; ABS, 17; Atlanta: Society of Biblical Literature, 2007), 173. Uehlinger, "Clio," 293–5.

83. Matty, *Sennacherib's Campaign*, 72. John Malcolm Russell notes that only three of the ten cities depicted are mentioned in Sennacherib's annals. Cf. John Malcolm Russell, *The Writing on the Wall: Studies in the Architectural Context of Late Assyrian Palace Inscriptions* (MS, 9; Winona Lake, IN: Eisenbrauns, 1999). Matty (*Sennacherib's Campaign*, 76) noted two more: "So there are five names mentioned in the annals, and five which are not." Matty suggests Lachish is not mentioned in the annals because "it was not a royal city; it was not annexed to Assyria; [and] Sennacherib did not resettle people in it" (82).

artists chose to portray "massive onslaught and violent attack."[84] Given that the stated function of Sennacherib's palace was to be filled "with splendor for the astonishment of all people," this choice of what to depict was to revel in Assyrian power and skill at war. No weakness is portrayed, and no alternative measures undertaken. In Assyrian memory, the enemy bowed to the power of Sennacherib in pitched battle, and Lachish is displayed as a prime example.

7.4.2 Assyrian War Aims Accomplished

Unlike Judahite perception of Assyrian war aims in the campaign, which was thought to include the taking of Jerusalem, the deportation of the people, and the deposing of Hezekiah (probably based on the rhetoric of the Rabshakeh and Assyrian practices of regime change elsewhere in the Levant during this campaign), from an Assyrian perspective essential war aims did *not* require the taking of Jerusalem, the total conquest of Judah and the deposing of Hezekiah. As we have seen, some scholars suggest as much. Elayi suggests, "It was useless to besiege and capture Jerusalem, but it was sufficient to leave troops there to continue the blockade of the city until Hezekiah understood the lesson and surrendered."[85] Matty argues that "the main object of the war was not the destruction or elimination of the enemy but the destruction of its opposition to Assyria."[86] Mayer opines, "Evidently, Sennacherib (and his successors) did not consider the city of Jerusalem worth the effort, unlike Lachish."[87] Knauf posits that "nobody wanted Jerusalem."[88] Rather, as Mayer suggests, "With Hezekiah chastized, Jerusalem returned to its vassal status intact."[89] He further proposes that "from the Assyrian point of view, launching a full-scale offensive against the capital of Jerusalem would have been superfluous and even senseless."[90] While in my opinion Knauf may go too far in suggesting "nobody wanted Jerusalem" (why would they not want Jerusalem?), Assyrian war aims likely did not *require* Jerusalem, though they may have desired it. Here the comparison with the War of 1812 is again helpful. As we have seen, American war aims in the War of 1812 may not have required the annexation of Canada, though there were doubtless some Americans (like the War Hawks) who wanted to expand American territory in that way. Regardless of the failure to take Canadian territory, the Americans viewed the war as successful for other reasons

---

84. Uehlinger, "Clio," 295.
85. Elayi, *Sennacherib*, 83.
86. Matty, *Sennacherib's Campaign*, 46.
87. Mayer, "Sennacherib's Campaign," 180.
88. Knauf, "Sennacherib at the Berezina," 146.
89. Mayer, "Sennacherib's Campaign," 181. Elayi (*Sennacherib*, 83) nearly identically opines that "after having chastised him [Hezekiah], Jerusalem returned to its vassal status intact."
90. Ibid., 184.

that were more important (the end of the British naval blockade, the practice of impressment, the respect earned, and the patriotism it stirred up).

While the conquest of Lachish is clearly a feather in Sennacherib's cap, one might well question how it is that the sacking of Lachish could be more important than the taking of Jerusalem, the Judahite capital. Again, the comparison with the War of 1812 may also serve well. In the War of 1812, from a US perspective, victory at Baltimore was more significant than the humiliating defeat at the capital (Washington, DC). Of course, in Canadian perspective burning the White House was more important than the defense of Baltimore, just as the preservation and survival of Jerusalem was doubtless deemed more significant than the defeat of Lachish from a Judahite perspective. It appears that Sennacherib considered "the conquest of Lachish to be his most important military achievement of the period prior to the construction of the palace."[91] Perhaps in Assyrian perspective, the conquest of Lachish meant that Sennacherib did not have to put Jerusalem to siege, so in that way it was the greatest victory. Why destroy the capital when it can be the source of future tribute? From the Assyrian perspective, the shocking capture of Lachish, its awe inducing splendor, and its terrible carnage was all that was needed to secure Assyrian war aims with Judah and the capitulation of its king.

Furthermore, in Assyrian perspective, the losses sustained in conflict with a Nubian-Egyptian force do not count as signaling a failed campaign. As we have seen, some reconstructions hold the battle at Eltekeh as a stalemate or an Assyrian setback/loss. Judahite scribes clearly remembered the conflict as an Assyrian defeat (if the angelic attack was the theological rendering of the defeat) that led to the Assyrian withdrawal.[92] However, here the comparison with the War of 1812 is helpful again. Just as American success at New Orleans had no effect on the outcome of the War of 1812, so the battle with Nubian-Egyptian forces had little effect on Assyrian success in the campaign. According to Knauf, "If the battle of Eltekeh was a draw, or not fought at all, the outcome would have been the same."[93] While the biblical text speaks of an angelic assault on the Assyrian camp, and Herodotus speaks of a plague of field mice on the Assyrian camp, losses in this conflict—however sustained—were deemed inconsequential from an Assyrian perspective. Enough was done to stop an Egyptian–Philistine alliance from dominating the land or gaining their independence from the Empire. Hezekiah and his people may have considered the turn of events to be advantageous or even serendipitous (a divine turn of events even), but Assyrian dominance remained.[94]

91. Ussishkin, "Sennacherib's Campaign," 354.

92. Evans, *Invasion of Sennacherib*, 192; Knauf, "Sennacherib at the Berezina," 144; Redford, *Egypt, Canaan, and Israel*, 351–3.

93. Knauf, "Sennacherib at the Berezina," 147.

94. The Assyrian perspective may have been similar to the claim in a Korean War-era manual that states, "Victory alone as an aim of war cannot be justified, since in itself victory does not always assure the realization of national objectives." Cf. Harry G. Summers, *On Strategy: A Critical Analysis of the Vietnam War* (Novato, CA: Presidio Press, 1982), 61–3, citing the army Field Manual 100-5- (1954), 6.

From that perspective Assyrian goals were met. The rulers of Phoenicia, Philistia, and Transjordan paid him homage. Sennacherib put an end to the troubles with Ashkelon, Ekron, and Eltekeh. He accepted Hezekiah's submission and payment. His loyal vassal Philistine king Padî had been restored to the throne and Sennacherib had distributed the lands Hezekiah had annexed back to the Philistines. The Assyrians had established the setting for a flourishing economic future that would enrich the empire further.

7.5 An Empire Perspective

Perhaps to better grasp the Assyrian perspective, one more perspective on the War of 1812 should be taken into account—that of Britain and the British Empire. In many ways Assyria should be compared to British perspective, not the Canadian (or the American). After all Britain was the Empire and United States the small rebellious country. In Assyrian perspective, the campaign against Judah was only a small cog in the wheel of Assyrian purposes. As Ehud Ben Zvi has written, the invasion of Judah was "part and parcel of the account of Sennacherib's third campaign, namely the one against the land of Hatti. In other words, the third campaign is one among others, and the campaign against Judah is a subset of this third campaign."[95] The Assyrian perspective on the third campaign had broader concerns and material aims than Hezekiah's Judah.

As Hickey writes of the British view of the War of 1812,

> Throughout this period Britain's focus was on Europe. Her overriding objective was to defeat Napoleonic France and all else was subordinated to this end. Great Britain's aim, in other words, was not to subvert American independence but to win the war in Europe.[96]

As noted, to Britain, the War of 1812 was only a small part of the larger war with Napoleon. When it came down to it, the main reasons for the War of 1812 was British policies of the impressment of American sailors and British shipping blockades (which incited action from the United States). Ironically, with the peace treaty of Ghent, Britain was not forced to change its policies whatsoever.[97] As Polner and Woods write, the "Treaty of Ghent ... included not a single word about any of the grievances for which the U.S. government had allegedly fought" (though the end of the war with Napoleon changed British practices in that regard anyway).[98] Therefore, from British perspective, they prevailed in the war. Similarly, Sennacherib's ostensibly incomplete success in Judah might be best understood

---

95. Ben Zvi, "Malleability and Its Limits," 78.
96. Hickey, *The War of 1812*, 115.
97. Ibid., 2.
98. Polner and Woods, *We Who Dared to Say No*, 3.

in terms of Realpolitik and the limited goals of the Assyrian empire. In the War of 1812, British priorities were not to humiliate America (by impressing sailors) or to stop American commercial enterprises (by blockading Americans from trading with France) but to win the war with France (impressing sailors to gain much needed manpower for the British fleet), after which both impressment and trading blockades were ended. Similarly, from the perspective of the Assyrian Empire, their priorities were not to completely conquer Judah or Jerusalem, or necessarily to depose the Judahite king, but to ensure the reinstatement of tribute in the Levant and to preserve order with Sennacherib established as the clear suzerain. As Crouch argues, "If an opponent could be relieved of its identification with chaos via a non-violent transfer of affiliation, this was sufficient to satisfy the Assyrian ideological requirements."[99] Once tribute was reestablished and the many kings of Hatti submitted, Hezekiah's retained monarchy mattered not to the empire if it ensured continued tribute was flowing to Assyrian coffers. Both the biblical text and Assyrian annals tell of Hezekiah's payment of such tribute to Sennacherib. What is more, going forward Assyrian annals tell of Hezekiah's successor, Manasseh, delivering tribute to Assyria as well. America may pat themselves on the back for their efforts in the war, and be glad of the patriotism it stirred up, but the British Empire really did not care about these things. They won the war with France, defended their territory, and were not forced to change any of their policies. Similarly, Judah may view Jerusalem's survival as evidence of Zion's inviolability, and Hezekiah's continued monarchy as fulfilling Yahweh's commitment to David (2 Kgs 19:34), but Assyria really did not care about these things. Sennacherib had successfully put down the rebellion in Hatti land, reestablished tribute, and recorded their glorious campaign for all to see (in mass-produced inscriptions and a palace relief).

7.6 The End of the War

Historian John Hattendorf sums up the resolution of the War of 1812:

> Although Britain had effectively thwarted all American offensive operations, both on land and at sea, pushing the United States to the brink of economic collapse through its naval blockade, the Americans achieved their fundamental war goal ... The resulting impasse was resolved only by the domestic political forces inside Britain.[100]

Something similar could be said of the end of the war of 701 BCE. Although Assyria had effectively thwarted all Judahite offensive operations, pushing Judah to the

---

99. Carly L. Crouch, *War and Ethics in the Ancient Near East: Military Violence in Light of Cosmology and History* (BZAW, 407; Berlin: Walter de Gruyter, 2009), 47.

100. Hattendorf, "The Naval War of 1812," 20.

brink of economic collapse through its blockade, the Judahites achieved their fundamental war goal. The resulting impasse was resolved only by the domestic political forces inside Assyria. With the Empire's objectives accomplished, Sennacherib and his forces returned to Assyria. Hezekiah could rest on his laurels at retaining his throne and his capital.

7.7 Summary

Given that even in an event as recent as 1812 with a plethora of sources and evidences at our fingertips, scholarly assessments differ on important historical questions, we should not be surprised that scholarly assessments on such questions on the war of 701 BCE differ as well.[101] What is more, given the value of perception as political commodity different assessments from those involved in the war should not be surprising either. In the next chapter, we will briefly consider the social location of modern scholars as we consider the differences in historical assessments of the war of 701 BCE and Hezekiah's rebellion in particular.

---

101. As Emory Elliott asserts, "The historian is not a truthteller, but a storyteller … and a nation's official history is ultimately no more than a story about which there is widespread agreement." Cf. Emory Elliott (ed.) *Columbia Literary History of the United States* (New York: Columbia University Press, 1988), xvii.

Chapter 8

SCHOLARLY ASSESSMENTS OF HEZEKIAH AND HIS REBELLION

Accompanying assessments of the extent of the success of each side in the war of 701 BCE are evaluations of the monarchs involved. A review of the relevant literature shows that scholarly evaluations of the reigns of the kings of Judah sometimes reverse the biblical viewpoint. Often, Ahaz, viewed very negatively in the Deuteronomsitic History and by the Chronicler, is seen in a sympathetic light by scholars, and his appeal to Assyria, so maligned in scriptural texts, is seen as a pragmatic move that in the end may have benefited his nation.[1] Another good example is Manasseh. Castigated by the Deuteronomist as the main reason that Judah is eventually exiled by Babylon (2 Kgs 21:12-16; 23:26-27), scholarly assessments have often viewed him as one of the most successful kings in Judahite history. For example, E. A. Knauf views Manasseh and Herod the Great as "the two best kings in Israel's history."[2] Hezekiah, on the other hand, while viewed very positively by the Deuteronomsitic History and the Chronicler alike, is often criticized by modern scholars as "rash," "reckless," and "foolhardy" due to his rebellion, which nearly led to the end of his dynasty and kingdom."[3]

---

1. E.g., As Na'aman writes, "Our historical evaluation of the two kings is quite the reverse: Ahaz successfully kept his kingdom intact during a stormy and dangerous period, whereas Hezekiah's bold policy brought about disastrous consequences for the kingdom and its inhabitants." Cf. Na'aman, "Let Other Kingdoms Struggle," 70. Cf. Gonçalves's (*L'expédition de Sennachérib*, 24–50) positive portrayal of Ahaz; Similarly, Peter R. Ackroyd, "The Biblical Interpretation of the Reigns of Ahaz and Hezekiah," in *In the Shelter of Elyon: Essays on Ancient Palestinian Life and Literature in Honor of G. W. Ahlstrom* (eds. Barrick and Spencer; JSOTSup, 31; Sheffield: JSOT Press, 1984), 257.

2. Ernst Axel Knauf, "The Glorious Days of Manasseh," in *Good Kings and Bad Kings* (ed. Grabbe; LHBOTS/JSOTSup, 393; ESHM 5; New York: T&T Clark, 2005), 173. Cf. Francesca Stavrakopoulou, *King Manasseh and Child Sacrifice: Biblical Distortions of Historical Realities* (BZAW, 338; Berlin: de Gruyter, 2004).

3. Gallagher, *Sennacherib's Campaign*, 263. E.g., Wildberger (*Isaiah 13–27*, 380) opines that it was "faulty political reasoning that led to the debacle of 701." Taking a view in favor of Ahaz and against Hezekiah, Ackroyd ("The Biblical Interpretation," 257) writes, "Hezekiah seems to have had a better press than he deserved."

In historical study, such reversals in opinions are often necessary as later perspectives provide different vantage points with which to view events and historical persons. Historians must reexamine older views and revise them accordingly to provide realistic assessments based on the best information available. But our approach must be cautious. As military historian Martin van Creveld writes,

> The point of the exercise must therefore be to look at the past through the glasses of the present, then to use the past in order to gain a better understanding of the nature of those very glasses. All this must be done without imposing the frame of reference of the present upon the past, thereby sacrificing veracity and reaching false conclusions, but at the same time without using the otherness of the past as an excuse to retreat into an ivory tower.[4]

We must attempt to look to the past without imposing our modern mores and assumptions on it. Therefore, to better assess modern evaluations of Hezekiah and his legacy, this study will now consider the social location of modern interpreters of Hezekiah and the possible influence it has on interpretation. This analysis of the reader (modern scholars) may be just as important as the analysis of ancient texts in assessing modern evaluations of the ancient Judahite king.[5] While a modern perspective may aid interpreters in many ways, it invariably blinds them to other dangers. In the end, the millennia between us and the eighth-century BCE may be a limitation not only due to the piecemeal knowledge we have of the ancient period but also due to biases of modern perspectives that cloud judgment in such a way that earlier, ancient perspectives are lost or at least not appreciated. Inescapably our assessments of history are colored by our own presuppositions and biases rooted in our own time and its concerns and mores.[6] In an effort to assess modern evaluations of Hezekiah, possible presuppositions should be explored. This chapter will suggest that recent negative assessments of Hezekiah are influenced by modern biases and presuppositions that are not relevant to the original writer and audience. Furthermore, taking into account the social location of scholars and historians in their evaluations of Hezekiah will help us better critique such modern evaluations and finally understand the assessment of the ancient Judahite king in positive ways.

---

4. Van Creveld, "Thoughts on Military History," 562.

5. As Peter W. Gray observes, historians "consider not only what may have happened in the past, but also attempt to infer what conditions were like." Cf. Gray, "XII. Why Study Military History?" *Def. Stud.* 5 (2005): 154. Yet, our own present conditions and mores often are imbued into our judgments about the past.

6. Howard argues that since history is narratives that individual historians write, historians are part of the process and that their work is imbued with their own cultural perspective and values. Michael Howard, *The Lessons of History* (New Haven, CT: Yale University Press, 1991), 11.

8.1 Modern Attitudes toward War

8.1.1 The Modern Context of "Peace"

Many in the West view the present world as on a peaceful trajectory, especially since the end of the Second World War.[7] Steven Pinker's recent book *The Better Angels of Our Nature* argued a thesis that the world is becoming less violent and that war is ever decreasing.[8] In his address to the United Nations, US president Barack Obama claimed that due to peace efforts "we take it as a given that great powers no longer fight world wars, that the end of the Cold War lifted the shadow of nuclear Armageddon, that the battlefields of Europe have been replaced by peaceful union."[9] Scholars have observed that

> ours is an unprecedented era of peace and progress. On the whole, humans today are living safer and more prosperous lives than their ancestors did. They suffer less cruelty and arbitrary violence. Above all, they seem far less likely to go to war. The incidence of war has been decreasing steadily, a growing consensus holds, with war between great powers becoming all but unthinkable and all types of war becoming more and more rare.[10]

Political scientist Michael Mousseau similarly opines that "the world is now in the endgame of a five-century-long trajectory toward permanent peace and prosperity."[11] While some[12] dispute this assessment and think it to be too early to come to that conclusion, there is somewhat of a consensus that permanent peace is coming to humankind. Looking back at the abolition of human sacrifice, infanticide, slavery, and the like, some suggest, "It could be argued that war, at least war in the developed world, is following a similar trajectory."[13]

The rise of "peacekeeping" in international conflicts evinces a significant change in modern attitudes toward war in the West. As Keegan writes, "The effort at peace-making is motivated not by calculation of political interest but by

---

7. John Mueller, "War Has Almost Ceased to Exist: An Assessment," *PSQ* 124 (2009): 297–321.

8. Pinker, *The Better Angels of Our Nature*.

9. Tanisha M. Fazal and Paul Poast, "War Is Not Over: What the Optimists Get Wrong About Conflict," *Foreign Aff.* 98 (2019): 74.

10. Ibid.

11. Michael Mousseau, "The End of War: How a Robust Marketplace and Liberal Hegemony Are Leading to Perpetual World Peace," *Int. Secur.* 44 (2019): 196.

12. Keegan admits that "it seems just possible to glimpse the emerging outline of a world without war" but asserts that "it would be a bold man who argued that war was going out of fashion." Cf. Keegan, *History of Warfare*, 58. Others take issue with the thesis entirely. See Fazal and Poast, "War Is Not Over," 74–83.

13. John Mueller, "Changing Attitudes to War. The Impact of the First World War," *Br. J. Polit. Sci.* 21 (1991): 21.

repulsion from the spectacle of what war does."[14] The humanitarian impulse that motivates this approach to conflict, through the United Nations, is evidence of the wide support for it among many international states who are "willing to show their commitment to the principle by the despatch [sic] of peace-keeping, and potentially peace-making forces to the seat of conflict."[15]

Some studies have shown that the context of peace has led to an antiwar ethos. Studies have shown that the more affected one was by a conflict, the more pro-war they are.[16] People from nations with internal wars who have been directly affected by war are *more* supportive of war and feel more loyalty to their nation's wars than those unaffected by conflicts.[17] Peoples who have endured political hardships "expressed ideological commitment that involved patriotic involvement in war, glorification of war and pessimistic attitudes toward peace."[18] Thus, this context of perceived peace in the West has led to a common antimilitary ethos.[19]

8.1.2 Popular Opposition to War

The impact of democratic societies and a global market are often seen to be the main reasons for this decline in war.[20] The elevation of standards of living, medicine, literacy, and social welfare all likely contribute to the cultural changes in attitudes toward wars.[21] However, Pinker attributes the decline of war to "the forces of modernity—reason, science, humanism, individual rights" and also chronicles the spread of a general belief that war is now seen as illegitimate.[22] Gwynne Dyer

---

14. Keegan, *History of Warfare*, 58.

15. Ibid.

16. R. L. Punamaki, S. Quota, and E. Sarrai, "Models of Traumatic Experiences and Children's Psychological Adjustment: The Roles of Perceived Parenting and the Children's Own Resources and Activity," *Child Dev.* 68 (1997): 718–28.

17. G. K. Jagodic, "Is War a Good or a Bad Thing? The Attitudes of Croatian, Israeli, and Palestinian Children toward War," *Int. J. Psychol.* 35 (2000); Saba Torabian and Marina Abalakina, "Attitudes toward War in the United States and Iran," *Iran. Stud.* 45 (2012): 464.

18. Torabian and Abalakina, "Attitudes toward War," 465 (referencing the study of R. L. Punamaki, "Can Ideological Commitment Protect Children's Psychological Wellbeing in Situations of Political Violence?" *Child Dev.* 67 (1996): 55–69.

19. Studies have also shown that in the United States views of war are determined in part by whether one has a family member or close friend in military service. Cf. James S. Krueger and Francisco I. Pedraza, "Missing Voices: War Attitudes among Military Service-Connected Civilians," *Armed Forces Soc.* 38 (2012): 391–412. Cf. Morten G. Ender, David E. Rohall, and Michael D. Matthews, "Intersecting Identities: Race, Military Affiliation, and Youth Attitudes towards War," *War & Society* 34 (2015): 230–46.

20. Oona Anne Hathaway and Scott Shapiro, *The Internationalists: How a Radical Plan to Outlaw War Remade the World* (New York: Simon & Schuster, 2017).

21. Keegan, *History of Warfare*, 58.

22. Pinker, *The Better Angels of Our Nature*, 694. Cf. Fazal and Poast, "War Is Not Over," 75.

asserts, "As a result of the two world wars, a majority of people everywhere have ceased to see war as an opportunity for personal and national glory, and come to see it instead as a very big and ugly problem."[23] Keegan observes that due to the aftermath of the world wars there is now a "deep antipathy to violence and to conflict" and "that the usefulness of future battle is widely doubted."[24] Hanson suggests that in the postmodern West, our widespread affluence and culture of leisure and entertainment have led to the opinion that any war is "retrograde and of no utility."[25] Dyer isolates two trends that he posits have combined to make people question the legitimacy (or necessity) of war:

> One is moral ... that is, killing foreigners for political reasons—might be simply wrong ...
> The other factor is severely practical: we will almost all die, and our civilization with us, if we continue to practise war.[26]

In a study of popular attitudes toward war, Paris concludes that "public tolerance of state violence in advanced societies has diminished."[27] Keegan further notes that in today's Western societies, "pacifism has been elevated as an ideal."[28] Some pacifistic circles today critique any who would view, or remember, war in a positive light as deceivers or ignorant. One author characterizes the remembering of a war positively as "military metaphysics" wherein war is presented in "a pleasing and glorious fashion."[29] Any commemoration of war is an example of where "war has been sanitized and romanticized almost beyond recognition by the sentimental, the loony patriotic, the ignorant, and the bloodthirsty."[30] Thus, from this modern

---

23. Dyer, *War: The New Edition*, 285. Dyer suggests most people now find the idea of war as "absurd or obscene" unless they are involved in running "the foreign policies of sovereign states or [serving] in their armed forces" (Ibid., 349).

24. John Keegan, *The Face of Battle* (London: Pimlico, 2004), 336. He notes that some suspect "that battle has already abolished itself."

25. Hanson, *Father of Us All*, 44.

26. Dyer, *War: The New Edition*, 2. Of course, other reasons for opposing war have also been observed, such as the fact that war "increases the size and power of government and leads to increases in taxation" (from "The Conservative Case against War"). Other studies have found important factors leading to antiwar attitudes such as "believing in the unity of all humanity and previous experiences of political violence." Cf. Torabian and Abalakina, "Attitudes toward War," 464. Alida S. Westman and Lisa M. Lewandowski, "How Empathy, Egocentrism, Kohlberg's Moral Development, and Erikson's Psychosocial Development Are Related to Attitudes toward War," *Psychol. Rep.* 69 (1991): 1123–7.

27. Michael Paris, *Warrior Nation: Images of War in British Popular Culture, 1850–2000* (London: Reaktion Books, 2000), 261.

28. Keegan, *History of Warfare*, 5.

29. Jamie Swift and Ian McKay, "False Memories of the War of 1812 or Glorifying War ... Then and Now," *Pace Magazine* 29 (2013): 16.

30. Ibid., 17.

peace perspective, remembering a war with honor is deemed "loony," "ignorant," or simply "bloodthirsty." As Keegan suggests war "may well be ceasing to commend itself to human beings as a desirable or productive, let alone rational, means of reconciling their discontents."[31]

8.1.3 The Decline of Military History in Academia

Historian John Keegan writes that "the written history of the world is largely a history of warfare, because the states within which we live came into existence largely through conquest, civil strife or struggles for independence."[32] Ancient historians focused on war. Assyrian stela, biblical narratives, Greek histories (Herodotus, Thucydides, Xenophon, Polybius, Livy, Caesar, etc.) all show how central wars were understood to be in the ancient world.[33] This continued in the medieval world, through to the modern world.[34] However, military historians today often lament that the study of military history, sometimes basically understood as "why one side wins in a battle and the other loses," is out of fashion on university campuses, despite the general public's continued fascination with war.[35] Some suggest that military history "is now often considered only barely respectable academically."[36] Others lament that during the twentieth century, "military history has fallen into relative disfavour and neglect, at least among serious historians."[37]

31. Keegan, *History of Warfare*, 59.
32. Ibid., 386.
33. Howard et al., "What Is Military History?" 9.
34. Van Creveld points out, "When Droysen helped 'found the modern discipline of' history around 1830, he chose Alexander the Great as one of the first topics which to apply the newly formulated principles." Cf. van Creveld, "Thoughts on Military History," 550. Howard offers an accessible history of the study of military history, noting how few embrace such a "disreputable a subject as military history." Howard et al., "What Is Military History?" 6.
35. Hanson, *Father of Us All*, 4. On the interest in war popularly see Michael Howard, "The Demand for Military History," *Times Literary Supplement* (13 November 1969). Nicholas J. D. Ombrain laments the emphasis on teaching over research for professors of history in the university in the modern quest "to seek their fortune in expanded student numbers." Cf. Nicholas J. D. Ombrain, "Comparative Studies and Military History: A Key to the Future of Historical Scholarship in the University," *Dalhous. Rev.* 51 (1971): 20. This has led to the perception that military history be "relevant" to avoid being antiquarian, which has affected how it is approached at the university.
36. Van Creveld, "Thoughts on Military History," 549. Cf. McNeill notes how military history is underdeveloped in Europe. Cf. William H. McNeill, "Modern European History," in *Past before Us: Contemporary Historical Writing in the United States*. (ed. Kammen; Ithaca, NY: Cornell University Press, 1980), 95–112. On neglect of military history and its importance see William E. Simons, "The Study of History and the Military Leader," *Mil. Aff.* 26 (1962): 22–7.
37. Howard et al., "What Is Military History?" 9.

Similarly, John Childs asserts that "prejudice against [military history] persists" and research into the conduct of war "produces a faintly unpleasant odour in the senior common room."[38]

"Make love, not war" is the mantra that has stuck since the 1960s. Some have attributed this academic disinterest in the subject to the nuclear pessimism of the Cold War and the post-Vietnam reaction against America's wars.[39] The "cultural turn" in history that began in the 1960s has greatly affected the study of military history. Yet the roots of this antipathy toward military history go back further than the peace movements of the 1960s. This change is often attributed to the rise of Marxist ideas and the belief in the importance of social and economic factors in shaping history, as opposed to military action and wars.[40] The long period of relative peace following 1815 in Europe created a movement away from the importance of kings and leaders to common people. With the industrial revolution, "military affairs in general and wars in particular for the first time no longer appeared as important as they had traditionally been."[41] In the academy particularly, Enlightenment ideas appear to have caused a decline in interest in military history in British and French intellectuals.[42]

Academic movements away from military history accelerated in the twentieth century as a reaction against the horrors of the world wars "forced a fundamental change of attitude that persists to this day."[43] Whereas war had been seen as perhaps the most important human endeavor, it became unfashionable among the academic elite. Traditional military history stressed "the significance of 'great captains' more than such aspects as war production, manpower allocation and civilian morale."[44] Subsequently, many valuable and more egalitarian histories are being written.[45] So much so that in vogue now in university departments are race,

---

38. Ibid., 10.

39. Hanson, *Father of Us All*, 6. Paul Kennedy, "The Fall and Rise of Military History" *J. Mil. Hist.* 3 (1991): 8–12.

40. Best notes the "unfashionability of military history" and the contributions of "left-wing" historians and Marxist influences on the diminishing of the study of military history. Cf. Howard et al., "What Is Military History?" 11; van Creveld, "Thoughts on Military History," 551. Cf. Bernard Semmel, *Marxism and the Science of War* (Oxford: Oxford University Press, 1981).

41. Van Creveld, "Thoughts on Military History," 551.

42. Ibid.

43. Ibid., 552. Chakravorty notes how military history fell out of favor after the Second World War. B. Chakravorty, "Military History," *USIJ* 107 (1978). See B. A. Clayton, "The Nature and Score of War Studies," *AQDJ* 101 (1971): 195–205.

44. Howard et al., "What Is Military History?" 7.

45. Peter Burke, *History and Social Theory* (Ithaca, NY: Cornell University Press, 2005). E.g., see Tony Ashworth, *Trench Warfare, 1914–1918: The Live and Let Live System* (New York: Holmes & Meier, 1980), which focuses on the experiences of ordinary troops in the trenches instead of commanders and generals.

class, and gender studies that underscore the nameless thousands who took to battle, rather than the generals or other powers-that-be who sent them.[46] As van Creveld surmises, "The rise of history as an academic discipline was accompanied by a gradual disappearance of wars and battles from the history books, their place being taken by constitutional and diplomatic, and increasingly also economic and social, history."[47] Such studies often turn to issues of identity and ideology rather than military tactics or the study of war itself.[48] This has been called the "socialising of military history."[49] As Morgan-Owen laments, "Historians engaged in the study of politics, power and military force find themselves firmly out of fashion and under-represented within the academy."[50]

Twentieth-century antipathy toward academic study of military history was invigorated by the rise of the *Annales* school in France.[51] Scholars following Braudel et al. have furthered the Marxist theory of the importance of environment in shaping human history and thus have minimized a "history as events" approach and instead focused on background causal elements like climate changes and geographical factors as primary in influencing human history.[52] Some from the *Annales* school have even "come to regard these changes as constituting almost the sole worthy subject of historical study; the result being so called 'eventless history' in which the stage rather than the play, much less a few principal actors, becomes

46. As Grabbe describes it as a "focus on the effect events had on individuals, the common people; to write the story of the ordinary soldier or the ordinary citizen; to recognize the common omission of women and other minorities from conventional histories." Cf. Lester L. Grabbe, *Ancient Israel: What Do We Know and How Do We Know It?* (London: T&T Clark, 2007), 26.

47. Van Creveld, "Thoughts on Military History," 552.

48. Hanson, *Father of Us All*, 8. As van Creveld ("Thoughts on Military History," 555) has observed, "Claiming that it is impossible to understand the history of warfare without a thorough prior examination of the political, economic and social foundations on which it rests, these men have produced much outstanding work and considerably deepened our understanding of those factors."

49. Colin Jones, "New Military History for Old? War and Society in Early Modern Europe," *European Studies Review* 12 (1982): 97–8.

50. David Morgan-Owen, "In Defence of Military History," *Defence in Depth*, July 22, 2016: https://defenceindepth.co/2016/07/22/in-defence-of-military-history/. Brian Bond has noted how there are "few established university posts in the subject." Howard et al., "What Is Military History?" 6.

51. As well as the rise of the New Social History, which drew on the insights of *Annales* and focused on large structural changes and uncovering the experiences of regular people. Cf. Charles Tilly, *Big Structures, Large Processes, Huge Comparisons* (New York: Russell Sage Foundation, 1984), 22. This approach has been criticized as "dogmatic" by some. See Peter Paret, "The New Military History," *Parameters* 21 (1991): 10–18.

52. Van Creveld, "Thoughts on Military History," 552. For an example of such an approach to a World War, see Marc Ferro (co-director of the *Annales* journal), *The Great War, 1914–1918*; London: Routledge & Kegan Paul, 1973).

the centre of attention."[53] While obviously more could be said about the merits of the *Annales* approach (as well as critiques), the change in focus in historical studies is likely at least partially attributable to this approach.[54] If history no longer focusses on events, then a focus on wars (or battles especially) is a non sequitur.[55] As Bond has observed, "There is a tendency now to focus on 'the context' at the expense of the heart of the matter: war and combat."[56] Best has commented that "even the best of [modern writing on war] may not include any proper military history at all."[57]

8.1.4 Modern Views of "Victory" in War

What counts as victory in war has changed over time. "Total war requires the goal of total victory."[58] Assessing victory in war is problematic to many today. Hanson observes that "in postmodern war, the word 'victory' often appears in such quotation marks as a philosophical construct; it is supposedly mired in complexities and spoken only by the near savage."[59] Lewis similarly notes the "moral climate" of today in which "the pursuit of victory" is seen as morally problematic.[60] Twentieth-century wars such as Vietnam War have left many disillusioned and skeptical that any war aims could be justified.[61] From some perspectives, it could be said that there is no such thing as victory in war.

At times, modern Westerners naively have come to think of victory in war as clear-cut and that a perfect military victory can be flawless. For example, late-twentieth-century Americans came to expect war to be less messy and expected nearly impeccable military victory success. As Hanson writes, "Victories in Grenada, Panama, Gulf War I, and the Balkans persuaded Americans that war could be redefined, at the end of history, as something in which the use of force ends quickly, is welcomed by locals, costs little, and easily thwarts tyranny."[62] Despite the fact that "the United States has not achieved an unambiguous military

---

53. Van Creveld, "Thoughts on Military History," 552.

54. Noting the importance of the *Annales* school, Grabbe observes, "There was a shift in emphasis to social and economic trends rather than the actions of individuals in the political sphere." Cf. Grabbe, *Ancient Israel: What Do We Know and How Do We Know It?* 26.

55. The New Military History arose from this intellectual climate and is often criticized for minimizing or excludes combat and battle as subjects. See Paret, "The New Military History," 10–18.

56. Howard et al., "What Is Military History?" 7.

57. Ibid., 11.

58. Dyer, *War: The New Edition*, 266.

59. Hanson, *Father of Us All*, 35.

60. Lewis, *Nothing Less Than Victory*, 2.

61. Hanson (*Father of Us All*, 263) suggests that popularly in the West "if American aims and conduct [in a war] were less than perfect, then they could not be good at all."

62. Ibid.

victory since 1945"[63] with wars of continual setbacks, mistakes, and unclear victories in Somali, Haiti, Iraq, and Afghanistan, the myth of the possibility of mistake-free wars of clear victory persists popularly. This perspective leads to an intolerance for unintended consequences and a lack of humility regarding human ability to wage and conclude war on their own terms. Walkover victories appear to be the only wars that are justified, but also the only wars that could be labeled clear victories. Thus, the current cultural climate evinces "impatience, historical amnesia, and utopian demands for perfection" in regard to assessments of war.[64] Such dispositions may affect not only how we assess modern warfare but how we assess the ancient variety as well. A perfect military victory in a flawless war has never existed. This should be remembered when considering who "won" the war of 701 BCE. Victory looks different from ancient diverse perspectives.[65]

8.2 Older Attitudes toward War

In an effort to not impose a modern frame of reference on the past, with our views of war and victory, it is worth briefly contrasting older perspectives on war with present mores and assumptions. Hanson suggests that "the greatest difference between our own world and the ancients' is this present-day notion that war itself—rather than particular wars per se—must be inherently evil."[66] As we should expect, the modern opposition to war both popularly and in the academy is clearly a more recent opinion. As Keegan writes, "Throughout much of the time for which we have a record of human behaviour, mankind [sic] can clearly be seen to have judged that war's benefits outweighed its costs."[67] As recently as the mid-nineteenth century, a popular militarism was common in the West. As Michael Paris writes, by the mid-1850s the mood was of "the widespread acceptance that the practice of war was a natural and legitimate activity, a new respect for the army and military-style organization and admiration for the soldier as a masculine ideal."[68] The modern antiwar sentiment today is some distance from the famous statement by nineteenth-century historian Helmuth von Moltke that "eternal peace is a dream, and not even a beautiful dream."[69] Positive views of wars popularly persisted into

63. Lewis, *Nothing Less Than Victory*, 1.
64. Hanson, *Father of Us All*, 265.
65. Fales ("The Road to Judah," 248) suggests that "Hezekiah lost his wager to obtain economic freedom and regionally-based prominence—but at least the oracle delivered by his God proved truthful." Could it be that the deliverance of Jerusalem and the fulfillment of Isaiah's salvation oracle was enough for Judahites to consider the conflict a victory?
66. Hanson, *Father of Us All*, 34.
67. Keegan, *History of Warfare*, 59.
68. Paris, *Warrior Nation*, 8.
69. Quoted in van Creveld, "Thoughts on Military History," 522. Similar quotations could fill these pages, though I will add one more here. That of Bridadier-General R. C. Hart who opined,

the twentieth century with novels, comics, movies, and other popular forms of entertainment perpetuating "the pleasure culture of war," but public opinion gradually followed that of academia in an opposition to war.[70] Paris has chronicled this "dramatic transformation" of public opinion in Britain, suggesting that the more recent wars "have been too morally ambiguous to be absorbed into the pleasure culture," which has led to significant change popularly.[71]

The nineteenth-century British philosopher John Stuart Mill famously said, "War is an ugly thing, but not the ugliest of things: the decayed and degraded state of moral and patriotic feeling which thinks that nothing is worth a war, is much worse."[72] As we have seen, Mill's opinion is not widely shared in the West today, which evinces largely an antimilitary bent in the academy and in popular opinion. However, Mill's opinion may be closer to that of ancient Judahites and their view of the conflicts instigated by Hezekiah's rebellion. In Judahite perspective, "the decayed and degraded state of moral and patriotic feeling" that prevailed under Hezekiah's father, Ahaz, may have been viewed as worse than an Assyrian invasion.

8.3 Modern Scholarly Assessments of Hezekiah in Light of Their Social Location

8.3.1 Does Peace Define Success?

In light of modern antiwar perspectives and assumptions, scholarly reassessments of ancient Judahite kings should not be surprising. Modern negative assessments of Hezekiah that view his actions that led to war as obviously foolish may be influenced by modern assumptions that "nothing could be worse than war." Avoidance of war is often seen as almost the highest ideal, and a measure with which to assess a political leader. I would suggest that this modern view of war and peace is held without conscious reflection on the part of many today and that it significantly influences their interpretation. This tendency to positively assess a leader if war is avoided can be seen in some scholars' appraisals of biblical kings. For example, Knauf concludes that "a good king is a king who brings as much, peace … to his

> Man [sic] has always been seeking after a Utopia where he will enjoy peace and plenty, ease, comfort and perfection in all things, but universal peace is an unattainable ideal which to practical men is a mere will-o-the-wisp … the means of improvement must be the same as in the past, namely war, relentless war of extermination of inferior individuals and nations. The process will be slower than in the past, because natural selection is hindered and thwarted by civilised man [sic].
>
> Cf. Paris, *Warrior Nation*, 13.

70. He writes, "The saturation bombing of cities, the Final Solution, atomic warfare and increasing political cynicism have taken their toll." Cf. Paris, *Warrior Nation*, 258.

71. Ibid., 261.

72. John Stuart Mill, "The Contest in America," *Fraser's Magazine* (Feb. 1862) 31.

people as his times allow."⁷³ Similarly, Stavrakopoulou argues that Manasseh was a success because there were no destruction layers found archaeologically that date during his reign, writing, "Significantly, this is a good indication of the success of Manasseh's reign, for it was a peaceful period."⁷⁴ This elevation of peace and denigration of conflict can be seen in Clements's study of Isaian oracles that are critical of Hezekiah, wherein he argues that Isaiah was angered at the rebellion and rejected Hezekiah's policies because they were "bound to involve Judah in conflicts."⁷⁵ However, there is a gap in reasoning here between understanding an oracle as critical of Hezekiah's policies and *assuming* that this criticism is due to the prophet's attempt at avoiding military conflict for Judah. If Isaiah did oppose the rebellion, was it for reasons of preserving the peace (striving above all for "peace in our time")? Clements seems to suggest that the prospect of *some hardship* was the determining factor for this opposition. Was Isaiah opposed *because* it would bring Judah into "conflict"? I think this view is difficult to support from the text. Based on the oracles, it appears the prophet was most concerned about an alliance with Egypt that showed a lack of trust in Yahweh. Clements's ascribing an "anti-conflict" ideal to Isaiah may be an example of reading modern mores into Isaiah.⁷⁶ Did Isaiah think nothing could be worse than hardship or conflict? Did Isaiah, like we in the modern West, think nothing is worth a war? Was Isaiah a pacifist? In the ancient mindset, there are worse things than military conflict. Avoidance of conflict was not the ultimate virtue.

8.3.2 Motivations for War

How can we best understand Hezekiah's decision to risk war with Assyria? As discussed above, in the postmodern West, our widespread affluence and culture of leisure and entertainment have led to the opinion that any war is "retrograde and of no utility."⁷⁷ Possibly due to the post-Marxist philosophy of materialism, the most widely understood explanations for wars are thought to be economic. But what of the ancient mindset of Judah in 701 BCE? The situation that led to Hezekiah's rebellion was no doubt one of economic hardship due to the burden of Assyrian tribute but also of low morale. Some suggest that the economic benefit of Assyria (despite the tribute) outweighed the dangers of rebellion and Pax Assyriaca is credited with the economic prosperity in the seventh-century BCE. While this is debatable, even if the economic benefits *may* have outweighed the required tribute, we must consider the undesirable situation of vassaldom in

---

73. Knauf, "The Glorious Days," 173.
74. Stavrakopoulou, *King Manasseh*, 106.
75. Clements, *Jerusalem and the Nations*, 92.
76. Elsewhere Clements (*Jerusalem and the Nations*, 92) suggests the prophet's stance against rebellion was due to the fact it was "likely to bring ruin" on Judah. In other words, he understands Isaiah's objections to be practical, not moral or theological.
77. Hanson, *Father of Us All*, 44.

regard to national pride and honor in that ancient context. We can see in military history that wars were often fought over such things and that economic concerns were not always primary causes of war and may not have been so in the ancient Judahite mind. As Keegan notes, "There is only so much moral sacrifice to be extracted from peoples."[78] We may misunderstand this due to a prevalent post-Marxist philosophy of materialism that always searches "in vain for a magic oil field or strategic concession that would explain the inexplicable wars."[79] War was not always about economics and material gain. As we saw in our study of the War of 1812, pride, honor, and anger are also important factors in entering a war.[80] Sometimes these factors were deemed worth the economic risk of conflict.

A twentieth-century example is helpful here. Following the Treaty of Versailles, which blamed Germany for the Great War (the First World War), reparations were laid out, wherein Germany would indemnify the victors in the war for the devastations suffered at their hand. The reparations to be paid became a point of contention in Germany to the point where outrage over such requirements became the wave on which Hitler and his Nazis rode to power. In reality, the reparations were very little, with merely 2 percent of German income going *out* of the country as compared to the 5.3 percent of the national income going *into* the country from foreign subsidies.[81] The problem was not economic, it was moral outrage at the insult to the nation.[82] As Marks writes, "The Germans from start to finish deemed reparations a gratuitous insult."[83] Rather than understanding the motivations as necessarily economic, the will to go to war is often about moral affront and insult. In post-First World War Germany, the national will opposed the reparations. In fact, the people were willing to risk economic disaster to recover their pride. As Lewis writes, "Many German leaders were willing to see their own economy collapse in order to avoid the political and moral affront of making payments to France and others."[84] Could it be that Hezekiah and the Judahites were willing to risk economic collapse to avoid "the political and moral affront" of paying the pagan nation of Assyria tribute? More than economics are involved. For example, explaining German and Soviet hostility in the Second World War does not come down to need for land or materials. Nazi Germany was receiving more materials through trade with the Soviet Union before the Second World War than they

---

78. Keegan, *The Mask of Command*, 4.
79. Hanson, *Father of Us All*, 58.
80. Berton, *The Invasion of Canada*, 24; Heidler and Heidler, *The War of 1812*, 5. As we saw, the peace treaty that ended the war did not deal with any of the economic issues that contributed to the war in the first place. Hickey, *The War of 1812*, 2; Polner and Woods, *We Who Dared to Say No*, 3. Cf. Hanson, *Father of Us All*, 36.
81. As Marks writes, "In the end the victor paid the bills." Sally Marks, "The Myths of Reparations," *CEH* 11 (1978): 254.
82. Lewis, *Nothing Less Than Victory*, 198.
83. Marks, "Myths," 255.
84. Lewis, *Nothing Less Than Victory*, 198.

gained through war with the USSR. Hanson explains the German hostility on the grounds that "they were proud peoples, stung by past slights and perceived grievances, who wanted deference from those whom they deemed inferior and weak."[85] Keegan similarly points to the Balkan and Transcaucasian conflicts of the twentieth century as examples of wars "fed by passions and rancours that do not yield to rational measures of persuasion or control; they are apolitical."[86] In some situations in some societies, there are things more important than economics that warrant a war in their perspective.

8.3.3 Assessments of Wartime Leaders

It may be that the modern cultural perspective that any war is "retrograde and of no utility" has influenced scholarly assessments of biblical kings and resulted in our failure to take into account the ancient cultural perspective. Due to our view of the futility of war (likely held without conscious reflection on our part), Hezekiah may be denigrated because he led his people into a war. Our ignorance of military history may lead us to think that a king who leads his people into a military conflict indicates that the leader was ignorant, a poor communicator, or deficient diplomat. Underlying this thinking is the belief that avoidance of conflict is always possible through civilized negotiations.[87] Yet military history shows that few wars break out due to poor communications or through disparaging diplomacy.[88]

Nevertheless, a modern "therapeutic mindset" exists concerning foreign policy today as popularly many expect that interstate problems "be discussed by equally civilized and peaceful rivals and solved without resorting to violence."[89] While it is true that good diplomatic leadership can encourage good relations with other peoples, they are not always enough to ensure the lack of conflict with rival states. As Hanson suggests, given the nature of humanity, the showing of restraint in conflict may invite ever "more contempt and audacity" on the part of an enemy.[90] Public signs of humiliation and weakness can lead to further aggression instead of better understanding between rival states. Famously, negotiation and appeasement

---

85. Hanson, *Father of Us All*, 37.

86. Keegan, *History of Warfare*, 58.

87. A good example can be seen in Norman F. Dixon, *On the Psychology of Military Incompetence* (London: Cape, 1976), which emphasizes the stupidity of prominent players in the war due to his lack of knowledge of war. Of Dixon's study, van Creveld ("Thoughts on Military History," 553) writes, "The author's lack of detailed knowledge of military affairs, however, causes him to lay too much emphasis on his heroes' stupidity and to neglect the objective problems of command, thus distorting the entire picture."

88. Hanson, *Father of Us All*, 17.

89. Ibid., 17. Keegan (*History of Warfare*, 5) has observed that "our culture looks for compromises and the compromise at which it has arrived over the issue of public violence is to deprecate its manifestation."

90. Hanson, *Father of Us All*, 40.

were the hallmark of the day under British prime minister Neville Chamberlain prior to the outbreak of war in Europe in 1939. Chamberlain's famous claim of "peace in our time" when Czechoslovakia was handed to Hitler in September 1938 is infamous of his foreign policy of diplomacy and appeasement. Though many have vilified him over his approach, it was "the culmination of a long policy of negotiation and compromise that had much support in Britain."[91] This is not to defend (or necessarily condemn) Chamberlain, but to provide a historical example illustrating that appeasement and negotiation are not always effective or reliable deterrents to military conflict. While modern academic culture tends "to cast moral aspersions" on those who "resorted to war" and think it "out of stupidity, greed, exploitation, vanity, or a quest for power,"[92] before we presume involvement in war was due to stupidity, greed, or power-mongering, we need to consider each situation independently and, in the case of Hezekiah, the ancient society and their perspective of the war. All this to say, before we condemn Hezekiah for his rebellion that led to the Assyrian invasion, we should reconsider our own preconceived notions. Military history shows us that war cannot always be prevented through diplomatic means.

Military leaders are often criticized when wars do not proceed as planned. It seems a safe assumption that Hezekiah's rebellion did not go as hoped (I assume he would rather have not lost Lachish), but should we for this reason criticize him? Military history should remind us that this is par for the course. Churchill famously said,

> Let us learn our lessons. Never, never, never believe any war will be smooth and easy, or that anyone who embarks on that strange voyage can measure the tides and hurricanes he will encounter. The Statesman who yields to war fever must realise that once the signal is given, he is no longer the master of policy but the slave of unforeseeable and uncontrollable events.[93]

Gallagher has made a good case to exonerate Hezekiah for rebellion, suggesting that from Hezekiah's perspective, it would have appeared to be the perfect time for a successful rebellion to free Judah from Assyrian hegemony with the tremendous burdens of vassaldom being a tremendous motivator.[94] Gallagher opines, "Only an exceptionally wise ruler could have resisted the temptation to rebel at this time."[95] Gallagher's assessment again seems to assume that the rebellion was, in fact, a mistake and that things would have gone better for Judah if Hezekiah had held to

---

91. Lewis, *Nothing Less Than Victory*, 185.
92. Hanson, *Father of Us All*, 83.
93. Similarly, Howard has noted how some knowledge of past war can problematically "create an unrealistic order of what is usually a chaotic situation." Cf. Michael Howard, "The Use and Abuse of Military History," *Parameters* 11 (1981): 9–14.
94. Gallagher, *Sennacherib's Campaign to Judah*, 272.
95. Gallagher, *Sennacherib's Campaign to Judah*, 272.

a policy of submission and Assyrian appeasement—but Gallagher suggests that Hezekiah should be forgiven for thinking otherwise. This approach has much to commend it. Criticisms of Hezekiah often use "contemporary wisdom or innate logic" in their assessments "rather than look to the history of past wars, which are frequently unpredictable and nearly inexplicable."[96] Some have pointed to divergent views of the wartime king in Isaian oracles to be decisive in their assessments. But examples from military history would suggest otherwise. Churchill's unpopularity after the War should not lead us to denigrate his achievements and leadership during the War that led to its victory. It should also caution us against viewing a leader negatively simply because citizens protested the conflict. Here it is possible that modern protest against America's wars are coloring our assessment of ancient war. Since some clearly protested Hezekiah's war, we should not for that reason necessarily assess him negatively.

8.4 Summary

While war was once thought to be a natural and necessary part of the human condition, it *could* be that humankind is finally beginning to move past this presupposition and be on a trajectory to peace. Regardless of the plausibility of this situation (as many dispute its reality), a broad consensus in academia and in popular culture in the West has an antiwar perspective that contrasts with premodern and many modern perspectives antedating the world wars of the twentieth century. Despite the sympathy that one may have with these perspectives (and I confess that my sympathies lie in an antiwar ethos), as historians we must attempt to view the past without imposing our own mores upon it. It seems likely this understandable recent view of the horrors of war has colored academic interpretations of ancient wars, and in this case, Hezekiah's role as the king who led his nation into conflict. While we are, of course, allowed our view of Hezekiah and his actions, and we may judge him negatively by our antiwar ethos, we should be careful not to understand our assessments as if shared by the ancients. As van Creveld has asserted, "The wars of the past could not be understood except within the context of historical circumstances very different from those prevailing."[97] Hezekiah was clearly a hero in some biblical texts, not due to deceptive reporting but due to different perspectives and presuppositions.[98]

---

96. Hanson, *Father of Us All*, 38.
97. Van Creveld, "Thoughts on Military History."
98. Young (*Hezekiah in History and Tradition*, 86) argues that Sennacherib himself credits Hezekiah's toughness with his keeping Jerusalem, writing, "Sennacherib in effect credits his formidable opponent for his own failure to take the city."

Chapter 9

CONCLUSION

The question that incited this study of the war of 701 BCE was how both Assyria and Judah could remember the war as their respective victory. To look for answers, we first surveyed archaeological and textual evidences to better understand both the perspectives of modern historians and the respective perspectives of Assyrian and Judahite sources. The survey of archaeological evidences showed that despite the widespread destruction left by Sennacherib's campaign, the devastation was *not* total, as some areas had only minor destructions, while others escaped unscathed. Furthermore, we noted that Judah's population zenith actually came after Sennacherib's withdrawal and that there was significant development and expansion soon after in the early seventh-century BCE. This growth is widely attributed to the so-called Pax Assyriaca, but we left open the question of whether Judahite perception might connect the growth with the perceived success of Hezekiah's rebellion.

We then examined Assyrian texts concerning Sennacherib's third campaign and found that it was presented as a grand success. The issue of the chronological presentation was discussed, with various proposals as to how to understand the actual progression of events (though there is not a clear consensus). Possibly, the battle of Eltekeh was narrated out of order to avoid suggestions that it led to the Assyrian withdrawal and the submission of Hezekiah presented at the end to purposefully conclude with the tribute collected from Judah, even though the earlier mention of the liberation of Padî from Jerusalem suggests that Hezekiah's submission occurred earlier. The Assyrian accounts were found to contain clear embellishments and exaggerations (the forty-six Judahite cities destroyed, the 200,105 captives taken). They ascribed their victory in battle to direct divine intervention (the "weapon of Assur"). They also seem to have glossed over less-than-ideal aspects of the campaign (e.g., the escape of the rebel king Lulî, the possible setback/defeat vs. Nubian-Egyptian forces, the failure to take Jerusalem or depose Hezekiah, and the Judahite payment being sent to Assyria only at a later date). This brought to the fore the issue of what qualifies a campaign to be understood as victorious. Did it have to be a total victory? Clearly, the Assyrians viewed the campaign a success despite aspects that could be understood as failures. These issues would be picked up later when we looked to other examples from military history to provide helpful perspectives on these questions.

We then examined the account of the war of 701 BCE from 2 Kings 18–19 to assess its claims. We found the narrative to be selective and careful in its presentation. Hezekiah is said to have a hostile relationship with Philistia, attacking them as far as the environs of Gaza. However, unlike Assyrian sources, the narrator does not mention Hezekiah's imprisonment of Padî, the king of Ekron, due to Hezekiah's apparent relationship with the Ekronites. The biblical presentation of Hezekiah defeating the Philistines was doubtless to cast him in the mold of David, his idealized forebear. Likewise, the avoidance of any mention of a foreign alliance was likely meant to distinguish him from the kings of Samaria whose foreign alliances and subsequent destruction by Assyria were chronicled in the previous chapter (2 Kings 17). Like the Assyrian accounts, the biblical account was found to contain embellishments and exaggerations (that "all" Judahite cities were taken, and that 185,000 Assyrians were slaughtered). Like the Assyrian annalistic account (and their references to the "weapon of Assur"), biblical accounts appeal to direct divine intervention to explain the defeat of the enemy (the "angel of Yahweh"). The chronological presentation of the biblical account was structured to villainize the enemy (with Sennacherib's demand for total surrender being subsequent to Hezekiah's submission) and lead to the climax of Sennacherib's withdrawal after a devastating loss. Of key importance to our research question were the stated war aims of Assyria as remembered from the words of the Rabshakeh (2 Kings 18): the destruction of the land of Judah (18:25), the taking of Jerusalem (18:30, 35) through a long siege (18:27), and the deportation of Jerusalem's inhabitants (18:32). We left open the possibility that the true Assyrian war aims were not the same as those communicated in these texts and would pick up this issue again later when we looked to other examples from military history. We also noted the issue of the supposed "defeat/setback" of Sennacherib's army (perhaps in conflict with Nubian-Egyptian forces at Eltekeh) being characterized by Judahite texts as the result of Yahweh's direct actions. While many scholars have suggested that this theological perspective evinces a much later theological reworking of the historical event, we questioned whether this was necessarily so and suggested that eighth-century Judahites were just as theological as sixth-century (or postmonarchic) scribes and that the departure of Sennacherib without taking Jerusalem was likely interpreted theologically at the time.[1] Again, we would look at other examples from military history where even very recent events were used mythologically or symbolically.

We then surveyed oracles from the book of Isaiah to consider what we might learn concerning how Hezekiah's leadership and rebellion might have been viewed historically. We found some prophetic oracles were clearly critical of Jerusalem's leadership during the Assyrian crisis leading up to the war of 701 BCE, though Hezekiah is not explicitly named. We also found oracles that were apparently

---

1. As Millard ("Sennacherib's Attack on Hezekiah," 76) opined, the miraculous conclusion of 2 Kgs 19:35 "could easily be a contemporary report written by a Judahite historian trained in the traditional outlook of orthodox Israelite faith."

positive toward the king, either setting out high hopes for his rule (7:10-17; 11:1-9), seemingly supporting Hezekiah's ambitions (8:23–9:6) and predicting/celebrating an Assyrian defeat (10:24–34), or otherwise evincing later positive reflections on his reign. While many have argued that these diverse perspectives are contradictory and cannot come from the same prophetic circles, we would later consider examples from military history where an assessment of leaders often changes in times of military crisis or war from opposition to support.

In order to gain a helpful perspective on the claims of both Assyrian and Judahite sources, we then drew on indirect evidence from the study of military history. In particular, we focused on the War of 1812 between Canada and the United States as an example of a disputed victory. We noted the reasons why both Canadians and Americans could perceive the war to be a victory for their respective sides. The war led to important American symbols and military lore, a national anthem, and led to the belief in the "Manifest Destiny" of America to expand and spread its dominion across North America. Interestingly, some sayings became symbols within a very short time frame, such as "Don't give up the ship!" uttered in June 1813 by the dying commander, James Lawrence (who lost the ship and the battle), which became a somewhat mythologized rallying point by the time of the battle of Lake Erie in September 1813.

We then compared our findings from the War of 1812 with what we know of the war of 701 BCE; we noted diverse and fluctuating support for wartime leaders in the War of 1812 that could be analogous to positive and negative oracles regarding Jerusalem's leadership during the war years. We found the reasons for perceiving victory in 1812 helpful for understanding possible reasons why both Assyria and Judah perceived victory in 701 BCE. In particular, US failure to achieve the war aims that were explicitly communicated to Canadians (to annex Canada into the United States) signified a victory to Canadians. Similarly, failure to achieve Assyrian war aims explicitly communicated to Judahites via the Rabshakeh's speech (the taking of Jerusalem and deportation of its inhabitants) signified a victory for Judah. We noted that the war aims communicated to the enemy were not always the true war aims. Nevertheless, from the Canadian and Judahite perspective, these communicated war aims failed, which meant they defeated the enemy. Both Canadian and American perspectives of success relied partially on the fact they did not lose any territory in the war. Both sides had gained territory in the war, but in the end, borders returned to their antebellum state. Similarly, Hezekiah's Judah appears to have returned to its antebellum borders following the Assyrian invasion, having only lost territory they had gained at Philistia's expense (2 Kgs 18:8). Furthermore, the issue of the importance of success in the last battle of a war was a key issue in determining victory. In the War of 1812, the United States won the last major victory at New Orleans, suggesting to them that they won the war. Canadians disregard that victory as of no consequence since terms of peace were already agreed upon before the conflict. Similarly, Judahites perceived Assyria to lose the last conflict of the war, likely with the Nubian-Egyptian forces at Eltekeh (interpreted as Yahweh's direct defeat of the enemy), suggesting a Judahite victory. It seems likely that Assyrians would have disregarded the importance of a loss or setback at Eltekeh as of no consequence, as some scholars have suggested. Their main goals in the campaign were achieved nonetheless.

One of the main issues involved in perceiving whether a war was worth it were intangible elements like regained prestige or renewed patriotism. In the United States and Canada, these types of elements were important outcomes of the war that both sides felt strengthened their respective national unity and pride. Similarly, despite the devastation to Judah, such intangibles were likely important for Judahites as well, and could have cast the rebellion and Hezekiah's leadership in a positive light. The legacy of the War of 1812 was important in the United States in particular for its strengthening the ideology of America's Manifest Destiny as well as originating other important legenda of US military lore. Similarly, in Judah, Zion theology likely originated or at least was immeasurably strengthened through Jerusalem's surprising survival in the face of the Assyrian war machine. The survival of Judah likely validated Yahwism (which was denigrated under the previous king, Ahaz), led to increased antipathy toward Assyria (as evinced in negative prophetic oracles like those in Nahum), and led to memories of Hezekiah's faithful leadership during the Assyrian crisis, with the story recounted three times in the OT/HB.

In Assyria, the campaign was also remembered fondly as seen in the mass production of its annalistic account (with seventy-four copies of the Rassam text produced in short order) recounting its memorable victorious battles (where Sennacherib himself apprehended princes' and kings' chariots)[2] and the submission of foreign rulers to his majesty, using epic mythological language to describe the victory and frequently attributing victory to the hand of their god (the "weapon of Assur"). Furthermore, pride in the campaign can be seen in the decoration of Sennacherib's palace with a relief depicting the siege of Lachish to impress those who visited the king.

It was suggested that the prosperity of Judah that followed Sennacherib's withdrawal likely contributed to the positive view of Hezekiah's rebellion. While many scholars often attribute Judah's growth and expansion following 701 BCE to the Pax Assyriaca, Judahites likely did not. Success is success. The growth and prosperity that followed the Assyrian withdrawal would have been interpreted as due to Hezekiah's successful rebellion wherein he trusted in Yahweh, defied the Empire, retained his throne, and led the nation to new prosperity.

From the Assyrian perspective, essential war aims were accomplished. As in 1812, where American war aims did not require the annexation of Canada, Assyrian war aims did not require the taking of Jerusalem, deporting its citizens, or deposing their king. Similar to how Canadians viewed the burning of the nation's capital in Washington, DC, as more important than the defense of Baltimore, Judahites viewed Jerusalem's survival as more significant than the loss of Lachish. But from an American perspective, the defense of Baltimore was more significant and not only stopped the British advancement but also led to the writing of the

---

2. RINAP 3.1:176, 22.iii.3–5.

national anthem. So, from an Assyrian perspective, the failure to take Jerusalem was inconsequential, but the taking of Lachish was a point of pride worth bragging about through the commissioned throne-room relief depicting the victory. The destruction of Lachish was all that was needed to compel Hezekiah to submit and pay the required tribute. From their perspective, Assyria was successful in achieving their essential war aims. The Assyrians established the setting for enriching their empire: the pacification of the Western rebels would lead to the economic flourishing of the region—Pax Assyriaca.

In the penultimate chapter of our study, we undertook an examination of the social location of modern scholarship in the West and suggested that modern assessments of Hezekiah and his rebellion may be influenced by the antiwar cultural bias today. The modern context of relative peace in the West, which has led to an antiwar and antimilitary ethos (evident popularly and in the academy) could account for some negative assessments of Judah's rebellion against Assyria in the late eighth-century BCE. I suggested that at times scholars have read modern mores into the prophet Isaiah in suggesting the prophet opposed Hezekiah's policies due to a desire to avoid conflict and his supposed belief that nothing would be worth a war. In surveying older opinions of war and its utility, we suggested that the ancient Judahite perspective may have been closer to opinions that saw war as necessary at times, as opposed to the antiwar ethos that prevails in the West today. Yet the modern assessment of biblical kings often seems to have at its core the supposition that peace at all costs is preferred. Manasseh is praised for the peace in his time, while Hezekiah is criticized for leading his nation into military conflict. Yet military history shows that conflict cannot always be avoided and that peace at all costs is not the ideal in the ancient world (or even in recent history). Our assessments of Hezekiah should take into account the unpredictability of war and not assume Hezekiah should have known better. Such assessments at times reveal ignorance of military history and/or assume modern mores in judging Hezekiah. The difference in social locations also helps explain how the ancient Judahites had such a positive view of Hezekiah, despite the devastation the Assyrian invasion brought.

In the end, the consideration of military history undertaken in the present study has supported the thesis that neither Assyrian nor biblical texts were principally deceptive in their presentation of the war of 701 BCE as their own victory. Similar to the War of 1812, both sides had reasons to see themselves as the victor in the conflict.[3] Furthermore, our assessments of Hezekiah's leadership and legacy should be cautious of imposing our modern mores onto the text or judging him too harshly due to our ignorance of military history.

When the Assyrians withdrew, no doubt some in Judah celebrated. In 1815, the reaction to the end of the War of 1812 was widespread in the United States. Many schools were closed, people stopped working, politicians adjourned their work,

---

3. As Amélie Kuhrt wrote, "Both accounts are probably 'true.'" Cf. Amélie Kuhrt, *The Ancient Near East: C. 3000–330 BC* (2 vols.; London: Routledge, 1995), 2:478.

and there was "boisterous celebration that ensued, bells were rung, buildings were illuminated, troops turned out to fire a salute, and cartmen with the word 'peace' on their hats led a procession of sleighs of the city."[4] Judah's celebration could be implied in Isa 22:1-2, but the reaction to Sennacherib's withdrawal is not described in biblical narratives. It could be that with Judah left licking its wounds in the wake of Assyrian withdrawal, opposition parties (as evinced in Isaianic criticisms) may have further strengthened their resolve against rebellion. Yet, despite the hardships of the war, the rebellion is remembered fondly and positively.[5] The situation might have been analogous to the aftermath of the War of 1812.

American historian Donald R. Hickey writes of the origins of the myth of the American victory in the War of 1812:

> As the years slipped by, most people forgot the causes of the war. They forgot the defeats on land and sea and lost sight of how close the nation had come to military defeat and financial collapse. According to the emerging myth, the United States had won the war as well as the peace. Thus, the War of 1812 passed into history not as a futile and costly struggle in which America had barely escaped defeat and disunion, but as a glorious triumph in which the nation had single-handedly defeated the conqueror of Napoleon and the Mistress of the Seas.[6]

Similarly, Canadian historian Pierre Berton writes of Canadian mythologizing,

> The war, or more properly the myth of the war, gave the rootless new settlers a sense of community. In the end, the myth became the reality. In the long run it did not matter who fought or who did not, who supported the cause or who disdained it. As the years went by and memories dimmed, as old scars healed and old grudges evaporated, as aging veterans reminisced and new leaders hyperbolized, the settlers began to believe that they had repelled the invader almost single-handed. For the first time, Upper Canadians shared a common tradition.

Mutis mutandis, as the years passed on following the Assyrian crisis of 701 BCE, Judahites appear to have forgotten about the hardships of the war. It did not matter anymore who had supported the rebellion or who opposed it. They ignore that the Philistine incursions ultimately failed to expand Judah's territory. They ignore that Assyria remained the Empire whose hegemony was still unrivalled in the ancient Near East. The memory was of a Judahite victory, achieved through reliance upon their God. The rebellion was remembered as successful. The fortifications created

---

4. Hickey, *The War of 1812*, 112.
5. Na'aman, "Voluntary Servitude," 52.
6. Hickey, *The War of 1812*, 121.

in preparation were remembered as sufficient to the task. Their God's salvation was remembered and celebrated as the cause of the Assyrian retreat.

Newspapers in America compared the US success of 1812 with that of the US War of Independence. The New York *National Advocate* referenced it as "this second war of independence," which it viewed as "illustrated by more splendid achievements than the war of the revolution."[7] Similarly, when the biblical "history" was compiled, Hezekiah's achievements are compared with none other than David (2 Kgs 18:3), the king who won Israel's independence. The Assyrian crisis passed into Judahite history not as a "futile and costly struggle" in which Judah "had barely escaped defeat" but as a "a glorious triumph" in which the God of this small nation had repulsed the great Empire and shown himself to be more powerful than Sennacherib or his gods.

---

7. Ibid., 113.

BIBLIOGRAPHY

Achenbach, Reinhard. "Jabâ und Atalja—zwei jüdische Königstöchter am assyrischen Königshof? zu einer These von Stephanie Dalley." *Biblische Notizen* 113 (2002): 29–38.

Ackroyd, Peter R. "The Biblical Interpretation of the Reigns of Ahaz and Hezekiah." Pages 247–59 in *In the Shelter of Elyon: Essays on Ancient Palestinian Life and Literature in Honor of G. W. Ahlstrom*. Edited by W. Boyd Barrick and John R. Spencer. Journal for the Study of the Old Testament: Supplement Series 31. Sheffield: JSOT Press, 1984.

Ackroyd, Peter R. "An Interpretation of the Babylonian Exile: A Study of II Kings 20 and Isaiah 38–39." Pages 152–71 in *Studies in the Religious Tradition of the Old Testament*. Edited by Peter R. Ackroyd. London: SCM, 1987.

Adams, Henry. *The War of 1812*. Edited by Harvey A. DeWeerd. 1st Cooper Square Press ed. New York: Cooper Square Press, 1999.

Aharoni, Miriam. "Arad: The Israelite Citadels." Pages 82–7 in *The New Encyclopedia of Archaeological Excavations in the Holy Land*. Edited by E. Stern. New York: Simon & Schuster, 1993.

Aharoni, Miriam, and Yohanan Aharoni. "Stratification of Judahite Sites in the 8th and 7th Centuries BCE." *Bulletin of the American Schools of Oriental Research* 224 (1976): 73–90.

Aharoni, Yohanan. "The Land of Gerar." *Israel Exploration Journal* 6 (1956): 26–32.

Aharoni, Yohanan. *The Land of the Bible: A Historical Geography*. Philadelphia, PA: Westminster, 1967.

Aharoni, Yohanan, ed. *Beer-Sheba I: Excavations at Tel Beer-Sheba, 1969–1971*. Vol. 2 of *Monographs of the Institute of Archaeology*. Tel Aviv: Tel Aviv University, 1973.

Aharoni, Yohanan. "The Stratification of the Site." In *Beer-Sheba I: Excavations at Tel Beer-Sheba, 1969–1971*. Monographs of the Institute of Archaeology. Tel Aviv: Tel Aviv University, 1973.

Aharoni, Yohanan. "Tel Haror." Pages 106–7 in *Moshé Stekelis Memorial Volume*. Eretz-Israel 13. Israel Exploration Society: Jerusalem, 1977.

Aharoni, Yohanan. *The Land of the Bible: A Historical Geography*. 2nd ed. Philadelphia, PA: Westminster, 1979.

Aharoni, Yohanan. *The Land of the Bible: A Historical Geography*. 2nd, Rev. and enlarged by A. F. Rainey ed. London: Burns & Oates, 1979.

Aharoni, Yohanan. *Arad Inscriptions*. Judean Desert Studies. Jerusalem: Israel Exploration Society, 1981.

Aharoni, Yohanan. *The Archaeology of the Land of Israel: From the Prehistoric Beginnings to the End of the First Temple Period*. Philadelphia, PA: Westminster, 1982.

Aharoni, Yohanan. "Ramat Rahel." Pages 1261–7 in *The New Encyclopedia of Archaeological Excavations in the Holy Land*, vol. 4. Edited by Ephraim Stern, Ayelet Lewinson-Gilboa, and Joseph Aviram. New York: Henrickson, 1993.

Aharoni, Yohanan, and Antonia Ciasca. *Università di Roma and Universiṭah ha-'Ivrit bi-Yerushalayim, Excavations at Ramat Raḥel, Seasons 1961 and 1962*. Serie Archeologica, 6. Roma: Centro die studi semitici, 1964.

Ahlström, Gösta W., Diana V. Edelman, and Gary Orin Rollefson. *The History of Ancient Palestine from the Palaeolithic Period to Alexander's Conquest*. Journal for the Study of the Old Testament: Supplement Series 146. Sheffield: JSOT Press, 1993.

Albright, William Foxwell. *The Excavation of Tell Beit Mirsim in Palestine*. The Annual of the American Schools of Oriental Research 12. New Haven, CT: Yale University Press, 1932.

Albright, William Foxwell. "Review of A. T. E. Olmstead, *History of Palestine and Syria to the Macedonian Conquest*." *Jewish Quarterly Review* 24/4 (1934): 370–1.

Albright, William Foxwell. "New Light from Egypt on the Chronology and the History of Israel and Judah." *Bulletin of the American Schools of Oriental Research* 130 (1953): 8–11.

Albright, William Foxwell. "Abram the Hebrew: A New Archaeological Interpretation." *Bulletin of the American Schools of Oriental Research* 163 (1961): 36–54.

Amit, D. "Farmsteads in Northern Judea (Betar Area), Survey." *Excavations and Surveys in Israel* 10 (1991): 147–8.

Anderson, A. A. *2 Samuel*. Word Biblical Commentary 11. Dallas, TX: Word, 1989.

Ashworth, Tony. *Trench Warfare, 1914–1918: The Live and Let Live System*. New York: Holmes & Meier, 1980.

Aster, Shawn Zelig. *The Unbeatable Light: Melammu and Its Biblical Parallels*. Alter Orient und Altes Testament 384. Münster: Ugarit-Verlag, 2012.

Aster, Shawn Zelig. *Reflections of Empire in Isaiah 1–39: Responses to Assyrian Ideology*. Ancient Near East Monographs 19. Atlanta, GA: SBL Press, 2017.

Aster, Shawn Zelig. "Isaiah 31 as a Response to Rebellions against Assyria in Philistia." *Journal of Biblical Literature* 136 (2017): 347–61.

Aster, Shawn Zelig. "The Historical Background of the Destruction of Judahite Gath in 712 BCE." Pages 436–44 in *Tell It in Gath: Studies in the History and Archaeology of Israel. Essays in Honor of Aren M. Maeir on the Occasion of His Sixtieth Birthday*. Münster: Zaphon, 2018.

Auld, A. Graeme, and M. L. Steiner. *Jerusalem*. Cities of the Biblical World. Cambridge: Lutterworth, 1996.

Ayalon, E. "Trial Excavation of Two Iron Age Stata at Tel 'Eton." *Tel Aviv* 12 (1985): 54–62.

Bagg, Ariel M. "Palestine under Assyrian Rule: A New Look at the Assyrian Imperial Policy in the West." *Journal of the American Oriental Society* 133 (2013): 119–44.

Bagg, Ariel M. "Assyria and the West: Syria and the Levant." Pages 268–74 in *Sennacherib at the Gates of Jerusalem: Story, History and Historiography*. Edited by Isaac Kalimi and Seth Francis Corning Richardson. Culture and History of the Ancient Near East, 71. Leiden: Brill, 2014.

Bányai, Michael. "Ein Vorschlag zur Chronologie der 25. Dynastie in Ägypten." *Journal of Egyptian History* 6 (2013): 46–129.

Bányai, Michael. "Die Reihenfolge der kuschitischen Könige." *Journal of Egyptian History* 8 (2015): 115–80.

Barbuto, Richard V. *Niagara, 1814: America Invades Canada*. Modern War Studies. Lawrence, KS: University Press of Kansas, 2000.

Barkay, G. "Royal Palace, Royal Portrait? The Tantalizing Possibilities of Ramat Rahel." *Biblical Archaeology Review* 32 (2006): 34–44.

Barnes, William. "A Fresh Interpretation of Isaiah 21:1–10." *Journal of Theological Studies* 1 (1900): 583–92.

Barnett, LeRoy, and Roger L. Rosentreter, *Michigan's Early Military Forces: A Roster and History of Troops Activated Prior to the American Civil War*. Great Lakes Books. Detroit, MI: Wayne State University Press, 2003.

Barton, George A. *Archaeology and the Bible*. Philadelphia, PA: American Sunday–School Union, 1916.

Barton, John. "Ethics in Isaiah." Pages 80–97 in *Writing and Reading the Scroll of Isaiah: Studies of an Interpretative Tradition, Volume 1*. Edited by Craig C. Boyle and Craig A. Evans. Supplements to Vetus Testamentum 70. Leiden: Brill, 1997.

Bates, Robert D. "Assyria and Rebellion in the Annals of Sennacherib: An Analysis of Sennacherib's Treatment of Hezekiah." *Near East Archaeological Society Bulletin* 44 (1999): 39–61.

Bates, Robert D. "Could Taharqa Have Been Called to the Battle of Eltekeh? A Response to William H. Shea." *Near East Archaeological Society Bulletin* 46 (2001): 43–63.

Beckerath, Jürgen von. "Ägypten und Der Feldzug Sanheribs Im Jahre 701 V Chr." *Ugarit-Forschungen* 24 (1993): 3–8.

Becking, Bob. *The Fall of Samaria: An Historical and Archaeological Study*. Studies in the History of the Ancient Near East 2. Leiden: Brill, 1992.

Becking, Bob. "Chronology: A Skeleton without Flesh? Sennacherib's Campaign as a Case-Study." Pages 46–72 in *"Like a Bird in a Cage": The Invasion of Sennacherib in 701 BCE*. Edited by Lester L. Grabbe. Journal for the Study of the Old Testament: Supplement Series 363; European Seminar on Historical Methodology 4. London: Sheffield Academic Press, 2003.

Begg, Christopher T. "Sennacherib's Second Palestinian Campaign: An Additional Indication." *Journal of Biblical Literature* 106 (1987): 685–6.

Beit Arieh, Itzhaq. "The Dead Sea Region: An Archaeological Perspective." Pages 249–51 in *The Dead Sea, the Lake and Its Setting*. Edited by T. M. Niemi, Z. Ben Avraham, and J. R. Gat. Oxford: Oxford University Press, 1997.

Beit Arieh, Itzhaq. "The Western Quarter." Pages 31–7 in *Beer-Sheba, Vol. 1, Excavations at Tel Beer-Sheba*, 1969–1971 Seasons. Edited by Yohanan Aharoni. Tel Aviv: Institute of Archaeology, Tel Aviv University, 1973.

Beit-Arieh, Itzhaq, Liora Freud, and Gregory H. Bearman. *Tel Malḥata a Central City in the Biblical Negev*. Sonia and Marco Nadler Institute of Archaeology Monograph Series 32. Winona Lake, IN: Eisenbrauns, 2015.

Ben Zvi, Ehud. "Who Wrote the Speech of Rabshakeh and When?" *Journal of Biblical Literature* 109 (1990): 79–92.

Ben Zvi, Ehud. "Malleability and Its Limits: Sennacherib's Campaign against Judah as a Case-Study." Pages 73–105 in *"Like a Bird in a Cage": The Invasion of Sennacherib in 701 BCE*. Edited by Lester L. Grabbe. Journal for the Study of the Old Testament: Supplement Series 363; European Seminar on Historical Methodology 4. London: Sheffield Academic Press, 2003.

Ben Zvi, Ehud. "Isaiah 1,4-9, Isaiah, and the Events of 701 BCE in Judah: A Question of Premise and Evidence." *Scandinavian Journal of the Old Testament* 5 (1991): 95–111.

Benn, Carl. *The Battle of York*. Belleville: Milan Publishing, 1984.

Benn, Carl. *The War of 1812*. Essential Histories. New York: Routledge, 2002.

Berges, Ulrich. *The Book of Isaiah: Its Composition and Final Form*. Hebrew Bible Monographs 46. Sheffield: Sheffield Phoenix, 2012.

Berlejung, Angelika. "The Assyrians in the West: Assyrianization, Colonialism, Indifference, or Development Policy?" Pages 21–60 in *Congress Volume Helsinki 2010*. Edited by Martti Nissen. Leiden: Brill, 2012.

Berton, Pierre. *The Invasion of Canada, 1812–1813*. Toronto: McClelland and Stewart, 1980.

Beuken, W. A. M. "Isa 29, 15–24: Perversion Reverted." Pages 43–64 in *The Scriptures and the Scrolls: Studies in Honour of A.S. van der Woude on the Occasion of his 65th Birthday*. Edited by F. García Martinez, A. Hilhorst, and C. J. Labuschagne. Supplements to Vetus Testamentum 49. Leiden: Brill, 1992.

Bienkowski, Piotr. "Transjordan and Assyria." Pages 44–53 in *The Archaeology of Jordan and Beyond: Essays in Honor of James A. Sauer*. Edited by Lawrence E. Stager, Joseph A. Greene, and Michael D. Coogan. Studies in the Archaeology and History of the Levant 1. Winona Lake, IN: Eisenbrauns, 2000.

Blakely, Jeffrey A., and James W. Hardin. "Southwestern Judah in the Late Eighth Century B.C.E." *Bulletin of the American Schools of Oriental Research* 326 (2002): 11–64.

Blenkinsopp, Joseph. *Isaiah 1–39*. Edited by David Noel Freedman. Anchor Bible, 19. New York: Doubleday, 2000.

Blenkinsopp, Joseph. "Judah's Covenant with Death (Isaiah XXVIII 14–22)." *Vetus Testamentum* 50 (2000): 472–83.

Blenkinsopp, Joseph. "Hezekiah and the Babylonian Delegation: A Critical Reading of Isaiah 39:1–8." Pages 107–22 in *Essays on Ancient Israel in Its Near Eastern Context: A Tribute to Nadav Na'aman*. Edited by Yairah Amit, Ehud Ben Zvi, Israel Finkelstein, and Oded Lipschits. Winona Lake, IN: Eisenbrauns, 2006.

Bloch-Smith, Elizabeth. "Assyrians Abet Israelite Cultic Reforms: Sennacherib and the Centralization of the Israelite Cult." Pages 35–44 in *Exploring the Longue Durée: Essays in Honor of Lawrence E. Stager*. Winona Lake, IN: Eisenbrauns, 2009.

Borger, Rykele. *Babylonisch-Assyrische Lesestücke*, 2nd ed. Rome: Pontifium Institutum Biblicum, 1979.

Borneman, Walter R. *1812: The War That Forged a Nation*. New York: HarperCollins, 2004.

Borowski, Oded. "Sennacherib in Judah—the Devastating Consequences of an Assyrian Military Campaign." Pages 33–40 in *Lawrence E, Stager Volume. Eretz-Israel: Archaeological, Historical and Geographical Studies*. Jerusalem: Israel Exploration Society, 2018.

Borowski, Oded. "Tell Halif—2009." *Hadashot Arkheologiyot/Excavations and Survey in Israel* 122 (2018). http://www.hadashot-esi.org.il/report_detail_eng.aspx?id=1362&mag_id=117.

Brandl, B. "Erani, Tel." Pages 256–8 in *The Oxford Encyclopedia of Archaeology in the Near East*. Edited by E. M. Meyers. New York: Oxford University Press, 1997.

Braun, Eliot, and Edwin C. M. van den Brink. "Tel 'Erani." Pages 124–5 in *Excavations and Surveys in Israel*. Jerusalem: Israel Antiquities Authority, 1997.

Bright, John. *A History of Israel*. 3rd ed. Philadelphia, PA: Westminster, 1981.

Brinkman, J. A. "Elamite Military Aid to Merodach-Baladan." *Journal of Near Eastern Studies* 24 (1965): 161–6.

Broekman, G. P. F. "The Order of Succession between Shabaka and Shabataka: A Different View on the Chronology of the Twenty-Fifth Dynasty." *Göttinger Miszellen* 245 (2015): 17–31.

Broshi, Magen. "Expansion of Jerusalem in the Reigns of Hezekiah and Manasseh." *Israel Exploration Journal* 24 (1974): 21–6.

Broshi, Magen, and Israel Finkelstein. "The Population of Palestine in Iron Age II." *Bulletin of the American Schools of Oriental Research* 287 (1992): 47–60.

Brueggemann, Walter, *Isaiah 1-39*. Westminster Bible Companion. Louisville, KY: Westminster John Knox Press, 1998.

Budge, E. A. Wallis. *A History of Egypt: From the End of the Neolithic Period to the Death of Cleopatra VII, B.C. 30, Vol. 6: Egypt under the Priest-Kings and Tanites and Nubians*. Books on Egypt and Chaldaea, 14. London: Kegan Paul, Trench, Trübner, 1902.

Bulbach, S. W. "Judah in the Reign of Manasseh." PhD Dissertation, New York University, 1981.

Bunimovits, Shelomoh, and Zvi Lederman. "The Archaeology of Border Communities: Renewed Excavations at Tel Beth-Shemesh Part I the Iron Age." *Near Eastern Archaeology* 72 (2009): 114-42.

Bunimovitz, Shlomo, and Zvi Lederman. "The Final Destruction of Beth Shemesh and the Pax Assyriaca in the Judean Shephelah." *Tel Aviv* 30 (2003): 3-26.

Bunimovitz, Shlomo, Zvi Lederman, and Raz Kletter. "Tel Bet Shemesh–1990." *Excavations and Surveys in Israel* 10 (1991): 142-4.

Burke, Peter. *History and Social Theory*. 2nd ed. Ithaca, NY: Cornell University Press, 2005.

Čapek, Filip, and Oded Lipschits, eds. *The Last Century in the History of Judah: The Seventh Century BCE in Archaeological, Historical, and Biblical Perspectives*. Ancient Israel and its Literature 37. Atlanta, GA: SBL Press, 2019.

Chakravorty, B. "Military History." *USI Journal* 107 (1978): 259-63.

Childs, Brevard S. *Isaiah and the Assyrian Crisis*. Studies in Biblical Theology 3. London: SCM, 1967.

Christensen, Duane L. "March of Conquest in Isaiah 10:27c-34." *Vetus Testamentum* 26 (1976): 385-99.

Clausewitz, Carl von. *On War*. Translated by E. Howard and P. Paret. New York: Routledge, 2004.

Clayton, B. A. "The Nature and Score of War Studies." *Army Quarterly and Defence Journal* 101 (1971): 195-205.

Clements, Ronald. "Ernest." *Jerusalem and the Nations: Studies in the Book of Isaiah*. Hebrew Bible Monographs, 16. Sheffield: Sheffield Phoenix Press, 2011.

Clements, Ronald. *Isaiah 1-39*. Edited by Ronald E. Clements. New Century Bible Commentary. Grand Rapids, MI: Eerdmans, 1980.

Clements, Ronald. *Isaiah and the Deliverance of Jerusalem: A Study of the Interpretation of Prophecy in the Old Testament*. Journal for the Study of the Old Testament: Supplement Series 13. Sheffield: University of Sheffield, 1980.

Cobb, William Henry. "Isaiah XXI. 1-10 Re-examined." *Journal of Biblical Literature* 17 (1898): 40-61.

Cogan, Mordechai. "Sennacherib's Siege of Jerusalem." Pages 302-3 in *The Context of Scripture*. Edited by William W. Hallo and K. Lawson Younger. Leiden: Brill, 1997.

Cogan, Mordechai. "Sennacherib's Siege of Jerusalem: Once or Twice?" *Biblical Archaeology Review* 27 (2001): 40.

Cogan, Mordechai. "Cross-Examining the Assyrian Witnesses to Sennacherib's Third Campaign: Assessing the Limits of Historical Reconstruction." Pages 51-74 in *Sennacherib at the Gates of Jerusalem: Story, History and Historiography*. Edited by Isaac Kalimi and Seth Francis Corning Richardson. Culture and History of the Ancient Near East, 71. Leiden: Brill, 2014.

Cogan, Mordechai, and Hayim Tadmor. *II Kings*. Anchor Bible, 11. Garden City, NY: Doubleday, 1988.

Cogan, Morton. *Imperialism and Religion: Assyria, Judah, and Israel in the Eighth and Seventh Centuries* B.C.E. Society of Biblical Literature Monograph Series 19. Missoula, MT: Society of Biblical Literature and Scholars Press, 1971.

Cohen, Chaim. "Neo-Assyrian Elements in the First Speech of the Biblical Rab-Saqê." *Israel Oriental Studies* 9 (1979): 32–48.

Creveld, Martin van. "Thoughts on Military History." *Journal of Contemporary History* 18 (1983): 549–66.

Cross, Frank Moore. "The Themes of the Book of Kings and the Structure of the Deuteronomistic History." Pages 274–89 in *Canaanite Myth and Hebrew Epic*. Cambridge, MA: Harvard University Press, 1973.

Crouch, Carly L. *War and Ethics in the Ancient Near East: Military Violence in Light of Cosmology and History*. Beihefte zur Zeitschrift für die Alttestamentliche Wissenschaft 407. Berlin: Walter de Gruyter, 2009.

Dagan, Yehudah. "The Shephelah during the Period of the Monarchy in Light of Archaeological Excavations and Surveys." MA thesis (Hebrew, with English abstract), Tel Aviv University, 1992.

Dagan, Yehudah. "The Settlement in the Judean Shephela in the Second and First Millennium BC: A Test-Case of Settlement Processes in a Geographic Region." PhD dissertation, Tel Aviv University, 2000.

Dalley, Stephanie. "Yabâ, Atalyā and the Foreign Policy of Late Assyrian Kings." *State Archives of Assyria Bulletin* 12 (1998): 97.

Dalley, Stephanie. *Esther's Revenge at Susa from Sennacherib to Ahasuerus*. Oxford: Oxford University Press, 2007.

Dalley, Stephanie. "The Identity of the Princesses in Tomb II and a New Analysis of Events in 701 BC." Pages 171–6 in *New Light on Nimrud: Proceedings of the Nimrud Conference, 11th–13th March 2002*. Edited by John Curtis. London: British Institute for the Study of Iraq; the British Museum, 2008.

Darr, Katheryn Pfisterer. "No Strength to Deliver: A Contextual Analysis of Hezekiah's Proverb in Isaiah 37:3b." Pages 219–56 in *New Visions of Isaiah*. Journal for the Study of the Old Testament: Supplement Series 214. Sheffield: Sheffield Academic Press, 1996.

Day, John. *Molech: A God of Human Sacrifice in the Old Testament*. University of Cambridge Oriental Publications, 41. Cambridge: Cambridge University Press, 1989.

de Groot, A. "Notes on the Development of Jerusalem." Page 21 in *The Fifteenth Archaeological Conference in Israel*. Jerusalem: Israel Exploration Society, 1989.

De Odorico, Marco. *The Use of Numbers and Quantifications in the Assyrian Royal Inscriptions*. State Archives of Assyria Studies 3. Helsinki: Neo-Assyrian Text Corpus Project, 1995.

Dever, William G. "Palestine in the Second Millennium BCE: The Archaeological Picture." Pages 70–120 in *Israelite and Judean History*. Edited by John H. Hayes and J. Maxwell Miller. Philadelphia, PA: Westminster, 1977.

Dever, William G. "Archaeology, Material Culture and the Early Monarchical Period in Israel." Pages 103–15 in *The Fabric of History: Text, Artifact and Israel's Past*. Journal for the Study of the Old Testament: Supplement Series 127. Sheffield: JSOT Press, 1991.

Dever, William G. *Beyond the Texts: An Archaeological Portrait of Ancient Israel and Judah*. Atlanta, GA: SBL Press, 2017.

Dhorme, P. "Le Désert de la Mer (Isaïe, XXI)." *Revue biblique* 31 (1922): 403–6.

Dietrich, Walter. *Prophetie und Geschichte; eine redaktionsgeschichtliche Untersuchung zum deuteronomistischen Geschichtswerk*. Forschungen zur Religion und Literatur des Alten und Neuen Testaments 108. Göttingen: Vandenhoeck & Ruprecht, 1972.

Dietrich, Walter. *Jesaja und die Politik*. Beiträge zur evangelischen Theologie 74. Münich: Kaiser, 1976.

Dillmann, August. *Der Prophet Jesaia*. Leipzig: Hirzel, 1890.

Dion, Paul-Eugène. "Sennacherib's Expedition to Palestine." *Èglise et thèologie* 20 (1989): 5–25.

Dixon, Norman F. *On the Psychology of Military Incompetence*. London: Cape, 1976.

Dodson, Aidan. *The Royal Tombs of Ancient Egypt*. Barnsley: Pen & Sword Archaeology, 2016.

Dodson, Aidan. "The Rescue of Jerusalem: A View from the Nile Valley." Pages 167–88 in *Jerusalem's Survival, Sennacherib's Departure, and the Kushite Role in 701 BCE: An Examination of Henry Aubin's Rescue of Jerusalem*. Edited by Alice Ogden Bellis. Perspectives on Hebrew Scriptures and Its Contexts 32. Piscataway, NJ: Gorgias Press, 2020.

Donner, Herbert. *Israel unter den Völkern: die Stellung der klassischen Propheten des 8. Jahrhunderts v. Chr. zur Aussenpolitik der Könige von Israel und Juda*. Supplements to Vetus Testamentum 11. Leiden: Brill, 1964.

Dougherty, Raymond P. "Sennacherib and the Walled Cities of Judah." *Journal of Biblical Literature* 49 (1930): 160–71.

Dressel, J. P. "Ramat Rahel." Pages 402–4 in *The Oxford Encyclopedia of Archaeology in the Near East*. Edited by Eric M. Meyers. Oxford: Oxford University Press, 1997.

Dubovský, Peter. *Hezekiah and the Assyrian Spies: Reconstruction of the Neo-Assyrian Intelligence Services and Its Significance for 2 Kings 18–19*. Biblica et Orientalia 49. Rome: Pontifical Biblical Institute, 2006.

Dubovský, Peter. "Assyrians under the Walls of Jerusalem and the Confinement of Padi." *Journal of Near Eastern Studies* 75 (2016): 109–26.

Dyer, Gwynne. *War: The New Edition*. Rev. ed. Toronto: Random House Canada, 2004.

Eaton, Joseph H. *Returns of Killed and Wounded in Battles or Engagements with Indians and British and Mexican Troops, 1790–1848, Compiled by Lt. Col J. H. Eaton*. Washington, DC: National Archives and Records Administration Microfilm Publications, 2000.

Eide, T., ed. *Fontes Historiae Nubiorum*. Bergen: Klassisk institutt, Universitetet i Bergen, 1994.

Eisenberg, Emanuel, and Alla Nagorski. "Tel Hevron (Er-Rumeidi)." *Hadashot Arkheologiyot* (2002): 91*–92*.

Eissfeldt, Otto. *The Old Testament, an Introduction: Including the Apocrypha and Pseudepigrapha, and Also the Works of Similar Type from Qumran: The History of the Formation of the Old Testament*. Oxford: Blackwell, 1965.

Elayi, Josette. *Sennacherib, King of Assyria*. Archaeology and Biblical Studies 24. Atlanta, GA: SBL Press, 2018.

Elliott, Emory, ed. *Columbia Literary History of the United States*. New York: Columbia University Press, 1988.

Ellis, James H. *A Ruinous and Unhappy War: New England and the War of 1812*. New York: Algora, 2009.

Elting, John Robert. *Amateurs, to Arms! A Military History of the War of 1812*. Major Battles and Campaigns 4. Chapel Hill, NC: Algonquin Books of Chapel Hill, 1991.

Emerton, John A. "The Historical Background of Isaiah 1:4–9." Pages 537–47 in *Studies on the Language and Literature of the Bible: Selected Works of J. A. Emerton*. Edited by Graham Davies and Robert Gordon. Supplements to Vetus Testamentum 165. Leiden: Brill, 2015.

Ender, Morten G., David E. Rohall, and Michael D. Matthews. "Intersecting Identities: Race, Military Affiliation, and Youth Attitudes Towards War." *War & Society* 34 (2015): 230–46.

Eph'al, Israel. "On Warfare and Military Control in the Ancient Near Eastern Empires: A Research Outline." Pages 88–106 in *History Historiography and Interpretation: Studies in Biblical and Cuneiform Literatures*. Edited by Moshe Weinfeld and Hayim Tadmor. Jerusalem: Magnes, 1983.

Eph'al, Israel. "The Assyrian Domination of Palestine." Pages 276–89 in *The World History of the Jewish People*. Edited by B. Mazar. Jerusalem: Rutgers University Press, 1979.

Erlandsson, Seth. *The Burden of Babylon: A Study of Isaiah 13:2–14:23*. Coniectanea Biblica: Old Testament Series 4. Lund: GWK Gleerup, 1970.

Eshel, Hanan. "A lmlk Stamp from Beth-El." *Israel Exploration Journal* 39 (1989): 60–2.

Evans, Carl D. "Judah's Foreign Policy from Hezekiah to Josiah." Pages 157–78 in *Scripture in Context: Essays on the Comparative Method*. Edited by Carl D. Evans, William W. Hallo, and John B. White. Pittsburgh, PA: Pickwick, 1980.

Evans, Paul S. "Sennacherib's 701 Invasion into Judah: What Saith the Scriptures?" Pages 57–77 in *The Function of Ancient Historiography in Biblical and Cognate Studies*. Edited by Patricia G. Kirkpatrick and Timothy Goltz. Library of the Hebrew Bible/ Old Testament Studies; Journal for the Study of the Old Testament 489. London: T&T Clark, 2008.

Evans, Paul S. "The Hezekiah-Sennacherib Narrative as Polyphonic Text." *Journal for the Study of the Old Testament* 33 (2009): 335–58.

Evans, Paul S. *The Invasion of Sennacherib in the Book of Kings: A Source-Critical and Rhetorical Study of 2 Kings 18–19*. Supplements to Vetus Testamentum 125. Leiden: Brill, 2009.

Evans, Paul S. "The Function of the Chronicler's Temple Despoliation Notices in Light of Imperial Realities in Yehud." *Journal of Biblical Literature* 129 (2010): 31–47.

Evans, Paul S. "Historia or Exegesis? Assessing the Chronicler's Hezekiah-Sennacherib Narrative." Pages 103–20 in *Chronicling the Chronicler: The Book of Chronicles and Early Second Temple Historiography*. Edited by Paul S. Evans and Tyler F. Williams. Winona Lake, IN: Eisenbrauns, 2013.

Fales, Frederick Mario. "The Enemy in Assyrian Royal Inscriptions: 'The Moral Judgment.'" Pages 425–35 in *Mesopotamien und seine Nachbaren*. Edited by H. J. Nissen and J. Renger. XXV Rencontre Assyriologique Internationale. Berlin: Deitrich Reimer, 1982.

Fales, Frederick Mario. "On Pax Assyriaca in the Eighth-Seventh Centuries BCE and Its Implications." Pages 17–35 in *Isaiah's Vision of Peace in Biblical and Modern International Relations: Swords into Plowshares*. New York: Palgrave Macmillan, 2008.

Fales, Frederick Mario. "To Speak Kindly to Him/Them' as Item of Assyrian Political Discourse." Pages 27–40 in *Of God(s), Trees, Kings, and Scholars. Neo-Assyrian and Related Studies in Honour of Simo Parpola*. Edited by Mikko Lukko, Saana Svärd, and Raija Mattila. Studia Orientalia 106. Helsinki: Finnish Oriental Society, 2009.

Fales, Frederick Mario. "The Road to Judah: 701 B.C.E. In the Context of Sennacherib's Political-Military Strategy." Pages 223–48 in *Sennacherib at the Gates of Jerusalem: Story, History and Historiography*. Edited by Isaac Kalimi and Seth

Francis Corning Richardson. Culture and History of the Ancient Near East, 71. Leiden: Brill, 2014.
Fales, Frederick Mario, and J. N. Postgate. *Imperial Administrative Records, II. Provincial and Military Administration*. State Archives of Assyria Studies 11. Helsinki: Neo-Assyrian Text Corpus Project, 1995.
Fantalkin, Alexander. "The Final Destruction of Beth Shemesh and the Pax Assyriaca in the Judahite Shephelah: An Alternative View." *Tel Aviv* 31 (2004): 245–61.
Farber, Zev, and Jacob L. Wright. *Archaeology and History of Eighth-Century Judah*. Edited by Zev Farber and Jacob L. Wright. Ancient Near East Monographs 23. Atlanta, GA: Society of Biblical Literature, 2018.
Faust, Avraham. "The Farmstead in the Highlands of Iron Age II Israel." Pages 91–104 in *The Rural Landscape of Ancient Israel*. Edited by A. Maeir, S. Dar, and Z. Safrai. Baris. Oxford: Archaeopress, 2003.
Faust, Avraham. "The Settlement of Jerusalem's Western Hill and the City's Status in Iron Age II Revisited." *Zeitschrift des Deutschen Palästina-Vereins* 121 (2005): 97–118.
Faust, Avraham. "The Interests of the Assyrian Empire in the West: Olive Oil Production as a Test Case." *JESHO* 54 (2011): 62–86.
Faust, Avraham. "Settlement and Demography in Seventh-Century Judah and the Extent and Intensity of Sennacherib's Campaign." *Palestine Exploration Quarterly* 140 (2008): 168–94.
Faust, Avraham. *The Archaeology of Israelite Society in Iron Age II*. Winona Lake, IN: Eisenbrauns, 2012.
Faust, Avraham. *Judah in the Neo-Babylonian Period: The Archaeology of Desolation*. Society of Biblical Literature Archaeology and Biblical Studies 18. Atlanta, GA: Society of Biblical Literature, 2012.
Faust, Avraham. "The Shephelah in the Iron Age: A New Look on the Settlement of Judah." *Palestine Exploration Quarterly* 145 (2013): 203–19.
Faust, Avraham, and Hayah Katz. "A Canaanite Town, a Judahite Center, and a Persian Period Fort: Excavating over Two Thousand Years of History at Tel 'eton." *Near Eastern Archaeology* 78 (2015): 88–102.
Faust, Avraham, and Hayah Katz. "Tel 'Eton Cemetery: An Introduction." *Hebrew Bible and Ancient Israel* 5 (2016): 171–86.
Faust, Avraham, and Ehud Weiss. "Judah, Philistia, and the Mediterranean World: Reconstructing the Economic System of the Seventh Century B.C.E." *Bulletin of the American Schools of Oriental Research* 338 (2005): 71–92.
Fawcett, Louise. "The Iraq War Ten Years On: Assessing the Fallout." *International Affairs* 89 (2013): 325–43.
Fazal, Tanisha M., and Paul Poast. "War Is Not Over: What the Optimists Get Wrong About Conflict." *Foreign Affairs* 98 (2019): 74–83.
Feig, Nurit. "New Discoveries in the Rephaim Valley, Jerusalem." *Palestine Exploration Quarterly* 128 (1996): 3–7.
Ferro, Marc. *The Great War, 1914–1918*. London: Routledge & Kegan Paul, 1973.
Finkelstein, Israel. "Environmental Archaeology and Social History: Demographic and Economic Aspects of the Monarchic Period." Pages 56–66 in *Biblical Archaeology Today, 1990: Proceedings of the Second International Congress on Biblical Archaeology, Jerusalem, June–July 1990*. Jerusalem: Palgrave Macmillan, 1993.
Finkelstein, Israel. "The Archaeology of the Days of Manasseh." Pages 169–87 in *Scripture and Other Artifacts: Essays on the Bible and Archaeology in Honor of Philip J. King*.

Edited by Michael D. Coogan, Cheryl J. Exum, and Lawrence E. Stager. Louisville, KY: Westminster John Knox, 1994.

Finkelstein, Israel, and Neil Asher Silberman. *The Bible Unearthed: Archaeology's New Vision of Ancient Israel and the Origin of Its Sacred Texts*. New York: Touchstone, 2001.

Finkelstein, Israel, and Nadav Na'aman. "The Judahite Shephelah in the Late 8th and Early 7th Centuries BCE." *Tel Aviv* 31 (2004): 60–79.

Fischer, Johann. *Das Buch Isaias*. Bonn: P. Hanstein, 1937.

Fohrer, Georg. *Das Buch Jesaja*. 3 vols. Zürcher Bibelkommentare. Zürich; Stuttgart: Zwingli Verlag, 1960.

Forest, Timothy S. "Epic Triumph, Epic Embarrassment, or Both? Commemorations of the War of 1812 Today in the Niagara Region." *Ontario History* 104 (2012): 96–122.

Frahm, Eckart. *Einleitung in die Sanherib-Inschriften*. Archiv für Orientforschung: Beiheft 26. Horn: Selbstverlag des Instituts für Orientalistik der Universität Wein, Druck F. Berger & Söhne, 1997.

Frahm, Eckart. *Historische und Historisch-Literarische Texte. Wissenschaftliche Veröffentlichungen Der Deutschen Orient-Gesellschaft 121*. Wiesbaden: Harrassowitz, 2009.

Frahm, Eckart. "Family Matters: Psychohistorical Reflections on Sennacherib and His Times." in *Sennacherib at the Gates of Jerusalem: Story, History and Historiography*. Edited by Isaac Kalimi and Seth Francis Corning Richardson. Culture and History of the Ancient Near East, 71. Leiden: Brill, 2014.

Frahm, Eckart. "The Neo-Assyrian Period (Ca. 1000–609 BCE)." in *A Companion to Assyria*. Edited by Eckart Frahm. Hoboken, NJ: John Wiley, 2017.

Friedman, Richard Elliott. *The Exile and Biblical Narrative: The Formation of the Deuteronomistic and Priestly Works*. Harvard Semitic Monographs, 22. Chicago, CA: Scholars Press, 1981.

Fritz, Stephen G. *Ostkrieg: Hitler's War of Extermination in the East*. Lexington: University Press of Kentucky, 2011.

Fuchs, Andreas. *Die Inschriften Sargons II. aus Khorsabad*. Göttingen: Cuvillier, 1994.

Fullerton, Kemper. "The Invasion of Sennacherib." *Bibliotheca Sacra* 63 (1906): 577–634.

Fullerton, Kemper. "Viewpoints in the Discussion of Isaiah's Hopes for the Future." *Journal of Biblical Literature* 41 (1922): 1–101.

Galil, Gershon. "A New Look at the 'Azekah Inscription." *Revue biblique* 102 (1995): 321–9.

Gallagher, William R. *Sennacherib's Campaign to Judah: New Studies*. Studies in the History and Culture of the Ancient Near East 18. Leiden; Boston, MA: Brill, 1999.

Gardiner, Alan. *Egypt of the Pharaohs: An Introduction*. Oxford: Clarendon Press, 1961.

Gianto, Agustius, and Peter Dubovský, eds. *The Changing Faces of Kingship in Syria-Palestine 1500–500 BCE*. Alter Orient und Altes Testament 459. Münster: Ugarit-Verlag, 2018.

Gibson, Shimon. "The Tell ej-Judeideh (Tel Goded) Excavations: A Re-Appraisal Based on Archival Records in the Palestine Exploration Fund." *Tel Aviv* 21 (1994): 194–234.

Ginsberg, Harold Lewis. "Judah and the Transjordan States from 734 to 582 B.C.E." Pages 347–68 in *Alexander Marx Jubilee Volume*. Edited by S. Lieberman. New York: The Jewish Theological Seminary of America, 1950.

Gitin, Seymour. "The Neo-Assyrian Empire and Its Western Periphery: The Levant, with a Focus on Philistine Ekron." Pages 77–103 in *Assyria 1995: Proceedings of the 10th Anniversary Symposium of the Neo-Assyrian Texts Corpus Project, September 7–11, 1995*. Edited by Simon Parpola and R. M. Whiting. Helsinki: University of Helsinki, 1997.

Gitin, Seymour. "The Effects of Urbanization on a Philistine City-State: Tel Miqne-Ekron in the Iron Age II Period." Pages 277–84 in *The Proceedings of the Tenth World Congress of Jewish Studies 1989*. Edited by D. Assaf. Jerusalem: World Union of Jewish Studies, 1990.

Gitin, Seymour. "Tel Miqne-Ekron in the Seventh Century B.C.: City Plan Development and the Oil Industry." Pages 219–42 in *Olive Oil in Antiquity: Israel and Neighbouring Countries from the Neolithic to the Early Arad Period*. Edited by David Eitam and Michael Heltzer. History of the Ancient Near East Studies 7. Padova: Sargon, 1996.

Gitin, Seymour. "The Philistines in the Prophetic Texts: An Archaeological Perspective." Pages 273–90 in *Hesed Ve-Emet: Studies in Honor of Ernest S. Frerichs*. Edited by J. Magness and S. Gitin. *Brown Judaic Studies*. Atlanta, GA: Scholars Press, 1998.

Gitin, Seymour. "Philistines in the Books of Kings." Pages 301–64 in *The Books of Kings: Sources, Composition, Historiography and Reception*. Edited by Baruch Halpern and Andre Lemaire. Supplements to Vetus Testamentum 129. Leiden: Brill, 2010.

Glantz, David M., and Jonathan M. House. *When Titans Clashed: How the Red Army Stopped Hitler*. Modern War Studies. Lawrence, KS: University Press of Kansas, 1995.

Glantz, David M. "The Soviet-German War 1941–1945: Myths and Realities." Paper presented as the 20th Anniversary Distinguished Lecture at the Strom Thurmond Institute of Government and Public Affairs. Clemson University, 2001.

Goldberg, Jeremy. "Two Assyrian Campaigns against Hezekiah and Later Eighth Century Biblical Chronology." *Biblica* 80 (1999): 360–90.

Gonçalves, Francolino J. *L'expédition de Sennachérib en Palestine dans la littérature hebraïque ancienne*. Etudes bibliques 7; Louvain-la-Neuve: Institut Orientaliste de l'Université catholique de Louvain. Paris: Gabalda, 1986.

Gonçalves, Francolino J. "Isaïe, Jérémie et la politique internationale de Juda." *Biblica* 76 (1995): 282–98.

Goosens, G. "Taharqa Le Conquérant." *Chronique d'Égypte* 22/44 (1947): 239–44.

Gosse, Bernard. *Isaïe 13,1–14,23: dans la tradition littéraire du livre d'Isaïe et dans la tradition des oracles contre les nations: étude de la transformation du genre littéraire*. Orbis biblicus et orientalis 78. Göttingen: Vandenhoeck & Ruprecht, 1988.

Glantz, David M., and Jonathan M. House. *When Titans Clashed: How the Red Army Stopped Hitler*. Modern War Studies. Lawrence, KS: University Press of Kansas, 1995.

Grabbe, Lester L. "Introduction." Pages 2–43 in *"Like a Bird in a Cage": The Invasion of Sennacherib in 701 BCE*. Edited by Lester L. Grabbe. Journal for the Study of the Old Testament: Supplement Series 363; European Seminar on Historical Methodology 4. London: Sheffield Academic Press, 2003.

Grabbe, Lester L. "Of Mice and Dead Men: Herodotus 2.141 and Sennacherib's Campaign in 701 BCE." Pages 119–40 in *"Like a Bird in a Cage": The Invasion of Sennacherib in 701 BCE*. Edited by Lester L. Grabbe. Journal for the Study of the Old Testament: Supplement Series 363; European Seminar on Historical Methodology 4. London: Sheffield Academic Press, 2003.

Grabbe, Lester L. "Reflections on the Discussion." Pages 308–23 in *"Like a Bird in a Cage": The Invasion of Sennacherib in 701 BCE*. Edited by Lester L. Grabbe. Journal for the Study of the Old Testament: Supplement Series 363; European Seminar on Historical Methodology 4. London: Sheffield Academic Press, 2003.

Grabbe, Lester L. "The Kingdom of Judah from Sennacherib's Invasion to the Fall of Jerusalem: If We Had Only the Bible…" Pages 78–122 in *Good Kings and Bad Kings*. Edited by Lester L. Grabbe. Journal for the Study of the Old Testament: Supplement

Series 393; European Seminar on Historical Methodology 5. New York: T&T Clark, 2005.

Grabbe, Lester L. *Ancient Israel: What Do We Know and How Do We Know It?* London: T&T Clark, 2007.

Grabbe, Lester L. "Israelite Interaction with Egypt During the Monarchy: A Context for Interpreting 2 Kings 19:8–13." Pages 189–210 in *Jerusalem's Survival, Sennacherib's Departure, and the Kushite Role in 701 BCE*. Edited by Alice Ogden Bellis. Perspectives on Hebrew Scriptures and Its Contexts 32. New Jersey: Gorgias Press, 2019.

Grant, Elihu, and G. Ernest Wright. *Ain Shems Excavations (Palestine): Part V (Text)*. Biblical and Kindred Studies 8. Haverford, PA: Haverford College, 1931.

Gray, George Buchanan. *A Critical and Exegetical Commentary on the Book of Isaiah, I-XXXIX*. International Critical Commentary on the Holy Scriptures of the Old and New Testaments. New York: C. Scribner, 1912.

Gray, John. *1 & 2 Kings*. Old Testament Library. Philadelphia, PA: Westminster, 1970.

Gray, Peter W. "XII. Why Study Military History?" *Defence Studies* 5 (2005): 151–64.

Grayson, Albert Kirk. "Problematic Battles in Mesopotamian History." Pages 337–42 in *Studies in Honor of Benno Landsberger on His Seventy-Fifth Birthday, April 25, 1965*. Edited by H. G. Güttersbock and Th. Jacobsen. Assyriological Studies 16. Chicago, CA: Chicago University Press, 1965.

Grayson, Albert Kirk. *Assyrian and Babylonian Chronicles*. Texts from Cuneiform Sources 5. Locust Valley, NY: J. J. Augustin, 1975.

Grayson, Albert Kirk. "Assyria: Sennacherib and Esarhaddon." In *Cambridge Ancient History: The Assyrian and Babylonian Empires and Other States of the Near East, from the Eighth to the Sixth Centuries B.C.* Edited by John Boardman, I.E.S. Edwards, N.G.L. Hammond, E. Sollberger, and C.B.F. Walker. Cambridge: Cambridge University Press, 1991.

Grayson, Albert Kirk, and Jamie R. Novotny. *The Royal Inscriptions of Sennacherib, King of Assyria (704–681 BC)*. The Royal Inscriptions of the Neo-Assyrian Period 3/1. Winona Lake, IN: Eisenbrauns, 2012.

Greenberg, R. "Beit Mirsim, Tell." Pages 177–80 in *The New Encyclopedia of Archaeological Excavations in the Holy Land*. Edited by E. Stern. New York: Simon & Schuster, 1993.

Greenberg, R. "Beit Mirsim, Tell." Pages 295–7 in *Oxford Encyclopedia for Archaeology in the Near East*. Edited by Eric M. Meyers. New York: Oxford University Press, 1997.

Greenblatt, Miriam. *War of 1812*. Edited by John Stewart Bowman. America at War. New York: Facts on File, 2003.

Gressmann, Hugo. *Der Messias*. Forschungen zur Religion und Literatur des Alten und Neuen Testaments 43. Göttingen: Vandenhoeck & Ruprecht, 1929.

Grimal, Nicolas-Christophe. *A History of Ancient Egypt*. Oxford: Blackwell, 1992.

Guidebook to the Historic Sites of the War of 1812. Toronto: Dundurn Press, 1998.

Hallo, William W. "Jerusalem under Hezekiah: An Assyriological Perspective." Pages 36–50 in *Jerusalem: Its Sanctity and Centrality to Judaism, Christianity, and Islam*. Edited by Lee I. Levine. New York: Continuum, 1999.

Halpern, Baruch. *David's Secret Demons: Messiah, Murderer, Traitor, King*. Bible in Its World. Grand Rapids, MI: Eerdmans, 2001.

Halpern, Baruch. "Jerusalem and the Lineages in the Seventh Century BCE: Kinship and the Rise of Individual Moral Liability." Pages 11–107 in *Law and Ideology in Monarchic Israel*. Edited by Baruch Halpern and Deborah W. Hobson. Journal for the Study of the Old Testament: Supplement Series 124. Sheffield: JSOT Press, 1991.

Halpern, Baruch, and Deborah W. Hobson. *Law and Ideology in Monarchic Israel.* Journal for the Study of the Old Testament Supplement Series 124. Sheffield: JSOT Press, 1991.

Hanson, Victor Davis. *The Father of Us All: War and History, Ancient and Modern.* New York: Bloomsbury, 2010.

Hardmeier, Christof. *Prophetie im Streit vor dem Untergang Judas: erzählkommunikative Studien zur Entstehungssituation der Jesaja- und Jeremiaerzählungen in II Reg 18–20 und Jer 37–40.* Berlin: de Gruyter, 1990.

Hasel, Michael G. *Domination and Resistance: Egyptian Military Activity in the Southern Levant, ca. 1300–1185 B.C.* Probleme der Ägyptologie 10. Leiden: Brill, 1998.

Hathaway, Oona Anne, and Scott Shapiro. *The Internationalists: How a Radical Plan to Outlaw War Remade the World.* New York: Simon & Schuster, 2017.

Hattendorf, John. "The Naval War of 1812 in International Perspective." *The Mariner's Mirror* 99 (2013): 5–22.

Hayes, John Haralson. "The Tradition of Zion's Inviolability." *Journal of Biblical Literature* 82 (1963): 419–26.

Hayes, John Haralson, and Stuart A. Irvine. *Isaiah, the Eighth Century Prophet: His Times and His Preaching.* Nashville, TN: Abingdon Press, 1987.

Heidler, David Stephen, and Jeanne T. Heidler. *The War of 1812.* Greenwood Guides to Historic Events, 1500–1900. Westport, CT: Greenwood Press, 2002.

Herbert, Arthur Sumner. *The Book of the Prophet Isaiah, Chapters 1–39.* The Cambridge Bible Commentary. Cambridge: Cambridge University Press, 1973.

Herzog, Ze'ev. "Beer-Sheba Valley: From Nomadism to Monarchy." Pages 122–49 in *From Nomadism to Monarchy* Edited by Israel Finkelstein and Nadav Na'aman. Jerusalem: Biblical Archaeology Society, 1994.

Herzog, Ze'ev. "Arad: Iron Age Period." Pages 174–6 in *The Oxford Encyclopedia of Archaeology in the Near East.* Edited by E. M. Meyers. Oxford: Oxford University Press, 1997.

Herzog, Ze'ev. "The Fortress Mound at Tel Arad: An Interim Report." *Tel Aviv* 29 (2002): 3–109.

Hickey, Donald R. *The War of 1812: A Forgotten Conflict.* Urbana, IL: University of Illinois Press, 2012.

Hickey, Donald R. *The War of 1812: A Short History.* Urbana, IL: University of Illinois Press, 2012.

Hoffmeier, James K. "Egypt as an Arm of Flesh: A Prophetic Response." Pages 79–97 in *Israel's Apostasy and Restoration: Essays in Honor of Roland K Harrison.* Grand Rapids, MI: Baker Book House, 1988.

Hoffmeier, James K. "Egypt's Role in the Events of 701 B.C. In Jerusalem." Pages 230–32 in *Jerusalem in Bible and Archaeology: The First Temple Period.* Edited by Andrew G. Vaughn and Anne E. Killebrew. Society of Biblical Literature Symposium Series 18. Leiden: Brill, 2003.

Høgenhaven, Jesper. "The Prophet Isaiah and Judaean Foreign Policy under Ahaz and Hezekiah." *Journal of Near Eastern Studies* 49 (1990): 351–4.

Holladay, John S., Jr. "Hezekiah's Tribute, Long-Distance Trade, and the Wealth of Nations ca. 1000–600 BC: A New Perspective." Pages 309–31 in *Confronting the Past: Archaeological and Historical Essays on Ancient Israel in Honor of William G. Devers.* Edited by Seymour Gitin, J. Edward Wright, and J. P. Dessel. Winona Lake, IN: Eisenbrauns, 2006.

Holloway, Steven W. "Harran: Cultic Geography in the Neo-Assyrian Empire and Its Implications for Sennacherib's 'Letter to Hezekiah' in 2 Kings." Pages

276–314 in *The Pitcher Is Broken: Memorial Essays for Gösta W. Ahlstrom*. Edited by Steven W. Holloway and Lowell K. Handy. Journal for the Study of the Old Testament: Supplement Series 190. Sheffield: Sheffield Academic Press, 1995.

Honor, Leo Lazarus. *Sennacherib's Invasion of Palestine: A Critical Source Study*. Contributions to Oriental History and Philology, 12. New York: Columbia, 1926.

Horn, Siegfried H. "Did Sennacherib Campaign Once or Twice against Hezekiah." *Andrews University Seminary Studies* 4 (1966): 1–28.

Howard, Michael. "The Demand for Military History." *Times Literary Supplement* (November 13, 1969).

Howard, Michael. "The Use and Abuse of Military History." *Parameters: U.S. Army War College* 11 (1981): 9–14.

Howard, Michael. *The Lessons of History*. New Haven, CT: Yale University Press, 1991.

Howard, Michael, Brian Bond, David Chandler, J. C. A. Stagg, John Childs, John Gooch, Geoffrey Best, and John Terraine. "What Is Military History?" *History Today* 34 (1984): 12.

Howes, Kelly King, and Julie Carnagie. *War of 1812*. Detroit, MI: UXL, 2002.

Huber, Friedrich. *Jahwe, Juda und die anderen Völker beim Propheten Jesaja*. Beihefte zur Zeitschrift für die alttestamentliche Wissenschaft 137. Berlin: de Gruyter, 1976.

Iggers, Georg G. *Historiography in the Twentieth Century: From Scientific Objectivity to the Postmodern Challenge*. Hanover, NH: Wesleyan University Press, 1997.

Irvine, Stuart A. *Isaiah, Ahaz, and the Syro-Ephraimitic Crisis*. Edited by David L. Petersen. SBL Dissertation Series 123. Atlanta, GA: Scholars Press, 1990.

Jagodic, G. K. "Is War a Good or a Bad Thing? The Attitudes of Croatian, Israeli, and Palestinian Children toward War." *International Journal of Psychology* 35 (2000): 1–257.

Jang, Sehoon. "Is Hezekiah a Success or a Failure? The Literary Function of Isaiah's Prediction at the End of the Royal Narratives in the Book of Isaiah." *Journal for the Study of the Old Testament* 42 (2017): 117–35.

Jenkins, A. K. "Hezekiah's Fourteenth Year: A New Interpretation of 2 Kings 18:13–19:37." *Vetus Testamentum* 26 (1976): 284–98.

Jeremias, Alfred, C. H. W. Johns, and C. L. Beaumont. *The Old Testament in the Light of the Ancient East*. London: Williams & Norgate, 1911.

Jones, Colin. "New Military History for Old? War and Society in Early Modern Europe." *European Studies Review* 12 (1982): 97–108.

Jones, Michael K. *The Retreat: Hitler's First Defeat*. New York: Thomas Dunne Books, 2010.

Jong, Matthijs J. de. *Isaiah among the Ancient Near Eastern Prophets: A Comparative Study of the Earliest Stages of the Isaiah Tradition and the Neo-Assyrian Prophecies*. Supplements to Vetus Testamentum 117. Leiden: Brill, 2007.

Jurman, Claus. "The Order of the Kushite Kings According to Sources from the Eastern Desert and Thebes. Or: Shabataka Was Here First!" *Journal of Egyptian History* 10 (2017): 124–51.

Kahn, Dan'el. "The Inscription of Sargon II at Tang-i Var and the Chronology of Dynasty 25." *Orientalia, Nova Series* 70 (2001): 1–18.

Kahn, Dan'el. "Taharqa, King of Kush and the Assyrians." *Journal of the Society for the Study of Egyptian Antiquities* 31 (2004): 109–28.

Kahn, Dan'el. "Tirhakah, King of Kush and Sennacherib." *Journal of Ancient Egyptian Interconnections* 6 (2014): 29–41.

Kahn, Dan'el. "The War of Sennacherib against Egypt as Described in Herodotus II 141." *Journal of Ancient Egyptian Interconnections* 6 (2014): 22–33.

Kahn, Dan'el. *Sennacherib's Campaign against Judah: A Source Analysis of Isaiah 36–37*. Society for Old Testament Study Monographs. Cambridge: Cambridge University Press, 2020.

Kaiser, Otto. *Isaiah 1–12: A Commentary*. Old Testament Library. Philadelphia, PA: Westminster, 1972.

Kaiser, Otto. *Der Prophet Jesaja; Kapitel 13–39*. Das Alte Testament Deutsch 18. Göttingen: Vandenhoeck & Ruprecht, 1973.

Kaiser, Otto. *Isaiah 13–39*. The Old Testament Library. Philadelphia, PA: Westminster, 1974.

Kalimi, Isaac. "Sennacherib's Campaign to Judah: The Chronicler's View Compared with His 'Biblical Sources.'" Pages 11–50 in *Sennacherib at the Gates of Jerusalem: Story, History and Historiography*. Edited by Isaac Kalimi and Seth Francis Corning Richardson. Culture and History of the Ancient Near East, 71. Leiden: Brill, 2014.

Katzenstein, H. Jacob. *The History of Tyre, from the Beginning of the Second Millennium B.C.E. Until the Fall of the Neo-Babylonian Empire in 538 B.C.E.* Jerusalem: Ben-Gurion of the Negev Press, 1997.

"Kawa IV (Khartoum SNM 2678 = Merowe Museum 52), ll. 7–9." Pls.7–8 in *The Temples of Kawa. Volume 1*. Edited by Miles Frederick Laming Macadam. Oxford University Excavations in Nubia. London: Oxford University Press, 1949.

"Kawa V (Ny Carlsberg Glyptotek Æ.I.N. 1712), ll. 22–27." Pls. 9–10 in *The Temples of Kawa. Volume 1*. Edited by Miles Frederick Laming Macadam. Oxford University Excavations in Nubia. London: Oxford University Press, 1949.

Keegan, John. *The Mask of Command*. London: Jonathan Cape, 1987.

Keegan, John. *A History of Warfare*. New York: Vintage Books, 1993.

Keegan, John. *The Face of Battle*. 2nd ed. London: Pimlico, 2004.

Kelle, Brad E. "Warfare Imagery." Pages 829–35 in *Dictionary of the Old Testament: Wisdom, Poetry & Writings*. Edited by Tremper Longman and Peter Enns. Downers Grove, IL: IVP Academic, 2008.

Kelm, George L., and Amihai Mazar. "Tel Batash (Timnah) Excavations: Second Preliminary Report (1981–1983)." Pages 93–120 in *Preliminary Reports of ASOR-Sponsored Excavations, 1981–83*. Edited by W. E. Rast. Bulletin of the American Schools of Oriental Research. Winona Lake, IN: Eisenbrauns, 1985.

Kelm, George L., and Amihay Mazar. *Timnah: A Biblical City in the Sorek Valley*. Winona Lake, IN: Eisenbrauns, 1995.

Kelm, George L., and Amihay Mazar. "Three Seasons of Excavations at Tel Batash—Biblical Timnah." *Bulletin of the American Schools of Oriental Research* 248 (1982): 1–36.

Kennedy, Paul. "The Fall and Rise of Military History." *Journal of Military History* 3 (1991): 8–12.

Keylor, William R. *The Legacy of the Great War: Peacemaking, 1919*. Problems in European Civilization Series. Boston, MA: Houghton Mifflin, 1998.

Kim, Hyun Chul Paul. "Isaiah 22: A Crux or a Clue in Isaiah 13–23?" Pages 3–18 in *Concerning the Nations: Essays on the Oracles against the Nations in Isaiah, Jeremiah and Ezekiel*. Edited by Andrew Mein. Library of Hebrew Bible/Old Testament Studies 612. London: Bloomsbury, 2015.

Kinnier Wilson, J. V. *The Legend of Etana: A New Edition*. Warminster: Aris & Phillips, 1985.

Kirkpatrick, A. F. *The Book of Psalms*. Cambridge: Cambridge University Press, 1902.

Kitchen, Kenneth A. *Ancient Orient and Old Testament*. Chicago, CA: InterVarsity Press, 1966.

Kitchen, Kenneth A. *Pharaoh Triumphant: The Life and Times of Ramesses II, King of Egypt*. Warminster: Aris & Phillips, 1982.

Kitchen, Kenneth A. "Egypt, the Levant and Assyria in 701 BC." Pages 243–53 in *ontes atque pontes: eine Festgabe für Hellmut Brunner*. Edited by Manfred Görg. Wiesbaden: Otto Harrassowitz, 1983.

Kitchen, Kenneth. A. *The Third Intermediate Period in Egypt (1100–650 B.C.)*. 2nd ed. Warminster: Aris & Phillips, 1986.

Kitchen, Kenneth A. "Egyptian Interventions in the Levant in Iron Age II." in *Symbiosis, Symbolism, and the Power of the Past: Canaan, Ancient Israel, and Their Neighbors from the Late Bronze Age through Roman Palaestina*. Edited by W. G. Dever and S. Gitin. Winona Lake, IN: Eisenbrauns, 2003.

Kletter, Raz. "Pots and Polities: Material Remains of Late Iron Age Judah in Relation to Its Political Borders." *Bulletin of the American Schools of Oriental Research* 314 (1999): 19–54.

Kloner, Amos, *Survey of Jerusalem: The Northeastern Sector, Introduction and Indices*. Archaeological Survey of Israel. Jerusalem: Israel Antiquities Authority, 2003.

Knauf, Ernst Axel. "Sennacherib at the Berezina." Pages 141–9 in *"Like a Bird in a Cage": The Invasion of Sennacherib in 701 BCE*. Edited by Lester L. Grabbe. Journal for the Study of the Old Testament: Supplement Series 363; European Seminar on Historical Methodology 4. London: Sheffield Academic Press, 2003.

Knauf, Ernst Axel. "The Glorious Days of Manasseh." Pages 164–88 in *Good Kings and Bad Kings*. Edited by Lester L. Grabbe. Journal for the Study of the Old Testament: Supplement Series 393. European Seminar on Historical Methodology 5. New York: T&T Clark, 2005.

Koch, Ido, and Oded Lipschits. "The Rosette Stamped Jar Handle System and the Kingdom of Judah at the End of the First Temple Period." *Zeitschrift des deutschen Palästina-Vereins* 129 (2013): 55–78.

Koch, Klaus. *The Prophets: Volume 1: The Assyrian Period*. Philadelphia, PA: Fortress, 1983.

Kochavi, Moshe. "Khirbet Rabûd = Debir." *Tel Aviv* 1 (1974): 2–33.

Kochavi, Moshe. "Rabud, Khirbet." Page 1252 in *The New Encyclopedia of Archaeological Excavations in the Holy Land*. Edited by Ephraim Stern, Ayelet Lewinson-Gilboa, and Joseph Aviram. New York: Hendrickson, 1993.

Kochavi, Moshe. "Rabud, Khirbet." Page 401 in *Oxford Encyclopedia for Archaeology in the Near East*. Edited by Eric M. Meyers. New York: Oxford University Press, 1997.

Kochavi, Moshe. "The Excavations at Tel Malhata—an Interim Report." *Qadmoniot* 115 (1998): 30–9.

Kooij, Arie van der. "Das assyrische Heer vor den Mauern Jerusalems im Jahr 701 v. Chr." *Zeitschrift des deutschen Palästina-Vereins* 102 (1986): 93–109.

Krueger, James S., and Francisco I. Pedraza. "Missing Voices: War Attitudes among Military Service-Connected Civilians." *Armed Forces & Society* 38 (2012): 391–412.

Kuhrt, Amélie. *The Ancient Near East: C. 3000–330 BC*. Routledge History of the Ancient World. London: Routledge, 1995.

Laato, Antti. "Hezekiah and the Assyrian Crisis in 701 BC." *Scandinavian Journal of the Old Testament* 2 (1987): 49–68.

Laato, Antti. *Who Is Immanuel? The Rise and the Foundering of Isaiah's Messianic Expectations*. Åbo, Finland: Åbo Akademy Press, 1988.

Laato, Antti. "Assyrian Propaganda and the Falsification of History in the Royal Inscriptions of Sennacherib." *Vetus Testamentum* 45 (1995): 198–226.
Lance, H. Darrell. "Royal Stamps and the Kingdom of Josiah." *Harvard Theological Review* 64 (1971): 315–32.
Lanskoy, Miriam. "When Personalities Clash: Assessing the 1994-1996 Russian-Chechen War." *Nationalities Papers* 28 (2000): 579–86.
Lapp, Nancy L. "Other Finds from the 1964 Campaign." Pages 109–13 in *Third campaign at Tell El-Ful: The Excavations of 1964*. Cambridge, MA: American Schools of Oriental Research, 1981.
Laxer, James. *Tecumseh and Brock: The War of 1812*. Berkeley, CA: House of Anansi Press, 2013.
Layard, Austen Henry. *Discoveries in the Ruins of Nineveh and Babylon*. London: J. Murray, 1853.
Le Moyne, J. "Les deux ambassades de Sennachérib à Jérusalem; Recherches sur l'évolution d'une tradition." Pages 149–53 in *Melanges bibliques rédigés en l'honneur de André Robert*. Paris: Bloud & Gay, 1957.
Leclant, Jean, and Jean Yoyotte. "Notes d'histoire et de civilisation éthiopiennes: À propos d'un ouvrage récent." *Bulletin de l'Institut français d'archéologie orientale* 51 (1952): 17–29.
Leeuwen, C. Van. "Sanchérib devant Jérusalem." *Old Testament Studies* 14 (1965): 245–72.
Lemche, Niels Peter. "On the Problems of Reconstructing Pre-Hellenistic Israelite (Palestinian) History." Pages 150–67 in *"Like a Bird in a Cage": The Invasion of Sennacherib in 701 BCE*. Edited by Lester L. Grabbe. Journal for the Study of the Old Testament: Supplement Series 363; European Seminar on Historical Methodology 4. London: Sheffield Academic Press, 2003.
Levenson, Jon Douglas. *Sinai and Zion: An Entry into the Jewish Bible*. New Voices in Biblical Studies. Minneapolis, MN: Winston Press, 1985.
Levine, Baruch A. "Assyrian Ideology and Israelite Monotheism." *Iraq* 67 (2005): 411–27.
Levine, Louis D. "Preliminary Remarks on the Historical Inscriptions of Sennacherib." Pages 58–75 in *History, Historiography and Interpretation*. Edited by Hayim Tadmor and Moshe Weinfeld. Jerusalem: Magnes, 1983.
Lewis, John David. *Nothing Less Than Victory: Decisive Wars and the Lessons of History*. Princeton, NJ: Princeton University Press, 2012.
Lichtheim, Miriam. *Ancient Egyptian Literature II: The New Kingdom*. Berkeley, CA: University of California Press, 1976.
Lipschits, Oded. *The Fall and Rise of Jerusalem: Judah under Babylonian Rule*. Winona Lake, IN: Eisenbrauns, 2005.
Lipschits, Oded. "The Changing Faces of Kingship in Judah under Assyrian Rule." Pages 116–38 in *The Changing Faces of Kingship in Syria-Palestine 1500–500 BCE*. Edited by Agustius Gianto and Peter Dubovský. Alter Orient und Altes Testament 459. Münster: Ugarit-Verlag, 2018.
Lipschits, Oded. "Judah under Assyrian Rule and the Early Phase of Stamping Jar Handles." Pages 337–55 in *Archaeology and History of Eighth-Century Judah*. Edited by Zev Farber and Jacob L. Wright. Ancient Near East Monographs 23. Atlanta, GA: SBL Press, 2018.
Lipschits, Oded. "The Long Seventh Century BCE: Archaeological and Historical Perspectives." Pages 9–44 in *The Last Century in the History of Judah: The Seventh Century BCE in Archaeological, Historical, and Biblical Perspectives*. Edited by Filip

Capek and Oded Lipschits, 2019. Ancient Israel and Its Literature 37. Atlanta, GA: SBL Press, 2019.

Lipschits, Oded, Omer Sergi, and Ido Koch. "Royal Judahite Jar Handles: Reconsidering the Chronology of the Lmlk Stamp Impressions." *Tel Aviv* 37 (2010): 3–32.

Lipschits, Oded, Yuval Gadot, Benjamin Arubas, and Manfred Oeming. *What Are the Stones Whispering? Ramat Rahel: 3000 Years of Forgotten History.* Winona Lake, IN: Eisenbrauns, 2017.

Lipschits, Oded, Yuval Gadot, Benny Arubas, and Manfred Oeming. "Palace and Village, Paradise and Oblivion: Unraveling the Riddles of Ramat Raḥel." *Near Eastern Archaeology* 74 (2011): 2–49.

Lipschits, Oded, Yuval Gadot, and Liora Freud. *Ramat-Raḥel III: Final Publication of Yohanan Aharoni's Excavations (1954, 1959–1962) 1–2.* Tel Aviv University, Sonia and Marco Nadler Institute of Archaeology Monograph Series 35. Winona Lake, IN: Eisenbrauns, 2016.

Liverani, Mario. *Israel's History and the History of Israel.* London: Equinox, 2005.

Lloyd, Alan B. "The Siege of Jerusalem by Sennacherib." Pages 211–20 in *Jerusalem's Survival, Sennacherib's Departure, and the Kushite Role in 701 BCE: An Examination of Henry Aubin's Rescue of Jerusalem.* Edited by Alice Ogden Bellis. Perspectives on Hebrew Scriptures and Its Contexts 32. Piscataway, NJ: Gorgias Press, 2020.

Luckenbill, Daniel David. *The Annals of Sennacherib.* University of Chicago Oriental Institute Publications, 2. Chicago, CA: University of Chicago Press, 1924.

Luckenbill, Daniel David. *Ancient Records of Assyria and Babylonia.* 2 vols. Chicago, CA: University of Chicago Press, 1926–1927. repr., New York: Greenwood, 1968.

Macadam, Miles Frederick Laming. *The Temples of Kawa.* Oxford University Excavations in Nubia. London: Oxford University Press, 1949.

Machinist, Peter. "Assyria and Its Image in the First Isaiah." *Journal of the American Oriental Society* 103 (1983): 719–37.

Machinist, Peter. "The Rab Saqeh at the Wall of Jerusalem: Israelite Identity in the Face of the Assyrian 'Other'." *Hebrew Studies* 41 (2000): 151–68.

Macintosh, A. A. *Isaiah XXI: A Palimpsest.* Cambridge: Cambridge University Press, 1980.

Magen, Y., and M. Dadon. "Nebi Samwil (Shmuel HaVani-Har Hasimha)." *Qadmoniot* 118 (1999): 62–77 (Hebrew).

Mahan, A. T. *Sea Power in Its Relations to the War of 1812.* London: S. Low, Marston, 1905.

Malcomson, Robert. *Historical Dictionary of the War of 1812.* Historical Dictionaries of War, Revolution, and Civil Unrest 31. Lanham, MD: Scarecrow Press, 2006.

Marks, Sally. "The Myths of Reparations." *Central European History* 11 (1978): 231.

Marti, Karl. *Das Buch Jesaja; Erklärt.* Edited by Karl Marti. Kurzer Hand-Commentar Zum Alten Testament 10. Tübingen: Mohr, 1900.

Martin, W. J. "Dischronologized' Narrative in the Old Testament." Pages 179–86 in *Congress Volume, Rome 1968.* Supplements to Vetus Testamentum 17. Leiden: Brill, 1969.

Master, Daniel M. "From the Buqeʿah to Ashkelon." Pages 305–17 in *Exploring the Longue Durée: Essays in Honor of Lawrence E. Stager.* Edited by J. David Schloen. Winona Lake, IN: Eisenbrauns, 2009.

Matty, Nazek Khalid. *Sennacherib's Campaign against Judah and Jerusalem in 701 B.C.: A Historical Reconstruction.* Beihefte zur Zeitschrift für die alttestamentliche Wissenschaft 487. Berlin: de Gruyter, 2016.

Mayer, Walter. *Politik und Kriegskunst der Assyrer.* Abhandlungen zur Literatur Alt-Syrien-Palästinas und Mesopotamiens 9. Münster: Ugarit, 1995.

Mayer, Walter. "Sennacherib's Campaign of 701 BCE: The Assyrian View." Pages 168–200 in *"Like a Bird in a Cage": The Invasion of Sennacherib in 701 BCE*. Edited by Lester L. Grabbe. Journal for the Study of the Old Testament: Supplement Series 393. European Seminar on Historical Methodology 5. London: Sheffield Academic Press, 2003.

Mayes, A. D. H. *The Story of Israel between Settlement and Exile: A Redactional Study of the Deuteronomistic History*. London: SCM Press, 1983.

Mazar, Amihai. "Three Israelite Sites in the Hills of Judah and Ephraim." *Biblical Archaeologist* 45 (1982): 167–78.

Mazar, Amihai. *Archaeology of the Land of the Bible: 10,000–586 BCE*. Anchor Bible Reference Library 1. New Haven, CT: Yale University Press, 1990.

Mazar, Amihai. "Batash, Tel." The Oxford Encyclopedia of Archaeology in the Near East. Edited by E. M. Meyers, vol. 1. New York: Oxford University Press, (1997): 281–3.

Mazar, Amihai. "The Divided Monarchy: Comments on Some Archaeological Issues." Pages 159–80 in *The Quest for the Historical Israel. Debating Archaeology and the History of Early Israel*. Edited by Israel Finkelstein and Amihai Mazar. Archaeology and Biblical Studies 17. Atlanta, GA: Society of Biblical Literature, 2007.

Mazar, Amihai, George L. Kelm, and Nava Panitz-Cohen. *Timnah (Tel Batash) II: The Finds from the First Millennium BCE (Text)*. Qedem 42. Jerusalem: Institute of Archaeology, Hebrew University of Jerusalem, 2011.

Mazar, B. "The Cities of the Territory of Dan." *Israel Exploration Journal* 10 (1960): 65–77.

McClellan, Thomas L. "Towns to Fortresses: The Transformation of Urban Life in Judah from 8th to 7th Century BC." *Society of Biblical Literature Seminar Papers* 13 (1978): 277–86.

McCown, Chester Charlton, Joseph Wampler, and William Frederic Badè. *Tell En-Nasbeh Excavated under the Direction of the Late William Frederic Badè*. Berkeley, CA: The Palestine Institute of Pacific School of Religion and the American Schools of Oriental Research, 1947.

McKenzie, Steven L. *The Chronicler's Use of the Deuteronomistic History*. Harvard Semitic Monographs 33. Atlanta, GA: Scholars Press, 1985.

McNeill, William H. "Modern European History." Pages 95–112 in *Past before Us: Contemporary Historical Writing in the United States*. Edited by Michael Kammen. Ithaca, NY: Cornell University Press, 1980.

Meinhold, Johannes. *Die Jesajaerzählungen, Jesaja 36–39: eine historisch-kritische Untersuchung*. Göttingen: Vandenhoeck und Ruprecht, 1898.

Mienis, H. K. "Molluscs." Pages 122–30 in *Excavations at the City of David 1978–1985, Vol. 3: Stratigraphical, Environmental, and Other Reports*. Edited by A. De Groot and D. T. Ariel. Qedem 33. Jerusalem: Institute of Archaeology, Hebrew University of Jerusalem, 1992.

Mill, John Stuart. *The Contest in America*. Reprinted from *Fraser's Magazine*. Boston, MA: Little, Brown and Company, 1862.

Millard, A. R. "Sennacherib's Attack on Hezekiah." *Tyndale Bulletin* 36 (1985): 61–77.

Millard, A. R. "Large Numbers in the Assyrian Royal Inscriptions." Pages 213–22 in *Ah, Assyria ... Studies in Assyrian History and Ancient Near Eastern Historiography Presented to Hayim Tadmor*. Edited by Mordechai Cogan and Israel Ephàl. Scripta Hierosolymitana 33. Jerusalem: Magnes Press, 1991.

Millard, A. R. *The Eponyms of the Assyrian Empire 910–612 BC*. State Archives of Assyria Studies 2. Helsinki: Neo-Assyrian Text Corpus Project, 1994.

Miller, James Maxwell, and John Haralson Hayes. *A History of Ancient Israel and Judah*. 1st ed. Philadelphia, PA: Westminster, 1986.

Mittmann, Siegfried. "Hiskia und die Philister." *Journal of Northwest Semitic Languages* 16 (1990): 91–106.

Montgomery, James A., and Henry S. Gehman. *A Critical and Exegetical Commentary on the Book of Kings*. International Critical Commentary. Edinburgh: T&T Clark, 1951.

Morgan-Owen, David. "In Defence of Military History," *Defence in Depth*, July 22, 2016: https://defenceindepth.co/2016/07/22/in-defence-of-military-history/

Motyer, J. A. *The Prophecy of Isaiah: An Introduction & Commentary*. Downers Grove, IL: InterVarsity Press, 1993.

Mousseau, Michael. "The End of War: How a Robust Marketplace and Liberal Hegemony Are Leading to Perpetual World Peace." *International Security* 44 (2019): 160–96.

Mowinckel, Sigmund. *He That Cometh*. Oxford: B. Blackwell, 1959.

Mowinckel, Sigmund. *Psalmenstudien*. Amsterdam: P. Schippers, 1966.

Mueller, John. "Changing Attitudes to War. The Impact of the First World War." *British Journal of Political Science*, 21 (1991): 1–28.

Mueller, John. "War Has Almost Ceased to Exist: An Assessment." *Political Science Quarterly* 124 (2009): 297–321.

Müller, Reinhard. *Ausgebliebene Einsicht: Jesajas "Verstockungsauftrag" (Jes 6,9–11) und die judäische Politik am Ende des 8. Jahrhunderts*. Biblisch-Theologische Studien 124. Neukirchen-Vluyn: Neukirchener Verlag, 2012.

Na'aman, Nadav. "Sennacherib's "Letter to God" on His Campaign to Judah." *Bulletin of the American Schools of Oriental Research* 214 (1974): 25–39.

Na'aman, Nadav. "Sennacherib's Campaign to Judah and the Date of the Lmlk Stamps." *Vetus Testamentum* 29 (1979): 61–86.

Na'aman, Nadav. "Historical and Chronological Notes on the Kingdoms of Israel and Judah in the 8th Century BC." *Vetus Testamentum* 36 (1986): 71–92.

Na'aman, Nadav. "Forced Participation in Alliances in the Course of the Assyrian Campaigns to the West." Pages 80–98 in *Ah, Assyria ... Studies in Assyrian History and Ancient Near Eastern Historiography Presented to Hayim Tadmor*. Edited by Mordechai Cogan and Israel Eph'al. Jerusalem: Magnes Press, 1991.

Na'aman, Nadav. "Population Changes in Palestine Following Assyrian Deportations." *Tel Aviv* 20 (1993): 104–24.

Na'aman, Nadav. "Hezekiah and the Kings of Assyria." *Tel Aviv* 21 (1994): 235–54.

Na'aman, Nadav. "The Deuteronomist and Voluntary Servitude to Foreign Powers." *Journal for the Study of the Old Testament* 65 (1995): 37–53.

Na'aman, Nadav. "Sargon II and the Rebellion of the Cypriote Kings against Shilta of Tyre." *Orientalia, Nova Series* 67 (1998): 239–47.

Na'aman, Nadav. "Ostracon 40 from Arad Reconsidered." Pages 199–204 in *Saxa loquentur: Studien zur Archäologie Palästinas/Israels: Festschrift für Volkmar Fritz zum 65. Geburtstag*. Edited by Cornelis Gijsbert den Hertog, Ulrich Hübner, and Stefan Münger. Alter Orient und Altes Testament, 302. Münster: Ugarit, 2003.

Na'aman, Nadav. "Updating the Messages: Hezekiah's Second Prophetic Story (2 Kings 19.9b–35) and the Community of Babylonian Deportees." Pages 200–20 in *"Like a Bird in a Cage": The Invasion of Sennacherib in 701 BCE*. Edited by Lester L. Grabbe. Journal for the Study of the Old Testament: Supplement Series 363; European Seminar on Historical Methodology 4. London: Sheffield Academic Press, 2003.

Na'aman, Nadav. *Ancient Israel and Its Neighbors: Interactions and Counteractions*. Winona Lake, IN: Eisenbrauns, 2005.

Na'aman, Nadav. "Let Other Kingdoms Struggle with the Great Powers–You, Judah, Pay the Tribute and Hope for the Best: The Foreign Policy of the Kings of Judah in the Ninth-Eighth Centuries BCE." Pages 55–73 in *Isaiah's Vision of Peace in Biblical and Modern International Relations: Swords into Plowshares*. New York: Palgrave Macmillan, 2008.

Nadali, Davide. "Sieges and Similes of Sieges in the Royal Annals: The Conquest of Damascus by Tiglath-Pileser III." *KASKAL* 6 (2009): 137–49.

Nelson, Richard D. *The Double Redaction of the Deuteronomistic History*. Journal for the Study of the Old Testament: Supplement Series 18. Sheffield: JSOT Press, 1981.

Nielsen, Kirsten. *There Is Hope for a Tree: The Tree as Metaphor in Isaiah*. Journal for the Study of the Old Testament Supplement Series 65. Sheffield: JSOT Press, 1989.

Oded, Bustenay. "'The Command of the God' as a Reason for Going to War in the Assyrian Royal Inscriptions." Pages 223–30 in *Ah, Assyria ... Studies in Assyrian History and Ancient Near Eastern Historiography Presented to Hayim Tadmor*. Scripta Hierosolymitana 33. Jerusalem: Magnes Press, 1991.

Ofer, Avi. "The Monarchic Period in the Judaean Highland: A Spatial Overview." Pages 14–37 in *Studies in the Archaeology of the Iron Age in Israel and Jordan*. Edited by Amihay Mazar. Journal for the Study of the Old Testament Supplement Series 331. Sheffield: Sheffield Academic Press, 2001.

Ollenburger, Ben C. *Zion: The City of the Great King*. Journal for the Study of the Old Testament Supplement Series 41. Sheffield: JSOT Press, 1987.

Ombrain, Nicholas J. D. "Comparative Studies and Military History: A Key to the Future of Historical Scholarship in the University." *Dalhousie Review* 51 (1971): 18–23.

Oren, E. D. "Sera', Tel." Pages 1329–35 in *The New Encyclopedia of Archaeological Excavations in the Holy Land*. Edited by E. Stern. New York: Simon & Schuster, 1993.

Oren, E. D. "Sera', Tel." Pages 1–2 in *The Oxford Encyclopedia of Archaeology in the Near East*. Edited by E. M. Meyers. New York: Oxford University Press, 1997.

Ortlund, Eric. "Reversed (Chrono-)Logical Sequence in Isaiah 1–39: Some Implications for Theories of Redaction." *Journal for the Study of the Old Testament* 35 (2010): 209–24.

Oswalt, John N. *The Book of Isaiah: Chapters 1–39*. New International Commentary on the Old Testament. Grand Rapids, MI: Eerdmans, 1986.

Panitz-Cohen, Nava. "A Salvage Excavation in the New Market in Beer-Sheba: New Light on Iron Age IIb Occupation at Beer-Sheba." *Israel Exploration Journal* 55 (2005): 143–55.

Paret, Peter. "The New Military History." *Parameters* 21 (1991): 10–18.

Paris, Michael. *Warrior Nation: Images of War in British Popular Culture, 1850–2000*. London: Reaktion Books, 2000.

Parker, Bradley J. *The Mechanics of Empire: The Northern Frontier of Assyria as a Case Study in Imperial Dynamics*. Helsinki: Neo-Assyrian Text Corpus Project, 2001.

Parker, Richard A. "The Length of the Reign of Amasis and the Beginning of the Twenty-Sixth Dynasty." *Mitteilungen des Deutschen Archäologischen Instituts, Abteilung Kairo* 15 (1957): 208–12.

Parpola, Simon. "Assyria's Expansion in the Eighth and Seventh Centuries and Its Long-Term Repercussions in the West." Pages 99–111 in *Symbiosis, Symbolism, and the Power of the Past*. Edited by William G. Dever and Seymour Gittin. Winona Lake, IN: Eisenbrauns, 2003.

Payraudeau, Frédéric. "Retour Sur La Succession Shabaqo-Shabataqo." *NeHet: Revue numérique d'Égyptologie* 1 (2014): 115–27.

Peckham, Brian. *The Composition of the Deuteronomistic History*. Harvard Semitic Monographs 35. Atlanta, GA: Scholars Press, 1985.

Person, Raymond F. *The Deuteronomic School: History, Social Setting, and Literature.* Studies in Biblical Literature 2. Atlanta, GA: Society of Biblical Literature, 2002.

Petrie, William Matthew Flinders. *Gerar.* Publications of the Egyptian Research Account 43. London: British School of Archaeology in Egypt, 1928.

Pinker, Steve. *The Better Angels of Our Nature: Why Violence Has Declined.* New York: Viking, 2011.

Polner, Murray, and Thomas E. Woods. *We Who Dared to Say No to War: American Antiwar Writing from 1812 to Now.* New York: Basic Books, 2008.

Pope, Jeremy. "Sennacherib's Departure and the Principle of Laplace." Pages 113–66 in *Jerusalem's Survival, Sennacherib's Departure, and the Kushite Role in 701 BCE: An Examination of Henry Aubin's Rescue of Jerusalem.* Edited by Alice Ogden Bellis. Perspectives on Hebrew Scriptures and Its Contexts 32. Piscataway, NJ: Gorgias Press, 2020.

Pritchard, James B. *Gibeon, Where the Sun Stood Still: The Discovery of the Biblical City.* Princeton, NJ: Princeton University Press, 1962.

Provan, Iain W. *Hezekiah and the Books of Kings: A Contribution to the Debate About the Composition of the Deuteronomistic History.* Beihefte zur Zeitschrift für die alttestamentliche Wissenschaft 172. Berlin: de Gruyter, 1988.

Punamaki, R. L. "Can Ideological Commitment Protect Children's Psychological Wellbeing in Situations of Political Violence?" *Child Development* 67 (1996): 55–69.

Punamaki, R. L., S. Quota, and E. Sarrai. "Models of Traumatic Experiences and Children's Psychological Adjustment: The Roles of Perceived Parenting and the Children's Own Resources and Activity." *Child Development* 68 (1997): 718–28.

Quinn-Miscall, Peter D. *Isaiah.* Readings: A New Biblical Commentary. Sheffield: Sheffield Phoenix Press, 2006.

Rad, Gerhard von. *Old Testament Theology.* Translated by D. M. G. Stalker. 2 vols. New York: Harper & Row, 1962.

Radner, K. "The Assyrian King and His Scholars: The Syro-Anatolia and the Egyptian Schools." in *Of God(S), Trees, Kings, and Scholars: Neo-Assyrian and Related Studies in Honour of Simo Parpola.* Edited by Mikko Luukko, Saana Svärd, and Raija Mattila. Studia Orientalia 106. Helsinki: Finnish Oriental Society, 2009.

Radner, K. "After Eltekeh: Royal Hostages from Egypt at the Assyrian Court." Pages 471–9 in *"Stories of Long Ago": Festschrift für Michael D. Roaf.* Edited by Kai Kaniuth Heather D. Baker, and Adelheid Otto. Alter Orient und Altes Testament 397 Münster: Ugarit-Verlag, 2012.

Rainey, Anson F. "Taharqa and Syntax." *Tel Aviv* 3 (1976): 38–41.

Rainey, Anson F. "Manasseh, King of Judah, in the Whirlpool of the Seventh Century B.C.E." Pages 147–64 in *Kinattiltu Sa Ddirdti. Raphael Kutscher Memorial Volume.* Edited by Anson F. Rainey. Tel Aviv: Institute of Archaeology. Tel Aviv: Occasional Publications, 1993.

Rainey, Anson F., and R. Steven Notley. *The Sacred Bridge: Carta's Atlas of the Biblical World.* Jerusalem: Carta, 2006.

Rawlinson, George. *The Five Great Monarchies of the Ancient Eastern World: The Second Monarchy: Assyria.* 4 vols. London: John Murray, 1864.

Rawlinson, Henry. "Assyrian Antiquities." *The Athenaeum* 1243 (August 23, 1851): 902–3.

Redford, Donald B. *Egypt, Canaan, and Israel in Ancient Times.* Princeton, NJ: Princeton University Press, 1992.

Redford, Donald B. "Taharqa in Western Asia and Libya." *EI* 24 (1993): 188–91.

Reich, Ronny, and Baruch Brandl. "Gezer under Assyrian Rule." *Palestine Exploration Quarterly* 117 (1985): 41-54.
Roberts, J. J. M. "Yahweh's Foundation in Zion (Isa 28:16)." *Journal of Biblical Literature* 106 (1987): 27-45.
Roberts, J. J. M. "Solomon's Jerusalem and the Zion Tradition." Pages 163-70 in *Jerusalem in Bible and Archaeology: The First Temple Period*. Edited by Andrew G. Vaughn and Ann E. Killebrew. Society of Biblical Literature Symposium Series 18. Leiden: Brill, 2003.
Roberts, J. J. M. "Egypt, Assyria, Isaiah, and the Ashdod Affair: An Alternative Proposal." Pages 265-83 in *Jerusalem in Bible and Archaeology: The First Temple Period*. Atlanta, GA: SBL Press, 2003.
Roberts, J. J. M. *First Isaiah: A Commentary*. Hermeneia. Minneapolis, MN: Fortress Press, 2015.
Rofé, Alexander. *The Prophetical Stories: The Narratives About the Prophets in the Hebrew Bible, Their Literary Types and History*. Publications of the Perry Foundation for Biblical Research in the Hebrew University of Jerusalem. Jerusalem: Magnes Press, Hebrew University, 1988.
Rogers, Robert William. *Cuneiform Parallels to the Old Testament*. New York: Eaton & Mains, 1912.
Rohland, Edzard. "Die Bedeutung der Erwahlungstraditionen Israels für die Eschatologie der alttestamentlichen Propheten." PhD Dissertation, Heidelberg University, 1956.
Römer, Thomas. *The So-Called Deuteronomistic History: A Sociological, Historical, and Literary Introduction*. London: T&T Clark, 2005.
Roosevelt, Theodore. *The Naval War of 1812*. Modern Library War. New York: Modern Library, 2004.
Rost, Paul. *Die Keilschrifttexte Tiglat-Pilesers III nach den Papierabklatschen und Originalen des Britischen Museums; neu hrsg*. Leipzig: Pfeiffer, 1893.
Routledge, Robin L. "The Siege and Deliverance of the City of David in Isaiah 29:1-8." *Tyndale Bulletin* 43 (1992): 181-90.
Rowley, Harold Henry. "Hezekiah's Reform and Rebellion." *Bulletin of the John Rylands University Library of Manchester* 44 (1962): 395-431.
Rudman, Dominic. "Is the Rabshakeh Also among the Prophets? A Rhetorical Study of 2 Kings XVIII 17-35." *Vetus Testamentum* 50 (2000): 100-10.
Russell, John Malcolm. *The Writing on the Wall: Studies in the Architectural Context of Late Assyrian Palace Inscriptions*. Mesopotamian Civilizations 9. Winona Lake, IN: Eisenbrauns, 1999.
Saggs, H. W. F. "The Nimrud Letters, 1952-Part I." *Iraq* 17 (1955): 21-56.
Saggs, H. W. F. "The Nimrud Letters, 1952-Part II." *Iraq* 17 (1955): 126-60.
Saggs, H. W. F. "The Nimrud Letters, 1952-Part III." *Iraq* 18 (1956): 40-56.
Saggs, H. W. F. *The Nimrud Letters, 1952*. Cuneiform Texts from Nimrud 5. London: British School of Archaeology in Iraq, 2001.
Sass, Benjamin. "Arabs and Greeks in Late First Temple Jerusalem." *Palestine Exploration Quarterly* 122 (1990): 59-61.
Sauren, Herbert. "Sennachérib, les Arabes, les déportés Juifs." *Die Welt des Orients* 16 (1985): 80-99.
Seger, Joe D. "Tel Halif." Pages 553-9 in *New Encyclopedia of Archaeological Excavations in the Holy Land*. Jerusalem: Israel Exploration Society, 1993.
Seitz, Christopher R. *Zion's Final Destiny: The Development of the Book of Isaiah: A Reassessment of Isaiah 36-39*. Minneapolis, MN: Fortress, 1991.

Seitz, Christopher R. "Account and the Annals of Sennacherib: A Reassessment." *Journal for the Study of the Old Testament* 58 (1993): 47–57.
Semmel, Bernard. *Marxism and the Science of War*. Oxford: Oxford University Press, 1981.
Shea, William H. "Sennacherib's Second Palestinian Campaign." *Journal of Biblical Literature* 104 (1985): 401–18.
Shea, William H. "The New Tirhakah Text and Sennacherib's Second Palestinian Campaign." *Andrews University Seminary Studies* 35 (1997): 181–7.
Shea, William H. "Jerusalem under Siege: Did Sennacherib Attack Twice?" *Biblical Archaeology Review* 25 (1999): 36.
Shea, William H. "Hezekiah, Sennacherib and Tirhakah: A Brief Rejoinder." *Near East Archaeological Society Bulletin* 45 (2000): 37–8.
Shiloh, Y. "South Arabian Inscriptions from the City of David." *Palestine Exploration Quarterly* 119 (1987): 9–18.
Simons, William E. "The Study of History and the Military Leader." *Military Affairs* 26 (1962): 22–7.
Smelik, Klaas A. D. "Distortion of Old Testament Prophecy: The Purpose of Isaiah XXXVI and XXXVII." *Oudtestamentische Studiën* 24 (1986): 70–93.
Smelik, Klaas A. D. "King Hezekiah Advocates True Prophecy: Remarks on Isaiah XXXVI and XXXVII//II Kings XVIII and XIX." Pages 93–128 in *Converting the Past: Studies in Ancient Israelite and Moabite Historiography*. Edited by Klaas A. D. Smelik. Old Testament Studies, 28. Leiden: Brill, 1992.
Smend, Rudolf. "Das Gesetz und die Völker: Ein Beitrag zur deuteronomistishen Redaktionsgeschichte." Pages 494–509 in *Probleme Biblischer Theologie: Festschrift Gerhard Von Rad*. Edited by Hans Walter Wolff. Munich: Chr. Kaiser, 1971.
Smith, George Adam. *Jerusalem; The Topography, Economics and History from the Earliest Times to A.D. 70*. 2 vols. London: Hodder and Stoughton, 1907.
Snow, Peter. *When Britain Burned the White House: The 1814 Invasion of Washington*. New York: Thomas Dunne Books, 2014.
Spalinger, Anthony. "Esarhaddon and Egypt: An Analysis of the First Invasion of Egypt." *Orientalia* 43 (1974): 296–326.
Spalinger, Anthony. "The Foreign Policy of Egypt Preceding the Assyrian Conquest." *Chronique d'Egypt* 53 (1978): 22–47.
Stade, Bernhard. "Miscellen: Anmerkungen zu 2 Kö. 15–21." *Zeitschrift für die alttestamentliche Wissenschaft* 6 (1886): 156–89.
Stager, Lawrence E. "Farming in the Judean Desert During the Iron Age." *Bulletin of the American Schools of Oriental Research* 221 (1976): 145–58.
Stager, Lawrence E. "The Impact of the Sea Peoples in Canaan (1185–1050 BCE)." Pages 332–48 in *The Archaeology of Society in the Holy Land*. Edited by Thomas E. Levy. London: Leicester University Press, 1995.
Stavrakopoulou, Francesca. *King Manasseh and Child Sacrifice: Biblical Distortions of Historical Realities*. Berlin: de Gruyter, 2004.
Stern, Ephraim. "Azekah." Pages 123–4 in *The New Encyclopedia of Archaeological Excavations in the Holy Land I*. Edited by Joseph Aviram, Ephraim Stern, and Ayelet Lewinson-Gilboa. New York: Simon & Schuster; Israel Exploration Society & Carta, 1993.
Stern, Ephraim. "Zafit, Tel." Pages 1522–4 in *The New Encyclopedia of Archaeological Excavations in the Holy Land IV*. Edited by Joseph Aviram, Ephraim Stern, and Ayelet Lewinson-Gilboa. New York: Simon & Schuster; Israel Exploration Society & Carta, 1993.

Stern, Ephraim. "The Eastern Border of the Kingdom of Judah." Pages 399–409 in *Scripture and Other Artifacts: Essays on the Bible and Archaeology in Honor of Philip J. King*. Edited by Michael D. Coogan, Cheryl J. Exum, and Lawrence E. Stager. Louisville, KY: Westminster John Knox, 1994.

Stern, Ephraim. *Archaeology of the Land of the Bible. Volume II: The Assyrian, Babylonian, and Persian Periods, 732–332 BCE*. Anchor Bible Reference Library 11. New York: Doubleday, 2001.

Stiglitz, Joseph, and Linda Bilmes. "The True Cost of the Iraq War: $3 Trillion and Beyond." *Washington Post*, September 5, 2010.

Strawn, Brent A. "Herodotus' History 2.141 and the Deliverance of Jerusalem: On Parallels, Sources, and Histories of Ancient Israel." Pages 210–38 in *Israel's Prophets and Israel's Past: Essays on the Relationship of Prophetic Texts and Israelite History in Honor of John H. Hayes*. Edited by Brad E. Kelle and Megan Bishop Moore. Library of Hebrew Bible/Old Testament Studies 446. New York: T&T Clark, 2006.

Streck, Maximilian. *Assurbanipal und die letzten assyrischen Könige bis zum Untergange Ninivehs*. Vorderasiatische Bibliothek 7 Stück. Leipzig: J. C. Hinrichs, 1916.

Summers, Harry G. *On Strategy: A Critical Analysis of the Vietnam War*. Novato, CA: Presidio Press, 1982.

Suriano, Matthew. "A Place in the Dust: Text, Topography and a Toponymic Note on Micah 1:10–12a." *Vetus Testamentum* 60 (2010): 433–44.

Swanson, Neil Harmon. *The Perilous Fight, Being a Little Known and Much Abused Chapter of Our National History in Our Second War of Independence and a True Narrative of the Battle of Godly Wood and the Attack on Fort McHenry, More Suitably Described as the Battle of Baltimore ... To Which Is Added Some Notice of the Circumstances Attending the Writing of the Star Spangled Banner ... Recounted Mainly from Contemporary Records by Neil H. Swanson*. New York: Farrar and Rinehart, 1945.

Sweeney, Marvin A. *Isaiah 1–4 and the Post-Exilic Understanding of the Isaianic Tradition*. Beihefte zur Zeitschrift für die alttestamentliche Wissenschaft 171. Berlin: Walter de Gruyter, 1988.

Sweeney, Marvin A. *Isaiah 1–39: With an Introduction to Prophetic Literature*. Forms of the Old Testament Literature 16. Grand Rapids, MI: Eerdmans, 1996.

Sweeney, Marvin A. *I & II Kings: A Commentary*. Old Testament Library. Louisville, KY: Westminster John Knox, 2007.

Swift, Jamie, and Ian McKay. "False Memories of the War of 1812 or Glorifying War ... Then and Now." *Pace Magazine* 29 (2013): 16.

Tadmor, Hayim. "The Campaigns of Sargon II of Assur: A Chronological-Historical Study." *Journal of Cuneiform Studies* 12 (1958): 77–100.

Tadmor, Hayim. "Philistia under Assyrian Rule." *The Biblical Archaeologist* 29 (1966): 86–102.

Tadmor, Hayim. "Sennacherib's Campaign to Judah: Historiographical and Historical Considerations." *Zion* 50 (1984): 65–80.

Tadmor, Hayim. *The Inscriptions of Tiglath-Pileser III, King of Assyria: Critical Edition, with Introductions, Translations and Commentary*. Jerusalem: Israel Academy of Sciences and Humanities, 1994.

Tadmor, Hayim. "Sennacherib's Campaign to Judah: Historiographical and Historical Considerations." Pages 653–75 in *"With My Many Chariots I Have Gone up the Heights of Mountains:" Historical and Literary Studies on Ancient Mesopotamia and Israel*. Edited by Mordechai Cogan. Zion. Jerusalem: Israel Exploration Society, 2011.

Tatum, Lynn. "King Manasseh and the Royal Fortress at Horvat 'Uza." *The Biblical Archaeologist* 54 (1991): 136–45.

"The Conservative Case against War." *Wilson Quarterly* 38 (2014): 16–18.

Thiele, Edwin R. *Mysterious Numbers of the Hebrew Kings: A Reconstruction of the Chronology of the Kingdoms of Israel and Judah*. Chicago, CA: University of Chicago Press, 1951.

Thureau-Dangin, F. *Une relation de la huitième campagne de Sargon (714 av. J.-C.)*. Musée du Louvre Département des antiquités orientales Textes cunéiformes 3. Paris: P. Geuthner, 1912.

Tilly, Charles. *Big Structures, Large Processes, Huge Comparisons*. Russell Sage Foundation 75th Anniversary Series. New York: Russell Sage Foundation, 1984.

Timm, Stefan. *Moab zwischen den Mächten: Studien zu historischen Denkmälern und Texten*. Ägypten und Altes Testament 17. Wiesbaden: O. Harrassowitz, 1989.

Toombs, Lawrence E. "Tell El-Ḥesi." Pages 555–8 in *Biblical Archaeology Today, 1990: Proceedings of the Second International Congress on Biblical Archaeology, Jerusalem, June-July 1990*. Jerusalem: Israel Exploration Society, 1993.

Torabian, Saba, and Marina Abalakina. "Attitudes toward War in the United States and Iran." *Iranian Studies* 45 (2012): 463–78.

Török, László. *The Kingdom of Kush: Handbook of the Napatan-Meroitic Civilization*. Handbuch der Orientalistik Erste Abteilung, Nahe und der Mittlere Osten 31. Leiden: Brill, 1997.

Tufnell, Olga. "Excavations at Tell Ed-Duweir, Palestine, Directed by the Late J. L. Starkey, 1932–1938." *Palestine Exploration Quarterly* 82 (1950): 65–80.

Tufnell, Olga, Margaret A. Murray, and David Diringer, eds. *Lachish III (Tell Ed-Duweir): The Iron Age*. Oxford: Oxford University Press, 1953.

Turner, Wesley B. *The War of 1812: The War That Both Sides Won*. Toronto: Dundurn Press, 2000.

Uehlinger, Christoph. "Clio in a World of Pictures—Another Look at the Lachish Reliefs from Sennacherib's Southwest Palace at Nineveh." Pages 221–305 in *"Like a Bird in a Cage": The Invasion of Sennacherib in 701 BCE*. Edited by Lester L. Grabbe. Journal for the Study of the Old Testament: Supplement Series 363; European Seminar on Historical Methodology 4. London: Sheffield Academic Press, 2003.

Uffenheimer, Benjamin. "The 'Desert of the Sea' Pronouncement (Isaiah 21:1–10)." Pages 677–88 in *Pomegranates and Golden Bells: Studies in Biblical, Jewish, and Near Eastern Ritual, Law, and Literature in Honor of Jacob Milgrom*. Winona Lake, IN: Eisenbrauns, 1995.

Ungnad, Arthur. "Die Zahl der von Sanherib deportierten Judäer." *Zeitschrift für die alttestamentliche Wissenschaft* 59 (1942): 199–202.

Ussishkin, David. *The Conquest of Lachish by Sennacherib*. Publications of the Institute of Archaeology 6. Tel Aviv: Tel Aviv University, Institute of Archaeology, 1982.

Ussishkin, David. "The Assyrian Attack on Lachish: The Archaeological Evidence from the Southwest Corner of the Site." *Tel Aviv* 17 (1990): 53–86.

Ussishkin, David. "A Synopsis of the Stratigraphical, Chronological and Historical Issues." Pages 50–119 in *The Renewed Archaeological Excavations at Lachish (1973–1994)*. Edited by David Ussishkin. Tel Aviv: Institute of Archaeology of Tel Aviv University, 2004.

Ussishkin, David. "Sennacherib's Campaign to Philistia and Judah: Ekron, Lachish, and Jerusalem." Pages 339–58 in *Essays on Ancient Israel in Its Near Eastern Context: A*

Tribute to Nadav Naʾaman. Edited by Yairah Amit, Ehud Ben Zvi, Israel Finkelstein, and Oded Lipschits. Winona Lake, IN: Eisenbrauns, 2006.

Ussishkin, David. "The Dating of the Lmlk Storage Jars and Its Implications: Rejoinder to Lipschits, Sergi, and Koch." *Tel Aviv* 38 (2011): 220–40.

Van Beek, Gus W. "Digging up Tell Jemmeh." *Archaeology* 36 (1983): 12–19.

Van de Mieroop, Marc. *A History of Ancient Egypt*. Blackwell History of the Ancient World. Chichester, West Sussex: Wiley-Blackwell, 2011.

Van der Brugge, Caroline. "Of Production, Trade, Profit and Destruction: An Economic Interpretation of Sennacherib's third campaign." *Journal of the Economic and Social History of the Orient* 60 (2017): 292–335.

Vaughn, Andrew G. *Theology, History, and Archaeology in the Chronicler's Account of Hezekiah*. Archaeology and Biblical Studies 4. Atlanta, GA: Scholars Press, 1999.

Vaughn, Andrew G. "Should All of the Lmlk Jars Still Be Attributed to Hezekiah? Yes!" Pages 357–62 in *Archaeology and History of Eighth-Century Judah*. Edited by Zev Farber and Jacob L. Wright. Ancient Near East Monographs 23. Atlanta, GA: SBL Press 2018.

Veijola, Timo. *Die ewige Dynastie: David und die Entstehung seiner Dynastie nach der deuteronomistischen Darstellung*. Annalae Academiae Scientiarum Fennica 193. Helsinki: Suomalainen Tiedeakatemia, 1975.

Vaughn, Andrew G. *Verheißung in der Krise: Studien zur Literatur und Theologie der Exilszeit anhand des 89. Psalms*. Annales Academiae Scientiarum Fennicae, Series B 220. Helsinki: Suomalainen Tiedeakatemia, 1982.

Vermeylen, Jacques. *Du prophète Isaïe à l'apocalyptique: Isaïe, I-XXXV, miroir d'un demi-millénaire d'expérience religieuse en Israël*. Etudes bibliques. Paris: J. Gabalda, 1978.

Vermeylen, Jacques. "Hypothèses sur l'Origine d'Isaïe 36–39." Pages 95–118 in *Studies in the Book of Isaiah*. Edited by J. van Ruiten and M. Vervenne. Leuven: Leuven University Press and Peeters, 1997.

Vidal, Jordi. "Some Remarks on the Battle of Altaqu." in *The Perfumes of Seven Tamarisks. Studies in Honour of Wilfred G.E. Watson*. Edited by Olmo Lete, Gregorio del, Jordi Vidal, and Nick Wyatt. Alter Orient und Altes Testament 394. Münster: Ugarit-Verlag, 2012.

Vogt, Ernst. *Der Aufstand Hiskias und die Belagerung Jerusalems 701 v. Chr.* Rome: Biblical Institute, 1986.

Wagner, Thomas. "From Salvation to Doom: Isaiah's Message in the Hezekiah Story." Pages 92–103 in *Prophecy and Prophets in Stories: Papers Read at the Fifth Message of the Edinburgh Prophecy Network, Utrecht, October 2013*. Edited by Bob Becking and Hans Barstad. Oudtestamentische Studiën 65. Leiden: Brill, 2015.

Wallace, W. Stewart. *The Story of Laura Secord: A Study in Historical Evidence*. Toronto: Macmillan, 1932.

Walt, Stephen. "Top 10 Lessons of the Iraq War." *Foreign Policy* (2012). https://foreignpolicy.com/2012/03/20/top-10-lessons-of-the-iraq-war-2/.

Wanke, Gunther, *Die Zionstheologie Der Korachiten in Ihrem Traditionsgeschichtlichen Zusammenhang*. Beihefte zur Zeitschrift für die alttestamentliche Wissenschaft 97. Berlin: Töpelmann, 1966.

Watts, John D. W. *Isaiah 1–33*. Word Biblical Commentary 24. Nashville, TN: Word Books, 1985.

Weber, William. "Dueling Narratives: Henry Adams's Alternative History of the War of 1812." Pages 99–120 in *Neither Victor nor Vanquished. America in the War of 1812*. Washington, DC: Potomac Books, 2013.

Wegner, Paul D. *An Examination of Kingship and Messianic Expectation in Isaiah 1–35*. Lewiston, NY: Edwin Mellen, 1992.

Weinfeld, Moshe. "Cult Centralization in Israel in the Light of a Neo-Babylonian Analogy." *Journal of Near Eastern Studies* 23 (1964): 202–12.

Weippert, Helga. *Palästina in vorhellenistischer Zeit*. Handbuch der Archäologie 2. Munich: C. H. Beck, 1988.

Westman, Alida S., and Lisa M. Lewandowski. "How Empathy, Egocentrism, Kohlberg's Moral Development, and Erikson's Psychosocial Development Are Related to Attitudes toward War." *Psychological Reports* 69 (1991): 1123–7.

Wildberger, Hans. *Jesaja 1–12*. Biblischer Kommentar, Altes Testament 10/1. Neukirchen-Vluyn: Neukirchener, 1972.

Wildberger, Hans. *Jesaja 13–27*. Biblischer Kommentar, Altes Testament 10/2. Neukirchen-Vluyn: Neukirchener, 1978.

Wildberger, Hans. *Jesaja 28–39*. BKAT, 10/3. Neukirchen-Vluyn: Neukirchener, 1982.

Wildberger, Hans. *Isaiah 1–12*. Continental Commentaries. Minneapolis, MN: Fortress Press, 1991.

Wildberger, Hans. *Isaiah 13–27*. Continental Commentaries. Minneapolis, MN: Fortress Press, 1997.

Williamson, H. G. M. *The Book Called Isaiah: Deutero-Isaiah's Role in Composition and Redaction*. Oxford: Oxford University Press, 1994.

Willis, John T. "An Important Passage for Determining the Historical Setting of a Prophetic Oracle: Isaiah 1:7–8." *Studia Theologica* 39 (1985): 151–69.

Wolff, Hans Walter. *Frieden ohne Ende: Jesaja 7, 1–17 und 9, 1–6 ausgelegt*. Biblische Studien 35. Neukirchen Kreis Moers: Neukirchener Verlag des Erziehungsvereins, 1962.

Wong, G. C. I. "Isaiah's Opposition to Egypt in Isaiah XXXI 1–3." *Vetus Testamentum* 46 (1996): 392–401.

Yeivin, Z. "'Erani, Tel." Pages 417–19, 421 in *The New Encyclopedia of Archaeological Excavations in the Holy Land*. Edited by E. Stern. New York: Simon & Schuster, 1993.

Young, Edward J. *The Book of Isaiah: The English Text, with Introduction, Exposition, and Notes*. The New International Commentary on the Old Testament. Grand Rapids, MI: Eerdmans, 1965.

Young, Robb Andrew. *Hezekiah in History and Tradition*. Supplements to Vetus Testamentum 155. Leiden; Boston, MA: Brill, 2012.

Younger, K. Lawson, Jr. "Yahweh at Ashkelon and Calah? Yahwistic Names in Neo-Assyrian." *Vetus Testamentum* 52 (2002): 207–18.

Younger, K. Lawson, Jr. "Assyrian Involvement in the Southern Levant at the End of the Eighth Century B.C.E." Pages 235–63 in *Jerusalem in Bible and Archaeology: The First Temple Period*. Edited by Andrew G. Vaughn and Ann E. Killebrew. Leiden: Brill, 2003.

Younger, K. Lawson, Jr. "Aubin's the Rescue of Jerusalem: An Assyriological Assessment." Pages 221–46 in *Jerusalem's Survival, Sennacherib's Departure, and the Kushite Role in 701 BCE*. Edited by Alice Ogden Bellis. Perspectives on Hebrew Scriptures and Its Contexts 32. New Jersey: Gorgias Press, 2019.

Yurco, Frank J. "Sennacherib's Third Campaign and the Coregency of Shabaka and Shebitku." *Serapis* 6 (1980): 221–40.

Yurco, Frank J. "The Shabaka-Shebitku Coregency and the Supposed Second Campaign of Sennacherib against Judah: A Critical Assessment." *Journal of Biblical Literature* 110 (1991): 35–45.

Zadok, R. "Neo-Assyrian Notes." Pages 312–30 in *Treasures on Camels' Humps: Historical and Literary Studies from the Ancient Near East Presented to Israel Eph'al*. Edited by Mordechai Cogan and Dan'el Kahn. Jerusalem: Magnes, 2008.

Zaslow, Morris, *The Defended Border*. Ontario Historical Society. Toronto: Macmillan Co. of Canada, 1964.

Zevit, Ziony. "Implicit Population Figures and Historical Sense: What Happened to 200,150 Judahites in 701 BCE?" Pages 357–66 in *Confronting the Past: Archaeological and Historical Essays on Ancient Israel in Honor of William G. Devers*. Edited by Seymour Gitin, J. Edward Wright, and J. P. Dessel. Winona Lake, IN: Eisenbrauns, 2006.

Zimhoni, Orna. "The Iron Age Pottery of Tel 'Eton and Its Relation to the Lachish, Tell Beit Mirsim and Arad Assemblages." *Tel Aviv* (1987): 63–90.

Zimmerli, Walther. "Jesaja und Hiskija." Pages 199–208 in *Wort und Geschichte: Festschrift für Karl Elliger zum 70. Geburtstag*. Edited by Karl Elliger, Hartmut Gese, and Hans Peter Rüger. *Alter Orient und Altes Testament*. Kevelaer: Neukirchen-Vluyn, 1973.

Zorn, J. R. "Nasbeh, Tell En-." Pages 1098–102 in *The New Encyclopedia of Archaeological Excavations in the Holy Land*. Edited by Ephraim Stern. New York: Israel Exploration Society; Simon & Schuster, 1993.

Zorn, J. R. "Nasbeh, Tell En-." in *Oxford Encyclopedia of Archaeology in the Near East*. Edited by Eric M. Meyers. New York: Oxford University Press, 1997.

Zukerman, Alexander. "The Royal City of the Philistines' in the 'Azekah Inscription' and the History of Gath in the Eighth Century BCE." *Ugarit-Forschungen* 38 (2006): 729–78.

AUTHOR INDEX

Abalakina, Marina 178 n.17, 179 n.26
Achenbach, Reinhard 17 n.71
Ackroyd, Peter R. 107 n.8, 175 n.1, 175 n.3
Adams, Henry 137, 138 n.79, 141 n.103
Aharoni, Miriam 29 n.1, 33 n.28, 34 n.30, 36, 36 n.53, 40 n.90, 47 n.145
Aharoni, Yohanan 29 n.1, 31 n.11, 33 n.28, 34, 34 n.30, 34 n.31, 36, 36 n.53, 39 n.87, 40, 40 n.90, 40 n.91, 44 n.122, 44 n.123, 45 n.128, 45 n.130, 47 n.145, 70, 70 n.66, 157 n.21
Ahlström, Gösta W. 68 n.43, 70 n.62, 73 n.81
Albright, William Foxwell 8 n.29, 8 n.30, 33 n.26, 45 n.130
Amit, D. 42 n.107
Anderson, A. A.. 163 n.50
Arubas, Benjamin 44 n.122
Ashworth, Tony 181 n.45
Aster, Shawn Zelig 30 n.7, 41 n.100, 85, 85 n.165, 113 n.37, 119 n.70
Auld, A. Graeme 55, 55 n.202
Ayalon, E. 38 n.71

Badè, William Frederic 43 n.113
Bagg, Ariel M. 16 n.67, 56 n.212
Bányai, Michael 9 n.34, 77 n.112
Barbuto, Richard V. 146 n.144, 147, 147 n.145
Barkay, G. 44 n.122, 44 n.123, 44 n.125, 45 n.127, 45 n.128
Barnes, Willliam 110 n.24
Barnett, LeRoy 143 n.115, 143 n.116, 143 n.118
Barton, George A. 8 n.29
Barton, John 113 n.37, 117 n.54, 119 n.65, 119 n.70
Bates, Robert D. 11 n.43
Bearman, Gregory H. 48 n.155
Beaumont, C. L. 7 n.29
Beckerath, Jürgen von 8 n.30

Becking, Bob 4 n.18, 12 n.43, 46 n.137, 52 n.186, 53 n.194, 78 n.113, 159, 159 n.29
Begg, Christopher T. 8 n.29
Beit Arieh, Itzhaq 39 n.88, 48 n.155, 48 n.156, 49 n.161
Ben Zvi, Ehud 13 n.54, 14 n.54, 66 n.28, 69 n.49, 72 n.73, 77 n.111, 78 n.114, 92 n.9, 95 n.23, 97, 97 n.32, 97 n.33, 97 n.34, 108 n.11, 171, 171 n.95
Benn, Carl 135 n.60, 136 n.62, 139 n.89, 140 n.96, 144 n.125, 144 n.127, 145 n.129, 145 n.134, 145 n.135, 145 n.136, 146 n.140, 150 n.169, 166 n.63
Berges, Ulrich 108 n.11
Berlejung, Angelika 56 n.212, 57, 57 n.216
Berton, Pierre 127 n.5, 129 n.15, 143 n.113, 149, 149 n.161, 150 n.167, 166, 166 n.62, 166 n.64, 187 n.80
Best, Geoffrey 19 n.81, 183
Beuken, W. A. M. 117 n.58
Bienkowski, Piotr 41 n.104
Bilmes, Linda 25 n.109
Blakely, Jeffrey A. 33 n.22, 33 n.28, 35, 35 n.43, 38 n.70, 40 n.89
Blenkinsopp, Joseph 106 n.6, 107 n.10, 108, 108 n.11, 108 n.13, 109 n.17, 111 n.29, 113 n.36, 113 n.37, 114 n.43, 116 n.53, 117 n.56, 117 n.58, 118 n.61, 118 n.63, 119 n.67, 121 n.84, 122 n.84, 126, 126 n.109
Bloch-Smith, Elizabeth 31 n.11, 34 n.32, 35 n.47, 36 n.51, 40 n.93, 42, 42 n.106, 42 n.109, 42 n.111, 45 n.126, 50 n.169, 157 n.21
Bond, Brian 19 n.81, 182 n.50, 183
Borger, Rykele 3 n.12
Borneman, Walter R. 128 n.7, 130 n.17, 132 n.35, 132 n.36, 134 n.47, 134 n.52, 135 n.56, 157 n.23
Borowski, Oded 33 n.21, 33 n.25, 39 n.76, 50 n.172, 51 n.175, 60 n.237, 84 n.159

Brandl, Baruch 35 n.48, 46 n.136, 46 n.137, 46 n.138
Braun, Eliot 35 n.47
Bright, John 8 n.29, 73 n.82, 76 n.107, 105 n.3, 126 n.108
Brinkman, J. A. 110 n.24
Broekman, G. P. F. 9 n.34, 77 n.112
Broshi, Magen 31 n.8, 50, 50 n.171, 52 n.185, 85 n.170, 100, 100 n.47
Brueggemann, Walter 116 n.50, 121 n.75
Budge, E. A. Wallis 7 n.29
Bulbach, S. W. 53 n.193
Bunimovits, Shelomoh 35 n.50, 36, 36 n.50, 36 n.52, 36 n.53, 36 n.54, 56 n.210, 57 n.215
Burke, Peter 181 n.45

Carnagie, Julie 130 n.25, 131 n.28, 132 n.38, 133 n.41, 133 n.45, 137 n.78
Chakravorty, B. 181 n.43
Chandler, David 19 n.81
Childs, Brevard S. 12, 12 n.44, 13, 13 n.53, 14, 14 n.56, 90, 97 n.31, 97 n.32, 101 n.57, 108 n.11, 112 n.29, 118 n.61, 122, 122 n.86, 124 n.96
Childs, John 19 n.81, 181
Christensen, Duane L. 124 n.98
Ciasca, Antonia 44 n.123
Clausewitz, Carl von 1, 21, 21 n.90
Clayton, B. A. 181 n.43
Clements, Ronald Ernest 12, 12 n.48, 13, 13 n.51, 13 n.52, 14 n.55, 15 n.64, 83 n.153, 97 n.38, 101, 102 n.58, 108 n.11, 109 n.18, 109 n.23, 111 n.29, 113 n.37, 114 n.44, 115 n.47, 115 n.48, 116 n.53, 117 n.55, 117 n.58, 118 n.59, 118 n.60, 118 n.63, 119 n.64, 119 n.69, 119 n.70, 120, 120 n.73, 121 n.80, 122, 122 n.87, 124 n.96, 156 n.13, 157, 157 n.52, 163 n.52, 186, 186 n.75, 186 n.76
Cobb, William Henry 110 n.24
Cogan, Mordechai 2 n.9, 4 n.18, 7 n.26, 11 n.40, 11 n.41, 11 n.42, 11 n.43, 14 n.54, 18, 18 n.74, 53 n.194, 63 n.4, 63 n.5, 63 n.7, 64, 64 n.11, 65 n.16, 65 n.22, 65 n.24, 66, 66 n.27, 67, 67 n.34, 67 n.37, 67 n.39, 68, 68 n.44, 68 n.46, 68 n.47, 69 n.50, 69 n.56, 69 n.58, 70 n.61, 70 n.62, 71 n.68, 72 n.78, 75, 75 n.93, 76 n.107, 77 n.111, 79 n.125, 80 n.126, 80 n.131, 83, 83 n.155, 84, 84 n.160, 85 n.164, 85 n.172, 86 n.180, 87 n.181, 94 n.20, 99 n.41, 102 n.61, 156 n.13, 158 n.26, 162 n.45, 167 n.68
Cogan, Morton 21 n.87
Cohen, Chaim 14 n.54, 97 n.32, 97 n.34
Creveld, Martin van 127, 127 n.1, 176, 176 n.4, 180 n.34, 181 n.40, 181 n.41, 182, 182 n.47, 182 n.48, 182 n.52, 183 n.53, 184 n.69, 188, 190, 190 n.97
Cross, Frank Moore 91 n.6
Crouch, Carly L. 172, 172 n.99

Dadon, M. 48 n.158
Dagan, Yehudah 31 n.12, 37 n.63, 37 n.68, 61 n.238
Dalley, Stephanie 17 n.71, 73 n.79
Darr, Katheryn Pfisterer 126 n.112
Day, John 116 n.52
de Groot, A. 39 n.86
De Odorico, Marco 50 n.170, 86, 86 n.175
Dever, William G 30 n.4, 30 n.5, 31 n.11, 32 n.15, 32 n.16, 33 n.22, 34 n.35, 35 n.42, 35 n.44, 38 n.70, 39, 39 n.79, 39 n.83, 40, 40 n.90, 40 n.92, 40 n.94, 40 n.97, 41 n.99, 43 n.115, 44 n.120, 44 n.125, 45 n.129, 45 n.130, 45 n.131, 46, 46 n.140, 47, 47 n.144, 47 n.148, 47 n.151, 48 n.160, 49 n.161, 51, 51 n.174, 51 n.177, 56 n.208, 56 n.209, 56 n.212, 57, 57 n.218, 58 n.219, 60 n.234, 61, 61 n.239, 61 n.240, 61 n.242, 84 n.161, 94 n.16, 157 n.21, 159 n.33, 165 n.56
Dhorme, P. 110 n.24
Dietrich, Walter 109 n.20
Dillmann, August 118 n.59
Dion, Paul-Eugène 74 n.91
Diringer, David 32 n.17
Dixon, Norman F. 188 n.87
Dodson, Aidan 9 n.34, 10 n.34, 77 n.112
Donner, Herbert 109 n.20, 116 n.53, 124 n.96
Dougherty, Raymond P. 8 n.29
Dressel, J. P. 44 n.123
Dubovský, Peter 64 n.9, 64 n.10, 65 n.18, 70 n.59, 70 n.63, 73 n.82, 73 n.83, 80, 80 n.128, 92 n.12, 95, 95 n.24, 96, 96 n.26, 99, 99 n.43, 100 n.44

Dyer, Gwynne 22 n.95, 179, 179 n.23, 179 n.26, 183 n.58

Eaton, Joseph H. 145 n.131
Edelman, Diana V. 68 n.43
Eide, T. 9 n.33
Eisenberg, Emanuel 39 n.80, 39 n.84
Eissfeldt, Otto 112 n.29
Elayi, Josette 11 n.41, 11 n.43, 16 n.67, 39 n.78, 48 n.157, 51 n.174, 58, 58 n.221, 58 n.224, 64 n.8, 64 n.10, 65 n.19, 65 n.22, 66 n.25, 66 n.27, 66 n.30, 67 n.35, 68, 68 n.41, 68 n.42, 69 n.54, 70 n.60, 71 n.67, 71 n.71, 71 n.72, 72 n.80, 76 n.102, 76 n.107, 79 n.121, 79 n.125, 82 n.152, 84 n.157, 101 n.49, 169, 169 n.85, 169 n.89
Elliott, Emory 173 n.101
Ellis, James H. 132 n.36, 132 n.37, 136 n.65, 136 n.68, 136 n.70, 139 n.93
Elting, John Robert 138 n.80
Emerton, John A. 108 n.11
Ender, Morten G. 178 n.19
Eph'al, Israel 60 n.236, 75 n.96, 101 n.54, 161, 162 n.43
Erlandsson, Seth 110 n.24
Eshel, Hanan 46 n.134
Evans, Carl D. 4 n.18, 11 n.43
Evans, Paul S. 6 n.21, 12 n.45, 78 n.115, 80 n.133, 89 n.1, 90 n.2, 90 n.3, 90 n.5, 96 n.25, 97 n.31, 97 n.33, 99 n.42, 154 n.5, 160 n.36, 170 n.92

Fales, Frederick Mario 16 n.66, 17 n.71, 56 n.212, 60 n.236, 73 n.81, 75 n.98, 80 n.129, 81 n.143, 107 n.10, 153 n.2, 157 n.19, 161 n.42, 167 n.69, 184 n.65
Fantalkin, Alexander 36, 36 n.55
Farber, Zev and Jacob L. Wright 30 n.6
Faust, Avraham 31 n.10, 32 n.13, 32 n.19, 32 n.20, 37, 37 n.65, 38 n.70, 38 n.71, 38 n.73, 38 n.74, 39, 39 n.82, 39 n.85, 40 n.90, 41 n.105, 42 n.107, 42 n.110, 42 n.112, 43 n.113, 43 n.114, 43 n.115, 43 n.116, 43 n.117, 43 n.118, 43 n.119, 45 n.127, 46 n.142, 47, 47 n.143, 47 n.144, 47 n.150, 47 n.151, 48 n.153, 48 n.158, 48 n.159, 49 n.162, 50, 50 n.168, 50 n.170, 51 n.175, 52, 52 n.179, 52 n.182, 52 n.185, 54 n.199, 54 n.200, 55, 56 n.207, 58 n.218, 84 n.159
Fawcett, Louise 25, 25 n.110, 26 n.118, 26 n.119
Fazal, Tanisha M. 177 n.9, 177 n.12, 178 n.22
Feig, Nurit 42 n.107
Ferro, Marc 182 n.52
Finkelstein, Israel 16 n.67, 31 n.8, 31 n.9, 33 n.23, 33 n.24, 33 n.25, 33 n.28, 34 n.31, 40 n.89, 47 n.147, 49 n.163, 50, 50 n.168, 50 n.171, 52, 52 n.178, 52 n.188, 53 n.192, 54, 54 n.197, 55 n.205, 55 n.206, 58 n.218, 85 n.170, 100, 100 n.47, 101 n.48, 159 n.31
Fischer, Johann 116 n.53
Fohrer, Georg 124 n.95
Forest, Timothy S. 127 n.2, 127 n.3, 143 n.113, 150, 150 n.164, 150 n.166, 150 n.168
Frahm, Eckart 3 n.13, 4 n.18, 6 n.22, 12 n.43, 15, 15 n.60, 15 n.63, 17 n.71, 26 n.117, 63 n.1, 63 n.5, 66 n.27, 68 n.47, 86 n.176, 102 n.61, 168 n.78
Freud, Liora 44 n.122, 48 n.155
Friedman, Richard Elliott 91 n.6
Fritz, Stephen G. 24 n.104
Fuchs, Andreas 4 n.18
Fullerton, Kemper 7 n.29, 105 n.2

Gadot, Yuval 44 n.122
Galil, Gershon 4 n.18
Gallagher, William R. 2 n.5, 4 n.18, 13 n.54, 16 n.69, 19, 19 n.79, 20 n.82, 50 n.170, 51 n.175, 64 n.15, 65, 65 n.18, 65 n.19, 65 n.23, 66, 66 n.31, 67, 67 n.33, 67 n.36, 67 n.39, 68, 68 n.42, 68 n.46, 69, 69 n.52, 69 n.56, 70, 70 n.62, 71 n.67, 71 n.70, 72 n.78, 74 n.90, 75, 75 n.95, 76, 76 n.101, 78, 78 n.113, 78 n.116, 79, 79 n.120, 79 n.122, 80, 80 n.129, 80 n.130, 81, 81 n.142, 82 n.146, 82 n.151, 83 n.154, 84, 84 n.158, 84 n.159, 86 n.180, 95, 95 n.22, 97 n.32, 101 n.53, 101 n.55, 110 n.24, 111 n.26, 111 n.28, 112 n.29, 112 n.30, 113 n.34, 153 n.3, 156 n.13, 158 n.26, 158 n.28, 167, 167 n.76, 175 n.3, 189, 189 n.94, 189 n.95, 190

Gardiner, Alan 10 n.40
Gehman, Henry S. 76 n.106
Gibson, Shimon 37, 37 n.64
Ginsberg, Harold Lewis 53 n.193
Gitin, Seymour 30 n.6, 57 n.214, 57 n.218
Glantz, David M. and Jonathan M. House 24 n.103, 24 n.104, 24 n.105
Glantz, David M. 24 n.105
Goldberg, Jeremy 4 n.18, 12 n.43
Gonçalves, Francolino J. 86 n.177, 105 n.1, 105 n.2
Gooch, John 19 n.81
Goosens, G. 74 n.91
Gosse, Bernard 1090 n.23
Glantz, David M. 24 n.103, 24 n.105
Grabbe, Lester L. 1 n.2, 17 n.71, 32, 32 n.18, 44 n.123, 45 n.127, 52 n.185, 53 n.194, 66 n.32, 67 n.32, 76, 77 n.108, 96, 96 n.27, 153 n.1, 156 n.13, 158 n.28, 163 n.48, 182 n.46, 183 n.54
Grant, Elihu 35 n.50
Gray, George Buchanan 111 n.27
Gray, John 76 n.106, 78 n.113, 102 n.59
Gray, Peter W. 176 n.5
Grayson, Albert Kirk 2 n.5, 3 n.13, 7, 7 n.29, 63 n.1, 77 n.111, 102 n.60
Greenberg, R. 34, 34 n.29, 34 n.31
Greenblatt, Miriam 131 n.34, 133 n.46, 134, 134 n.50, 135 n.60, 137 n.72, 138 n.81, 142 n.112, 143 n.117, 144 n.119, 145 n.136, 147, 147 n.148, 147 n.149, 147 n.150
Gressmann, Hugo 125 n.100
Grimal, Nicolas-Christophe 23 n.97

Hallo, William W. 15 n.65
Halpern, Baruch 14, 14 n.58, 42 n.108, 50 n.167
Hanson, Victor Davis 20 n.85, 131 n.32, 155 n.10, 179, 179 n.25, 180 n.35, 181 n.39, 182 n.48, 183, 183 n.59, 183 n.61, 184, 184 n.64, 184 n.66, 186 n.77, 187 n.79, 187 n.80, 188, 188 n.85, 188 n.88, 188 n.90, 189 n.92, 190 n.96
Hardin, James W. 33 n.22, 33 n.28, 35, 35 n.43, 38 n.70, 40 n.89
Hardmeier, Christof 11 n.43
Hasel, Michael G. 23 n.99
Hathaway, Oona Anne 178 n.19

Hattendorf, John 138 n.85, 172, 172 n.100
Hayes, John Haralson 4 n.18, 56 n.210, 58 n.225, 59, 59 n.226, 59 n.230, 60, 60 n.236, 73 n.82, 109 n.18, 110 n.24, 163 n.50, 163 n.51
Heidler, David Stephen 127 n.3, 128 n.6, 129 n.11, 130 n.22, 130 n.24, 131 n.27, 131 n.30, 132 n.40, 133 n.42, 134 n.53, 136 n.64, 136 n.66, 136 n.68, 136 n.71, 143 n.115, 144 n.120, 144 n.126, 144 n.128, 145 n.130, 145 n.135, 146, 146 n.137, 146 n.142, 146 n.143, 149 n.159, 187 n.80
Heidler, Jeanne T. 127 n.3, 128 n.6, 129 n.11, 130 n.22, 130 n.24, 131 n.27, 131 n.30, 132 n.40, 133 n.42, 134 n.53, 136 n.64, 136 n.66, 136 n.68, 136 n.71, 143 n.115, 144 n.120, 144 n.126, 144 n.128, 145 n.130, 145 n.135, 146, 146 n.137, 146 n.142, 146 n.143, 149 n.159, 187 n.80
Herbert, Arthur Sumner 118 n.61
Herzog, Ze'ev 43 n.115, 47 n.146, 50 n.167
Hickey, Donald R. 128 n.4, 128 n.7, 128 n.8, 129 n.10, 129 n.12, 129 n.16, 130, 130 n.20, 130 n.24, 131 n.33, 132, 132 n.36, 132 n.39, 133 n.43, 133 n.45, 134 n.48, 134 n.54, 135 n.56, 135 n.57, 137 n.73, 137 n.76, 137 n.77, 139 n.88, 139 n.89, 139 n.90, 139 n.95, 140, 140 n.98, 141 n.105, 142 n.110, 142 n.111, 144 n.123, 146 n.140, 148 n.152, 148 n.154, 149 n.160, 154 n.4, 157 n.22, 157 n.23, 159 n.35, 160 n.37, 165, 165 n.58, 171, 171 n.96, 187 n.80, 196, 196 n.4, 196 n.6
Hoffmeier, James K. 9 n.31, 111 n.29, 118 n.61
Høgenhaven, Jesper 109 n.21, 118 n.61, 118 n.62, 119 n.70, 123 n.93, 126, 126 n.110
Holladay Jr., John S. 55, 55n 203
Holloway, Steven W. 97 n.32
Honor, Leo Lazarus 68 n.40, 68 n.48, 103 n.63, 112 n.29, 114 n.41
Horn, Siegfried H. 11 n.43
House, Jonathan M. 24 n.103, 24 n.105
Howard, Michael 19 n.81, 176 n.6, 180 n.33, 180 n.34, 180 n.35, 180 n.37,

181 n.40, 181 n.44, 182 n.50, 183 n.56, 189 n.93
Howes, Kelly King 130 n.25, 131 n.28, 132 n.38, 133 n.41, 133 n.45, 137 n.78
Huber, Friedrich 109 n.20

Iggers, Georg G. 18, 18 n.75
Irvine, Stuart A. 109 n.18, 110 n.24, 124 n.96, 163 n.51

Jagodic, G. K. 178 n.17
Jang, Sehoon. 107 n.7
Jenkins, A. K. 11 n.43, 12 n.43, 53 n.194
Jeremias, Alfred 7 n.29
Johns, C. H. W. 7 n.29
Jones, Michael K. 24 n.102
Jones, Colin 182 n.49
Jong, Matthijs J. de 119 n.70
Jurman, Claus 9 n.34, 77 n.112

Kahn, Dan'el 9 n.31, 9 n.33, 10 n.39, 11 n.43, 18 n.76, 76 n.102, 77, 77 n.108, 77 n.109, 77 n.112, 89 n.1, 161 n.42
Kaiser, Otto 106 n.5, 109 n.22, 109 n.23, 111 n.29, 112 n.32, 116 n.51, 116 n.53, 117 n.58, 118 n.61, 118 n.62, 119 n.66, 120 n.70, 121 n.82, 124 n.95
Kalimi, Isaac 1 n.3, 2 n.6
Katz, Hayah 38 n.70, 38 n.73, 38 n.74, 39 n.78
Katzenstein, H. Jacob 67 n.39, 69, 69 n.50, 69 n.51
Keegan, John 22 n.94, 24 n.104, 24 n.105, 24 n.106, 177, 177 n.12, 178 n.14, 178 n.21, 179, 179 n.24, 179 n.28, 180, 180 n.31, 184, 184 n.67, 187, 187 n.78, 188, 188 n.86, 188 n.89
Kelle, Brad E. 21 n.92, 22 n.92
Kelm, George L. 34 n.33, 34 n.34, 35, 35 n.38
Kennedy, Paul 181 n.39
Keylor, William R. 22 n.93
Kim, Hyun Chul Paul 113 n.35
Kinnier Wilson, J. V. 167 n.75
Kirkpatrick, A. F. 163 n.49
Kitchen, Kenneth. A. 8 n.31, 10 n.35, 10 n.36, 11 n.43, 75 n.94, 76, 76 n.105
Kletter, Raz 36 n.53, 46 n.137, 53, 53 n.189, 159 n.32

Kloner, Amos 38 n.69
Knauf, Ernst Axel 6 n.23, 7 n.7, 14 n.57, 15, 15 n.60, 16, 16 n.68, 20 n.82, 21 n.88, 24 n.107, 31 n.10, 57 n.217, 59, 59 n.227, 64, 64 n.9, 64 n.10, 67 n.39, 70, 70 n.64, 71 n.69, 74 n.90, 75, 75 n.96, 75 n.97, 75 n.99, 76, 76 n.102, 78 n.115, 79, 79 n.124, 80 n.133, 81 n.145, 83 n.153, 85 n.164, 96, 96 n.29, 97 n.38, 101 n.54, 156 n.13, 158 n.27, 161 n.39, 161 n.41, 165 n.57, 166 n.67, 169, 169 n.88, 170, 170 n.92, 170 n.93, 175, 175 n.2, 185, 186 n.73
Koch, Ido 30 n.6, 49 n.163, 49 n.165
Koch, Klaus 118 n.61
Kochavi, Moshe 39 n.77, 41 n.104, 48 n.156
Kooij, Arie van der 8 n.30, 81 n.145
Krueger, James S. 178 n.19
Kuhrt, Amélie 195 n.3

Laato, Antti 4 n.18, 78 n.113, 105 n.1, 123 n.88, 123 n.95, 125 n.100, 125 n.107, 126 n.109
Lance, H Darrell 46 n.134
Lanskoy, Miriam 20, 20 n.84
Lapp, Nancy L. 46 n.141
Laxer, James 142 n.110, 143 n.114
Layard, Austen Henry 6, 6 n.24
Lederman, Zvi 36 n.50, 36, 36 n.50, 36 n.52, 36 n.53, 36 n.54, 56 n.210, 57 n.215
Le Moyne, J. 8 n.29
Leclant, Jean 9 n.31
Leeuwen, C. Van 8 n.29, 9 n.31
Lemche, Niels Peter 15, 15 n.61
Levenson, Jon Douglas 163 n.51
Levine, Baruch A. 156 n.13, 157, 157 n.19
Levine, Louis D. 3 n.10
Lewandowski, Lisa M. 179 n.26
Lewis, John David 20 n.83, 21 n.86, 21 n.89, 183, 183 n.60, 184 n.63, 187 n.82, 187 n.84, 189 n.91
Lichtheim, Miriam 23 n.98
Lipschits, Oded 30 n.4, 30 n.6, 37 n.63, 44 n.122, 45 n.126, 45 n.129, 49 n.163, 49 n.165, 56 n.210, 56 n.212, 57 n.217, 58 n.220
Liverani, Mario 76 n.105

Lloyd, Alan B 77 n.110, 100 n.46, 101, 101 n.50
Luckenbill, Daniel David 3, 3 n.11, 3 n.13, 10 n.38, 59 n.228, 63 n.1, 80 n.129, 81 n.141, 93 n.13

Macadam, Miles Frederick Laming 8 n.30
Machinist, Peter 14 n.54, 97 n.32, 97 n.34, 101 n.57, 111 n.29, 124 n.97, 154, 154 n.7
Macintosh, A. A. 109 n.22
Magen, Y. 48 n.158
Mahan, A. T. 142 n.108
Malcomson, Robert 131 n.31, 146 n.144
Marks, Sally 187, 187 n.81, 187 n.83
Marti, Karl 111 n.29, 116 n.53
Martin, W. J. 100 n.45
Master, Daniel M. 52 n.181
Matthews, Michael D. 178 n.19
Matty, Nazek Khalid 16 n.68, 53 n.194, 64 n.8, 64 n.14, 65 n.18, 74 n.89, 82, 82 n.147, 82 n.149, 83 n.154, 84, 84 n.163, 85, 85 n.166, 162 n.44, 167 n.71, 168, 168 n.83, 169 n.86
Mayer, Walter 3 n.13, 4 n.18, 5 n.20, 6, 7, 7 n.26, 15, 15 n.62, 51 n.175, 64, 64 n.12, 65, 65 n.21, 65 n.23, 67 n.39, 69 n.55, 69 n.56, 69 n.57, 70 n.62, 72 n.77, 73 n.84, 74 n.90, 75 n.92, 77 n.110, 79, 79 n.123, 80, 80 n.133, 80 n.134, 81, 81 n.136, 82, 82 n.150, 83 n.153, 84 n.159, 84 n.162, 85, 85 n.171, 92, 92 n.11, 95 n.20, 96, 96 n.28, 97 n.38, 101 n.52, 156 n.13, 169, 169 n.87, 169 n.89
Mayes, A. D. H. 91 n.6
Mazar, Amihai 34 n.33, 34 n.34, 35, 35 n.38, 79, 79 n.121
Mazar, B. 40 n.96, 43 n.113, 50 n.168, 168 n.82
McClellan, Thomas L. 50 n.167
McCown, Chester Charlton 43 n.113
McKay, Ian 179 n.29
McKenzie, Steven L. 91 n.6
McNeill, William H. 180 n.36
Meinhold, Johannes 89 n.1
Mienis, H. K. 54 n.200
Mill, John Stuart 185, 185 n.72
Millard, A. R. 3 n.13, 12, 12 n.46, 82 n.151, 86 n.177, 192 n.1

Miller, James Maxwell 4 n.18, 56 n.210, 58 n.225, 59, 59 n.226, 59 n.230, 60, 60 n.236, 73 n.82
Mittmann, Siegfried 5 n.19, 41 n.101
Montgomery, James A. 76 n.106
Morgan-Owen, David 182, 182 n.50
Motyer, J. A. 106 n.5, 107 n.9, 112 n.31, 120 n.74, 121 n.83
Mousseau, Michael 177, 177 n.11
Mowinckel, Sigmund 121 n.79, 125 n.102, 163 n.50
Mueller, John 177 n.7
Müller, Reinhard 108 n.12
Murray, Margaret A. 32 n.17

Naʾaman, Nadav 3, 3 n.15, 4, 4 n.17, 4 n.18, 5 n.19, 13, 13 n.50, 16 n.66, 16 n.68, 18 n.72, 19, 19 n.77, 33 n.23, 33 n.24, 33 n.25, 33 n.28, 34 n.31, 37, 37 n.59, 37 n.60, 40 n.89, 41 n.101, 48 n.155, 49, 49 n.163, 49 n.164, 49 n.166, 50 n.167, 53 n.194, 54 n.194, 55 n.205, 65 n.19, 74 n.90, 101 n.57, 114 n.43, 118 n.61, 119 n.70, 126 n.112, 175 n.1, 196 n.5
Nadali, Davide 81, 81 n.139, 81 n.143
Nagorski, Alla 39 n.80, 39 n.84
Nelson, Richard D. 91 n.6
Nielsen, Kirsten 123 n.95, 124 n.96, 154 n.8, 155 n.8
Notley, R. Steven 31 n.11, 51 n.175, 73 n.81, 76 n.105, 84 n.159, 157 n.21
Novotny, Jamie R. 2 n.5, 3 n.13, 63 n.1

Oded, Bustenay 73 n.83
Oeming, Manfred 44 n.122
Ofer, Avi 31 n.12, 52 n.183
Ollenburger, Ben C. 163 n.51
Ombrain, Nicholas J. D. 180 n.35
Oren, E. D. 40 n.93, 40 n.95
Ortlund, Eric 108 n.15
Oswalt, John N. 106 n.6, 107 n.6, 112 n.33, 116 n.49, 118 n.63

Panitz-Cohen, Nava 34 n.33, 34 n.36
Paret, Peter 182 n.51, 183 n.55
Paris, Michael 179 n.27, 184, 184 n.68, 185, 185 n.69, 185 n.70
Parker, Bradley J. 57 n.212
Parker, Richard A. 8 n.30

Parpola, Simon 56 n.212
Payraudeau, Frédéric 9 n.34, 77 n.112
Peckham, Brian 91 n.6
Pedraza, Francisco I. 178 n.19
Person, Raymond F. 91 n.7
Petrie, William Matthew Flinders 40 n.96, 45 n.130
Pinker, Steve 56 n.211, 177, 177 n.8, 178, 178 n.22
Poast, Paul 177 n.9, 177 n.12, 178 n.22
Polner, Murray 128 n.9, 135, 135 n.59, 144 n.124, 145 n.132, 146 n.139, 146 n.141, 147 n.153, 171, 171 n.98, 187 n.80
Pope, Jeremy 77 n.112, 158 n.24
Postgate, J. N. 60 n.236
Pritchard, James B. 43, 43 n.118, 43 n.119
Provan, Iain W. 91 n.6
Punamaki, R. L. 178 n.16, 178 n.18

Quinn-Miscall, Peter D. 114 n.42
Quota, S. 178 n.16

Radner, K. 76 n.102, 78 n.113
Rainey, Anson F. 9 n.31, 31 n.11, 51 n.175, 53 n.193, 70, 70 n.66, 73 n.81, 76 n.105, 84 n.159, 157 n.21
Rawlinson, George 6, 6 n.25, 7, 7 n.27, 53 n.194
Rawlinson, Henry 2, 2 n.9, 3 n.10, 6, 63 n.2
Redford, Donald B. 8 n.30, 10 n.40, 12 n.43, 76, 76 n.104, 78 n.115, 101 n.56, 161 n.40, 161 n.41, 170 n.92
Reich, Ronny 46 n.136, 46 n.137, 46 n.138
Roberts, J. J. M. 109 n.19, 116 n.53, 116 n.53, 117 n.53, 121 n.78, 163 n.50
Rofé, Alexander 101 n.57
Rogers, Robert William 8 n.29
Rohall, David E. 178 n.19
Rohland, Edzard 163 n.50
Rollefson, Gary Orin 68 n.43
Römer, Thomas 91 n.8
Roosevelt, Theodore 136 n.62, 136 n.63, 139, 139 n.93
Rosentreter, Roger L. 143 n.115, 143 n.116, 143 n.118
Rost, Paul 3 n.14, 4 n.16
Routledge, Robin L. 117 n.57
Rowley, Harold Henry 94 n.20

Rudman, Dominic 13 n.54, 14 n.54, 97 n.32, 97 n.33
Russell, John Malcolm 168 n.83

Saggs, H. W. F. 13 n.53
Sargon and F. Thureau-Dangin 82 n.146
Sarrai, E. 178 n.16
Sass, Benjamin 55 n.201
Sauren, Herbert 86 n.177
Seger, Joe D. 33 n.22, 33 n.25
Seitz, Christopher R. 12, 12 n.47, 89 n.1, 115 n.46, 118 n.61, 122 n.85
Semmel, Bernard 181 n.40
Sergi, Omer 30 n.6
Shapiro, Scott 178 n.19
Shea, William H. 5 n.18, 8 n.29, 10 n.40, 11 n.43
Shiloh, Y. 55 n.201
Silberman, Neil Asher 16 n.67, 53 n.192
Simons, William E. 180 n.36
Smelik, Klaas A.D. 14 n.54, 90 n.3, 97 n.32, 106 n.4
Smend, Rudolf. 91 n.6, 91 n.7
Smith, George Adam 7 n.29
Snow, Peter 147 n.151
Spalinger, Anthony 18 n.73, 74 n.91, 75 n.94, 101 n.53
Stade, Bernhard 12, 12 n.44, 90
Stager, Larwence E. 41 n.100, 54 n.196, 54 n.198, 58 n.219
Stagg, J. C. A. 19 n.81
Stavrakopoulou, Francesca 175 n.2, 186, 186 n.74
Steiner, M. L. 55, 55 n.202
Stern, Ephraim 2 n.7, 29 n.2, 33 n.23, 33 n.25, 33 n.28, 35, 35 n.39, 35 n.45, 35 n.47, 35 n.47, 35 n.49, 36 n.52, 37 n.58, 37 n.61, 37 n.62, 37 n.66, 38, 38 n.72, 38 n.75, 41, 41 n.100, 41 n.102, 44 n.121, 45 n.127, 46, 46 n.135, 46 n.139, 47, 47 n.143, 47 n.144, 47 n.149, 47 n.152, 48 n.154, 48 n.159, 49 n.163, 49 n.166, 53 n.190, 54, 54 n.195, 55 n.204, 57 n.213, 58 n.218, 58 n.220, 59 n.226, 59 n.229, 60 n.235, 60 n.236, 61, 61 n.241, 166 n.65
Stiglitz, Joseph 25 n.109
Strawn, Brent A. 77 n.108, 78 n.114
Streck, Maximilian

Summers, Harry G. 170 n.94
Suriano, Matthew 31 n.11
Swanson, Neil Harmon 148 n.156
Sweeney, Marvin A. 82 n.152, 83 n.152, 90 n.3, 95 n.23, 101 n.57, 107 n.8, 108 n.15, 110 n.25, 112 n.30, 113, 113 n.38, 114 n.39, 114 n.44, 116 n.49, 116 n.53, 117 n.58, 118 n.61, 118 n.62, 118 n.63, 119 n.68, 119 n.69, 119 n.70, 120, 120 n.71, 120 n.74, 121 n.76, 121 n.77, 124 n.96
Swift, Jamie 179 n.29

Tadmor, Hayim 2 n.8, 4 n.18, 6 n.22, 11 n.41, 14 n.54, 18 n.74, 40 n.197, 53 n.194, 63 n.7, 64, 64 n.13, 64 n.14, 64 n.15, 67 n.39, 71 n.69, 71 n.71, 75 n.94, 76 n.107, 79 n.119, 80 n.133, 81 n.135, 81 n.144, 82 n.151, 94 n.20, 101 n.53
Tatum, Lynn 52 n.184, 52 n.188, 53 n.193, 159 n.31
Terraine, John 19 n.81
Thiele, Edwin R. 54 n.194
Tilly, Charles 182 n.51
Timm, Stefan 4 n.18
Toombs, Lawrence E. 35 n.42
Torabian, Saba 178 n.17, 179 n.26
Török, László 9 n.33
Tufnell, Olga 29 n.1, 32 n.17
Turner, Wesley B. 128 n.5, 131 n.26, 136 n.61, 137 n.76, 138 n.86, 139 n.88, 139 n.92, 139 n.94, 141 n.102, 142 n.109, 143 n.113, 146, 146 n.143, 147 n.149, 148 n.155, 148 n.157, 149 n.158, 160 n.37, 162 n.46, 165 n.59, 166, 166 n.61

Uehlinger, Christoph 81 n.140, 168, 168 n.80, 168 n.82, 169 n.84
Uffenheimer, Benjamin 109 n.22
Ungnad, Arthur 85 n.173
Ussishkin, David 30 n.6, 32 n.14, 32 n.17, 32 n.20, 80 n.133, 170 n.91

Van Beek, Gus W. 40 n.96, 40 n.97, 40 n.98
Van de Mieroop, Marc 23 n.99, 23 n.100
Van den Brink, Edwin C. M. 35 n.47
Van der Brugge, Caroline 72 n.74, 75 n.94
Vaughn, Andrew G. 30, 30 n.4, 30 n.6, 30 n.6, 37 n.67, 42 n.107, 44 n.123, 45 n.127, 55 n.206

Veijola, Timo 91 n.7
Vermeylen, Jacques 106 n.4, 124 n.96, 125 n.101
Vidal, Jordi 74 n.90
Vogt, Ernst 81 n.145, 101 n.57
von Rad, Gerhard 125 n.100

Wagner, Thomas 115 n.45
Wallace, W. Stewart 145 n.133
Walt, Stephen 25 n.115
Wampler, Joseph 43 n.113
Wanke, Gunther 163 n.49
Watts, John D. 106 n.6, 112 n.33, 113 n.38, 114 n.42
Weber, William 141 n.104
Wegner, Paul D. 123 n.88
Weinfeld, Moshe 14 n.54, 97 n.32, 97 n.34, 154 n.5
Weiss, Ehud 54 n.199, 54 n.200
Weippert, Helga 52 n.187, 159 n.30
Westman, Alida S. 179 n.26
Wildberger, Hans 108 n.16, 108 n.17, 109 n.20, 109 n.22, 109 n.23, 111 n.25, 111 n.26, 111 n.27, 111 n.28, 111 n.29, 113 n.36, 113 n.37, 114 n.40, 115 n.47, 118 n.59, 121 n.81, 123 n.91, 123 n.93, 124, 124 n.96, 124 n.97, 124 n.98, 154 n.7, 175 n.3
Williamson, H. G. M. 117 n.58
Willis, John T. 108 n.14
Wilson, J. V. Kinnier 167 n.75
Wolff, Hans Walter 123 n.92
Wong, G. C. I. 119 n.70
Woods, Thomas E. 128 n.9, 135, 135 n.59, 144 n.124, 145 n.132, 146 n.139, 146 n.141, 147 n.153, 171, 171 n.98, 187 n.80
Wright, G. Ernest 35 n.50

Yeivin, Z. 35 n.48
Young, Edward J. 124 n.99
Young, Robb Andrew 9 n.31, 10 n.36, 11 n.43, 98 n.40, 123, 123 n.89, 123 n.94, 125 n.103, 154, 154 n.6, 157 n.20, 190 n.98
Younger, K. Lawson, Jr. 4 n.18, 17 n.71, 64, 64 n.13, 64 n.15, 65 n.17, 79 n.125, 98 n.39
Yoyotte, Jean 9 n.31

Yurco, Frank J. 5 n.18, 9 n.31, 11 n.43

Zadok, R. 17 n.71
Zaslow, Morris 166 n.60
Zevit, Ziony 22 n.96, 23 n.96, 29 n.3, 31 n.11, 50, 51 n.173, 52, 52 n.180, 86, 86 n.177, 101 n.51, 156 n.13, 157 n.21

Zimhoni, Orna 34 n.31, 38 n.70, 38 n.71
Zimmerli, Walther 105 n.2, 109 n.20
Zorn, J. R. 43 n.114, 43 n.115
Zukerman, Alexander 4 n.18, 5 n.19

INDEX OF REFERENCES

BIBLE

Deuteronomy
8:2-4	120

2 Samuel
8:1	93

2 Kings
6:19-20	96
6:21	96
11:1	54 n.194
16	164
17	93, 192
17:4	93, 99
17:9	92, 93
18	122, 192
18:1	54 n.194
18:2	54 n.194
18:3	164, 197
18:5	164
18:7	122, 125, 162, 164
18:7-8	93
18:8	72, 92, 93, 158, 164
18:1-8	91
18:9	125
18:9-10	53n, 54 n.194
18:9-12	93
18:13	53 n.194, 54 n.194, 89 n.1, 93, 121, 160
18:13-16	12, 100
18:13–19:37	93
18:14	94, 95
18:14-16	12 n.43, 89 n.1
18:14, 17	32
18:15-16	95
18:16	95 n.20
18:17	96 n.30
18:17-37	95
18:17–19:9a, 36-37	12
18:17–19:37	15
18:19-35	16, 83, 156
18:22	154
18:25	97 n.37, 156, 192
18:27	16, 83, 97, 156, 157, 192
18:29	99
18:30	98, 192
18:30, 35	97
18:32	16, 83, 97, 98, 156, 192
18:35	156, 192
18–19	1, 15, 31, 78 n.30, 87, 89, 90, 99 n.43, 105, 112 n.30, 192
19:7	98, 102
19:8	98
19:9	8, 10, 74, 78, 98, 161
19:9b-35	12
19:10	99
19:14	99
19:34	172
19:35	99, 100, 162, 192 n.1
19:37	102
20	83 n.152, 106, 110 n.24, 153
20:6	53 n.194
20:20	113
21:12-16	175
23:26-27	175

2 Chronicles
29–32	155
32	1, 89
32:1	160
32:3-5, 27-30	113
32:9	32

Isaiah

Reference	Pages
1:4-9	1, 108
1:4-26	108
1:7-8	108 n.14
1:8	108
1:11-17	108
1:23	111 n.28
1–4	108 n.15
1–12	123 n.91, 124 n.96
1–33	112 n.33, 113 n.38, 114 n.42
1–35	123 n.88
1–39	108 n.11, 109 n.17, 110 n.25, 112 n.30, 113 n.38, 114 n.43, 115 n.47, 116 n.49, 117 n.58, 118 n.61, 119 n.70, 120 n.71, 121 n.75, 124 n.96, 126, 154
2:6-17	108
3:14	111 n.28
5:11-12, 22-3	111 n.28
7	164
7:1-17	123n
7:10-17	125, 193
7:18-25	107n
8:11-18	123n
8:23–9:6	123, 193
9	119
9:1-6	123 n.92
9:4	119
9:5	119
9:6	123
10:5	164
10:5-19	1, 13 n.54
10:12	165
10:24-34	193
10:27c-34	124 n.98
11:1-9	125, 193
11:11-16	125
13:1–14:23	109 n.23
13:2–14:23	110 n.24
13–23	113 n.35
13–27	108 n.16, 109 n.22, 111 n.25, 113 n.36, 114 n.40, 175 n.3
13–39	109 n.23, 111 n.29, 112 n.30, 116 n.49, 117 n.58, 118 n.61, 119 n.66, 120 n.70, 121 n.82
14:4-21	1
14:28-32	110 n.24
15, 16	110 n.24
17	110 n.24
18:1-2	1, 108, 118
18, 19	110 n.24
20:6	107 n.10
21:1b-2	112
21:1-10	1, 109, 110 n.24
21:2	110 n.24, 112 n.29
21:3-4	110 n.24, 111, 112 n.29
21:5	112 n.29
21:5-6	110 n.24
21:6	112 n.29
21:6-10	110 n.24
21:7, 9	112 n.29
21:11-17	110 n.24
22	112 n.33, 113 n.34, 123
22:1-2	196
22:1-2, 13	113
22:1-14	110 n.24, 111
22:1b-3	112 n.29
22:4	112 n.29
22:5	112 n.29
22:6, 7	112 n.29
22:11	113
22:13	111, 112 n.29
22:14	112 n.29
22:9-11	1
22:15-25	113
27:14-22	116 n.53
28:1-4	115
28:7-13	117 n.53
28:14-22	116
28:16	117 n.53
28–31	1, 114, 115
28–32	122
28–39	115 n.47, 118 n.59, 121 n.81, 154 n.7
29:1-8	115 n.45, 117 n.57
29:1-10	117
29:15-16	117
29:15-24	117 n.58
29:17-21	118 n.60

30:1-5	115 n.45	26:1-6	164 n.53
30:1-5, 15-17	105 n.1	37:6-8	99
30:1-7	99	46:25	99
30:2	117 n.57		
30:15	118	**Ezekiel**	
30:15-17	119	29:6-7	99
30:31-32	119		
30:33	119	**Hosea**	
31	113 n.37	12:2	99
31:1	117 n.57, 120		
31:1, 3	99	**Micah**	
31:1-3	105 n.1, 115 n.45, 119	1:8-16	31
31:4-6	120	**Psalms**	
31:8	121	47:3	21 n.92
33	121	68:21	21 n.92
33:7-9	121	110:1	21
36:1	89 n.1		
36–37	1, 15, 89, 90, 105, 112, 122	OTHER ANCIENT SOURCES	
		Annals of Sennacherib	
36–38	125	1–2	3, 10, 26, 32, 34–35, 50, 58, 63–87, 93–95, 99, 100, 103, 120, 156–8, 160, 162, 167, 172, 192, 194
36–39	107 n.7		
37:3	121 n.83		
37:3b	126 n.112		
38–39	107 n.8		
39	106, 107 n.7, 110n		
39:5-8	107 n.7		
39:1-8	106, 110	**Josephus Antiquities**	
40	107 n.7	10:1-23	2
Jeremiah		**Herodotus Historia**	
7:1-15	164 n.53	2:141	2, 76–78, 170

INDEX OF SUBJECTS

Annales school 182–3
Ashdod 57, 72, 79, 158
Ashkelon 57, 69, 71, 86, 171

Babylon 11, 58, 59, 97n.31, 106n.5, 107n.7, n.10, 110–11, 121, 153–4, 157n.16, 165, 175
Battle of
  Baltimore 138, 170, 194
  Bladensburg 148
  Borodino 22
  Champlain 139
  Chateaugay 145–6
  Crysler's Farm 146
  Eltekah 10, 16, 59, 71, 74–6, 78, 98–9, 101–3, 170–1, 191, 193–4
  Fort Erie 147
  Lachish 75
  Lake Erie 136–7, 193
  Lundy's Lane 137, 146–7, 160
  Qadesh 23
  Queenstown Heights 144
  Moraviantown 137
  Moscow 24
  New Orleans 140, 149, 161, 170, 193
  Put-in-Bay 136–7, 193
  Sortie from Fort Erie 139, 141, 147
  Stoney Creek 144
  The Thames 137
  Tyre 68
blockade 6, 73, 81, 169–73
British
  advancement 194
  blockade 165, 170
  bombardment 141
  burned by 147
  casualties 137, 139, 144
  concessions 156
  criticism of 142
  defeat of 149
  empire 164
  forces 143, 145, 148
  guns 138, 146, 160
  occupation 133, 140
  perspective 171
  practices/policies 128–30
  priorities 172
  problems 153
  regulars 135
  removal of threat 134
  retreat 140
  settlement with 132
  taken by 136
  terms 159
  weaken 131

Canada (Canadian)
  annexation of 157, 169, 194
  conquer of 142
  conquest of 133–4
  promise of protection of 134, 157
  unification of 150
  victory in 1812 142–51
Churchill, Winston 155, 189–90

defeat
  Assyrian 6–7, 11–12, 15, 78, 98, 100, 103, 119, 157, 161–2, 193
  British 139
  Ekron 72
  Egypt 73
  Philistine 73
  U.S. 25, 138, 144–5, 147
deportation 97, 103, 156
Deuteronomistic History 90, 106, 175

Ekron 5, 34, 36, 57, 65, 69, 72, 79, 92–3, 102, 158, 167, 171
Egypt (Egyptian)
  aid from 71, 118, 120
  allied with 73, 93, 99, 105, 115, 119
  approach of 101

dynasty in 59
expedition 98
hegemony 36
influence 23
incursion of 98
invasion of 77
forces 5, 16, 23, 71, 74, 76, 78–9, 98–9, 161–2, 167, 170, 191–3
negotiations with 108
policies favoring 109
records 8
reliance upon 115, 120, 122
scarabs from 55
story 77
summoned to 9–10
support from 119
unreliable 99

Fall of
   Assyria 121
   Babylon 109–10, 154
   Jerusalem 117
   Samaria (722 BCE) 30, 46, 93, 116, 192
fortified cities 5, 51, 84, 93–4, 100, 103, 157–8, 160
French Revolution 21, 131

Gaza 69, 71, 87, 92, 103, 158

Hezekiah
   achievements 197
   allied with 65, 93, 103, 105–8, 110n.24, 115, 119–20, 153–4, 186, 192
   ambition of 193
   annexed by 46
   anti-Assyrian policies of 123
   assault (or attack of) of 72, 79, 92
   assessment of 27
   Assyrian critique of 79–80
   breaking of treaty 121
   captured by 41, 92
   centralized worship 164
   critique of 106–9, 113, 116–19, 122, 126, 154, 176, 185–6, 188, 190, 195
   death of 66
   Immanuel 125
   imprisonment by 192
   kingdom (territory) of 34, 167
   last days of 54
   negotiations of 96
   paid tribute 6, 7, 85, 87, 99–100, 103, 172, 195
   rebuilt by 45
   rebellion 16, 18–19, 38, 60–1, 86, 104–5, 109, 114, 118, 122, 154–5, 158, 162, 164–6, 173, 175, 185–6, 189, 194–5
   reign of 53, 163
   rejected policies of 117
   released by 72
   risk of 187
   root of Jesse 125
   siege preparation 30
   submission of 73, 80, 83, 94, 103, 157, 171, 191–2, 195
Hitler, Adolf 24, 187, 189
Hussein, Saddam 24–5

inscriptions
   Assyrian Royal Inscriptions 14
   Azekah 3–4
   Bull 4 63, 86
   Bull Colossus No. 2 67
   Bull Inscriptions 2, 83
   Chicago Prism 3, 63, 70, 168
   Cylinder C 66, 80
   Jerusalem Prism 168
   Rassam Cylinder 3, 63, 65–6, 68, 70, 75, 80–1, 84, 86, 102–3, 168
   Sennacherib 2
   Stelae from Cush 8
   Taylor Prism 3, 63, 70, 168
Isaiah
   critique from 111–12, 154
   opposition of 126, 186, 195
   oracles from 105–26, 164
   prophecy of 98, 102, 105, 119, 121–2, 125, 163

Jay Treaty 127, 129
Josiah 12, 121, 123, 125, 154

Lulî (King of Sidon) 65–9, 79, 87, 102–3, 156, 191

Madison, James (President) 130–1, 133, 154
manifest destiny 141, 163, 193–4
Manasseh 11, 53–4, 59, 172, 175, 186, 195

Index of Subjects

maritime concessions 135, 142
Merodach-Baladan 75, 82n.152, 110n.24, 116n.53, 153
military history 20–6, 180–3, 187–9, 193–5
mythologizing 102, 135, 141, 150, 167, 196

Napoleon 21–2, 153, 171, 196
negotiations 73, 75, 89, 93, 98–9, 103, 108

oracles 122, 193, 115–20, 192

Padî (King of Ekron) 5, 72–3, 78–9, 86, 92–4, 96, 99–100, 103, 171, 191–2
Pax Assyriaca 33, 56–7, 61, 165–6, 186, 194–5
peace, permanent 177, 195–6
Pearl Harbor 155
Philistia 31, 34–5, 40, 54, 57–8, 60–1, 65, 70, 92–4, 158–9, 171, 192
Phoenicia 5, 60, 64–5, 68–9, 171
propaganda 15, 86

Rabshakeh 13, 16, 83, 97–100, 122, 154–5, 157–8, 160, 169, 192–3
rebellious coalition 72, 93, 111, 119
Roosevelt, Theodore (President) 139, 155

Secord, Laura 144–5, 150
siege of
  Detroit 143
  Jerusalem 5, 55, 80–1, 83, 96–7, 100, 103, 114, 117, 169–70, 192
  Lachish 84, 168, 194
Sennacherib
  building of 96
  capture by 194
  claims 158, 162
  conquest of 71, 170
  demands surrender 95
  deposed by 157
  distribution by 171
  failure of 66
  hears report 98–9
  inscription of 37
  invasion of 33–4, 42–3, 45, 47–8, 100, 105–6, 120, 124
  less powerful than God 197
  liberated by 73

murder 59, 98, 102–3
power of 169
received tribute 82, 95
reign 168
the relief of 32
retreat of 76
return of 82, 98, 173
submission to 65, 70, 95, 167
suzerain 172
withdrawal 100, 108, 159, 164, 166, 191–2, 194, 196
Sennacherib's Campaigns 121, 158, 191
  Fifth Campaign 58
  Fourth Campaign 58
  Second Campaign 11
  Third Campaign 1, 5, 18, 27, 29, 31, 63, 86, 101–2, 167–8, 171, 191
  Two Campaign reconstruction 6, 11
Shalmaneser III 77
Ṣidqâ of Ashkelon 70–1, 80, 84, 156–7
Ṣil-Bēl (King of Gaza) 72, 92
sites
  Arad 47
  Azekah (Tel Zakariah) 37–8, 61
  Beersheba (Tell es-Saba') 39, 45
  Beth-Zur 47, 94
  Gibeon 43, 94
  Hebron (Al-Khalil) 39, 42, 44, 47
  Khirbet el Kom (Makkedah) 47, 94
  Khirbet Rabud (Debir) 39, 42
  Lachish 2, 29, 32, 36–8, 47–8, 55, 94, 98–9, 168–70, 189, 194–5
  Mareshah 37–8
  Nebi-Samuel 48, 94
  Ramet Raḥel (Hirbet Salih) 43–4, 94, 96
  Rishon le-Zion 60
  Ruqeish 60
  Sheikh Zuweid 60
  Shephelah 31, 38, 41, 54–5, 83, 96, 157
  Tel Batash 38, 61
  Tel Beit Mirsim 33, 38
  Tel Beth Shemesh 35–6, 38, 61
  Tel el-Ful (Gibeah) 46, 94
  Tel el Hesi 35, 38
  Tel en-Naṣbeh (Mispah) 42–3, 94
  Tel es-Safi (Gath) 41
  Tel 'Erani 35, 38
  Tel 'Eton (Eglon) 38
  Tel Gezer 46

Tel Goded 37
Tel Halif 33
Tel Haror (Gerar) 45, 60, 94
Tel Ira 48
Tel Jemmeh 40, 60
Tel Malḥata (Moladah) 48, 94
Tel Sera' (Ziklag) 40, 60
Timnah 34
Sortie from Fort Erie 139, 147
stalemate 16, 76, 79, 99, 101, 161, 170
surrender 97-8

Taba'lu (King of Sidon) 69, 70, 156
Tiglath-Pileser 14, 35, 46, 81, 116
Tirhakah/Taharqa/Taharqo (King of Cush) 8-10, 74, 76, 78, 98-9, 103, 161
Treaty of Ghent 140, 143, 149, 159, 171
Treaty of Versailles 22, 187
tribute 6, 7, 12, 65, 69, 81-4, 94-5, 162, 167, 172, 186

United States
  morale 136
  retreat 146
  victory in 1812 127, 135-42, 146-9, 150, 160, 184, 193
  war aims 133-5
  war motives 128-30
  withdrawal 160

vassal 65, 82, 86, 158, 164, 167, 169, 171, 186
victory (or success)
  Assyrian 6, 17-18, 71, 77, 83, 86, 98, 101, 170, 191
  British 148, 171-2
  by capture 20-1, 52, 68, 71, 83, 93-4, 98, 100-1, 135, 137, 147, 160, 170, 192, 194

Canada 127, 147, 150, 160
by deportation 98, 100-1, 169, 192, 194
disputed 127, 156, 193
Egyptian 23, 76, 99
Hezekiah 92-3, 103, 126, 155
historical perspective 24
by humiliation 21, 148, 172
by increased prosperity 141, 165-7, 194
Judah 18, 26, 98, 115, 160, 166, 193
Nubian Egyptian 99
by patriotism 142, 166, 185, 194
perfect 184
by Prestige 141, 162, 194
Sennacherib 75, 80, 93, 103, 167
by taking territory 23, 52, 72-3, 86, 137, 140, 158-60, 169
United States 127, 135, 137-40, 146-9, 184, 193
war aims 22, 25, 83, 97-101, 103, 133-5, 142, 156-7, 169-71, 173, 183, 192-5
by Winning Last Battle 23, 94, 100-1, 140, 149, 161, 193

War
  of 1812 127-51, 154-8, 160, 162-5, 169-72, 193-6
  Devastation caused by 165-6, 194
  Great (WWI) 187
  of Iraq 24-6, 184
  motivations for 186-8
  Napoleonic 131, 137, 153, 171
  opposition to 131, 154, 178-80, 184
  world 179, 181
Washington D. C. 133, 138, 140, 147-8, 170, 194

Yahwism 164, 194

Zion 123, 163-5, 172, 194

www.ingramcontent.com/pod-product-compliance
Lightning Source LLC
Chambersburg PA
CBHW062133300426
44115CB00012BA/1911